GW00724698

Lost in Change

Studies in Language Companion Series (SLCS)

ISSN 0165-7763

This series has been established as a companion series to the periodical *Studies in Language*.

For an overview of all books published in this series, please see *benjamins.com/catalog/slcs*

Founding Editor

Werner Abraham
University of Vienna / University of Munich

Editors

Werner Abraham
University of Vienna / University of Munich

Elly van Gelderen
Arizona State University

Editorial Board

Bernard Comrie
University of California, Santa Barbara

William Croft
University of New Mexico

Östen Dahl
University of Stockholm

Gerrit J. Dimmendaal
University of Cologne

Ekkehard König
Free University of Berlin

Christian Lehmann
University of Erfurt

Elisabeth Leiss
University of Munich

Marianne Mithun
University of California, Santa Barbara

Heiko Narrog
Tohuku University

Johanna L. Wood
University of Aarhus

Debra Ziegeler
University of Paris III

Volume 218

Lost in Change
Causes and processes in the loss of grammatical elements and constructions
Edited by Svenja Kranich and Tine Breban

Lost in Change

Causes and processes in the loss of
grammatical elements and constructions

Edited by

Svenja Kranich
University of Bonn

Tine Breban
University of Manchester

John Benjamins Publishing Company
Amsterdam / Philadelphia

The paper used in this publication meets the minimum requirements of the American National Standard for Information Sciences – Permanence of Paper for Printed Library Materials, ANSI z39.48-1984.

DOI 10.1075/slcs.218

Cataloging-in-Publication Data available from Library of Congress:
LCCN 2021009612 (PRINT) / 2021009613 (E-BOOK)

ISBN 978 90 272 0863 7 (HB)
ISBN 978 90 272 5996 7 (E-BOOK)

© 2021 – John Benjamins B.V.
No part of this book may be reproduced in any form, by print, photoprint, microfilm, or any other means, without written permission from the publisher.

John Benjamins Publishing Company · https://benjamins.com

Table of contents

Lost in Change[1]

Svenja Kranich & Tine Breban

University of Bonn / University of Manchester

1. Introduction

The central question of this volume, how and why linguistic elements are lost, has not been put center stage in diachronic linguistics so far. Instead, the study of language change has focused on the emergence and spread of new elements and new categories. A telling example is the highly-active research tradition on grammaticalization at the turn of the twentieth century. Even though early contributions sketched out a path ultimately leading to loss (e.g., clines in Givón 1979 and Hopper & Traugott 1993), subsequent descriptive and theoretical contributions developed the earlier stages of the grammaticalization process, i.e., the development of new grammatical elements out of lexical material or the acquisition of new grammatical functions by grammatical elements. These changes have been studied extensively and robust generalizations concerning paths, processes and motivations have been formulated and tested based on a wide variety of languages from around the world. Solid insights into the demise and eventual loss of grammatical elements and categories are, by contrast, still lacking. Possible explanations for this imbalance may be the tendency to use a synchronic starting point for diachronic investigations: we observe a noteworthy construction in the present stage of a language and wish to know how it came into being. What is not there in the present stage might thus be more easily overlooked; or the fact that, in an area of linguistics that by necessity draws extensively on real language data, latterly in the form of historical corpora, it is easier to study what is attested than what is not.

That is not to say that there are no previous studies of loss in diachronic linguistics. To the contrary, certain language-specific phenomena, e.g., for English,

1. We would like to thank Hanna Bruns and Katharina Scholz for their very helpful assistance in the editing process.

the loss of grammatical gender (cf. Curzan 2003; Dolberg 2019) and the loss of verb second word order (amongst many others Kroch et al. 2000; Haeberli 2002; van Kemenade 2012), have attracted large amounts of scholarly attention. But these studies are clearly scarcer overall, and they tend to be devoted to particular loss stories in a specific language rather than aimed at finding generalizations and formulating hypotheses about loss as a unified phenomenon. A notable exception is a recent study by Leung and van der Wurff (2018), whose starting point is a corpus study of the decline of two English anaphoric nominal constructions, *the said N* and *the same*. Leung and van der Wurff use the contrasting facts surrounding the demise of the two constructions as a springboard to propose a wide-ranging list of possible motivations for loss (Leung and van der Wurff 2018: 177). It includes language-internal factors, e.g., competition with and replacement by functionally equivalent items, high processing costs due to the multi-functional load of the element, low-frequency, and various types of mismatches (such as mismatch between form and function, incompatibility between different uses of the element, mismatch with the syntactic context); as well as external factors, e.g., negative social or stylistic attitudes and loss of a similar element in a contact language. The present volume is a further step in the systematic study of loss. The contributions all use their individual cases of loss to reflect on general processes and motivations for loss and advance the methods for studying loss.

This investigation is long overdue as loss in language change is as manifold as is emergence. All fields of a language can exhibit loss: To take the example of phonology, one may observe the loss of specific phonemes (e.g., English /x/), the loss of combinatory possibilities (e.g., English /kn-/) as well as the loss of distinctions, i.e., merger of two different phonemes (cf. Labov 1994: Chapter 11), and finally, one can also observe languages losing a complete category (e.g., loss of tone, cf. Gussenhoven 2004: 42). The same is true for other fields of language: Losses range from the most specific, i.e., the loss of a specific element, via loss of combinatory possibilities and loss of distinctions within a category to the most general, i.e., the loss of a whole category. Table 1 presents an overview and gives examples of losses in different fields and different levels to chart the ubiquity of loss, citing examples from the contributions to this volume where possible.

This overview also gives the reader an impression of the scope of the studies in this volume, most of which started out as contributions to the workshop we organized under the auspices of the DGfS conference in Stuttgart (6–8 March 2018). The studies cover syntactic, morphological and lexical loss. Even though most of the contributions present case studies from English and German, there are also typologically very different languages, such as Chinese (Kuo), and lesser studied languages, such as Koĭc (Borchers), among the languages investigated, as well as a paper that presents a typological classification of loss in the field of morphology (Sims-Williams & Baerman). Even though we would have liked to

Table 1. Types of losses in the different fields of language

Field	Level of specificity of loss	Example
Phonology	Individual	Loss of /x/ in English
	Combinatory	Loss of /kn-/ in English
	Distinction	Merger
	Category	Loss of tone
Morphology (cf. *Sims-Williams & Baerman* for a survey)	Individual	Loss of *-ung* (marker of the verbal noun and deverbal nominalization morpheme in Old English) in English
	Combinatory	English *-ly* specialized to adverbs, lost as adjective-deriving morpheme
	Distinction	Loss of biactantial marking in Koĭc verb paradigm (cf. *Borchers*), loss of adnominal genitive in Alemannic (cf. *Rehn*)
	Category	Loss of grammatical gender in English
Lexicon	Individual	Loss of *cweðan* in English, demise of *very* in New Zealand English (NZE) (cf. *Schweinberger*)
	Combinatory	Loss of multi-word expressions (cf. *Tichý*)
	Distinction	Loss of distinctions in a semantic field
	Category	Loss of a semantic field (not common, but would be possible e.g., if a certain cultural practice falls into disuse)
Syntax	Individual	Loss of the *so*-relative construction in German (cf. *Kempf*), loss of an avertive construction in Chinese (cf. *Kuo*), loss of the *so*-adj-*a* construction in English (cf. *Rudnicka*)
	Combinatory	Loss of *be* as auxiliary in the perfect construction (cf. *Hundt*), demise of combination modal *may* + verb of saying as a hedging construction (cf. *Kranich*)
	Distinction	Fixation of SVO word order in English leading to loss of information-structural distinctions
	Category	Loss of whole highly schematic construction type, e.g., English impersonals (cf. *Čermák*)
Pragmatics	Individual	Loss of specific pragmatic markers (e.g., English *prithee, pray*)
	Combinatory	Loss of the so-called "Hamburger Sie" (use of Christian name but formal pronoun of address)
	Distinction	Loss of distinctions within a category (e.g., demise of the *polite formal* in Hungarian, cf. Östör 1982)
	Category	Loss of T/V distinction in English

be able to include a broader variety of languages and phenomena, the present studies are a fruitful starting point to embark on the systematic study of loss in diachronic linguistics. The remainder of this introduction is organized in two sections. In Section 2, we introduce the central topics and questions we presented to the contributors for consideration: data and methods for studying loss, modeling of loss in different linguistic frameworks, different steps in the process of loss, potential causes and motivations of loss, and potential universals. All of them are discussed against the background of similarities and differences with what we know about the emergence of new elements and categories. In Section 3, we introduce the individual contributions. The contributions are grouped into two sets, studies which primarily focus on descriptive generalizations, models and methods and those which first and foremost address the question of causes and motivations for loss.

2.   Studying loss: Hypotheses and generalizations

2.1   Data and methods for studying loss

As the study of loss is relatively uncharted terrain, several studies in this volume present the reader with promising new data sources and methods for the study of loss. Rudnicka discusses and applies a typology of five criteria that can be used to determine loss of grammatical constructions (see also Rudnicka 2018). Tichý proposes and tests a new quantitative method to identify obsolescing multi-word units in corpus data. Schweinberger and Hundt apply statistical models such as logistic regression (Schweinberger), variability-based neighbor clustering, random forests, and conditional inference trees (Hundt). Čermák explores the added value and shortcomings of 'updated' Old English for the study of loss and innovation.

2.2   Modelling loss: Classifications and theories

Other contributions seek to work out classification schemes and determine how to best model loss in different linguistic frameworks. Sims-Williams and Baerman propose a classification of loss in the area of inflectional morphology based on a broad typological survey, which is intended as an initial step towards theory-formation. Rehn takes an explicit generative approach and is, amongst others, interested in competition as a factor in loss (cf. Kroch 1994). Kuo's analysis is couched within Diachronic Construction Grammar. He proposes that whereas innovation (constructionalization) is characterized by increase in productivity, increase in schematicity and loss of compositionality (Traugott & Trousdale 2013), loss involves losses with regard to these three parameters.

2.3 The process of loss

Many contributions address the internal make-up of the process of loss. This topic offers the most obvious area of comparison between emergence and loss, as diachronic linguistics has made significant in-roads into understanding the process of emergence. Many studies make a distinction between the actual innovation and the subsequent spread, with the latter usually being separated into spread through the language system and spread through the community (see for example Hopper & Traugott 1993: 46–50; McMahon 1994: 248–252 going back to Weinreich et al. 1968 and Timberlake 1977). As for emergence, the first instance of loss will prove impossible to observe for linguists, as that would be represented by the first speaker not using a particular element or the first speaker not even acquiring that element. The advances in the study of the two types of spread (through the language and through the community), by contrast, provide contributors to this volume with interesting hypotheses. Spread in both areas has been shown to be gradual and incremental (e.g., Labov 1994; Traugott & Trousdale 2010). The questions that pose themselves are whether loss, after its (imperceptible) initial manifestation, is gradual and incremental? And if so, whether the process is a mirror-image of the spread involved in emergence, i.e., whether it involves progressive restrictions of linguistic contexts and progressive constraint in terms of sociolinguistic and register usage. With regard to the latter, one could hypothesise that the element being lost is increasingly restricted to older speakers and to more formal and/or archaic registers. Table 2 sketches potential parallels:

Table 2. Suggested process of emergence vs. loss

Emergence	Loss
1. Innovation of new element (difficult/impossible to observe)	1. Decline begins: first speaker not using or not even acquiring element (difficult/impossible to observe)
2. New element is observed. It is limited to certain linguistic contexts and socially/regionally/stylistically marked.	2. Decline of an element is observed. Decline is limited to certain linguistic contexts and socially/regionally/stylistically marked.
3. Rise in frequency – Spread through speech community: Sociolinguistic or registerial restrictions become less marked or vanish. – Spread through language system: Used in more and more linguistic contexts.	3. Further decrease in frequency – Acquires sociolinguistic restrictions or registerial restrictions. – Becomes more restricted with respect to the range of linguistic contexts it is used in.

The answers to the questions diverge intriguingly. The main purpose of Schweinberger's study is to test whether loss in a replacement scenario, intensifier renewal, proceeds in an incremental way with a systematic addition of language-internal, social and cognitive constraints, mirroring the innovation process shown by intensifiers. He finds that it is almost exclusively the variable age that is significant, so that in this case, one can assume a uniform loss pattern where younger speakers across the board prefer other intensifiers. Hundt considers the interaction of a variety of sociolinguistic and system-internal factors in the demise of the *be*-perfect in Late Modern English. She finds that the sociolinguistic factors tend to not affect the use of the construction, while the impact of language-internal factors is crucial. The most significant finding is that the construction is lost at different speeds with different lexical verbs. She therefore proposes that the loss of the *be*-perfect displays lexical attrition, the mirror-image of lexical diffusion. Similarly, Kranich shows in her analysis of the loss of modals *must* and *may* that they seem to decrease faster with certain types of verbs and shows how this is connected to their falling into disuse most clearly in specific constructions, such as the *we may say* construction, and genres, e.g., scientific writing. Rudnicka finds evidence for loss of paradigmatic combinatory potential and genre-restrictions for the *so*-adj-*a* construction. Kuo's study further supports the notion of gradual decline across the language system, in that different constructions representing the same abstract schema are lost at different times. Kempf's paper discusses the impact of region, style and genre in the demise of the *so*-relative as starting point for a discussion of changing socio-cultural practices as explanation.

2.4   Causes and motivations for loss

Causes and motivation factors for loss is another topic that can build on a strong tradition of research on emergence. In many case studies, an innovative element is shown to replace an older element, and the discussion of causes and motivations also includes hypotheses as to why the older element is replaced. Causes of loss are expected to reflect causes of language change in general. In line with existing discussions, we distinguish language-internal and language-external factors behind language change. The contributions in this volume identify and discuss a large number of potential factors. We give a brief overview here.

Among the language-internal factors, competition is addressed specifically by Rehn and Rudnicka. While Rehn proposes that competition is a necessary but not sufficient factor for loss in her case study, Rudnicka argues that for the *so*-adj-*a* construction, potential competitors did not play a major role in the loss. Kranich points out that in the case of the modals and later semi-modals in English, an explanation in terms of replacement is too simplistic, and the process is influenced by factors such as contexts of use and genre. A second language-internal factor discussed by several contributors is functional load or multi-functionality. With regard to this factor, the jury is still out as to whether multi-functionality of an element prevents its loss or whether it may actually be a factor contributing to its loss, e.g., because the multiple functions inhibit straightforward interpretation, as also argued by Leung and van der Wurff (2018). Rehn and Kempf offer different perspectives on this intriguing question, with Rehn supporting the idea that multi-functionality makes an element resistant to loss, and Kempf analysing the multi-functionality of German *so* as one of the factors that led to its loss as a relative pronoun. All these factors together point to the prominent role of economy in loss and language change (e.g., Keller 1994; van Gelderen 2004). This is not unexpected given what we know about e.g., ease of production leading to loss of difficult phoneme combinations, avoidance of syncretism leading to loss of specific morphemes, or syncretism leading to the loss of distinctions within a category.

Another factor that featured prominently in the overview of possible causes proposed by Leung and van der Wurff (2018: 177) is form-function mismatch. In our volume, the distinction between form and meaning plays an essential role in the typology of losses in inflectional morphology proposed by Sims-Williams and Baerman. While it is possible for form and function to be both lost, they show many cases to be driven initially by loss of either form or function. The idea of form-function match and mismatch is also crucial to Kuo's constructional analysis. He argues that abstract constructions, such as the adverse avertive schema in Chinese, can be lost when the 'best-match semantic' (sub)construction decreases in frequency. Put differently, abstract constructions can be lost when they are semantically demotivated by the loss of a prototypical concrete construction.

A further observation is that changes in one field may trigger changes in another field. Take for example, the loss of phonemic distinctions in short unstressed syllables in Old English that led to case syncretism, which can be seen as a major factor in the loss of morphological case marking in English or the repercussions of morphological change on syntax as described in a.o. Lightfoot (2002). In this volume, Čermák highlights the interplay between the lexical and syntactic level in so far that the loss of the English impersonal construction is stalled by the replacement of obsolete lexical verbs by other verbs with similar meanings. It could be argued that Tichý's paper points in a similar direction: he proposes amongst other motivations that an obsolete word can be responsible for the loss of a multi-word pattern.

A further factor featured in multiple contributions is extravagance (cf. Haspelmath 1999: 1055). As Keller has stated in his classic discussion of motivations for language change, speakers tend to follow, among other maxims, the maxim "Talk in such a way that you are noticed" (cf. Keller 1994: 101). This means that when a linguistic element is overused and becomes bleached of its expressivity, replacement by a new, more expressive element is likely to happen and the bleached element is likely to fall into disuse. Both in Schweinberger's study of New-Zealand English intensifiers and in Kuo's study of Chinese adverse avertive constructions, the once prototypical member of the category is on its way out. It is particularly in regard to elements that have a strong attitudinal force, as is the case in intensification and adverse avertive constructions, that the factor extravagance as a motivation for innovation and its counterpart loss of expressivity as a motivation for decline and loss plays a role. Rudnicka discusses extravagance as motivation for the use of the grammatically peculiar *so*-adj-*a* construction and argues that not so much the loss of expressivity, but the association with more negative attitudes such as old-fashionedness and jocularity are factors explaining the loss.

A final factor that is maybe somewhat more controversial is the notion of typological drift. Sapir's (1921) notion of a tendency for changes in a language to move into a certain direction (e.g., a change from synthetic to analytic in various domains of the English language, cf. Baugh and Cable 1993: 60, but cf. Szmrecsanyi 2012 for a critical view of the textbook story). Čermák discusses the notion of typological change in English with regard to the loss of impersonal constructions. In Kempf's paper, the general tendency of the German language to become more favourable to overt as opposed to hidden complexity (cf. Bisang 2015) is named as one factor supporting the loss of *so* as relative pronoun, which can also be seen as a type of 'drift-based explanation'.

Among the language-external factors, language contact immediately springs to mind because of its important role in language change (e.g., Weinreich 1953; Thomason & Kaufman 1988; Van Coetsem 2000; Matras 2009). It can be presumed to also play an important role in loss, be it because speakers of language A borrow a new construction from language B (cf. Thomason & Kaufman 1988: 65–95) and thus stop using the indigenous construction they originally used for the same function, be it because speakers of language A grammaticalize a new construction under contact conditions (cf. Heine & Kuteva 2005) and as a consequence stop using older markers that are in competition with the newly grammaticalized construction, or be it that younger speakers no longer acquire the full spectrum of constructions in a language A because language B has become dominant in their territory so that a whole part of a language gets lost in the younger 'semi-bilingual' generation (cf. Sasse 1992). Language contact could motivate the loss of linguistic elements in multiple different ways. Borchers explores this factor as a potential explanation for the loss of biactantial marking in Koĭc – as speakers of Koĭc are bilingual with Nepali, which does not have biactantial indexing, it seems a plausible cause for their demise in Koĭc. Leung and van der Wurff (2018) provide a different causation, where the fact that a particular element is no longer reinforced by a similar element when a situation of language contact ends, could have played a role in its decline.

A further set of language-external factors which have been shown to play a role in language change and innovation involving replacement are prescriptivism, changes in language attitudes, as well as socio-cultural changes and changes in fashion. Kempf discusses changes in stylistic tastes as one potential factor in the demise of *so* as relative marker: As the Chancery style was no longer considered a model and fell out of fashion, constructions associated with it could lose appeal as well (though this by no means affected all relevant constructions). Looking at more recent times, democratization and colloquialization (Mair 2006) can act as trends that disfavor the use of linguistic elements associated with formal styles or with an overt attention to social hierarchies. Kranich shows that the use of a deferential hedging construction in scientific writing is decreasing in frequency, presumably because of changes in the simulated author-reader-interactions in these texts due to changes in social norms.

2.5   Potential universals

An ultimate purpose pursued in the study of loss is to investigate whether there is evidence for or against potential universals of loss. While, of course, based on the limited number of studies and the limited number of languages investigated, it is impossible to have firm evidence for a particular universal, it is possible to find evidence against suggested universals – as, one could argue, even one case is enough to revoke a universal in the proper sense of the term or, at least, prompt a thorough re-investigation of the universal, in less strict interpretation.

One universal specific to loss that we are aware of claimed that "when a grammatical distinction is given up, it is the more frequent category that survives" (Haspelmath 2004: 18). Contrary to this prediction, Kuo's study of Chinese adverse avertive constructions shows that in this case, it is the most frequent (and most prototypical) item that is affected by loss. Furthermore, this type of loss, as Kuo shows, can then, in fact, trigger the loss of the whole schematic construction. Likewise, in Schweinberger's investigation of intensifiers in New-Zealand English, the variant on the verge of loss, at least in the colloquial use of the younger generation, is the previously highly frequent *very*. The reason for this specific and other parallel cases of loss and innovation has been mentioned above: While high frequency leads to a high degree of entrenchment favoring retention in the language (cf. Bybee 2010), high frequency can also lead to bleaching and loss of expressive force, which may make an element less suitable for fulfilling its intended function and therefore prone to loss.

Frequency is not the only factor that sometimes protects against and sometimes promotes loss. Contributions to this volume identify similar ambivalence with regard to multi-functionality. While in Rehn's study of loss and retention in

Alemannic, multi-functionality seems to help the item to be preserved, in Kempf's study, multi-functionality rather seems to be among the factors promoting the loss of *so* as relative pronoun because of ambiguity and high-processing cost.

Other open questions are whether some languages are more prone to loss than others (if one compares English to other Germanic languages, English may seem to be more prone to loss, possibly because of the greater amount and intensity of language contact situations in its history (cf. Thomason & Kaufman 1988: 306–321 for a controversial discussion)), and, if contact does play a considerable role, whether more isolated languages would be less likely to lose elements over time. As a matter of course, a first set of contributions on a topic, such as those provided in this volume, can only scratch the surface, but we do hope that the insights that can be gained from them will pique interest in and stimulate further discussion of loss.

3.   Summaries of the contributions in this volume

PART I – Modelling loss: Description, theory and method

The aim of **Helen Sims-Williams and Matthew Baerman** in the paper 'A typological perspective on the loss of inflection' is to draw up a typology of operations of inflectional loss based on a survey of data from a typologically, genetically and areally diverse set of languages. The origin of inflectional morphology has been extensively studied, but its loss much less so and Sims-Williams and Baerman set out to provide a descriptive basis for future theory development and discussion of explanations and motivations. They tease apart how inflectional change happened to propose fine-grained but highly significant distinctions whilst recognising that these distinctions are not always possible to make with the data available. Their typology consists of three main types. The first is the loss of forms or formal distinctions through convergence or replacement. In this type, loss itself is a by-product as are consecutive changes to features or feature values. The second type involves loss of contrast between feature values. Under this process forms persist without functional motivation, which can result in free variation, lexical and paradigmatic redistribution, or the formal contrast is reinterpreted. The third type are cases in which form and content are lost together: the form is lost and the function is no longer expressed inflectionally. Sims-Williams and Bearman conclude that notwithstanding the ubiquitous interplay between form and function, their typology shows it is possible and instructive to conceptualise loss in inflectional morphology in terms of discrete operations anchored in meaning or in form.

In the paper '*So*-adj-*a* construction as a case of obsolescence in progress', **Karolina Rudnicka** applies the framework she developed for the analysis of grammatical obsolescence (Rudnicka 2018) to the *so*-adj-*a* construction, which has also been referred to as the Big Mess Construction in the literature. Using the Corpus of Historical American English, Rudnicka shows that this construction has undergone a steep decline in the past 200 years. This matches the first, necessary, criterion for grammatical obsolescence in the framework, i.e., a negative correlation between time and frequency of use. Rudnicka tests whether the construction also displays the four further symptomatic criteria: distributional fragmentation, i.e., restriction to particular (typically formal) genres; paradigmatic atrophy, where a construction's potential for combinations at the paradigmatic level is reducing; competition at constructional level; and evidence of higher-order motivations, e.g., socio-cultural processes. Rudnicka finds some evidence for distributional fragmentation and paradigmatic atrophy but rules out competition. She speculates about possible higher-order motivations and points out that the *so*-adj-*a* construction has always had a very specific rhematic function but may have lost expressivity and instead became associated with a more archaic and jocular character.

In the paper 'The impersonal construction in the texts of Updated Old English', **Jan Čermák** revisits the loss of the English impersonal construction which is known to have been a drawn-out process by and large spanning the entire Middle English period. Čermák focuses on the early part of the period, on the transition between Old and Middle English. This turbulent period is famously underrepresented in the historical corpus. An important goal of Čermák's paper is to explore to what extent texts cataloged and classified as Updated Old English (1060–1220), i.e., post-Conquest edited copies of Old English texts, are useful for the linguistic study of change, and for the study of morphosyntactic change in particular. Čermák gives a detailed description of the types of changes typically attested when comparing the updated texts and their originals. He finds that even though less conspicuous than in the areas of lexis or morphology, there is evidence that scribes changed syntax. He warns of the complexities presented by the structural and sociolinguistic context of this particular data set, e.g., scribes made both archaic and innovative interventions. Specifically, for the impersonal construction, Čermák finds further evidence supporting Möhlig-Falke's (2012) observation that at this early stage in its decline the impersonal construction was maintained and kept productive by the replacement of obsolescing lexical pivots.

Ondřej Tichý's paper 'Corpus driven identification of lexical bundle obsolescence in Late Modern English' reports on a project to develop a quantitative methodology for the study of a particular type of lexical obsolescence, the obsolescence of multi-word sequences or lexical bundles, i.e., of multi-word units that were once common but that radically decreased in frequency. One particularly striking example is the loss and replacement of the expression *a right line* by *a straight line* in the period under study. Tichý focuses on the Late Modern English period and uses the Google NGrams data set because this provides him with a sufficiently large data set for this type of investigation. The proposed methodology combines the Obsolescence Index (Tichý 2018) for lexical obsolescence with a bottom up approach to calculating association measures in multi-word sequences inspired by Wahl & Gries (2019). A first part of the paper carefully discusses drawbacks of the data set and the thorny issue of deciding thresholds. The second part qualitatively explores the sequences identified as obsolete by the methodology: they can be grouped into scientific terminology, "quasi terminology" (fixed expressions for concepts outside the realm of science, e.g., *Primitive Fathers* which is replaced by *Early Church Fathers*), appellations, legal and administrative phrases, dating expressions, pragmatic markers, lexical replacements in collocations, changes in countability of nouns, changes to complex verb phrases. These, interestingly for wider thinking about loss, cover processes of lexical and grammatical change. Tichý concludes that the methodology is successful, but also identifies further points for improvement.

Yueh Hsin Kuo's paper 'A constructional account of the loss of the adverse avertive schema in Mandarin Chinese' uses a case study from Chinese to explore the defining characteristics of loss as opposed to emergence in the framework of Diachronic Construction Grammar. The well-chosen case study involves an instance of loss at schema level (i.e., a high-level grammatical construction – the loss of which means that an abstract pattern [ADVERB (NEG) VP] is no longer productively used to express a specific grammatical meaning, the adverse avertive meaning). Kuo argues that where schema emergence, or constructionalisation, has been characterised by increase in productivity and schematicity and loss of compositionality, schema loss is characterised by loss across all three parameters. He draws particular attention to the role played by different subschemata. Following Goldberg (2006 and other works), he argues that a constructional schema is motivated and cognitively anchored by its most prototypical subschematic member, which provides the 'constructional meaning supply'. In the case of the Chinese avertive construction, there was a clear decrease in frequency of the subschema which provided the best semantic match with the adverse avertive schema. At the same time, another subschema, the semantics and pragmatics of which did not provide a transparent match with the adversity meaning, gained in frequency and as a result became the most frequent subschema. This process constituted a change where the constructional meaning supplier changed from a subschema that motivated the schema as a whole to one that demotivates it, leading to the loss of the schema. Kuo concludes that constructional loss, like constructional emergence, involves interacting changes affecting constructions of different levels of schematicity within a network.

PART II – Motivations and explanations for loss: Language-internal and external factors

Alexandra Rehn is interested in the role of competition and the availability of an alternative means of expression in loss. In the paper 'Loss or variation? Functional load in morpho-syntax – three case studies', she investigates three distinctive cases of decline in German dialects, in particular Alemannic, resulting in loss (adnominal genitive), optionality (adjectival inflection marking) and variation (relative clause introducers). The data are drawn from the SynALM project, which used questionnaires to collect data on certain syntactic phenomena in Alemannic. The study is couched in a generative approach to syntactic analysis and language change. Comparing the different outcomes of the three case studies, Rehn concludes that the availability of an alternative strategy of expression is a necessary but not a sufficient factor for loss. It is important that the two strategies are in direct competition. Rehn argues that an item can be protected from loss even when there is a direct competitor when it has a high functional load, i.e., when the same item appears in multiple morphosyntactic contexts. The adnominal genitive differs from the other two cases in that it is restricted to one very specific morpho-syntactic context. The multiple contexts in Rehn's case studies on adjectival inflection and relative clause introducers are clearly distinct and therefore do not give rise to ambiguity. Rehn notes that a similar constraint on loss has been observed in phonology (cf. Wedel, Kaplan & Jackson 2013).

Marianne Hundt's paper '"*The next Morning I got a Warrant for the Man and his Wife, but he was fled*": Did sociolinguistic factors play a role in the loss of the BE-perfect?' revisits a well-known case of loss in the history of English whereby the verb *be* is gradually completely replaced as a perfect auxiliary by *have*. In the period under study, Late Modern English, *be* as a perfect auxiliary is declining in its last stronghold, in combinations with change of state and motion verbs. Hundt is particularly interested in the potential role played by sociolinguistic factors and investigates these with a variationist corpus analysis of data from the Old Bailey Corpus. Hundt conducts a number of statistical analyses, Variability-based Neighbour Clustering to determine relevant periodization, and random forests and conditional inference trees to assess the relative importance and interactions of the selected predictor variables. The independent variables included are sex, class, role (e.g., defendant, witness, lawyer) as well as verb (12 change of state and change of place verbs) and morphological form of the auxiliary. Hundt finds that social factors only play a minor role in the change. The language-internal predictors and the predictor verb, in particular, outweigh the social predictors. Hundt suggests this could be because the change is below the level of speakers' awareness (cf. Anderwald 2014). The significance of the factor verb is interpreted as evidence for *lexical attrition*, the mirror image of lexical diffusion seen in morphosyntactic innovation. Equally intriguing is Hundt's finding that the analysis does not show the expected trend of step-wise loss based on Sorace's (2000) Auxiliary Selection Hierarchy.

Martin Schweinberger looks at intensifier renewal from the perspective of loss in the paper 'On the waning of forms – a corpus-based analysis of decline and loss in adjective amplification'. The specific case of loss and renewal he focuses on is the replacement of *very* by *really* in New Zealand English. The process of innovation involved in intensifier renewal has been extensively studied in variationist sociolinguistic publications. These studies found the innovation process to proceed in a systematic way by sequentially undoing language-internal, social and cognitive constraints. Schweinberger sets out to investigate whether decline and loss proceed in a similar systematic way. He uses The Wellington Corpus of Spoken New Zealand English to extract data for a binominal mixed-effects regression analysis including a range of language-internal (related to the adjective; adjective, function, gradability, emotionality, semantic category, frequency), social (age, gender, education) and cognitive (priming) factors. The regression reveals that age is the most important factor determining the use of *very* with other significant factors largely absent in the final minimal adequate model. Schweinberger concludes that the absence of other significant predictors indicates a uniform process and an absence of a systematic, stepwise loss of *very*. In this particular instance, morphosyntactic loss is not incremental in the way innovation is.

Svenja Kranich turns her attention to a well-known change in English, the decline in frequency of the core modals, in her paper 'Decline and loss in the modal domain in recent English'. Previous studies have shown that an explanation in which the core modals are replaced by semi-modals is too simplistic (e.g., Leech 2013). Kranich and Gast (2015) showed that the functions of the modals are a crucial factor and that the modals are much more robust in their epistemic function than in their deontic uses. In addition, the decline appears to be highly sensitive to genre. Kranich confirms and builds on these findings with a new study of *may* and *must* using the Corpus of Historical American English and argues that the decline of core modals includes the demise of certain modal constructions, which decline at different rates. She illustrates this with a micro-study of the construction *we + may + verb* of speaking/reasoning, which contributed to the more rapid decline rate of *may* in non-fiction texts. Kranich proposes the reasons behind this construction's decline and that of *must* and *may* in general are socio-cultural developments, e.g., democratization, which result in changes to discourse-pragmatic practices. She ends her paper by making a plea for an integrated approach to the study of loss combining corpus studies with socio-cultural and discourse-pragmatic analyses.

In the paper 'German *so*-relatives: lost in grammatical, typological, and sociolinguistic change', **Luise Kempf** takes an in-depth look at the rapid and complete decline of the particle *so* as a relativiser in New High German. She conducts a corpus study using the GermanC corpus, which allows to investigate differences in genre and regional distribution in a systematic way. Based on her findings, she carefully reassesses, contextualises and complicates factors proposed in the literature. She convincingly argues that the decline cannot simply be explained by the demise of 'chancery language' (*Kanzleisprache*). *So*-relatives were not only used in genres associated with chancery languages, but more widely in high register genres. While *so*-relatives disappeared from the language, other constructions found in chancery style were not. Kempf suggests more general sociocultural changes were also responsible for the decline of *so*-relatives. The Enlightenment and democratization of writing and written language resulted in a demand for clearer and more precise language visible in a general typological drift towards overtness and morphosyntactic complexity. *So*-relatives, which are both grammatically and semantically imprecise, clashed with this new stylistic demand.

The paper 'Loss of object indexation in verbal paradigms of Koïc (Tibeto-Burman, Nepal)' by **Dörte Borchers** describes a case of morphological loss in Koïc, a language of the Kiranti branch of the Tibeto-Burman family. Kiranti languages typically have biactantial indexing systems and index both subject and object on transitive verbs. Recent data for modern Koïc collected by Borchers (2008), and a contemporaneous grammar (Rapacha 2005), do not evidence biactantial indexing but contain different subject indexes for different conjugations. These findings are contrasted with the data collected by Genetti (1988), which do contain verbal paradigms with both subject and object indexes alongside paradigms with only the former. Borchers shows that there is a systematic morphological and semantic relationship between the biactantial indexes and the subject indexes of modern Koïc. However, the available data for Koïc are not sufficient to reconstruct the loss of object indexing. Borchers looks at language contact as an explanation for the change; speakers of Koïc are bilingual with Nepali, which does not have biactantial indexing. Borchers identifies Silva-Corvalán's (1994) study of bilingual Spanish speakers in Los Angeles as presenting a potential model as it involves a comparable sociolinguistic context.

References

Anderwald, Lieselotte. 2014. The decline of the be-perfect, linguistic relativity, and grammar writing in the nineteenth century. In *Late Modern English Syntax*, Marianne Hundt (ed.), 13–27. Cambridge: CUP. https://doi.org/10.1017/CBO9781139507226.004

Baugh, Albert C. & Cable, Thomas. 1993. *A History of the English Language*, 4th edn. London: Routledge. https://doi.org/10.4324/9780203994634

Bisang, Walter. 2015. Hidden complexity - The neglected side of complexity and its implications. *Linguistics Vanguard* 1: 177–187. https://doi.org/10.1515/lingvan-2014-1014

Borchers, Dörte. 2008. *A Grammar of Sunwar. Descriptive Grammar, Paradigms, Texts and Glossary* [Languages of the Greater Himalayan Region 5.7]. Leiden: Brill.

Bybee, Joan L. 2010. *Language, Usage and Cognition*. Cambridge: CUP. https://doi.org/10.1017/CBO9780511750526

van Coetsem, Frans. 2000. *A General and Unified Theory of the Language Transmission Process in Language Contact*. Heidelberg: Winter.

Curzan, Anne. 2003. *Gender Shifts in the History of English*. Amsterdam: John Benjamins. https://doi.org/10.1017/CBO9780511486913

Dolberg, Florian. 2019. *Agreement in Language Contact. Gender Development in the Anglo-Saxon Chronicle*. [Studies in Language Companion Series 208]. Amsterdam: John Benjamins. https://doi.org/10.1075/slcs.208

van Gelderen, Elly. 2004. *Grammaticalization as Economy* [Linguistik Aktuell/Linguistics Today 71]. Amsterdam: John Benjamins. https://doi.org/10.1075/la.71

Genetti, Carol. 1988. Notes on the structure of the Sunwari transitive verb. *Linguistics in the Tibeto-Burman Area* 11 (2): 62–92.

Givón, Talmy. 1979. *On Understanding Grammar*. New York NY: Academic Press.

Goldberg, Adele E. 2006. *Constructions at Work. The Nature of Generalization in Language*. Oxford: OUP.

Gussenhoven, Carlos. 2004. *The Phonology of Tone and Intonation*. Cambridge: CUP. https://doi.org/10.1017/CBO9780511616983

Haeberli, Eric. 2002. Inflectional morphology and the loss of verb-second in English. In *Syntactic Effects of Morphological Change*, David W. Lightfoot (ed.), 88–106. Oxford: OUP. https://doi.org/10.1093/acprof:oso/9780199250691.003.0005

Haspelmath, Martin. 1999. Why is grammaticalization irreversible? *Linguistics* 37 (6): 1043–1068. https://doi.org/10.1515/ling.37.6.1043

Haspelmath, Martin. 2004. On directionality in language change with particular reference to grammaticalization. In *Up and Down the Cline. The Nature of Grammaticalization* [Typological Studies in Language 59], Olga Fischer, Muriel Norde & Harry Perridon (eds), 17–44. Amsterdam: John Benjamins. https://doi.org/10.1075/tsl.59.03has

Heine, Bernd & Kuteva, Tania. 2005. *Language Contact and Grammatical Change*. Cambridge: CUP. https://doi.org/10.1017/CBO9780511614132

Hopper, Paul & Traugott, Elizabeth Closs. 1993. *Grammaticalization*. Cambridge: CUP.

Keller, Rudi. 1994. *On Language Change. The Invisible Hand in Language*. London: Routledge.

van Kememade, Ans. 2012. Rethinking the loss of verb second. In *The Oxford Handbook of the History of English*, Terttu Nevalainen & Elizabeth Closs Traugott (eds), 1182–1199. Oxford: OUP.

Kranich, Svenja & Gast, Volker. 2015. Explicitness of epistemic modal marking: Recent changes in British and American English. In *Thinking Modally. English and Contrastive Studies on Modality*, Juan Rafael Zamorano-Mansilla, Carmen Maíz, Elena Domínguez & Maria Victoria Martín de la Rosa (eds), 3–22. Newcastle upon Tyne: Cambridge Scholars.

Kroch, Anthony. 1994. Morphosyntactic variation. In *Papers from the 30th Regional Meeting of the Chicago Linguistics Society. Parasession on Variation and Linguistic Theory*, Katharine Beals (ed.), 180–201. Chicago IL: Chicago Linguistics Society.

Kroch, Anthony, Taylor, Ann & Ringe, Donald. 2000. The Middle English verb-second contsraint: A case study in language contact and language change. In *Textual Parameters in Older Languages* [Current Issues in Linguistic Theory "https://www.benjamins.com/

catalog/cilt" 195], Susan C. Herring, Pieter van Reenen & Lene Schøsler (eds), 353–391. Amsterdam: John Benjamins. https://doi.org/10.1075/cilt.195.17kro

Labov, William. 1994. *Principles of Linguistic Change, Vol. I: Internal Factors*. Oxford: Blackwell.

Leech, Geoffrey. 2013. Where have all the modals gone? An essay on the declining frequency of core modal auxiliaries in recent standard English. In *English Modality. Core, Periphery and Evidentiality*, Juana I. Marín-Arrese, Marta Carretero, Jorge Arús Hita & Johan vander Auwera (eds), 95–115. Berlin: Mouton De Gruyter. https://doi.org/10.1515/9783110286328.95

Leung, Alex Ho-Cheong & van der Wurff, Wim. 2018. Anaphoric reference in Early Modern English: The case of said and same. In *The Noun Phrase in English. Past and Present* [Linguistik Aktuell/Linguistics Today 246], Alex Ho-Cheong Leung & Wim van der Wurff (eds), 143–186. Amsterdam: John Benjamins. https://doi.org/10.1075/la.246.06leu

Lightfoot David W. 2002. *Syntactic Effects of Morphological Change*. Oxford: OUP. https://doi.org/10.1093/acprof:oso/9780199250691.001.0001

Mair, Christian. 2006. *Twentieth Century English. History, Variation, and Standardization*. Cambridge: CUP. https://doi.org/10.1017/CBO9780511486951

Matras, Yaron. 2009. *Language Contact*. Cambridge: CUP. https://doi.org/10.1017/CBO9780511809873

McMahon, April M.S. 1994. *Understanding Language Change*. Cambridge: CUP. https://doi.org/10.1017/CBO9781139166591

Möhlig-Falke, Ruth. 2012. *The Early English Impersonal Construction. An Analysis of Verbal and Constructional Meaning*. Oxford: OUP. https://doi.org/10.1093/acprof:oso/9780199777723.001.0001

Östör, Ákos. 1982. Terms of address and Hungarian society. *Language Sciences* 4 (1): 55–69. https://doi.org/10.1016/S0388-0001(82)80013-2

Rapacha, Lal. 2005. A Descriptive Grammar of Kirānti-Kõits. PhD dissertation, Jawaharlal Nehru University.

Rudnicka, Karolina. 2018. Variation of sentence length across time and genre: Influence on the syntactic usage in English. In *Diachronic Corpora, Genre, and Language Change* [Studies in Corpus Linguistics 85], Richard Jason Whitt (ed.), 219–240. Amsterdam: John Benjamins. https://doi.org/10.1075/scl.85.10rud

Sapir, Edward. 1921. *Language. An Introduction to the Study of Speech*. New York, NY: Harcourt, Brace and Co.

Sasse, Hans-Jürgen. 1992. Language decay and contact-induced change: Similarities and differences. In *Language Death. Factual and Theoretical Explorations with Special Reference to East Africa*, Matthias Brenzinger (ed.), 7–30. Berlin: Mouton de Gruyter.

Silva-Corvalán, Carmen. 1994. *Language Contact and Change. Spanish in Los Angeles*. Oxford: Clarendon Press.

Sorace, Antonella. 2000. Gradients in auxiliary selection with intransitive verbs. *Language* 76 (4): 859–890. https://doi.org/10.2307/417202

Szmrecsanyi, Benedikt. 2012. Analyticity and syntheticity in the history of English. In *The Oxford Handbook of the History of English*, Terttu Nevalainen & Elizabeth Closs Traugott (eds), 654–665. Oxford: OUP.

Thomason, Sara G. & Kaufman, Terrence. 1988. *Language Contact, Creolization, and Genetic Linguistics*. Berkeley CA: University of California Press.

Tichý, Ondřej. 2018. Lexical obsolescence and loss in English: 1700–2000. In *Applications of Pattern-Driven Methods in Corpus Linguistics*, [Studies in Corpus Linguistics 82], Joanna Kopaczyk & Jukka Tyrkkö (eds), 81–103. Amsterdam: John Benjamins. https://doi.org/10.1075/scl.82.04tic

Timberlake, Alan. 1977. Reanalysis and actualization in syntactic change. In *Mechanisms of Syntactic Change*, Charles N. Li (ed.), 141–177. Austin TX: University of Texas Press.

Traugott, Elizabeth Closs & Trousdale, Graeme (eds). 2010. *Gradualness, Gradience, and Grammaticalization* [Typological Studies in Language 90]. Amsterdam: John Benjamins. https://doi.org/10.1075/tsl.90

Traugott, Elizabeth Closs & Trousdale, Graeme. 2013. *Constructionalization and Constructional Changes*. Oxford: OUP. https://doi.org/10.1093/acprof:oso/9780199679898.001.0001

Wahl, Alexander & Gries, Stefan T. 2020. Computational extraction of formulaic sequences from corpora: Two case studies of a new extraction algorithm. In *Computational Phraseology* [IVITRA Research in Linguistics and Literature 24], Gloria Corpas Pastor & Jean-Pierre Colson (eds), 84–110. Amsterdam: John Benjamins. https://doi.org/10.1075/ivitra.24.05wah

Wedel, Andrew, Kaplan, Abby & Jackson, Scott. 2013. High functional load inhibits phonological contrast loss: A corpus study. *Cognition* 128 (2): 179–186. https://doi.org/10.1016/j.cognition.2013.03.002

Weinreich, Uriel. 1953. *Languages in Contact. Findings and Problems*. New York NY: Linguistic Circle of New York.

Weinreich, Uriel, Labov, William & Herzog, Marvin. 1968. Empirical foundations for a theory of language change. In *Directions of Historical Linguistics*, Winfred P. Lehmann & Yakov Malkiel (eds), 95–188. Austin TX: University of Texas Press.

PART I

Modelling loss: Description, theory and method

CHAPTER 1

A typological perspective on
the loss of inflection[1]

Helen Sims-Williams & Matthew Baerman
University of Surrey

The loss of inflectional morphology is a diachronic process which has played a major role in shaping our linguistic landscape, but has never been the target of focussed research in the same way that the origin of inflectional morphology has been. We offer here a preliminary typology of the operations involved in inflectional loss, distinguishing three change types: the loss of forms, the loss of features, and loss of both at the same time – that is, the loss of entire paradigm cells. These are illustrated with examples from a typologically, genetically and areally diverse set of languages.

Keywords: typology, inflection, analogy, morphology

1. Introduction

The role played by inflection has been a major parameter in linguistic typology ever since the traditional model of morphological typology which divides languages into isolating, fusional and agglutinative types (see Schwegler 1990: chapter 1 for a historical overview). Understanding the pathways along which grammatical structures move between these types is vital to explaining how and why individual languages end up with their particular typological profiles. Research on grammaticalisation has made significant advances in our understanding of how linguistic expressions transition from isolating to agglutinative to fusional structures (e.g., Hodge 1970; Heine et al. 1991; Hopper & Traugott 2003; Heine & Reh 1984;

1. This research reported here is a product of the project 'Loss of Inflection', funded by the Arts and Humanities Research Council (UK) under grant number AH/N00163X/1. Their support is gratefully acknowledged. We would also like to thank two anonymous reviewers, whose comments have helped us clarify our presentation and argumentation.

© 2021 John Benjamins Publishing Company

Lehmann 2015). Yet the opposite process, the loss of inflection, which has equally been a powerful shaping force in the history of many languages, is still poorly understood. While zero marking is typically regarded as the end point of a grammaticalisation cline (e.g., Hopper & Traugott 2003: 172–174; Lehmann 2015: 15), the transition from inflectional morphology (or morphophonology) to zero is not typically conceived of as part of the grammaticalisation process, and is often dismissed as the result of phonological attrition (e.g., Givón 1979: 209), with the implication that it lacks theoretical interest in its own right.[2]

This lack of recognition of the problem is partly because the loss of inflection involves change and reorganisation at multiple linguistic levels which can be difficult to tease apart. Inflection fundamentally relies on formal and functional contrasts operating in parallel. The *loss* of inflection necessarily involves the disruption of both formal and morphosyntactic contrasts, but it can be difficult to distinguish cause and effect. Similarly, the loss of inflection is often accompanied by syntactic changes – for example, the breakdown of case in the history of English is often associated with the move towards a fixed SVO word order. We can look at this in two ways – either the change in word order made inflectional case redundant, precipitating its loss, or the loss of case marking made a fixed basic word order necessary in order to disambiguate arguments (e.g., Allen 2006; Fischer 2010). Finally, the loss of inflection is often attributed to morphological simplification as the result of language contact (e.g., Kusters 2003, 2008; McWhorter 2007; Bentz & Winter 2013; Maitz & Neémeth 2014; Klein & Perdue 1997; Lupyan & Dale 2010; Trudgill 2012) and/or language attrition or death (Dorian 1978; Campbell & Mutzel 1989; Polinsky 1995), through imperfect learning by L2 learners or semi-speakers (Dorian 1980). It is unclear whether these phenomena are essentially the same or different from the 'internal' loss of inflection.

Such questions concern the mechanisms and reasons underlying the loss of inflection. Before we can embark on the task of explaining the loss of inflection, however, we must first be able to describe it. The routes taken by some individ-

---

2.   Within research on grammaticalisation there are exceptions to this attitude: e.g., the work of Norde on 'deflexion' in Swedish (2000, 2001, 2002). Apart from the loss of formatives, other aspects of grammaticalisation may also involve loss of inflection; in particular the loss of inflectional contrasts is a common effect of an item's transition from lexical to functional status (see discussion in § 5). Moreover, the term 'degrammaticalisation' has been applied to a diverse range of phenomena (see Heine 2003; Norde 2009), some of which can be regarded as the loss of inflection, in the sense that an inflectional marker ceases to be an inflectional marker and gains a new derivational, syntactic or lexical status (e.g., the development of the s-genitive in English and Mainland Scandinavian from inflectional affix to phrasal clitic (Norde 1997), which constitutes a loss of paradigm cells (see § 4) in the terms of this typology), potentially via a stage in which the marker serves no function (cf. Lass 1990 on 'exaptation').

ual languages have been well documented: e.g., Mørck (2005) and Naumann & Teleman (2002) on Scandinavian, Hogg (1992) and Lass (1992) on English, Wahström (2015) on Balkan Slavic, Herman (1967) on Early Romance and Schøssler (1984) on Old French, or Bloch (1934) on Indo Aryan. Yet as far as we know, so far there has been no published attempt to describe the possible diachronic pathways leading to the loss of inflection from a typological perspective. In this paper, our aim is to map out this possibility space in descriptive terms – that is, given the basic notions of inflectional functions and inflectional forms, how can we describe the transition between two diachronic states? – in order to lay out the configurations that any theory would need to cover. A given theory of change may of course favour one type over another in cases where they overlap, or indeed reject some of the types out of hand.

Our typology consists of three basic change types: loss of forms (§ 2), loss of features (§ 3), and loss of paradigm cells, i.e., the simultaneous loss of features and forms (§ 4). We illustrate these types with examples drawn from individual language histories. These languages have been chosen with typological, genetic and areal diversity in mind, but our sample is necessarily limited to languages for which sufficient historical data is available. Finally in § 5, we summarise our observations.

2.   Loss of forms

Some cases of the loss of inflection can be described as the loss of forms or formal distinctions, with changes to the system of morphosyntactic or morphosemantic features and values as a result. Here we distinguish two types: convergence (§ 2.1), where forms within an inflectional paradigm fall together by phonological or morphological change, and replacement (§ 2.2), where one form replaces another (or others). In either case, the result is the loss of a formal contrast which was previously responsible for conveying the distinction between two or more inflectional values.

2.1   Convergence

Phonological or morphological change may lead to the coincidence of two or more word forms, consequently reducing the inventory of distinct forms in the paradigm. The most obvious and familiar reason for this is phonological erosion (§ 2.1.1), given that inflectional material is often in a peripheral position in the word form and prone to weakening effects seen, for example, in final syllables. But there are also examples where such changes are not strictly phonological, which can be described instead as the explicit omission of an inflectional formative (§ 2.1.2). The defining characteristic of this type in either case is that the change can be described locally, in terms of the properties of individual forms, such as being vowel-final, or containing a particular morphological affix. The consequent paradigmatic effects are a secondary by-product of these changes.

2.1.1   *Phonological change*

Phonological change may cause the outright deletion of segments which bear grammatical information, as in Geʿez (Ethiosemitic; Hasselbach 2013: 28), where suffixes marking the nominative and genitive singular were affected by a sound change which first merged short *i* and *u* as schwa, then deleted schwa in word-final position (Table 1). These regular phonological changes created a marking pattern which opposed a marked accusative with an unmarked nominative/genitive in the singular, and removed all case endings in the feminine plural. In this case, evidence from the rest of the language shows that the change is most economically described in terms of the loss of a phonological contrast, causing the loss of the morphological suffixes as a side-effect.

Table 1. The effect of the phonological rule -a/i > -ə > ø on the Geʿez noun

	Proto-Semitic		Geʿez
	SG		SG
NOM	-u	>	-ø
ACC	-a		-a
GEN	-i		-ø

Phonological change may also lead to the loss of formal contrast not by deleting morphological elements, but merely by neutralising phonological contrasts within them. In Classical Greek, the indicative mood had been distinguished from the subjunctive primarily by the vowel length of the suffixes marking person and number of the subject (Table 2). Because the perfective and future active were both signalled by a suffix -*s*, this meant that for regular verbs, which lacked stem alternations in their paradigms, vowel length was the only feature distinguishing most future active indicative forms from their aorist active subjunctive counterparts. When contrastive vowel length was lost by phonological change, these forms became identical. We can see clearly that this change was phonologically motivated because contemporary spelling errors show us that contrastive vowel length was lost everywhere, regardless of morphological category, while on the other hand the future indicative and aorist subjunctive remained distinct where the contrast between the two was also marked by irregular stem alternations, e.g., for verbs like *légō* 'say' with future stem *ere-* and a perfective stem *eip-*.

Table 2. The effect of loss of vowel quantity on the Greek future and aorist

	500 BC			100 BC	
future indicative	pau-s-ei	ere-ei	>	pau-s-ei	ere-ei
aorist subjunctive	pau-s-ēi	eip-ēi		pau-s-ei	eip-ei

2.1.2 *Morphological change*

There are also cases where the loss of inflectional material has no obvious phonological basis, and looks instead as if formatives have simply been dropped off from inflected words. We are aware of at least one example which, at least at first glance, seems to be of this type. In Old Malayalam (Dravidian), a single set of verbal subject endings (Table 3) was attached to the different tense/polarity stems (present, past, future and negative), with deletion of the final vowel, e.g., the present stem *pookunnu-* 'leave' plus the 2SG ending *-aay* yields *pookunn-aay* 'you (SG) leave.PRS'. The forms shown in Table 3 are taken from Andronov (1993: 22, 114f); Ramaswami Ayyar (1936: 52); some variant forms have been omitted for clarity.

Table 3. Verb subject endings in Old Malayalam

1SG	-een
2SG	-aay
3SG M	-aan
3SG F	-aaḷ
3SG N	-atu
1PL	-oom
2PL	-iir
3PL M/F	-aar
3PL N	-(an)a

In Modern Malayalam these subject endings have all been dropped, so that the verb inflects only for tense/polarity. This is particularly striking, because Malayalam has not undergone any drastic phonological changes in the period since these endings started to be lost in the 14th century. For example, markers of nominal case, which like verbal subject is expressed suffixally, have continued relatively unchanged since Malayalam split from Tamil in around the 8th century (Tamil also retains the full set of subject endings on verbs). Comparison of the Modern Malayalam and Tamil forms in Table 4 shows that relatively few phonological changes are needed to derive the cognate case suffixes from a common ancestor; certainly not the widespread loss of final syllables that would be required to account for the loss of the Malayalam verbal subject suffixes by phonological means.

Table 4. Tamil and Malayalam case inflection compared

	Tamil	Malayalam
	'rod' (Asher & Annamalai 2002: 228)	'fire' (Andronov 1993: 52)
NOM	taḍi	tii
ACC	taḍiy-e	tiiy-e
DAT	taḍi-kki	tii-kku
SOC	taḍiy-ooḍa	tiiy-ooṭu
LOC	taḍi-le	tiiy-il
INSTR	taḍiy-aale	tiiy-aal
GEN	taḍiy-ooḍa	tiiy-uṭe
ABL	taḍi-le-rundu	----------

The evolution of the verbal system shown in Table 3 and that of Modern Malayalam has been portrayed as the gradual omission of subject markers, leaving only the bare stem. Ramaswami Ayyar (1936: 52) writes:

> This absence of terminations gradually affects more and more categories of finites with the passing of time. There is a gradualness in the dropping of personal endings from period to period. [...] This gradualness may have been purely literary; but it is quite possible that it may have mirrored, though chronologically at belated stages, a gradually increasing tendency in the regional and communal colloquials to drop these personal endings.

A crucial point is that the resulting form, consisting of the bare verb stem without any subject marker, is portrayed as a morphological innovation derived by dropping off the subject markers. The bare stem was not a member of the original paradigm. A single uninflected form will have emerged as the by-product of this change being applied separately to each individual form, eroding them down to their core. Ramaswami Ayyar's description (1936: 53–62) of the course of events is summarised in Table 5.

Although this account reflects the scenario as presented by Ramaswami Ayyar's description (1936), there are reasons to doubt this is the whole story (see § 2.2.1). Equally, although on the face of it is a simple change to describe, convincing examples of inflectional affixes simply being dropped off are few and far between. Nevertheless there are good reasons to believe it can and does happen.

One simple illustration of this comes from Anong, a Nungish (Sino-Tibetan) language of China. Sun and Liu (2009) describe both a conservative and an innovative variety of the language. In the innovative variety, the verbal paradigm has eliminated syllabic number suffixes in verbs (Table 6, from Sun & Liu 2009: 138). As a result the seven-cell paradigm has been reduced to three forms. All three of

Table 5. Evolution of subject markers in the present and past in Malayalam

	Old M.		by 14th c		by 15th c		by 16th	
	PRS	PST	PRS	PST	PRS	PST	PRS	PST
1SG	-een	-een	-een	-een	-een	-een	-een	-een
2SG	-aa(y)	-aa(y)	-aa(y)	-aa(y)	-aa(y)	-aa(y)	-aa(y)	-aa(y)
3SG M	-aan	-aan	----	-aan	----	-aan	----	-aan
3SG F	-aaḷ	-aaḷ	----	-aaḷ	----	-aaḷ	----	-aaḷ
3SG N	-adu	-adu	----	-adu	----	----	----	----
1PL	-oom	-oom	-oom	-oom	-oom	-oom	----	----
2PL	-iir	-iir	-iir	-iir	----	----	----	----
3PL M/F	-aar	-aar	----	-aar	----	----	----	----
3PL N	-(an)a	-(an)a	-(an)a	-(an)a	----	----	----	----

these forms were members of the original paradigm, making it possible to describe the change in terms of certain forms (which happen to be unsuffixed) replacing suffixed forms, rather than the loss of suffixes *per se*. Under the latter explanation, however, both the survival only of unsuffixed forms and the resulting patterns of syncretism are expected. In contrast, if we explain this change in terms of replacement (cf. examples in § 2.2), the loss of all syllabic suffixes has to be regarded as mere coincidence, and the resulting patterns of syncretism are more unexpected, since they require a replacement of other numbers by singular in the second person, but 1st by 3rd person in the plural.[3]

Table 6. Reduction of number distinctions in Anong (verb 'hit')

	A		B
1SG	$a^{31}n̠ɛŋ^{35}$	1SG	$a^{31}n̠ɛŋ^{35}$
2SG	$ŋa^{31}n̠ɛ^{33}$	2	$ŋa^{31}n̠ɛ^{33}$
3	$a^{31}n̠ɛ^{33}$	3/1PL	$a^{31}n̠ɛ^{33}$
1DU	$a^{31}n̠ɛ^{33}sɛ^{55}$		
2DU	$ŋa^{31}n̠ɛ^{33}sɛ^{55}$		
1PL	$a^{31}n̠ɛ^{33}i^{31}$		
2PL	$ŋa^{31}n̠ɛ^{33}ŋɯ^{31}$		

---

3. Superscript numbers represent tone: high level (55), high falling (53), mid level (33), mid falling (31) and mid rising (35).

A more complex variant of this occurs in various languages of the Caucasus. One of the areal features of these languages is a tendency towards group inflection, where only the final member of a nominal group is inflected, be it conjoined nouns or modifier + noun (Chirikba 2008: 55). In a telling variation on this, nominals that undergo stem alternations on top of case (and possibly number) suffixation lose the suffixes in non-final position, but retain the stem alternation. For example, in the Nakh languages, here illustrated by Tsova-Tush in Table 7, the absolutive of fully inflected nominals is unsuffixed, formed from the bare absolutive stem, and all the other cases are suffixed and formed from the oblique stem. The deletion of the case suffixes lays bare the oblique stem, meaning that this synchronic alternation is one in which the wholesale neutralisation of case distinctions is not due to the generalisation of one of the existing forms of the paradigm, but rather to a morphological process whose result is a barely inflected form marking only a binary distinction between absolutive and oblique case.

Table 7. Tsova-Tush (Holisky & Gagua 1994: 171f)

	Adjective in final position 'bad one'	Attributive adjective 'bad child'	
ABS	mos:i^n	mos:i^n	bader
GEN	muis:čo-^{n}	muis:čo	badre-^{n}
ERG	muis:čo-v	muis:čo	badre-v
DAT	muis:čo-n	muis:čo	badre-n

Georgian prenominal adjectives (or attributive nouns) show a similar pattern, one which can to some extent be traced historically. In this case at least (there is of course no reason to suppose that the origins of the pattern will have been the same as in the Nakh languages) its evolution appears to have involved the interplay of different processes, and not simply the dropping of terminal formatives. In Modern Georgian (Table 8), prenominal adjectives show reduced case suffixes: they lack the final consonant found elsewhere, or, in the case of the adverbial, the entire suffix is missing. Where an adjective is in final position, either because it has been substantivised or because it is post-posed (a rare alternative word order), it takes the full case suffix paradigm.

While the full paradigm is close to what was found in Old Georgian, both for nouns and adjectives, the reduced paradigm is an innovation. Boeder (1987) illustrates the various stages in the evolution of such paradigms (Table 9), drawing in part on Žanašia (1936). Type I was found in Old Georgian and represents a completely unreduced paradigm; the only difference compared to the modern full paradigms is the final /n/ of the ergative. Type II was found in the early 19th century. Compared

Table 8. 'Tall woman' in Modern Georgian (Hewitt 1995: 45f)

	'tall	woman'
NOM	maġal-i	kal-i
DAT	maġal	kal-s
ERG	maġal-ma	kal-ma
GEN	maġal-i	kal-is
INS	maġal-i	kal-it
ADV	maġal	kal-ad
VOC	maġal-o	kal-o

Table 9. Inflectional patterns of attributive adjectives in Georgian, illustrated by 'red' (Boeder 1987: 29f, 33–35)

	I	II	III	IV	V
VOC	c'itel-o	c'itel-o	c'itel-o	c'itel-o	c'itel-i
NOM	c'itel-i	c'itel-i	c'itel-i	c'itel-i	c'itel-i
ERG	c'itel-man	c'itel-ma	c'itel-ma	c'itel(-ma)	c'itel-i
GEN	c'itl-is(a)	c'itl-is	c'itel-i	c'itel	c'itel-i
INS	c'itl-it(a)	c'itl-is	c'itel-i	c'itel	c'itel-i
DAT	c'itel-s(a)	c'itel-s	c'itel	c'itel	c'itel-i
ADV	c'itl-ad	c'itel-s	c'itel	c'itel	c'itel-i

to type I what has happened is that certain forms in the paradigm have been replaced by other forms, as described in § 2.2 below: the instrumental by the genitive, and the adverbial by the dative. Type III, characteristic of the modern literary language, lacks both the final /s/ and the stem-vowel syncope (*c'itel-* ~ *c'itl-*) of type II, which could be understood either as the levelling of the paradigm to a single stem, or the extension of the nominative form to the genitive and instrumental. Type IV, which is also the typical pattern for titles (such as 'professor' or 'president'), has an unsuffixed form in most or all of the oblique cases. Type V, found in some dialects, has a single uninflected form throughout, corresponding to what in phrase-final position would be a nominative form. The whole process looks as if both the paradigm-internal replacement of forms and the (phonologically conditioned?) truncation of suffixes conspired to yield a barely or completely uninflected form.[4]

---

4.   Boeder (1987: 38, fn 5) notes that some Kartvelian dialects display a loss of word-final //s/. He cites Činčarauli (1960: 183) on Khevsuretian dialect, where it appears to be lost when

2.2   Replacement

One form may simply replace another in the paradigm. In contrast to convergence as described in the preceding section, the loss of formal distinction between forms is inherent to the change, rather than being the by-product of more general processes that happen to yield a formal identity. We distinguish two types: functionally motivated change (2.2.1), and formally motivated change (2.2.2).

2.2.1   *Functionally motivated change*

By functionally motivated change we mean replacement that can be described directly in terms of feature values. For example, in Mand (Sogeram family, Trans New Guinea phylum), the 3SG form is in the process of replacing other subject forms in all the verbal subparadigms (Daniels 2015). For example, (1a) shows 1SG agreement, while (1b), three clauses earlier in the same text, shows 3rd person agreement with the same subject. (2a) shows 1PL agreement, while (2b) shows a 1PL subject taking 3rd person agreement.

(1)   a.   api akaji-rɨn.
              I   wait-FPST.1SG
              'I waited.'   (Daniels 2015: 501)

       b.   api agra-rɨd.
              I   run.SG-FPST.3SG
              'I ran away.'   (Daniels 2015: 448)

(2)   a.   Awaŋ ka-c   arhw   gok-i   j-emɨ-nhw.
              sago FD-TOP 1PL   break-SS eat-MPST-1PL
              'The sago, we broke it and ate it.'   (Daniels 2015: 468)

       b.   Kɨmohr-i, ya   mɨŋ na-n   arhw k-ebi.
              sit.PL-SS speech true ND-ACC 1PL   talk-MPST.3
              'We sat down and spoke this language.'   (Daniels 2015: 478)

The spread of 3rd person forms is systematic, in that it embraces multiple subparadigms with different morphology. Table 10 shows the relevant paradigms, with statistics drawn from the Mand corpus provided by Daniels.

---

the following word begins in a consonant: compare *c'itl-is araq'-it* 'red brandy' (instrumental case) with *c'itl-i badag-it* 'red grapes' (instrumental case), where vowel syncope shows that it is indeed the expected reduced instrumental form of paradigm type II minus the final /s/ and not the /i/-final form of paradigm type III. It is unclear however how closely we should connect this more-or-less contemporary alternation to the rise of the /s/-less forms of paradigm type III, since this was already attested in the 10th century (Boeder 1987: 8).

Table 10. Subject marking suffixes with 1st or 2nd person subjects in Mand, with statistics from Daniels' corpus

		singular	plural	agreement with 1st or 2nd person subj.	
				marked for 1st or 2nd person	marked for 3(SG)
IMM PST	1	-in	-inhw	44	5
	2	-n	-e-n		
	3	-i(d)[i]	-e-d		
MPST	1	-emɨ-n	-emɨ-nhw	10	8
	2	-emɨ-n	-emɨ-n		
	3	-eb-i	-eb-i		
FPST	1	**-rɨ-n**	**-rɨ-nhw**	45	12
	2	**-rɨ-n**	-eu-rɨ-n		
	3	-r(ɨ-d)[i]	-e(u)-r(ɨ-d)[i]		
FUT	1	-ŋar-in	-ŋar-inhw	35	10
	2	-ŋara-n	-ŋar-e-n		
	3	-ŋar-i(d)[i]	-ŋar-e-d		
HAB	1	-cɨ-n	-cɨ-nhw	6	0[ii]
	2	-cɨ-n	-e-cɨ-n		
	3	-cɨ-n	-e-cɨ-n		

[i]The elements in parentheses appear to be optional (they are absent in many instances).
[ii]Daniels (2015: 486) notes however that the 3SG is strongly preferred in elicitation.

We have been unable to find any lexical, syntactic or discourse factors that play any role here, though perhaps this might be revealed by a larger corpus. As it stands, it looks like the incipient loss of subject agreement across the board through the generalisation of the 3SG form, affecting a morphologically heterogeneous set of forms.

Borchers (this volume) describes a similar situation in Koïc, a Kiranti language of Nepal. Transitive verbs once had a complex and partly portmanteau system of forms that marked person and number of both subject and object, but the original 3SG object forms have now been generalized throughout. This means that object agreement has effectively been lost, even though the forms themselves can be traced to ones which originally reflected object agreement features.

Borchers suggests this can be attributed to intensive contact with Nepali, and in a similar vein, Daniels suggests that the loss of agreement in Mand may be due to language attrition:

> Villagers under the age of 30 appear to be fluent only in Tok Pisin, although they
> possess varying degrees of passive fluency in Mand. Older villagers show consid-
> erable variation in their language ability.   (Daniels 2015: 439)

That said, the same applies to four of the five other closely-related Sogeram languages studied by Daniels, none of which display this loss of agreement. But generalisation of a single form in the paradigm appears to be common both in cases
of language death (e.g., Polinsky 1995; Klein & Purdue 1997) and in the initial
stages of pidgin formation (Mühlhäusler 1986), which is unified with language
attrition/death by speakers' reduced access to a target language. During subsequent stabilisation each lexeme tends to settle on a single invariant form.[5] For
example, Palenquero has generalised the 3SG form of the Spanish verb. Haitian
Creole has generalised the form of the French 2PL and/or infinitive (McWhorter
1998). Tây Bôi (a French/Vietnamese pidgin) generalised the French infinitive as
an uninflected verb form (examples from Bickerton 1995). Further examples can
be found in Bakker (2003):

(3)   Lui **avoir** permission repos   (French: *Il a la permission de se réposer*)
      'He has permission to rest.'

      Lui la **frapper**   (*Il l'a frappé*)
      'He hits her.'

      Assez, pas **connaître**   (*Assez, je n'en sais rien*)
      'Enough, I don't know.'

This type of change is not limited to such sociolinguistic scenarios, but can also
be found in cases of 'internal' change. In the predecessor of the Northern West
Germanic dialects (Old English, Old Frisian and Old Saxon) 3PL forms were generalised to 1st and 2nd person plural (Table 11). Although we do not have direct
access to intermediate stages of this merger, we might speculate that the loss of
person agreement in the plural was preceded by a stage at which agreement was
optional, as in Mand.

---

5.   Some writers seem to imply that the loss of inflection in pidgin/creole formation happens
through inflectional affixes simply being lost from words in the lexifier language, leaving only
the lexical stems. E.g., Allen (1997), arguing that the loss of case in English should not be
regarded as creolisation, says "the reduction of case-marking forms in English was not just
a matter of substituting an uninflected form for the inflected ones." We have not found any
examples of uninflected forms replacing inflected ones, except when the bare stem is also a
member of the paradigm in its own right.

Table 11. Generalisation of 3PL forms in West Germanic

	Proto West Gmc strong past	Northern West Gmc strong past		Middle English strong past
		Paradigm 1	Paradigm 2	
1SG	*laih-Ø	*laih-Ø	*laih-Ø	-Ø
3SG				
2SG	*liw-ī	*liw-ī	*liw-ī	-est
1PL	*lig-um	*lig-um	*lig-un	
2PL	*lig-ud	*lig-ud	*lig-un	-en
3PL	*lig-un	*lig-un	*lig-un	

The Malayalam developments which are described in the preceding section as resulting from the loss of affixes may alternatively be interpreted in the same way, as replacement rather than convergence. Forms realizing third person singular are affected first, an asymmetry that would be unsurprising if what we were looking at were the extension of a 3SG form, as in Mand (§ 2.2.1). And in fact, there are also similar examples attested from older texts in Malayalam, with forms bearing an overt 3rd person suffix being extended to other persons, as in *ñaan keeṭṭiiṭin-aan* 'I heard' *nii conn-aan* 'you.SG said' or *naam vaaṇ-aan* 'we lived', all with the 3SG masculine suffix *aan* (Andronov 1993: 116).

But particularly significant is the fact that the future tense and negative paradigms appear to have evolved along the same trajectory, but under different morphological circumstances. In both of the paradigms a participial form encroached and ultimately spread to supplant the original subject-marked forms. The development of the future is shown in Table 12, again summarizing the account given by Ramaswami Ayyar (1936). The history of the negative form is similar. In the oldest texts the participial ending *-aa* has already replaced the 3rd person neuter singular (Andronov 1993: 113, Ramaswami Ayyar 1936: 56), and later takes over the whole paradigm.

The changes across all four tense/polarity paradigms thus find a unified interpretation if we suppose that a morphological change first affected 3rd person forms (perhaps, more specifically, 3rd person neuter singular forms), which then spread throughout the paradigm. The nature of that morphological change will have differed within the different paradigms (deletion of suffix, substitution of participial form), but the trajectory of its spread will have been similar. In that case we can only say that, in the present and past, the ending was truly dropped in only one form, while for the rest of the paradigm what looks like the dropping of an ending is in fact replacement by a form which *happens* to coincide with the underlying stem.

Table 12. Evolution of subject markers in the future in Malayalam

	up to 14th c.	by 15th c	by 16th c
1SG	-een	-an	-an
2SG	-aa(y)	-aa(y)	-um
3SG M	-aan	-aan	-um
3SG F	-aaḷ	-aaḷ	-um
3SG N	-adu	-um	-um
1PL	-oom	-oom	-oom
2PL	-iir	-um	-um
3PL M/F	-aar	-um	-um
3PL N	-(an)a	-um	-um

2.2.2   Formally motivated change

If the morphological replacements described in the preceding section can be understood as having arisen *ex nihilo*, other instances appear to take their motivation from an already established morphological pattern. This is most clearly the case where that pattern is itself the result of prior phonological convergence: the replacement of forms only commences once the morphological pattern has been put into place. For example, in Geʿez, the syncretism between the nominative and genitive (§ 2.1.1) was extended beyond its original environment by transferring it to the plural (Table 13; Hasselbach 2013).

Table 13. Analogical spread of a marking pattern caused by phonological change in Geʿez

	Proto-Semitic				-a/i > -ǝ > ø				Geʿez		
	SG	(F) PL	(M) PL		SG	PL			SG	PL	
NOM	-u	-āt-u	-ū	>	-ø	-āt -ø	-ū	→	-ø	-āt -ø	-ø
ACC	-a	-āt-i	-ī		-a	-āt -ø	-ī		-a	-āt -a	-a
GEN	-i	-āt-i	-ī		-ø	-āt -ø	-ī		-ø	-āt -ø	-ø

Similarly in Greek, the syncretism of aorist subjunctive and future indicative was extended through the lexicon, attracting verbs which had originally had distinct aorist and future stems (Table 14).

Table 14. Analogical extension of syncretism in the Greek future and aorist

	500 BC			100 BC			AD 300	
future indicative	pau-s-ei	ere-ei	>	pau-s-ei	ere-ei	→	pau-s-ei	eip-ei
aorist subjunctive	pau-s-ēi	eip-ēi		pau-s-ei	eip-ei			

The analogical spread of syncretism is one way that formal loss can occur through the morphological convergence of forms. However, it is restricted in a way that the other mechanisms listed here are not: syncretism can only spread by analogy if it has already been introduced by some other mechanism elsewhere in the language. Analogy is essentially pattern-copying, and for a pattern to be copied, it must already exist somewhere. Therefore analogy cannot trigger a loss of formal contrast, but once syncretism has been established, it can play a big role in extending it through the morphology.

To illustrate the way that analogy interacts with sound change in the loss of inflection, consider the loss of case marking in French (Sornicola 2011). The loss of final -*m* and other sound changes caused widespread syncretism in the noun declensions inherited from Latin. Subsequently, the analogical loss of subject/oblique marking in the plural of the feminine 1st declension assimilated it to the pattern of the corresponding singular forms, where it is the result of final -*m* being lost, and to the third declension, where the syncretism is inherited.

Table 15. Old French development of the Latin feminine 1st and 3rd declensions

| | Late Latin | | | (Intermediate) | | | Old French | |
	1st decl	3rd decl		1st decl	3rd decl		1st decl	3rd decl
NOM SG	filia	matre		fille	medre		fille	medre
ACC SG	filiam	matrem	>	fille	medre	→	fille	medre
NOM PL	filiae	matrēs		fille	medres		filles	medres
ACC PL	filiās	matrēs		filles	medres		filles	medres

Compare the development of third declension nouns with original stem alternations between the nominative singular and other forms, where the nominative plural is clearly based on the singular, rather than the accusative plural (Table 16). This maintained a subject/oblique contrast in the plural for some feminine nouns, by extending a formal alternation with the singular forms, at the expense of syncretism in the plural forms.

Table 16. Old French development of the Latin feminine 3rd declension

	Late Latin			(Intermediate)			Old French	
NOM SG	soror	matre		suer	medre		suer	medre
ACC SG	sororem	matrem	>	seror	medre	→	suer	medre
NOM PL	sororēs	matrēs		serors	medres		**suers**	medres
ACC PL	sororēs	matrēs		serors	medres		serors	medres

In contrast, masculine nouns of the Latin third declension aligned with the pattern of the second declension, confirming the analogical nature of these changes:[6]

Table 17. Old French development of the Latin masculine 2nd and 3rd declensions

	Late Latin		(Intermediate)		Old French	
	2nd decl	3rd decl	2nd decl	3rd decl	2nd decl	3rd decl
NOM SG	murus	patre	murs	pedre	murs	pedres
ACC SG	murum	patrem	mur	pedre	mur	pedre
NOM PL	muri	patrēs	mur	pedres	mur	pedre
ACC PL	murōs	patrēs	murs	pedres	murs	pedres

Unlike the feminine nouns, the development of masculine nouns with stem alternations can't be based on the nominative singular:

Table 18. Old French development of the Latin masculine 3rd declension

	Late Latin		(Intermediate)		Old French	
NOM SG	latro	patre	ledre	pedre	ledres	pedres
ACC SG	latronem	patrem	ladron	pedre	ladron	pedre
NOM PL	latronēs	patrēs	ladrons	pedres	**ladron**	pedre
ACC PL	latronēs	patrēs	ladrons	pedres	ladrons	pedres

Here we see the gradual analogical extension of syncretism caused by sound change, both through morphosyntactic environments (cf. Ge'ez, where case syncretism was

---

6.   This is a simplification of the situation in Old French texts (Sornicola 2011, van Reenen and Schøsler 2000 for more details). Both masculine and feminine nouns descended from the Latin third declension show variation between -s and zero in the subj. singular. Part of this variation is inherited from Latin: cf. *finis* vs *mater* (both fem), *comes* vs *pater* (both masc), but the presence or absence of -s does not necessarily reflect etymology and depends on time, place and textual tradition. The tendency seems to be for feminine 3rd declension nouns to lose -s in nouns where it would be etymologically justified (e.g., *fins* or *fin* for Latin *finis*, but not *medres* for Latin *mater*), but for masculines to add -s where Latin had none (*pedre/ pedres* for Lat. *pater*, but not *con* for Lat. *comes*). This suggests that third declension nouns were attracted analogically into either the first and second declensions depending on their gender. This attraction is already necessary to explain why OF has e.g., *pedre* (masc) in the subj. pl instead of *pedres* (the expected outcome of Latin *patrēs*), but *medres* (fem) < *matrēs* (not *medre*).

extended to the plural from the singular) and through lexical categories (cf. Greek, where future indicative/aorist subjunctive syncretism was extended from regular to irregular verbs). In all of these examples, the loss of formal contrasts eventually led to the loss of a functional contrast as well: in Old French, the later generalisation of the accusative forms led to the loss of case marking altogether.[7] When a formal contrast is lost everywhere, the result is loss of content as well as form, because the language no longer furnishes sufficient evidence for either speakers or grammarians to construct the relevant category distinctions.[8]

3. Loss of features

The processes described in § 2 have been characterised as changes applied to forms, with the neutralisation of features or of feature value contrasts as a by-product. Alternatively, change may be understood as targeting the feature system itself. This can be understood as loss of contrast between feature values. Left unresolved, this would lead to free variation between forms now voided of their functional motivation (§ 3.1). Ultimately these forms may find a stable place through lexical (§ 3.2) or paradigmatic (§ 3.3) redistribution. Alternatively, we can identify cases where a feature has been lost not through loss of contrast, but through a transformation of its meaning or function profound enough that we are in fact faced with a different feature (§ 3.4).

3.1 Free variation

In Late Egyptian, textual evidence suggests that the original distinction between 3SG masculine and feminine is no longer maintained in stative verb inflection, with the original masculine and feminine forms persisting (e.g., *sdm.w* 'hears.3SG.M', *sdm.t* 'hears.3SG.F'), but used interchangeably for subjects of either gender (Sethe 1899: 25f). In broad terms this development could also be characterised as replacement as in § 2.2.1, but in contrast to what is described there, the replacement is complementary.

---

7.   According to van Reenen and Schøsler (2000) this was because the masculine pattern, with syncretism between the subject and oblique forms of opposing numbers, was 'conceptually too complicated'. But this explanation may be superfluous, given that the pattern X (SG) ~ Xs (PL) was already well established in the feminine nouns.

8.   Naturally a lost category distinction can later be formally renewed or reintroduced. Some Modern Ethiopian languages have reintroduced case distinctions, and both the subjunctive and future were renewed in Medieval Greek by new analytic constructions.

A more extensive instance of this comes from the Oceanic language Anejom̃:
(Lynch 1995, 2000: 89–96), involving its preverbal markers of person, number and
tense. An example of one of these markers is shown in (4).

(4)   ki   apan añak
      1SG.INCP go   I
      'I'll be going'

In the system as recorded in the 19th century, there were three tenses marked, each
of which distinguished four numbers (singular, dual, trial and plural) and four
person values (with a distinction between first person inclusive and exclusive).
Between then and the 20th century the language underwent rapid change, probably due to disturbances in transmission due a drastic drop in population resulting
from disease and natural disasters (with possible language contact effects as well).
Table 19 shows the 19th century system and Table 20 the 20th century system.

Table 19. Preverbal tense markers in Anejom̃: the 19th century system

		SG	DU	TR	PL
AOR	1INC	—	intau	intaj	inta
	1	ek	ecrau	ektaj, ektij	ecra
	2	na	ekau	ahtaj	eka
	3	et	erau	ehtaj	era
PST	1INC	—	intis	intijis	imjis
	1	kis	ecrus	ektijis	ecris
	2	as	akis	ahtijis	akis
	3	is	erus	ehtijis	eris
INCEP	1INC	—	tu	tiji	ti
	1	(in)ki	ecru	tiji	ecri
	2	an	eru	tiji	aki
	3	(in)yi	eru	tiji	eri

Note: The syncretic forms in the inceptive may be errors in the original material (because there are
distinctions in the 20th century attestations)

In part the 20th century system is characterised by innovations in form, mostly the
truncation of markers or their transformation into prefixes. But the old forms have
also persisted, typically with an expanded paradigmatic distribution. What is of
interest here is that in some cases the distribution of distinct affixes ends up overlapping or coinciding completely (Table 21). For example, in the aorist, the original 1PL *ekra* and 3PL *era* are both found used for any non-singular person, while
in the past, the original 1PL *ekris* is also used for 2nd or 3rd person non-singular,
and the original 3PL *eris* is found for all 1st and 3rd person non-singular values, as

Table 20. Preverbal tense markers in Anejom̃: the 20th century system

		SG	DU	TR	PL
AOR	1INC	—	tau, ta, ekra, erau, era, rai-	taj, ta, ekra, era, rai-	ta, ekra, era, rai-
	1	ek, k-	ekrau, ekra, erau, era, rai-	ettaj, ekra, era, rai-	ekra, era, rai-
	2	na, nai, n-	erau, ekra, era, rai-	ettaj, ekra, era, rai-	eka, ekra, era, eri, rai-
	3	et, t-	erau, ekra, era, rai-	ettaj, ekra, era, rai-	era, eri, ekra, rai-
PST	1INC	—	tus, tu, kis, is, s-	tijis, kis, is, s-	eris, kis, is, s-
	1	kis, is-, s-	eris, is, s-	eris, is, s-	ekris, eris, is, s-
	2	as, na, is, s-	ekris, ekrus, arus, is, s-	atijis, ekris, is, s-	akis, ekris, is, s-
	3	is, s-	erus, eris, ekris, is, s-	etijis, ekris, eris, is, s-	eris, ekris, is, s-
INCEP	1INC	—	tu, ti, yi, ri	tiji, ti, ri	ti, ri
	1	ki	ekru, ri	etiji, ekri, ri	ekri, ri
	2	an, ni	aru, ra, ri	atiji, ra, ri	aki, ra, ri
	3	iñiyi, (in)yi, y-	eru, ru, ra, ri	etiji, eri, ra, ri, yi	eri, ra, ri

well as 1INCL plural. In addition, the original 3sg is also found for any past tense value. As Lynch (2000: 95) points out, the overall impression one gets is that while tense distinctions have remained robust, all person-number distinctions outside of the singular have been neutralised. The original forms persist, but with a seemingly random distribution, constituting a kind of overabundance (Thornton 2011).

Table 21. Overlapping distribution of inherited non-singular markers in Anejom̃

		DU	TRIAL	PL
AOR	1INC			
	1			ekra
	2			
	3			era
PST	1INC			
	1			ekris
	2			
	3			eris

Note: eris = ▨, ekris = ☐; forms are shown in their original position within the paradigm

3.2   Lexical redistribution

The examples described in § 3.1 involve the retention of distinct inflectional forms, but without any functional motivation for their formal contrast. The resulting over-abundance may persist, at least temporarily, but the forms may also be redistributed between mutually exclusive sections of the lexicon, as occurred with Greek perfect and aorist verb forms. The two aspectual values became synonymous via a familiar path of semantic reanalysis (the 'aoristic drift', e.g., Bybee & Dahl 1989). At first, this resulted in a significant period of apparently fairly free variation between the two sets of forms, although later each verb settled on a single variant: usually the origi-nal aorist, but sometimes the perfect (where it fitted into an existing aorist template, with a stem ending in -*ēk*). Because these latter verbs do not form a natural class by any semantic or formal criteria, the formal distinction between the aorist and perfect forms ended up as a new type of lexically idiosyncratic allomorphy.

(5)   500 BC. *hēúron* 'I found', *hēúrēka* 'I have found'; *épausa* 'I stopped', *pépauka* 'I have stopped'.

   Byzantine Greek. *ēúra, ēúrēka* 'I (have) found'; *épausa/pépauka* 'I (have) stopped'.

   Modern Greek. *bréka* 'I found' (< *ēúrēka*); *épapsa* 'I stopped' (< *épausa*).

A similar development is also seen in Egyptian, following the changes described in § 3.1. By the Coptic period the original 3sG masculine and feminine forms that were in free variation had replaced all subject person-number-gender values. But instead of being in free variation, they became lexically segregated, with a handful of verbs displaying the feminine form, the rest the masculine form (Sethe 1899: 27).

3.3   Paradigmatic redistribution

In § 3.2 we saw examples where morphological forms were redistributed lexically following the loss of a feature distinction. In a similar way, the remaining morpho-logical forms may accommodate themselves to a changed feature system by being redeployed to the realisation of other features or values. For example, in the Gur language Ncam (Niger-Congo, Cox 1998; also rendered as *nñcàm̃* and *Ntcham*), verbal number is in the course of being lost as a feature, and the original marking is being repurposed as a supplementary marker of aspect. Verbs in Ncam originally distinguished two moods, realis and irrealis, and within the realis, two aspects, perfective and imperfective (the irrealis can be considered inherently perfective); these may be distinguished by a stem alternation.[9] Cross-cutting these distinctions of aspect and mood, there was a verbal number distinction, with the plural value

---

9.   The labels 'realis' and 'irrealis' are adapted from Naba's (1994) description of another Gur lan-guage (Gulmancema), as they are more familiar than the terms Cox (1998) uses (*venu* and *virtuel*).

indicating either multiple events or, in the imperfective, an ongoing process. Verbal plurality is marked by suffixes, which show a great deal of lexically-conditioned allomorphy; the most common is -*ti*, others include -*fi*, -*ki*, -*n*, -*l*, and -*b*.

Cox (1998: 79) reports that the number distinction is disappearing: prior to 1980, a speaker born in 1936 recalled the plural forms for about 25% of verbs, a speaker born in 1959 only knew a handful. Crucially though, it is not just that the plural form is being eliminated, rather in the perfective realis and (inherently perfective) irrealis the singular form is generalised, in the realis imperfective the plural form is generalised. Presumably this was due to an association between verbal plurality and imperfectivity that is evident in a number of languages, as documented by Dressler (1968).

Table 22 shows the implied evolution, based on paradigms given by Cox (1998). The verb 'suckle' represents the original state of affairs, while 'stick one's hand into' has lost the singular imperfective form and uses the plural perfective forms only marginally. 'Bite' continues the trend, with the verbal number distinction extinguished entirely, but with the original plural marker retained as a supplementary marker of imperfective aspect.

Table 22. Reanalysis of verbal plural markers in Ncam (Cox 1998: 85, 87)

a. 'suckle'

	IRR	REALIS	
	(PFV)	PFV	IPFV
SG	mɔ́	mɔ́	mô:
PL	mō:-tì	mó:-tì	mó:-tí

b. 'stick one's hand into'

	IRR	REALIS	
	(PFV)	PFV	IPFV
SG	bɔ́	bɔ́	—
PL	(bō:-tì)	(bó:-tì)	bō:-tí

c. 'bite'

	IRR	REALIS				IRR	REALIS	
	(PFV)	PFV	IPFV			(PFV)	PFV	IPFV
				>				
SG	jú	jú	—		SG	jú	jú	jún-tí
PL	—	—	jún-tí		PL			

3.4   Rebranding

Arguably one could speak of the loss of a feature even where the forms continue to express a morphosyntactic contrast. An example of this comes from the Dagestanian language Dargwa. Most varieties of Dargwa have distinct first and second person markers on their verbs, e.g., Aqusha Dargwa *w-ak'-i-ra* M-come.PFV-AOR-<u>1</u> 'I (masculine) came' vs. *w-ak'-i-ri* M-come.PFV-AOR-<u>2</u> 'you (masculine) came' (Sumbatova 2011: 137). In Mehweb Dargwa (Sumbatova 2011: 143), which is isolated from other varieties of the language, only the first person markers have been retained, and have been reinterpreted as the conjoint marker in a conjoint/disjoint system, used for the first person in declarative sentences and for the second person in questions.

(6)   a.   sija   b-iq'-UWE   le-w-<u>ra</u>   ħu?
              what(ABS)   n-do.IPFV-PRS.CVB   COP-M-<u>CONJ</u> you.SG(ABS)

      b.   bazal-li-cče   ar-q'ʕ-ül   χalq'
              market-OBL-super   el-go.IPFV-PRS.ATR   people(ABS)

              ħark'-i-če-di   χ:was:ar   b-iq'-uwe   le-w-<u>ra</u>
              river-OBL-SUPER-PROL   rescue   N-do.IPFV-PRS.CVB   COP-M-<u>CONJ</u>

      a.   'What are <u>you</u> doing?'
      b.   '<u>I</u> am accompanying people going to the market across the river.'

One might then claim that Mehweb Dargwa has lost person inflection, not because it has lost (all) the forms, but because one inflectional feature has been replaced by another.

4.   Loss of cells

We have already seen in § 2.2.2 one way both form and content can be lost together, when a formal contrast is neutralised in the only or final place that it exists, as with the loss of case contrasts in French. At least logically, this seems to involve the loss of form then loss of content as a result. This section deals with cases where neither the loss of form or content are logically prior, but both are lost together.

Where the morphological marking of some function is lost, this does not necessarily mean it becomes inexpressible; but if it is retained, the means for doing so are no longer inflectional. Other means are used instead, such as periphrastic multi-word constructions. In the modern Scandinavian languages a number of adjectives, often those which have also lost gender and number agreement, lack the usual synthetic comparatives and superlatives (Table 23). For these adjectives, the types of gradation inherited from Old Norse (1–3 below) have been replaced by a new periphrastic construction using the uninflected adjective and comparative and 'more', 'most' (4) (Sims-Williams and Enger 2021).

Table 23. Ways of marking adjective degree in modern Norwegian *Bokmål*.

	Positive	Comparative	Superlative	Gloss	Gradation type
1 (most adjectives)	*dum*	*dummere*	*dummest*	'dumb, stupid'	Suffixation by -ere and -est
2 (few members)	*tung*	*tyngre*	*tyngst*	'heavy'	Suffixation by -re and -st + umlaut
3 (few members)	*god*	*bedre*	*best*	'good'	suppletion
4	*stille*	*mer stille*	*mest stille*	'quiet'	periphrasis

In this case, the encroachment of the new construction is gradual only in the sense that it has affected only a subset of lexemes. In similar cases where a new construction gradually encroaches on the functional territory of an inflectional competitor, this type of change can actually lead to the creation of new contrasts. In Basque (7), the progressive value of the inherited synthetic imperfective is being replaced by a periphrastic construction, using an auxiliary and a nominalised verb in the locative case, leaving the synthetic form available only in habitual contexts (Jendraschek 2003).

(7)   a.   Aitor etxe-ra   doa
          Aitor house-ALL   go.PRS.3.SG
          'Aitor goes/is going home'

      b.   Aitor etxe-ra   joa-te-n   da
          Aitor house-ALL   go-NOUN-LOC   PRS.3.SG
          'Aitor is going home'

In one sense, something is lost, because the inherited synthetic imperfective loses part of its functional range, which is taken over by a new construction from outside the paradigm (whether we regard such constructions as members of inflectional paradigms or not, we can agree that they *originate* outside the paradigm). But at the same time, a new morphological contrast between two different readings of imperfective (habitual vs. progressive) is created. While there is no immediate loss of form, this may be the end result, if the new construction continues to usurp values of the old inflectional form. Compare the German construction using auxiliary 'have' or 'be' followed by a past participle, which first replaced the inflectional preterite in resultative or stative uses (as in English 'I have eaten', etc.), but went on to oust the preterite altogether for the majority of verbs, in all but the most conservative and formal styles. The end result is thus a loss of both form and function, in that the inflectional form disappears, and its function is no longer expressed inflectionally.

5.   Grammaticalisation and the loss of inflection

The loss of inflection is commonly understood as a possible side effect of grammaticalisation (Norde 2019). When an inflected lexeme becomes a functional item, it may lose the grammatical properties associated with the lexical class it originally belonged to. For example, the grammaticalisation of the verb 'want' into a future tense particle within the Balkan Sprachbund has been accompanied by the loss of subject agreement marking in some of the languages (Greek, Bulgarian, Macedonian, and some adjacent dialects of Serbian) through the generalisation of the 3sg form (Sandfeld 1930: 180–83). Since this occurred precisely in constructions which also employed a finite lexical verb, the result was the elimination of double marking of the subject. Compare the Serbian sentence in (8), where the future marker 'will' takes subject agreement, with the Bulgarian sentence in (9), where its cognate *šte* is invariant (Mišeska-Tomić 2006: 477, 509).[10]

(8)   Ja   ću   da   vam   to pokaž-em.
      I   will.1sg that   2pl.dat it   show-prs.1sg
      'I will show it to you.'

(9)   Šte   ti   go   da-m.
      fut   2sg.dat it.acc give-prs.1sg
      'I will give it to you.'

In this case, the inflectional marking that has been lost as a result of grammaticalisation was redundant, since the subject continues to be marked on the lexical verb, but this is not always so. For example, in older Estonian, verbal negation was expressed through a construction consisting of a negative auxiliary inflected for subject features, and an invariant participle (Ziegelmann 2001). Subject inflection on the auxiliary was then lost, turning it into an invariant negative particle. As a result, all finite verbs are now uninflected for subject features when negated.

In these examples the loss of inflection appears to be driven by what Hopper and Traugott (2003) call *decategorialisation*. By contrast, the examples discussed in § 2-§ 4 have not changed their status: verbs remain verbs, nouns remain nouns, and adjectives remain adjectives. But so far as the evidence allows us to judge, the pathways along which inflection is lost are the same in either case. Thus in Serbian dialects where the verb 'want' is becoming a future particle, in the 1sg the original form and the 3sg are still in competition (Mišeska-Tomić 2006: 509), reminiscent of what is seen in Mand (§ 2.2.1). In Estonian, as reconstructed by Ziegelmann

---

10.   The loss of the complementiser *da* is an ongoing process in southwest Serbian dialects that are adjacent to Bulgarian and Macedonian (Mišeska-Tomić 2006: 509).

(2001: 420–22), the paradigm was gradually dismantled in the fashion described in § 2.2.2. First the plural forms were replaced by singular forms (Table 24b), possibly encouraged by the regular loss of final vowels which made the first and second person forms more similar to each other. Then the first person form was replaced by the third person (Table 24c), possibly triggered by the regular loss of final /n/ which rendered the first person form phonologically weak. Finally, the third person form prevailed throughout. (The form *ei* currently used in Standard Estonian is from a southern variety whose history was not recorded, but some northern dialects still preserve a form *eb* or *ep*.) Note that this development was unique to the negative auxiliary – other verbs maintain the six-way distinction.

Table 24. Development of the Estonian negative auxiliary

	a. Stage 1		b. Stage 2	c. Stage 3	d. Stage 4
	SG	PL	SG/PL	SG/PL	SG/PL
1	en	emme	en	eB	
2	et	ette	et	et	eB
3	eB	evat	eB	eB	

Note: *B* represents a weak voiceless bilabial stop

6.   Conclusion

While the rise of inflection can and has been described as a linear process of grammaticalisation that builds up both morphosyntactic and paradigmatic complexity, the loss of inflection takes this morphological complexity as its starting point and somehow breaks it apart. It presents particular challenges for historical morphology, not least the question of motivation: is it the loss of meanings or the loss of forms which drives the change? Even while we acknowledge the back-and-forth interplay of factors in any historical process, the descriptive and conceptual mechanisms we have at our disposal as linguists compel us to speak in terms of discrete operations anchored either in meaning or in form. The typology we have presented here is not intended so much as a catalogue of change types as an exploration of possible descriptions of change. While we offer tentative interpretations of a number of examples, they are meant chiefly as illustrations; we are only too aware that for any example multiple interpretations are possible, and indeed that multiple overlapping mechanisms may well be in operation simultaneously. Judging between these alternative interpretations will depend on various criteria, particularly descriptive and theoretical economy. If syncretism can be fully predicted by a sound change that is already needed to explain phonological developments in a language, for example, we need not posit any additional functional motivation. Similarly, if all examples of morphological affix loss (2.1.2) turn out to be amenable to some other analysis, we need not include it in our toolbox of change mechanisms. Before we can start grappling with these questions seriously, though, we need to accumulate a sufficient empirical base of examples of the loss of inflection, and use them to derive an inventory of possible change types. The goal of this typological survey has thus been to lay the groundwork for a more comprehensive theory of the loss of inflection, by setting out what phenomena need to be accounted for, and what the elements of this account will consist of.

References

Allen, Cynthia. 2006. Case syncretism and word order change. In *The Handbook of the History of English*, Ans van Kemenade & Bettelou Los (eds), 201–223. Oxford: Blackwell. https://doi.org/10.1002/9780470757048.ch9

Allen, Cynthia. 1997. Middle English case loss and the 'creolization' hypothesis. *English Language and Linguistics* 1: 63–89. https://doi.org/10.1017/S1360674300000368

Andronov, Mixail Sergeevič. 1993. *Jazyk malajalam*. Moscow: Nauka.

Bakker, Peter. 2003. Pidgin inflectional morphology and its implications for creole morphology. In *Yearbook of Morphology 2002*, Geert Booij & Jaap van Marle (eds), 3–33. Dordrecht: Kluwer. https://doi.org/10.1007/0-306-48223-1_2

Bentz, Christian & Winter, Bodo. 2013. Languages with more second language learners tend to lose nominal case. *Language Dynamics and Change*, 3 (1): 1–27. https://doi.org/10.1163/22105832-13030105

Bickerton, Derek. 1995. *Language and Human Behavior*. Seattle WA: University of Washington Press.

Boeder, Winfried. 1987. Einfachheit und Komplexität in der Geschichte der Kartvelsprachen. *Annual of Ibero-Caucasian Linguistics XIV*: 23–64.

Bybee, Joan L. & Dahl, Östen. 1989. The creation of tense and aspect systems in the languages of the world. *Studies in Language* 13 (1): 51–103. https://doi.org/10.1075/sl.13.1.03byb

Campbell, Lyle & Muntzel, Martha. 1989. The structural consequences of language death. In *Investigating Obsolescence*, Nancy C. Dorian (ed.), 181–196. Cambridge: CUP. https://doi.org/10.1017/CBO9780511620997.016

Chirikba, Viacheslav. 2008. The problem of the Caucasian Sprachbund. In *From Linguistic Areas to Areal Linguistics* [Studies in Language Companion Series 90], Pieter Muysken (ed.), 25–93. Amsterdam: John Benjamins. https://doi.org/10.1075/slcs.90.02chi

Činčarauli, A. 1960. *Xevsurulis taviseburebani, ṭeksṭebita da indeksit (Features of Khevsuretian, with texts and index)*. Tbilisi: SMa gam-ba.

Cox, Monica. 1998. Description grammaticale du ncàm, langue Gourma du Togo et du Ghana. PhD dissertation, École Pratique des Hautes Études, Paris.

Daniels, Don. 2015. A Reconstruction of Proto-Sogeram. PhD dissertation, UC Santa Barbara.

Dorian, Nancy C. 1978. The fate of morphological complexity in language death: Evidence from East Sutherland Gaelic. *Language* 54 (3): 590–609. https://doi.org/10.1353/lan.1978.0024

Dorian, Nancy C. 1980. Language shift in community and individual: The phenomenon of the laggard semi-speaker. *International Journal of the Sociology of Language* 25: 85–94.

Dressler, Wolfgang. 1968. *Studien zur verbalen Pluralität.* Vienna: Bühlau in Kommission.

Fischer, Susann. 2010. *Word-order Change as a Source of Grammaticalisation* [Linguistik Aktuell/Linguistics Today 157]. Amsterdam: John Benjamins. https://doi.org/10.1075/la.157

Givón, Talmy. 1979. *On Understanding Grammar.* New York NY: Academic Press. Also published as Givón, T. 2018. *On Understanding Grammar.* Revised Edition. Amsterdam: John Benjamins. https://doi.org/10.1075/z.213

Hasselbach, Rebecca. 2013. *Case in Semitic: Roles, Relations, and Reconstruction.* Oxford: OUP. https://doi.org/10.1093/acprof:oso/9780199671809.001.0001

Heine, Bernd. 2003. On degrammaticalisation. In *Historical Linguistics 2001* [Current Issues in Linguistic Theory 237], Barry J. Blake & Kate Burridge (eds) 163–180. Amsterdam: John Benjamins. https://doi.org/10.1075/cilt.237.12hei

Heine, Bernd, Claudi, Ulrike & Hünnemeyer, Friederike. 1991. *Grammaticalisation: A Conceptual Framework.* Chicago IL: University of Chicago Press.

Heine, Bernd & Reh, Mechthild. 1984. *Grammaticalisation and Reanalysis in African Languages.* Hamburg: Helmut Buske.

Hewitt, B. George. 1995. *Georgian: A Structural Reference Grammar* [London Oriental and African Language Library 2]. Amsterdam: John Benjamins. https://doi.org/10.1075/loall.2

Hodge, Carleton. 1970. The linguistic cycle. *Linguistic Sciences* 13: 1–7.

Holisky, Dee Ann & Gagua, Rusudan. 1994. Tsova-Tush (Batsbi). In *North East Caucasian Languages (Part 2), Rieks Smeets* (ed.), 147–212. Delmar NY: Caravan Books.

Hopper, Paul J. & Traugott, Elizabeth. 2003. *Grammaticalisation.* 2nd edition. Cambridge: CUP. https://doi.org/10.1017/CBO9781139165525

Jendraschek, Gerd. 2003. When old paradigms die, new paradigms are born: On the eternal cycle of morphological change and its importance for language typology. *Journal of Universal Language* 4(2): 27–59. https://doi.org/10.22425/jul.2003.4.2.27

Klein, Wolfgang & Perdue, Clive. 1997. The basic variety (or: Couldn't natural languages be much simpler?). *Second Language Research* 13 (4): 301–347. https://doi.org/10.1191/026765897666879396

Kusters, Walter. 2008. Complexity in linguistic theory, language learning, and language change. In *Language Complexity: Typology, Contact, Change* [Studies in Language Companion Series 94], Matti Miestamo, Kaius Sinnemäki & Fred Karlsson (eds), 4–22. Amsterdam: John Benjamins. https://doi.org/10.1075/slcs.94.03kus

Kusters, Walter. 2003. Linguistic Complexity: The Influence of Social Change on Verbal Inflection. PhD Dissertation, University of Leiden.

Lass, Roger. 1990. How to do things with junk: Exaptation in language evolution. *Journal of linguistics* 26 (1): 79–102. https://doi.org/10.1017/S0022226700014432

Lehmann, Christian. 2015. *Thoughts on Grammaticalisation* [Classics in Linguistics 1], 3rd edn. Berlin: Language Science Press.

Lupyan, Gary & Dale, Rick. 2010. Language structure is partly determined by social structure. *PloS one* 5(1). https://doi.org/10.1371/journal.pone.0008559

Lynch, John. (2000). *A Grammar of Anejom̃.* Canberra: Australian National University.

Maitz, Peter & Németh, Attila. 2014. Language contact and morphosyntactic complexity: Evidence from German. *Journal of Germanic Linguistics* 26(1): 1–29. https://doi.org/10.1017/S1470542713000184

McWhorter, John. H. 1998. Identifying the creole prototype: Vindicating a typological class. *Language* 74 (4): 788–818. https://doi.org/10.2307/417003

Mišeska-Tomić, Olga. 2006. *Balkan Sprachbund Morpho-syntactic Features*. Dordrecht: Springer. https://doi.org/10.1007/1-4020-4488-7

Mühlhäusler, Peter. 1986. *Pidgin and Creole Linguistics*. Oxford: Blackwell.

Norde, Muriel. 1997. The History of the Genitive in Swedish. A Case Study in Degrammaticalisation. PhD dissertation, University of Amsterdam

Norde, Muriel. 2000. Deflexion as a counterdirectional factor in grammatical change. *Language Sciences* 23(2–3): 231–264. https://doi.org/10.1016/S0388-0001(00)00022-X

Norde, Muriel. 2001. The loss of lexical case in Swedish. In *Grammatical Relations in Change* [Studies in Language Companion Series 56], Jan Terje Faarlund (ed.), 241–272. Amsterdam: John Benjamins. https://doi.org/10.1075/slcs.56.11nor

Norde, Muriel. 2002. The final stages of grammaticalisation: Affixhood and beyond. In *New Reflections on Grammaticalization* [Typological Studies in Language 49], Ilse Wischer & Gabriela Diewald (eds), 45–66. Amsterdam: John Benjamins. https://doi.org/10.1075/tsl.49.06nor

Norde, Muriel. 2009. *Degrammaticalisation*. Oxford: OUP. https://doi.org/10.1093/acprof:oso/9780199207923.001.0001

Norde, Muriel. 2019. Grammaticalization in morphology. In *Oxford Research Encyclopedia of Linguistics: Morphology*, Rochelle Lieber (ed.). Oxford: OUP. <oxfordre.com/linguistics/page/morphology/the-oxford-encyclopedia-of-morphology> (9 November 2020).

Polinsky, Maria. (1995). Cross-linguistic parallels in language loss. *Southwest Journal of Linguistics* 14 (1): 87–123.

Ramaswami Ayyar, L. Vishwanatha. 1936. *The Evolution of Malayalam Morphology*. Cochin: Government Press.

van Reenen, Pieter & Schøsler, Lene. 2000. Declension in Old and Middle French: Two opposing tendencies. In *Historical Linguistics 1995, Vol. 1* [Current Issues in Linguistic Theory 161], John Charles Smith & Delia Bentley (eds), 327–344. Amsterdam: John Benjamins. https://doi.org/10.1075/cilt.161.21ree

Sandfeld, Karl. 1930. *Linguistique balkanique: Problèmes et résultats*. Paris: Champion.

Schwegler, Armin. 1990. *Analyticity and Syntheticity*. Berlin: Mouton de Gruyter. https://doi.org/10.1515/9783110872927

Sethe, Kurt. 1899. Das aegyptische Verbum im Altaegyptischen, Neuaegyptischen und Koptischen:*Formenlehre und Syntax der Verbalformen*, Vol. 2. Leipzig: J.C. Hinrichs.

Sims-Williams, Helen & Enger, Hans-Olav (2021). The loss of inflection as grammar complication: Evidence from Mainland Scandinavian. *Diachronica* 38(1): 111–150.

Sornicola, Rosanna. 2011. Romance linguistics and historical linguistics: Reflections on synchrony and diachrony. In *The Cambridge History of the Romance Languages*, Martin Maiden, John Charles Smith & Adam Ledgeway (eds), 1–49. Cambridge: CUP.

Sumbatova, Nina. 2011. Person hierarchies and the problem of person marker origin in Dargwa: Facts and diachronic problems. In *Tense, Aspect, Modality and Finiteness in East Caucasian Languages*, Gilles Authier & Timur Maisak, 95–130. Bochum: Brockmeyer.

Sun, Hongkai & Liu, Guangkun. 2009. *A Grammar of Anong: Language Death under Intense Contact*. Leiden: Brill.

Thornton, Anna M. 2011. Overabundance (multiple forms realizing the same cell): A non-canonical phenomenon in Italian verb morphology. In *Morphological Autonomy*, Martin

Maiden, John Charles Smith, Maria Goldbach & Marc-Olivier Hinzelin (eds), 358–81. Oxford: OUP.

Trudgill, Peter. 2012. On the sociolinguistic typology of linguistic complexity loss. In *Potentials of Language Documentation: Methods, Analyses, and Utilization*, Frank Seifart, Geoffrey Haig, Nikolaus P. Himmelmann, Dagmar Jung, Anna Margetts & Paul Trilsbeek (eds), 91–96. Honolulu HI: University of Hawai'i Press.

Ziegelmann, Katja. 2011. Die Verneinung im Estnischen: Zum Abbau des finiten Verneinungsverbs im älteren Schriftestnischen. PhD dissertation, Göttingen University.

CHAPTER 2

So-adj-*a* construction as a case of obsolescence in progress

Karolina Rudnicka
University of Gdańsk

The main focus of this study is the *so*-adj-*a* construction seen as an instantiation of grammatical obsolescence in progress. Starting at where Klégr's (2010) synchronic study of the construction's local grammar and syntactic functions leaves it, the present work provides a diachronic account of changes in the frequency of use in the last two centuries; their implications; and an overview of possible causes that had led to the situation in which the construction became considerably rare in Present Day English. Methodologically, the paper features quantitative and statistical analyses of corpus data. The work uses the framework for the investigation of grammatical obsolescence designed in the author's doctoral thesis (Rudnicka 2019). Additionally, the present chapter suggests extravagance as a cognitive motivation behind the emergence of the *so*-adj-*a* construction.

Keywords: grammatical obsolescence, *so*-adj-*a* construction, big mess construction, syntactic loss, extravagance

1. Introduction

The aim of this work is to present a case of grammatical obsolescence in progress using the *so*-adj-*a* construction as the studied variable. The paper builds on the framework for the investigation and description of grammatical obsolescence recently developed in Rudnicka (2019), and used by e.g., Imel (2019) and Kempf (this volume).

The construction in question has been displaying a consistent decrease in the frequency of use over the last two hundred years (see Section 2.2.2), its most frequent variant being currently 33.5 times less frequent than in 1810. This drastic decrease makes it a promising variable to be studied in the context of grammatical

https://doi.org/10.1075/slcs.218.02rud
© 2021 John Benjamins Publishing Company

obsolescence, a process in the course of which previously productive and popular constructions disappear, become fossilized or residual (Rudnicka 2019: 4).

The present work subscribes to the Construction Grammar (CxG) approach and adopts the definition of constructions from Hilpert according to which constructions "are defined as linguistic generalizations that speakers internalize" (2014: 22) and "form meaning pairs which either have non-predictable formal characteristics, non-compositional meanings, or a high enough frequency to be remembered as such" (Goldberg 2006: 5, quoted in Hilpert 2014: 22).

The chapter is structured as follows. After the first section discussing the *so*-adj-*a* construction in terms of its structure and function, Section 2 moves on to the diachronic development of the construction's frequency. Section 3 introduces the notion of grammatical obsolescence. In the literature, the phenomena which might instantiate obsolescence are referred to as e.g., *loss, decline, demise* or *death*. Section 4 explores the hypothesis whether *so*-adj-*a* sequence could be, according to the framework applied, seen as an instantiation of grammatical obsolescence in progress. The concluding Section 5 sums up the findings of the previous sections.

2. *So*-adj-*a* construction – an example of the *Big Mess Construction*

Noun phrases with *so*-adj predeterminers, exemplified by (1) below, are atypical and irregular when it comes to their structure and features. According to Klégr (2010: 95), "the position of the indefinite article after attributive adjectives preceded by *so*" can be seen as one of the peculiarities of English article usage. Jespersen (1933: 178; quoted in Klégr 2010) notes that "[t]he indefinite article naturally precedes an adjective" and lists *so* as one of the exceptions to this rule (together with *how, however, as, too* and *no less*), as it seems to attract the adjective and take the position in front of it.

> (1)   I have never seen so <u>black a shadow</u>.
>
> (COHA: 2007; FIC; "Dance of Shadows")

Furthermore, in the research literature, the *so*-adj-*a* construction is not always referred to in a consistent way. Among different terms under which the construction exemplified in (1) is found, there are: *so*-adj-*a* construction, *so*-adj-*a* NOUN, noun phrases with *so*-adj predeterminers, complex predetermination phenomenon (Kay & Sag 2009), and the Big Mess Construction (sometimes not capitalized). This last term is used, above all, by the representatives of head-driven phrase structure grammar – a generative grammar theory – and it has first been used by Berman (1974) to point to "the challenges to syntactic theory the phenomenon generates" (Osborne 2019). The label Big Mess Construction, contrary to its singular form, does not apply to a single sequence or pattern, but to all adjectival phrases which are introduced by *as*, *so*, *too*, *how*, *this* and *that* occurring in nominals which contain the indefinite article (van Eynde 2007: 416).

This complicated terminological picture could result in a situation in which many authors of recent studies were, most likely, unaware of the existence of other works on the construction in question. For instance, Klégr's (2010) study on the *so*-adj-*a* construction, which aims at providing a comprehensive overview of research on the noun phrases with *so*-adj predeterminers does not mention any of the studies in which they are investigated under the label of Big Mess Construction. Analogically, recent works which focus on the Big Mess Construction (such as Aniya 2016; Kim & Sells 2011) do not mention Klégr's study.

The present work looks both at studies subscribing to the usage-based approach and to generative grammar as it is believed the insights of scholars representing different approaches can complement each other. Thus, in most parts of this work the studied variable is referred to as the *so*-adj-*a* construction, but wherever authors representing generative grammar are cited, the terms used might also change – e.g., to an instantiation of Big Mess Construction.

2.1   Noun phrases with *so*-adj predeterminers – their characteristics

Among remarks on the construction made in traditional grammars, one needs to mention:

i.   that the *so*-adj-*a* sequence is stylistically restricted to rather formal contexts (Quirk et al. 1985; Swan 2005; quoted in Klégr 2010: 99);
ii. it is not compatible with the zero article and plural noun phrases (Quirk et al. 1985; Huddleston & Pullum 2002; quoted in Klégr 2010: 98), compare (2) to ungrammatical Examples (3) and (4) below;
iii. it is compatible only with the indefinite article (Swan 2005; quoted in Klégr 2010: 99), see an ungrammatical Example (5).

(2) He'd been foolish to send one man on <u>so dangerous a mission</u>.
                                    (COHA: 2003; FIC; "Enchantress")

(3) *There are less dangerous ways to give soldiers <u>so important information</u>.

(4) *He'd been foolish to send one man on <u>so dangerous missions</u>.

(5) *He'd been foolish to send one man on <u>so dangerous the mission</u>.

Klégr's empirical study (2010: 99), conducted on a dataset from the British National Corpus (BNC for short), reveals there are more variants of the sequence than just the basic type *so*-adj *a/an* N (e.g., *so black a shadow*) traditionally referred to in the literature (e.g., Jespersen 1933; Quirk et al. 1985; Swan 2005). Among the four main types of the construction Klégr identifies, there are:

i.   Type A – *so*-adj *a/an* N, see (1), (2) and (6);
ii. Type B – *so*-adj and adj-*a/an*-N, see (7);
iii. Type C – *so*-adv-adj-*a/an*-N, see (8);
iv. Type D – *so*-adj-*a/an*-adj-N, see (9).

> (6)   I wish I could take <u>so benign a view</u>.   (COHA: 1994; FIC; "White Walls")
>
> (7)   It was his privilege to address <u>so large and generous an audience</u>.
>   (COHA: 1975; FIC; "The Last Valley")
>
> (8)   It was <u>so thoroughly American a place</u>, everything so shiny and
>   neat (…).   (COHA: 2002; FIC; "The Drive-In Puerto Rico")
>
> (9)   You are not <u>so strong a little boy</u> as I thought.
>   (COHA: 1904; NF; "Bits of Talk about Home Matters")

The types B, C and D are shown to be decidedly rarer than the basic A type – in Klégr's BNC sample (2010: 100) there are 572 instances of type A, compared to 32, 7 and 22, respectively.

   As for their syntactic functions, noun phrases with a *so*-adj-*a* construction do not seem to be restricted (Klégr 2010: 107,108). They are most often used as: object (37,4% of the cases), adverbial (24,3%), subject complement (18,4%), subject (10,5%), modifier (7,5%). Due to the fact that three most frequently observed functions can be said to be typically rhematic[1], Klégr claims that "[t]his finding is in keeping with the potentially rhematizing nature of the intensifying *so* and the indefinite article". Aniya (2016) expresses a similar view on this matter claiming that the inverted constituent order of the Big Mess Construction is a "way of producing an emphatic effect" (2016: 8). She compares it to how WH-exclamations (e.g., *What a beautiful dress you are wearing!*) and changes in the intonation work (2016: 8).

3.   Diachronic account

The main goal of the present section is to answer the call for a diachronic study made by Klégr (2010: 118) and to provide an addition to the research literature on *so*-adj-*a* by presenting a hypothesis concerning the origin of the construction in question.

---

1.   Rhematic elements introduce new information or have significant semantic content; the notions *theme* and *rheme* tend to be paraphrased as *topic* and *comment* (Wales 2001: 344).

3.1   The construction's origin: A handy stylistic device from the very beginning?

In the literature, one does not find much on the *so*-adj-*a* construction's beginnings. However, there are a few facts which might provide important indications and point in a certain direction towards answering the question about how and why the construction came into being. Firstly, according to the Oxford English Dictionary (OED Online)[2], the first attestation of the *so*-adj-*a* construction can be found in the late 14th-century Middle English chivalric romance "Sir Gawain and the Green Knight". Secondly, according to Klégr (2010: 117) the intensifying *so* and the indefinite article have a (potentially) rhematising nature (introducing important semantic content, having a commenting function), which is also reflected by the most frequent functions exercized by the construction. Thirdly, Aniya (2016: 8) expresses a similar view, namely, that the main aim of the construction is to produce an emphatic effect. Furthermore, Aniya makes two more interesting claims pertaining to the semantics of the Big Mess Construction, of which the *so*-adj-*a* construction is an instantiation, namely that (i) it "naturally carries a contrastive meaning since it obligatorily contains an adjective together with a degree word" (2016: 11); and (ii) "a highlighted object is new information rather than old information" (2016: 10).

If we add these facts together, we arrive at a situation in which the *so*-adj-*a* construction might have very likely been introduced to the written language as a handy stylistic device which enables the writer to e.g., make a comment with a high pragmatic load. The atypical, non-canonical order of the constituents makes the comment and the construction stand out from the text. Exactly this way of reasoning is applied by Petré (2017), who describes the concept of extravagance, which he defines as "the desire to talk in such a way that one is noticed" (2017: 228), as a possible cognitive motivation behind the spread of emphatic progressive [BE Ving]. In his work he argues that the novel use of [BE Ving] is motivated by extravagance and refers to other scholars, who are also writing about the same or very similar kinds of cognitive motivations (2017: 228):

> Keller (1994) has argued for the importance of expressivity as a trigger of change in his formulation of the social maxim 'talk in such a way that you are noticed'. Haspelmath (1999) and Detges and Waltereit (2002) reiterate on this with their notions of extravagance and expressivity, and have pointed out that a number of phenomena, such as redundancy or the replacement of short expressions by longer ones (e.g., with a hammer > by means of a hammer), can be directly related to this.

---

2.   OED Online, Oxford University Press, s.v. *so*, retrieved on March 30, 2019 from <http://www.oed.com>

To be completely sure that it is extravagance and that a desire to "talk in such a way that you are noticed" motivated the emergence of the *so*-adj-*a* noun construction, one could analyse texts created by writers of the 14th and 15th century to follow the exact path of how the construction in question spread across texts and genres. However, the clear stylistic value, which the construction had from its first attestation (in a literary work) and which it still has now ("a useful stylistic device" according to Klégr (2010:117)) together with the fact that it did not become especially frequent and did not lose its atypical flair, with its main use being the introduction of comments and notes on the side, do make extravagance a likely hypothesis explaining the construction's origins.

3.2   Frequency of use

The *so*-adj-*a* construction has often been looked at as something slightly peculiar. But are the noun phrases with *so*-adj predeterminers actually something rare? Were they more frequent in the past? To answer these questions, the Corpus of Historical American English (COHA) is consulted.

3.2.1   *Methodology*

COHA is the largest diachronic multi-genre corpus of American English containing 400 million words of text from the time period 1810–2009, belonging to four genres (*fiction, magazine, newspaper, non-fiction*). The fact that it is rich in data, freely available online and POS-tagged makes it an adequate source to turn to.

Since the aim of the present study is to gain insight into the frequency development of the *so*-adj-*a* construction across time, the value we are interested in is the normalized frequency of use. One has to note that for each of the four types described in Section 2.1, two searches need to be done, namely one for the version with the indefinite article *a* and one for the version with *an*.

3.2.2   *Results and discussion*

Table 1 contains the normalized frequencies obtained via the online interface of COHA. Spot checks prove that the search procedure has a high degree of precision. The number of false positives and e.g., double hits is kept at a reasonably low level, amounting to less than 2%, depending on the sophistication of the construction we are searching for (it is higher for types C and D).

As we can see, the first basic type of the construction is and has probably always been, by far, the most frequent one. In the first decade of 2000 type A was 47 times more frequent that type B, 23.5 times more frequent than type C and 27.65 times more frequent than type D. In the very beginning of the studied period, namely in the decade of 1810, type A was 26.5, 185.2 and 55.1 times more

Table 1. Frequency per million words across the time period 1810–2009 – four types of the *so*-adj-*a* sequence.

Decade	Type A so-adj-a/an-N	Type B so-adj and adj-a/an-N	Type C so-adv-adj-a/an-N	Type D so-adj-a/an-adj-N
1810	157.46	5.93	0.85	1.69
1820	115.64	10.10	0.58	0.87
1830	106.57	6.76	1.02	0.87
1840	100.13	7.29	0.74	1.68
1850	105.52	8.01	1.21	1.70
1860	88.48	6.33	1.00	0.94
1870	79.68	4.74	1.62	0.91
1880	69.01	5.47	1.13	1.18
1890	64.51	5.29	1.16	1.02
1900	56.29	3.26	0.81	1.18
1910	43.88	2.55	0.88	0.75
1920	34.38	1.68	0.27	0.86
1930	26.46	1.58	0.49	0.85
1940	21.11	1.31	0.25	0.57
1950	18.42	0.89	0.24	0.41
1960	14.05	1.17	0.42	0.55
1970	12.60	0.84	0.33	0.25
1980	10.15	0.44	0.20	0.24
1990	4.36	0.36	0.18	0.15
2000	4.70	0.10	0.20	0.17

frequent than types B, C and D respectively. Especially types C and D can be said to have been really rare throughout the studied period, the highest frequency of use being, for each of them, a little more than 1.6 per million words.

Figure 1 presents the results in the form of four line plots. Apart from making the dominance of the type A construction even more noticeable, the visualization of the data shows how steep the decline in frequency has been over the last two hundred years, at least in the case of the most frequent type A.

Because of the frequency scale used in Figure 1, which is adjusted to the most frequent variant, we are unable to trace the frequency developments for types B, C and D. Figure 2, which contains four bar plots, one for each type, addresses this problem.

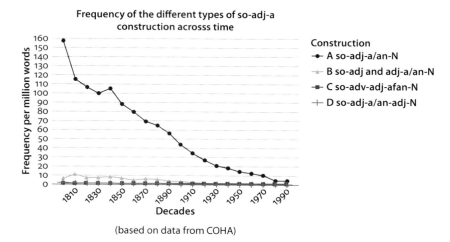

Figure 1. Frequency across time (Part I): four types of the *so*-adj-*a* construction in the time period 1810–2009.

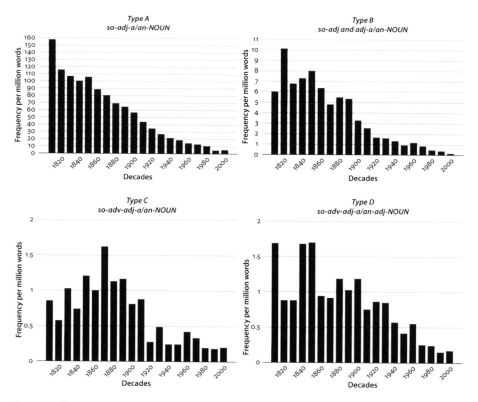

Figure 2. Frequency across time (Part II): four types of the *so*-adj-*a* construction in the time period 1810–2009.

As is shown, there is a decrease in the frequency of occurrence in the case of each of the four variants. The rarest of them, namely C and D, display the highest fluctuations, which, given their very low frequency of use (starting from the second decade of the 20th century below 0.9 per million words), is fully understandable.

The decrease visualized in Figure 1 and Figure 2 is so steep that naturally following questions could be "does this mean that the construction is on the way out?" and "is it even going to be represented in the corpus in e.g., 50 years?". The next section introduces the framework and methodology that can be applied to investigate this inquiry in more detail.

4.   Grammatical obsolescence

Grammatical obsolescence is a notion encompassing phenomena, which, in the literature, are referred to as *loss*, *demise* and *decline*. According to the definition in Rudnicka (2019: 4), it can be explained as:

> [A] situation in which a previously popular and productive construction is, often gradually, losing its productivity and popularity over time until the construction disappears or there are only residues or fossilised forms left. The function of the obsolescent construction may discontinue or continue to be (fully or partially) expressed by alternative means.

It has to be noted that the adjective *obsolescent* is different from the adjective *obsolete*, as the first one describes a process in which the construction is used less and less frequently as time passes, but the construction as such is still acceptable and would be judged as grammatical by the language community. The second one, on the contrary, describes a state in which the construction is already "out" – not acceptable to the language users (Rudnicka 2019: 10).

Figure 3 presents the criteria catalogue designed for the investigation of obsolescence. According to the chart, there are five criteria that should be looked at while describing a potentially obsolescent construction, namely (i) the presence of a negative correlation between time and frequency; (ii) distributional fragmentation – a situation in which the construction becomes "genre-restricted" and tends to occur in more formal genres; (iii) paradigmatic atrophy (when the construction's paradigmatic potential is shrinking)[3]; (iv) competition with other constructions, both a symptom and a cause of obsolescence; (v) the presence of higher-order

---

3.   It can be summarized as a growing restriction of lexical or grammatical items to certain morphological forms and syntactic environments (e.g., Hundt 2014). A development which might be considered as paradigmatic atrophy is e.g., "the increasing rarity of the negative contraction in -n't with some (though not all) modals" (Leech et al. 2009: 81).

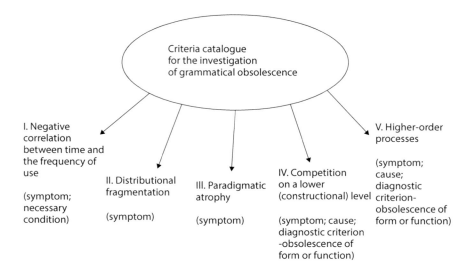

Figure 3. Criteria catalogue for investigation of obsolescence (taken from Rudnicka 2019: 31).

processes (changes happening above the constructional level, sometimes referred to as system dependency), also both a symptom and a potential cause. The fulfilment of the first criterion, namely the presence of negative correlation between time and frequency of use is suggested as a *necessary condition*[4] for the presence of grammatical obsolescence. Each of the following five subsections (4.1–4.5) deals with one of the criteria presented in Figure 3.

4.1   Negative correlation between time and the frequency of use

To test for the presence of a negative correlation between time and the frequency of use, we turn to the data presented in Table 1 (Section 3.2.2). The testing itself and the interpretation of the results are conducted with the use of R, a programming language and software environment for statistical computing and graphics, and R Studio – which is a set of integrated tools for R.[5]

Correlation testing conducted with the use of Kendall's tau test reveals the presence of a negative correlation between time and the frequency of use[6] for all

---

4.   According to Schustack (1988: 93) "a necessary condition for some outcome is a condition that must always be present for the outcome to be present, that is a condition whose absence will prevent that outcome".

5.   R is freely available at <https://cran.r-project.org/mirrors.html> and RStudio at <https://www.rstudio.com/products/rstudio/download/>

6.   The negative correlation between time and the frequency of use is to be interpreted as "the later the decade, the less instances of a given word or construction there are".

of the studied variants. Table 2 presents the results. In each case, the results are highly statistically significant, however, the strongest negative correlation has been detected for the most frequent type A. This is in line with our observation, based on visualization of the diachronic frequency trends in Figure 2, that the frequency histograms show more fluctuations in the less frequent types of the construction.

Table 2. Results of correlation testing in R.

Type	Correlation	Tau and p-value
A *so*-adj-*a/an*-N	Negative correlation	tau = −0.979 p-value < 2.2e-16 ***
B *so*-adj and adj-*a/an*-N	Negative correlation	tau = −0.884 p-value = 3.687e-11 ***
C *so*-adv-adj-*a/an*-N	Negative correlation	tau = −0.565 p-value = 0.000514 ***
D *so*-adj-*a/an*-adj-N	Negative correlation	tau = −0.709 p-value = 1.348e-05 ***

4.2   Distributional fragmentation

In the present subsection we look at the distribution of the *so*-adj-*a* sequence across different genres represented in the COHA corpus, namely *fiction*, *magazine*, *newspaper* and *non-fiction*. The aim is to add more pieces of information to what we know about the construction itself and to have a closer look at claims made in the research literature about the restriction of the construction to more formal textual environments (e.g., Quirk et al. 1985; Swan 2005). Is it really the case, and if it is, has it always been like that or has the construction once had a more even distribution across different text types? The answer to this question is relevant because signs of distributional fragmentation, understood as a situation in which a certain construction is increasingly restricted to formal or academic genres, point in the direction of possible obsolescence (e.g., Hundt & Leech 2012). However, this is only the case if the construction in question used to be more evenly distributed across different genres in the past (Rudnicka 2019).

4.2.1   *Methodology*

Following Rudnicka (2019: 136–137), the data will be processed and analysed in a way suitable for variables which are shown to be decreasing in frequency over time and which have already become considerably rare. The method measures *genre-related concentration* – the degree to which a given variant is concentrated (or overrepresented) in some genres, while being underrepresented in others.

The analysis envisages the use of raw frequencies extracted from the corpus which are later extrapolated so that we obtain a picture of what the genre-related distribution would look like if each of the four genres actually made up 25% of the corpus. As Rudnicka writes (2019: 136) "[d]ue to this approach the fact that the constructions decrease in the overall frequency of use will not interfere with what we want to observe". The results obtained this way can be summarized as providing an answer to the question "If we draw a random instance of *so-adj-a* construction from a corpus in which all four genres are balanced, what are the probabilities that it will stem from each of the four genres in each of the represented decades (time period 1860[7]-2000)?"

For the purpose of manageability, the present study is only conducted for the basic type (A) of the *so-adj-a* construction. It is assumed that results obtained for type A will possibly reflect tendencies that can be ascribed to other types.

4.2.2 Results and discussion

Table 3 presents the results obtained for three equidistant points in time, namely the decades 1880, 1940 and 2000. Figure 4 shows the changes of genre-related concentration across the whole time period represented in COHA.

For the decade of 1880 we see a more or less even probability of coming across an instance of the *so-*adj*-a* construction in the four genres – the probabilities oscillate around 25% which is the exact value we should have in an idealized scenario in which the construction is free from signs of concentrating in one particular genre. Sixty years later, in the decade of 1940, one can notice that there is a higher chance of finding noun phrases with *so-*adj predeterminers in the most formal[8] genre, namely *non-fiction books*. During the following period of sixty years, the tendency gets stronger, now the probability that a random instance of the *so-*adj*-a* construction found in the corpus belongs to the genre *non-fiction books* equals 43.6 %. On the other hand, the construction seems to be underrepresented in the genre of *newspaper* (for both the decades of 1940 and 2000) and *magazine* (the tendency is stronger in 2000 than in 1940). The probability of finding the construction in *fiction* is more or less the same for the first two points in time (22.1% in 1880, 22% in 1940) and there is a slight increase in the probability calculated for the last decade of COHA, namely 31.5%.

---

7. Only the time period of 1860–2009 is dealt with because the genre *newspaper* has been included in COHA no earlier than in 1860.

8. Out of the four genres represented by COHA, *non-fiction books* is assumed to be the most formal one, as it contains more texts exemplifying the formal language (Leech & Svartnik, 2013: 30), such as official reports and academic writing, than any other genre.

Table 3. Probability of finding an instance of the *so*-adj-*a* construction across four
COHA genres in the decades of 1880, 1940 and 2000.

Decade	Genre	Probability of finding an instance of *so*-adj-*a* construction across genres in percentage
1880	*fiction*	22.14%
	newspaper	23.54%
	magazine	27.63%
	non-fiction	26.70%
1940	*fiction*	22.01%
	newspaper	12.67%
	magazine	26.12%
	non-fiction	39.19%
2000	*fiction*	31.55%
	newspaper	7.98%
	magazine	16.83%
	non-fiction	43.64%

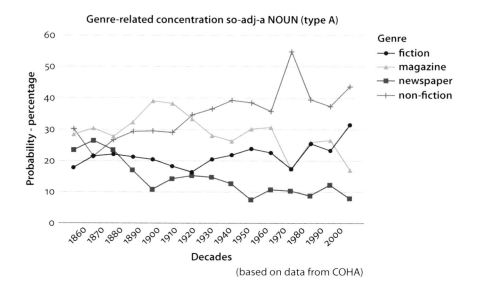

Figure 4. Probability of finding an instance of the *so*-adj-*a* construction in particular genres of
COHA across time.

To sum up the results presented in this subsection, Quirk et al. (1985) and Swan (2005) are, at least to some extent, right about the fact that the *so*-adj-*a* construction has some preference to more formal texts. This preference can be observed from the end of the 19th century onwards (see Figure 4). However, it is hard to talk about a "restriction" to formal contexts, as the construction is present in every genre included in the corpus. An example of an obsolescent construction, which shows a much higher degree of distributional fragmentation can be provided by *in order that* – a finite purpose subordinator, for which according to Rudnicka (2019: 141), in the last decade represented in COHA "we have more than 85% of chance that a random *in order that* found in the corpus belongs to the non-fiction genre. In the case of *newspaper* and *magazine,* the probability of occurrence gradually goes down and in the decade 2000 it equals zero".

This is also the case for the instances found in the Corpus of Contemporary American English[9] (COCA) featuring texts from the time period of 1990–2017. The contents of COCA are equally divided into five genres, four of them roughly corresponding to COHA genres (*fiction, popular magazines, newspapers* and *academic texts*), and one genre which is not represented in the historical corpus, namely *spoken.*[10] Because of the even division of the content into genres, it is easier to gain insight into genre-related distribution of the *so*-adj-*a* construction. Table 4 contains the frequencies (per million words) of noun phrases with *so*-adj-*a* (type A) across the different COCA genres. These results are also given in the form of percentages in the last column of Table 4.

Table 4. Distribution of the *so*-adj-*a* construction across COCA genres.

	Frequency per million words	Distribution across genres in percentage
COCA genres	*so*-adj-*a/an* NOUN	*so*-adj-*a/an* NOUN
spoken	0.98	6.86%
fiction	5.13	35.94%
popular magazines	3.25	22.80%
newspapers	1.31	9.20%
academic texts	3.60	25.20%

According to the results, the *so*-adj-*a* sequence is most often found in the genre of *fiction* (35.94% of all the instances). The genres *academic texts* (25.20%)

9.   The Corpus of Contemporary American English (COCA) contains more than 520 million words of text. Website: <https://www.english-corpora.org/coca/>

10.   Much more on the COCA genres can be read in e.g., Rudnicka (2019: 129).

and *popular magazine* (22.80%) follow. Significantly smaller probabilities can be seen in the case of *newspapers* and *spoken* genres – 9.20% and 6.86%. Especially, this last genre seems to be an unfavourable environment for noun phrases with *so*-adj-*a*. Figure 5 presents a visualization of the results.

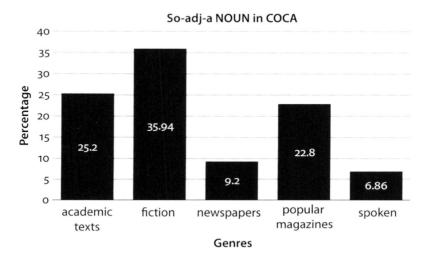

Figure 5. *So*-adj-*a* construction across different COCA genres.

Even though noun phrases with *so*-adj predeterminers are more frequent in written genres, and, judging by the trends detected in historical data, they seem to become more typical for formal genres (Table 3 & Figure 4), it is hard to talk about a concrete restriction to formal contexts. Still, we should bear in mind that the diachronic study features extrapolated frequencies from COHA, but the over-all frequency of the construction in question is decreasing, so in fact it is far from being a typical feature of formal genres in later periods.

As we can see in the data extracted from COCA (Table 4 & Figure 5), the *so*-adj-*a* construction is, even in modern times, represented in each of the COCA genres. Moreover, its most preferred genre is not *academic texts* but *fiction*, the latter being considered less formal than the former.

4.3 Paradigmatic atrophy

In the literature among the examples of paradigmatic atrophy at work there is e.g., "the increasing rarity of the negative contraction in -n't with some (though not all) modals" (Leech et al. 2009: 81). One idea could be to see types B, C and D (see Section 1.1) as parts of the paradigmatic potential of the basic type A *so*-adj-*a* construction. Under this assumption their demise (see Figure 2 and Table 1) might be seen as a symptom of the overall obsolescence of the *so*-adj-*a* construction. One other idea could be to identify a recent restriction to certain semantic functions, however, as Klégr (2010: 107, also see Section 2.1) emphasizes, this does not seem to be the case. The fact that the construction usually fulfils rhematising functions should not be seen as a symptom of paradigmatic atrophy, as that has probably been its main function from the very beginning. To sum up, the construction might display some signs of paradigmatic atrophy, but it is not that noticeable and it definitely should not be seen as one of the main symptoms of obsolescence.

4.4   Competition on the constructional level

Moving to the criterion of competition, we have to first define the prerequisites of treating competition (on the constructional level) as a serious possibility and as the explanation of what we observe. In Rudnicka (2019: 84) I have argued:

> As Hundt (2014: 171) has said, there are two prerequisites for competition to be seen as a plausible factor playing a role in an observed language change process. The (potentially) competing constructions have to be functionally equivalent (Lass 1997), and there has to be a direct reflection of competition in the observed frequencies of use of the two (potentially) competing constructions (Hundt & Leech 2012: 176).

However, in the case of the *so*-adj-*a* construction it is hard to point to any natural and obvious competitors. The next two subsections (4.4.1 and 4.4.2) are devoted to two constructions, which, at least at first sight, might seem to be potential competitors, namely the *that*-adj-*a* construction and the *such-a*-adj construction.

4.4.1   That-*adj*-a *construction*
The *so*-adj-*a* construction as such is an atypical one and one of the few alternatives which tends to be used in the same context, but, surprisingly does show some increase in the frequency of use, especially from the middle of the twentieth century onwards (see Table 5), is the *that*-adj-*a* noun construction, exemplified in (10).

(10)   It is not <u>that big a deal</u>.   (COHA: 1995; FIC; "Nondestructive testing")

Table 5. Frequency of the *that*-adj-*a* noun construction in the time period 1930–2000.[11]

	that-adj-*a/an* noun	
Decade	Raw frequency	Frequency per million words
1930	7	0.28
1940	4	0.16

11.   Data retrieved from COHA on April 13, 2019 from <https://www.english-corpora.org/coha/>

Table 5. (*Continued*)

	that-adj-*a/an* noun	
Decade	Raw frequency	Frequency per million words
1950	7	0.28
1960	13	0.54
1970	18	0.76
1980	36	1.42
1990	27	0.97
2000	34	1.15

However, the *that*-adj-*a* construction is frequently preceded by a negation or a negative context, see (11).

(11)   I'd never been all <u>that big a fan</u> of Marybeth's in the first place.
(COHA: 2009; FIC; "A slice of murder")

So its main area of semantic specialization is different from the one typical for the *so*-adj-*a* noun. Also, if we take into account the frequency figures from Table 1 – we see that the increase in the frequency of use of the *that*-adj-*a* construction is still not high enough to fully account for the frequency decrease observed in the case of *so*-adj-*a* construction. Table 6 presents the frequency gains and losses in the case of the two constructions during the time period 1930–2000.

Table 6. Changes in the frequency of the *so*-adj-*a* construction and the *that*-adj-*a* construction.[12]

Decades	Changes in the frequency (per million words) of the *so*-adj-*a* construction (type A)	Changes in the frequency (per million words) of the *that*-adj-*a* construction
1930 – 1940	−5.35	−0.12
1940 – 1950	−2.69	+0.12
1950 – 1960	−4.37	+0.26
1960 – 1970	−1.45	+0.22
1970 – 1980	−2.45	+0.66
1980 – 1990	−5.79	−0.45
1990 – 2000	−0.34	+0.18

---

12.   Data retrieved from COHA on February 4, 2020 from <https://www.english-corpora.org/coha/>

4.4.2   *Competition with the* that-adj-*a construction: An explanation*

If we assume the *that*-adj-*a* construction to be a potential competitor of the *so*-adj-*a* construction, why couldn't we see a direct reflection of the competition in the frequency of use of the two constructions (Table 6)? For a potential explanation, let us now have a look at Hilpert's (2012) conclusions concerning *many-a* noun. Importantly, he attempts to explain the demise of the *many-a* noun construction by checking for any reflection of potential competition between it and the canonical pattern *many* noun[PL] (*many a dog owner* vs. *many dog owners*). According to his findings, clues suggesting a frequency trade-off are very scarce. His explanation for this is the following (2013: 374) "The *many a noun* construction was, from its beginning, a stylistically marked, peripheral grammatical device. Hence, its diachronic demise does not cause substantial ripple effects".

The same might actually be true for the *so*-adj-*a* construction. Although it seems to have always, from its very beginning in the late 14th century, functioned as a stylistic device used to make comments and catch the readers' attention, it has never made it to the mainstream. This is why, even though its function is still there, realized by different constructions (one of which might actually be *that*-adj-*a* noun, at least for the variant preceded by *not*, as in (12)), we are not able to point to "a direct reflection of competition in the observed frequencies of use of the two (potentially) competing constructions" (Hundt & Leech 2012: 176).

(12)   Crossing the ocean in a balloon is <u>not so difficult a feat after all</u>.
                                    (COHA: 2003; FIC; "On glorious wings: the best
                                    flying stories of the century")

4.4.3   Such-a-*adj construction*

The *such-a*-adj construction, exemplified by (13), might, at first sight, appear to be a less atypical, but functionally similar alternative for the *so*-adj-*a* construction.

(13)   They are surprised and embarrassed to be uncovered in <u>such a private
        moment</u>.   (COHA: 2000; FIC; "Staging Coyote's Dream")

However, as has been argued in this chapter (see Section 2.1), a crucial feature of the *so*-adj-*a* construction is its stylistic function, which might result from the inverted order of the adjective and the determiner. This non-canonical grammatical form gives the construction a certain undertone, it is a "special-purpose" construction used to emphasize, catch the attention of a reader or introduce comments as side notes. The *such-a*-adj construction does not share this characteristic with the *so*-adj-*a* construction and that is why it is not treated as a possible genuine competitor.

4.5   Larger changes

The fifth criterion from the catalogue in Figure 3 is the presence of higher-order processes – namely processes happening above the constructional level. Rudnicka (2019: 189) differentiates between internally- and externally-motivated higher-order processes and gives one example for each kind:

i.   *the rise of the* to-*infinitive* for the former, which is very likely one of the main causes behind for the obsolescence of the finite purpose subordinator *in order that* (Rudnicka 2019: 193); and

ii. *socio-cultural changes of the 19th and 20th centuries* for the latter, which might be responsible for the decrease in popularity of the elaborate non-finite purpose subordinators such as *so as to* and *in order to* (e.g., Rudnicka 2019: 183).

Is it possible that any of these processes might be influencing the *so*-adj-*a* construction? The fact that the *so*-adj-*a* sequence is judged as rather restricted to formal contexts (Quirk et al. 1985; Swan 2005; quoted in Klégr 2010: 99) might suggest that the externally-motivated higher-order process of socio-cultural changes of the 19th and 20th centuries is not working in its favour. Figure 6 presents the hierarchical schema showing particular levels on which changes are happening. According to it, the main "big" externally-motivated process gives rise

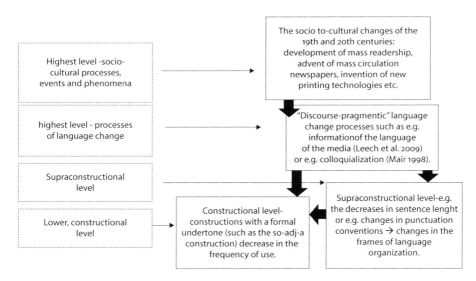

Figure 6. Socio-cultural changes of the 19th and 20th centuries influencing the constructional level – a hierarchical schema (based on Rudnicka 2019: 188).

to e.g., discourse-pragmatic language change processes such as colloquialization (Mair 1998). The discourse-pragmatic language change processes, in turn, influence both the supraconstructional and the constructional level of language. An example of such influence is, for instance, the shortening of the sentence length in words (Rudnicka 2018). Apart from influencing the supraconstructional level, also the constructional level is being influenced by e.g., the decisions made by the language users, such as the choice of less formal, more colloquial expressions over the sophisticated and elaborate ones, which could exactly be one of the reasons for the *so*-adj-*a* construction's loss of popularity.

Interestingly, also Kempf (this volume), who studies the loss of the relative particle *so* in the early stages of New High German, identifies a hierarchy of major societal and linguistic changes which appear to be playing a fundamental role in the obsolescence of *so*-relatives, among them "democratization, the Enlightenment, and literalization". All of these processes could be subsumed under the label of externally-motivated higher-order changes which by themselves, and by means of other processes, exert influence on the constructional level.

4.6   Summary of the results

To conclude, the *so*-adj-*a* construction can be treated as an instantiation of grammatical obsolescence in progress. It does not only fulfil the necessary condition (the presence of negative correlation between time and the frequency of use), but it (i) also shows signs of distributional fragmentation (Section 4.3); (ii) its other variants (type B, C and D) are already nearly extinct (see Table 1 and Figure 2), which might point in the direction of paradigmatic atrophy; (iii) and there is at least one higher-order process which is not "in line" with the construction in question (see Figure 6).

5.   Conclusions and outlook

As already mentioned, the investigation of the *so*-adj-*a* construction with the use of the applied framework shows that the construction in question is very likely an instantiation of grammatical obsolescence in progress. Its decline seems to have been gradual, but at the same time, the decrease in the frequency of use is really dramatic (see Figure 1). Although, as pointed out by e.g., Jespersen (1933), Quirk et al. (1985), Swan (2005) and Klégr (2010), the construction is, and has always been, atypical, somewhat unusual and "one of the many peculiarities of English article usage", it seems to have fulfilled its rhematic function quite successfully for a few centuries. What can its demise be attributed to? Judging by the low number of natural competitors, and by the story of a similar construction, namely *many a* noun construction (Hilpert 2012: 374, quoted in Section 4.4), competition on the constructional level is not always the right explanation. Are the higher-order processes (see Section 4.5) "to blame"? This does seem to be the right direction. Still, what has been suggested about the origins of *so-adj-a* noun is that its "birth" might have been motivated by extravagance (Section 3.1), or, in different words, by the desire of the writer to grab more attention of the reader. This reasoning is in line with the main rhematic function fulfilled by the *so-adj-a* sequence. A natural question following from there is "How long may a construction be extravagant?". The "freshness effect" cannot, by definition, last forever. The construction described by Petré (2017), namely [BE Ving] construction (or simply the progressive), has managed to spread across many different functions in the language and it definitely belongs to the linguistic mainstream nowadays. On the way there, however, due to the process of secondary grammaticalization (Kranich 2015), the progressive lost most of its emphatic, speaker-based, attitudinal shades of meaning. *So-adj-a* noun has not been as successful as the progressive. It seems that the construction in question did fulfil the need for which it was intended for a few centuries, but once more time has passed, and the conditions slightly changed (due to e.g., colloquializa-tion), it lost its finesse and got an archaic, old-fashioned and formal undertone. This, however, does not necessarily mean that it lost its function, and will disappear in the immediate future. On the contrary, the case might be that it will stay around for at least a few more decades and its function will still probably be to draw the readers' attention but this time not to the content or the comment it is introducing but to itself, exactly because of the formal, archaic and jocular touch it provides.

Acknowledgements

I would like to express my most sincere thanks to (i) the two anonymous reviewers for their thorough reviews which helped to make this chapter much better than it was at first; (ii) to Aleš Klégr for his second opinion and "a bit of polishing languagewise"; (iii) to Tine Breban and Svenja Kranich – for their work and commitment while organising the "Lost in change" work-shop at the 40th Annual Conference of the German Linguistic Society and during the process of getting the present volume ready.

Language corpora

Davies, Mark. 2008. The Corpus of Contemporary American English (COCA): 560 million words, 1990-present. <https://www.english-corpora.org/coca/>
COHA Davies, Mark. 2010. The Corpus of Historical American English: 400 million words, 1810–2009. <http://corpus.byu.edu/coha/>

Software

R Core Team. 2013. *R: A Language and Environment for Statistical Computing*. R Foundation for
Statistical Computing, Vienna, Austria.

References

Aniya, Sosei. 2016. The Big Mess Construction straightened out. *Studies in Human Sciences Bulletin of the Graduate School of Integrated Arts and Sciences, Hiroshima University* 11, 1–12.
https://doi.org/10.15027/42543
Berman, Arlene. 1974. Adjectives and Adjective Complement Constructions in English. PhD
dissertation, Harvard University.
Detges, Ulrich & Waltereit, Richard. 2002. Grammaticalization vs. reanalysis: A semantic-
pragmatic account of functional change in grammar. *Zeitschrift für Sprachwissenschaft* 21:
151–195.
Fowler, Henry W. & Butterfield, Jeremy (ed.). 2015. *Fowler's Dictionary of Modern English Usage*,
4th edn. Oxford: OUP.
Goldberg, Adele. 2006. *Constructions at Work*. Oxford: Oxford University Press.
Haspelmath, Martin. 1999. Why is grammaticalization irreversible? *Linguistics* 37: 1043–1068.
Hilpert, Martin. 2012. Diachronic collostructional analysis meets the noun phrase. Study-
ing *many a* noun in COHA. In *The Oxford Handbook of the History of English*, Terttu
Nevalainen & Elizabeth Closs Traugott (eds), 233–244. Oxford: OUP.
Hilpert, Martin. 2014. *Construction Grammar and its Application to English*. Edinburgh: Edin-
burgh University.
Huddleston, Rodney & Pullum, Geoffrey. 2002. *The Cambridge Grammar of the English Lan-
guage*. Cambridge: Cambridge University Press.
Hundt, Marianne & Leech, Geoffrey. 2012. Small is beautiful: On the value of standard reference
corpora for observing recent grammatical change. In *The Oxford Handbook of the History
of English*, Terttu Nevalainen & Elizabeth Closs Traugott (eds), 175–88. Oxford: OUP.
Hundt, Marianne. 2014. The demise of the *being to V* construction. *Transactions of the Philologi-
cal Society* 112(2): 167–187. https://doi.org/10.1111/1467-968X.12035
Imel, Brock. 2019. Sa nature proveir se volt: A New Examination of Leftward Stylistic
Displacement in Medieval French through Textual Domain, Information Structure, and
Oral Représenté. PhD dissertation, University of California, Berkeley.
Jespersen, Otto. 1933. *Essentials of English Grammar*. London: Allen and Unwin.
Kay, Paul & Sag, Ivan. 2012. Discontinuous dependencies and complex determiners. In *Sign-
Based Construction Grammar*, Hans Boas & Ivan Sag (eds), 229–256. Stanford CA: CSLI.
Kempf, Luise. 2021. German *so*-relatives: Lost in grammatical, typological, and sociolinguistic
change. In *Lost in Change. Causes and Processes in the Loss of Grammatical Elements and
Constructions* [Studies in Language Companion Series 218], Svenja Kranich & Tine Breban
(eds). Amsterdam: John Benjamins. (This volume) https://doi.org/10.1075/slcs.218.10kem
Keller, Rudi. 1994. *On Language Change: The Invisible Hand in Language*. London: Routledge.
Kim, Jong-Bok & Sells, Peter. 2011. The Big Mess Construction: Interactions between the lexicon and constructions. *English Language and Linguistics* 15 (2): 335–362.
https://doi.org/10.1017/S1360674311000062

Klégr, Aleš. 2010. Noun phrases with *so*-adj predeterminers: So complicated a matter. In ... *for thy speech bewrayeth thee. A Festschrift for Libuše Dušková*, Markéta Malá & Pavlína Šaldová (eds), 93–119. Praha: Filozofická Fakulta.

Kranich, Svenja. 2015. The impact of input and output domains: Towards a function-based categorization of types of grammaticalization. In *What Happens after Grammaticalization? Secondary Grammaticalization and Other Late Stage Processes in Grammaticalization*, Tine Breban & Svenja Kranich (eds). *Special issue of Language Sciences* 47(B), 172–187.

Lass, Roger. 1997. *Historical Linguistics and Language Change*. Cambridge: CUP.
https://doi.org/10.1017/CBO9780511620928

Leech, Geoffrey, Hundt, Marianne, Mair, Christian & Smith, Nicholas. 2009. *Change in Contemporary English. A Grammatical Study*. Cambridge: CUP.
https://doi.org/10.1017/CBO9780511642210

Leech, Geoffrey & Svartnik, Jan. 2013. *A Communicative Grammar of English*. London: Routledge. https://doi.org/10.4324/9781315836041

Mair, Christian. 1998. Corpora and the study of major varieties in English: Issues and results. In *The Major Varieties of English: Papers from MAVEN 97*, Hans Lindquist, Staffan Klintborg, Magnus Levin & Maria Estling (eds), 139–157. Växjö: Acta Wexionensia.

Osborne, Timothy. 2019. Noun phrases rooted by adjectives: A dependency grammar analysis of the Big Mess Construction. *Proceedings of the Fifth International Conference on Dependency Linguistics* (Depling, SyntaxFest 2019), 49–59. Stroudsburg PA: Association for Computational Linguistics.

Petré, Peter. 2017. The extravagant progressive: An experimental corpus study on the history of emphatic [BE Ving]. In *Cognitive Approaches to the History of English*, Thomas Hoffmann & Alexander Bergs (eds). *Special issue of English Language & Linguistics* 21 (2): 227–250.

Quirk, Randolph, Greenbaum, Sidney, Leech, Geoffrey & Svartvik, Jan. 1985. *A Comprehensive Grammar of the English Language*. London: Longman.

Rudnicka, Karolina. 2018. Variation of sentence length across time and genre: Influence on the syntactic usage in English. In *Diachronic Corpora, Genre, and Language Change* [Studies in Corpus Linguistics 85], Richard Jason Whitt (ed.), 219–240. Amsterdam: John Benjamins.
https://doi.org/10.1075/scl.85.10rud

Rudnicka, Karolina. 2019. *The Statistics of Obsolescence: Purpose Subordinators in Late Modern English* [NIHIN Studies]. Freiburg: Rombach.

Schustack, Miriam W. 1988. Thinking about causality. In *The Psychology of Human Thought*, Robert J. Sternberg & Edward E. Smith (eds.), 92–116. Cambridge: Cambridge University Press.

Stefanowitsch, Anatol. 2013. Collostructional analysis. In *The Oxford Handbook of Construction Grammar*, Graeme Trousdale & Thomas Hoffmann (eds), 290–306. Oxford: OUP.
https://doi.org/10.1093/oxfordhb/9780195396683.013.0016

Swan, Michael. 2003. *Practical English Usage*. Oxford: OUP.

van Eynde, Frank. 2007. The Big Mess Construction. In *Proceeding of the 14th International Conference on Head-Driven Phrase Structure Grammar*, Stefan Müller (ed.), 415–433. Stanford CA: CSLI.

Wales, Katie. 2001. *A Dictionary of Stylistics*, 2nd edn. Harlow: Longman.

CHAPTER 3

The impersonal construction in the texts of Updated Old English

Jan Čermák
Charles University

This chapter explores the methodological relevance of a recently systematized linguistic source of data on early English, the so-called Updated Old English contained in the edited copies of pre-Conquest texts produced in the late twelfth and the early thirteenth century. The analytical focus of the chapter is on the interplay of linguistic processes affecting the form and functional status of the impersonal construction in these texts. The continued appearance of the impersonal construction at this time is seen against the backdrop of the linguistic variation in the Updated Old English texts that heralds the typological transformation of English in grammar, word-formation and the structure of lexis.

Keywords: impersonal construction, Updated Old English, language typology, inflectional morphology, derivational morphology, lexical obsolescence, obsolescent morphology

1. Introduction

The idea to write this chapter was sparked by Cynthia L. Allen's observation (Allen 1997) that the Old English verb *behōfian* ('to need') started developing impersonal uses (in the sense of 'to befit') only in the late eleventh and early twelfth centuries, a transitional phase between Old English and Middle English syntax. This observation was later confirmed by Möhlig-Falke (2012), author of the most comprehensive account of the impersonal construction in the history of English to date,[1] who

---

1. Möhlig-Falke's findings were based on the *DOEC* data on impersonal verbs with a diachronic outlook based on the *MED* data. Another diachronic monograph on the impersonal construction in the history of English is Miura (2015), which, however, narrows its focus on interactions between syntax and meaning of Middle English verbs of emotion.

https://doi.org/10.1075/slcs.218.03cer
© 2021 John Benjamins Publishing Company

showed that Old English *behōfian* did indeed not as yet display the extension to the expression of obligation such as came with the Middle English verb *behoven*.

This individual observation highlights the potential relevance, for the study of impersonal constructions in early English, of texts now catalogued and classified as Updated Old English (1060–1220). These post-Conquest edited copies of Old English texts provide us with the earliest manifestations of the most dramatic structural change in the history of English, marking the beginnings of its typological transformation from the fusional (inflectional) to the isolating type and being datable to a time that in many respects embodies "the textual black hole" (Curzan 2003: 55) in the history of the language.[2] This body of texts, still awaiting conversion into the form of a language corpus, has thus far been explored somewhat unevenly by philologists and linguists, and this also relates to the history of the English impersonal construction. Even though the wealth of recent literature on the English impersonal construction does contain studies that have worked with twelfth-century documents (including, notably, those of Allen herself, cf. especially Allen 1995, 1997), the texts of Updated Old English as systematically collated to their Old English predecessors represent a source of data that has not yet been fully exploited and a missing link in the chronological coverage of the English impersonal construction.[3]

---

2.   Complementary linguistic evidence for this period comes from changes to pre-Conquest English texts made principally in the twelfth century and described as alterations. These alterations possibly show the scribes working on (mainly homiletic) texts with a greater degree of linguistic spontaneity than the scribes who were responsible for the Updated Old English material proper, discussed here. The alterations were probably made when the scribes prepared their texts for preaching or when they emended texts ready to be copied (Faulkner 2012).

3.   To the best of my knowledge, the vast literature on the subject does not as yet include comprehensive treatment of the long twelfth century texts based on systematic collation of post-Conquest copies to their Old English precedents. Allen (1997) first "completely examined" (1997: 16) a selection of Middle English texts of the twelfth and thirteenth centuries for occurrences of *behoven* and then compared those to their respective Old English textual counterparts. Allen (1995) contains substantial chapters on the syntax of experiencer verbs in Old and Early Middle English (1995: 96–157 and 1995: 222–290, in particular), but, again, her vast coverage of diverse Middle English texts examined for the loss of case marking does not contain analysis based on systemic collation of Old English texts and their post-Conquest copies (with the latter listed in Section B of her appendix C). Even though Allen says in the discussion of her twelfth century material that "[O]ne reason why these MSS are useful to us is that a comparison of the homilies found in these MSS and the extant OE originals shows some consistent changes in inflection" (Allen 1995: 167), she adduces but one instance based on such a collation – the verb *behoven* again (Allen 1995: 167).

Making use of this newly available data source, under-represented still even in major lexicographic historical resources such as the *Middle English Dictionary* (*MED*) and *Oxford English Dictionary* (*OED*), this methodological and qualitative study looks into the profile of the impersonal construction at this dramatic moment in the history of English. It attempts to achieve two aims: first, to assess the status of the impersonal construction in the selected Updated Old English texts as part of what was to become the complex story of the loss of the English impersonal construction, a story that had come to an end after 1500, and, second, to trace some of the mechanisms which Updated Old English used to maintain the impersonal construction even in copied texts that display diverse variation when compared to their Old English originals. While the construction studied is a poster child example of loss in the history of English and while the Updated Old English material provides new data to study diverse cases of loss, it will be shown that tracing the impersonal construction through the Updated texts provides evidence for the resilience and renewal of the impersonal construction where especially the resolution of lexical loss is crucial to its maintenance.

Section 2 offers a profile of Updated Old English, discusses practices of the updating scribes and characterizes the data sample in its linguistic context; Section 3 brings a nutshell story of the impersonal construction in the history of English; Section 4 analyses the lexico-semantic and syntactic features of the sampled impersonal verbs as well as alterations in the recording of the impersonal construction by the updating scribes. Section 5 contains a discussion of the results and concluding remarks.

2.   Updated Old English

"Pre-Conquest manuscripts did not languish in *armaria*, but continued to be read, annotated and used" (Faulkner 2012: 181), so that the period after the Norman Conquest did not mean a break with the Anglo-Saxon textual and literary tradition. These Old English texts, catalogued now under the heading of Updated Old English, were "variously copied, recopied, excerpted, re-contextualised, rewritten" (Dance 2014: 181) to serve a variety of uses in the post-Conquest period. Today they survive in over 200 manuscripts containing Old English and in more than 25 manuscripts composed principally of Updated Old English material – homilies, hagiographic, educational and devotional writings, laws and prognostications – produced between the Norman Conquest and the beginning of the thirteenth century. They are described in a searchable catalogue created by Mary Swan, Elaine Treharne and others under the project *The Production and Use of English Manuscripts 1060 to 1220* (2005–2010), available at <http://www.le.ac.uk/ee/em1060to1220>.

Witnesses to the active reuse of Old English materials many decades after the Norman Conquest, these texts offer much potential for providing a missing link in the period of the history of English still only partially covered by corpora and dictionaries. Standard academic understanding finds it "reasonable to expect to find linguistic updating" in these texts to make them "understandable to a late twelfth or early thirteenth-century audience" (Swan 1997: 8). On the other hand, precise characteristics, conditions and circumstances of such updating are extremely hard to retrieve in their systemic entirety or precise chronology. This may be the primary reason why these resources have been studied mainly by manuscript scholars (e.g., Swan 1997, 2006, 2007; Treharne 2006; Swan & Treharne 2000; Da Rold & Swan 2012; Irvine 1993; McColl Millar & Nicholls 1997; Clayton 2013), interested in textual transmission and in the dynamics of English literary culture of the long twelfth century, while linguistic exploration of the Updated Old English texts has so far been rather uneven. There has been much ground-breaking work on lexical change (e.g., Fischer 1996; Dance 2011, 2012, 2014), on multilingualism (e.g., Conti 2007) and on phonology and dialectology (e.g., Kitson 1992, 1997), but other aspects – such as morphology, syntax, word-formation – and interactions of all of them in an overall description and assessment of Updated Old English remain fairly underexplored.

2.1   Scribal practices followed in Updated Old English

Updated Old English material offers new perspectives on the decisive period in the typological transformation of English over time, when so much appears to have happened offstage, and on the subtle, quasi-synchronic mechanics of language variation and change generally. When scrutinizing the material, however, the linguist faces a number of serious methodological challenges.

Scribal responses to inherited material in the twelfth century were hugely complex. English linguistic and cultural identity was not only preserved but also developed. In the words of Mary Swan (2006: 152), in the scribal activity of that time continuity and transformation were interwoven. A primary impulse in the scribes surely was to produce a faithful version, but that impulse did not result in slavish copying. There was another important end for them to meet: for all their faithfulness, they can be seen as responding to differences between the language of their exemplars and the English of their day in an effort to produce faithful copies that would be, at the same time, fully intelligible to the readership and audiences of their time. Scribes of these texts made changes to the lexis and structural features of the originals, thereby presenting a glimpse into their own dialects and linguistic competences, i.e., offering a perspective on what they as individual language users found to be too archaic or perhaps even incomprehensible in the texts they copied. On the other hand, they engaged with these texts in a variety of ways, never smoothing them out systematically so that their products would read like newer ones.

A fairly typical textual configuration in Example 1, collating the Old English 'original' (1a) with two of its later updated versions (1b and 1c), may look like this:

(1) a. *God nele þæt we beon grædige gitseras. Ne eac for woruldgilpe forworpan ure <u>æhta</u>. ac dælan hi mid <u>gesceade</u>. swa swa hit <u>drihtne</u> licige.*
        (Cambridge Corpus Christi College, MS. 178; Morris 1868: 297.30–32)[4]

     God not desires.3.sg that we.nom.pl be.1.pl.sbjv greedy.nom.pl misers.nom.pl, nor also for worldly_praise.acc.sg waste.1.pl.sbjv our.acc.pl property.acc.pl; but deal_ out.pl.sbjv them.acc.pl with discretion.dat.sg so that it.nom.sg Lord.dat.sg may_ be_ pleasing.3.sg.sbjv.

     b. *God nyle þæt we beon grædige gitseres, ne eac for wurldgelpe forwurpen ure <u>æhte</u>, ac dælen heo mid <u>gescade</u>, swa swa hit <u>gode</u> lichige.*
        (Cotton Vespasian D.XIV; Warner 1917: 18.5–7)

     c. *God nele þet we beon gredie gitseras. ne ec for weorld gelpe forworpan ure <u>ehtan</u> ah dele we ure <u>ehtan</u> mid <u>wisdom</u>. swa þet hit <u>drihtne</u> likie.*
        (Lambeth 487; Morris 1868: 105.14–16)

     'God does not desire that we be greedy misers, or that we waste our property for worldly praise; but let us deal it wisely so that it may be pleasing to the Lord.'

The two updated versions in Example 1 agree in accommodating a number of spelling and sound departures from the Old English version, typically in what were unstressed syllables, though they do by no means share all of them. The most conspicuous morphological difference is the *ehtan* of Lambeth 487 (1c) that has added an analogical –*n* to the noun to mark unequivocally its plural reference. Lambeth 487 is here, as well as generally, more innovative than Vespasian D.XIV. (1b). In Example 1, this is apparent primarily from two kinds of evidence. Firstly, the Lambeth version replaces *gescead*, a word that was by then very probably on its way out of the lexis as in the *MED* it is attested only in a narrow range of texts prior to 1200. Secondly, the Lambeth scribe spends time and energy trying to make his text as clear as possible to the reader or listener. In the last but one clause, he not only re-introduces the subject of *dele* but also replaces the pronominal object

---

4. Citations are provided both with an interlinear translation and a free translation into Present-Day English. The references to editions are given by page and line number. Caroline and insular g's have been unified under the Caroline form. Items that are discussed specifically have been underlined.

of his exemplar (*hi*) with an explanatory noun phrase, repeating *ure ehtan*. On the other hand, a lexical replacement can be spotted in the Cotton Vespasian D. XIV version as well, even though the reason for it appears to have been a stylistic one: *God* and *drihten* of the final clause in 1b and 1c will continue being used as synonyms in Middle English. This particular instance is important for us to realize that what seems to be a diachronic updating due to obsolescence may simply have been dictated by dialectal, stylistic or pragmatic reasons or may have been due to shifts in theological emphasis. Interestingly, the syntactic structure of this clause had been left intact by the later scribes, including the dative case marking on the words for 'the Lord' in the semantic role of experiencer.

It is clear, then, that the twelfth-century scribes took a whole range of approaches to copying and that their copies represent a cline from extreme conservatism to partial (and selective) modernization. While some of the scribes were literatim copyists, others "worked editorially, modernising the language and adapting the content of the works they copied" and "the majority adopted an intermediate approach" (Faulkner 2012: 182). The kind of approach the scribes selected crucially depended not only on the content and form of their exemplars, on the dialect of Middle English they spoke themselves and on the levels of their linguistic awareness, but also on their motivations and the purposes of copying. This is the kind of background scholars can hope to reconstruct only piecemeal through interdisciplinary effort. The scribal approach certainly varied in relation to a number of other variables (and/or their combinations) as well. It depended on the form of the scribes' exemplars, which may have been themselves of a composite nature, or with which they worked by way of rearranging the material into new composite pieces. Also, the approach of the scribes was shaped by the use for which they were preparing and adapting their texts – whether this was public or private, preaching or devotional. Very importantly, this generally happened in a new context, the scribes possibly engaging with broader, and therefore less sophisticated, audiences than before the Conquest. Further to this, the textual approach of the scribes was determined by the extent to which they engaged with the tradition of the late West Saxon *Schriftsprache*, a factor that was likely to have a conservative effect on the levels of variation in the Updated texts. In addition, the scribes' approach also depended on how intelligible they found the language of their exemplars. Last but not least, we can rarely be sure that an Updated text in the form in which we have it was originally composed for the manuscript context in which it is now found. Numerous and complex as these factors are, they are certainly not the only ones operating on the cline between seemingly archaic, verbatim copying and the innovative reworking of a text, including abridgments, paraphrases, and excisions of extraneous material. Current scholarship should be prepared to consider the parts played by scribal motivation to sound deliberately archaic, transmission of text by memory, parallel influence of original post-Conquest texts, hypercorrection, and a host of linguistic variables (dialectal features, genre and register, multilingualism, idiolect, prosody and others). All of these were potentially relevant in the "multitude of interconnected aspects of textual revision" (Dance 2012: 172–173) in real scribal behaviour, limiting the scope of scholarly possibilities of looking for conscious and purposeful substitutions in the Updated Old English texts.

It is therefore not difficult to see why this body of evidence has so far been trawled for linguistic data only relatively sparsely. Defying easy periodization, these texts create their own context of interpretation because they are not "unambiguously 'contemporary' documents" (Dance 2014: 182). Containing a blend of archaic form and current usage whose full characteristics and relationships are not immediately tractable, the Updated texts have frequently been considered insufficiently spontaneous and up-to-date in that they do not represent an accurate representation of the speech of any region at any period.

On the other hand, given the general patchiness of the English record in the period under scrutiny, there are significant reasons why gleaning data from the Updated Old English material should be a worthwhile linguistic exercise. The textual changes made by the editing scribes come across as being of a comprehensive nature, with an effect on every level of linguistic description, not only the traditional domain of orthography. Some of the data have been used, in methodologically convincing ways, for thorough explorations of syntactic developments (cf. e.g., Allen 1995, 1997) and changes in the lexis of Early Middle English (e.g., Dance 2012). The consistency with which some of the differences between the various updated texts and their 'originals' recur suggests that, indeed, in a number of instances we are dealing with deliberate, meaningful acts of revision that reflect processes symptomatic of subtle, incipient but ongoing diachronic change. An early editor of these texts described the process as one not of "transliteration", but of "translation" (Morris 1868: xi). Much can therefore be learnt in systematic ways from these texts, limited in number and length as they are, if they are treated with caution (Allen 1995: 166). Once they have been collected in a corpus, full comparison with both Old English texts and original post-Conquest creations will be possible with an ambition to refine the history of English in the twelfth century, including a classification of the Updated Old English texts in terms of chronological, dialectal, intertextual and sociolinguistic characteristics.[5] Until that stage

---

5.   Two such corpus projects are currently underway: *An Electronic Corpus of Anonymous Homilies in Old English* is being developed at the University of Göttingen <https://www .uni-goettingen.de/en/electronic+corpus+of+homilies+in+old+english/556598.html> (2018– 2023), while Mark Faulkner reports work on the *Trinity Corpus of Old English from the Twelfth*

has been reached, however, it is reasonable to analyse the volumes of language variation and incipient change only by manual collation of these texts with their originals.

2.2   The Updated Old English data for the present study

The data for this chapter comprise a textual corpus of 57,680 words altogether. They come from forty Updated Old English texts of variable length collected in four manuscripts. London, British Library Cotton Vespasian D. xiv, which was copied almost entirely by one scribe in the mid-twelfth century, possibly in Canterbury, provided manuscript items 3, 4–7, 8–12, 14–25, 30–31, 37–41, 43, 49, 51 and 52, as edited by Warner (1917). From MS. Bodley 343, composed in the second half of the twelfth century near Worcester or Hereford and edited by Belfour (1909), items 19, 31, 72 and 84 were used. London, Cotton Vespasian A. xxii, another manuscript from the South, copied around c. 1200 probably in Rochester, contains Updated items no. 1 and 4, and these were edited by Morris (1868). The final four Updated items come from MS. London, Lambeth Palace 747 (no. 2, 9–11), copied in south-west Midlands also around c. 1200, and also edited by Morris (1868). In terms of Middle English dialect geography, these texts represent South-East and West. By genre, the bulk of the textual material is homiletic. It contains homilies mainly by Ælfric, one (incomplete) piece by Wulfstan (*Be godcundre warnunge*, Lambeth 487, item 2) and the rest of an anonymous nature. The few items that complement the homilies are of a devotional, epistolary, hagiographic and generally educational nature, represented e.g., by a portion of Ælfric's *Letter to Sigefyrð* and by the *Dicts of Cato* in Cotton Vespasian D. xiv. Most of them were collated to their Old English exemplars in complete form, but several items allowed for only partial collation. The Old English original versions were used based on the editions by Assmann (1889), Clemoes (1997), Crawford (1969), Fehr (1966), Godden (1979), Pope (1967–1968), Scragg (1992), Skeat (1881–1900) and Thorpe (1844–1846).

2.3   The data in their linguistic context

In order to be able to appreciate variation affecting impersonal constructions in the Updated textual sample, it is necessary to contextualize them in linguistic terms. In the following we will therefore illustrate, by means of selected examples, the

Century (*TOXIIC*) <http://peoplefinder.tcd.ie/Profile?Username=FAULKNEM> (2017–2019). On this webpage, Faulkner also specifies the volume of his material as comprising "29 manuscripts, collectively containing 471 texts and just over 1.25 million words of English".

general volume of variation within which the constructions are embedded in the selected Updated texts, exemplifying at least some of the linguistic features that are typically subject to modification by the updating scribes in reference to variation and change they perceived in the language of the time. These features come from all the linguistic levels, ranging from spelling innovation and sound change to replacements due to lexical obsolescence, and heralding, albeit to a varying degree determined by the cline between conservatism and innovation, profiles of change known from the later history of English.

(2)   a.   (*se ealda mann...*) *biþ þam treowe gelic. þe leaf byrð and blostman*
                                                                   (Morris 1868: 299.23)

           (the.NOM.SG old.NOM.SG man.NOM.SG...) is the.DAT.SG tree.DAT.SG like
           that leaf.ACC.SG bears.3.SG.IND and blossom.ACC.SG

     b.   (*þe alde mon...*) *biþ iliche þan treo þe bereð lef and blosman*
                                                                   (Morris 1868: 109.10)

           '(the old man...) is like the tree that bears leaf and blossom'

This is an unusually rich example. Though not particularly informative as regards (expected) changes in orthography (as is the use of the digraph *ch* in *iliche*) or phonology of both stressed and unstressed syllables (cf. *ealda* > *alde*; *leaf* > *lef*), this example presents a number of morphophonological and syntactic modifications responsive to phonological changes (i.e., changes in unstressed syllables and in the nature of stress) and reflecting the incipient typological transformation of the language structure. The forms *þe* (as opposed to *se* in the bracketed noun phrase), *treo* (cf. the allomorphy *trēo-/trēow-* in Old English) and *bereð* of the Updated b-version illustrate, each in its own way, the tendency to abolish paradigmatic allomorphy, characteristic of the fusional type of language structure. The simplification of the consonant cluster in *blosman* can also be seen as typologically relevant.[6] The persistence of case marking on *þan* illustrates the continuity of

---

6.   Updated Old English texts feature a number of instances that reflect growing sensitiveness of the word-structure to consonant clusters and consonant combinations. Though often difficult to assess against the welter of spelling forms, two tendencies appear to be operative here. One manifests itself in the simplification of consonant clusters through ultimate loss of a consonant, as in *bloSTMa* > *bloSMa*, *riHTLæcan* > *riHLechen*, *aNDSete* > *aNSete* (with affected consonant groups capitalized). The other tendency is reflected in the simplification of consonant clusters by vowel insertion (anaptyxis), often on the basis of morphological analogy motivated again, at least in some cases, by the tendency to remove allomorphy from inflectional paradigms: *forligre* > *forligEre, syngian* > *synEgian; wiglung* > *wigElung* (with the inserted vowel capitalized). In effect, these developments are similar to the case of desyncopation and levelled mutation in *bereð* of Example 2 above. Although these two tendencies oppose one another in their results, they jointly

lexically assigned case on the determiner, but, at the same time, the Updated noun (*treo*) is not marked for case any longer. This illustrates the economy of grammatical marking in the noun phrase by which the language system responds to the ongoing dramatic developments in non-tonic syllables. Among the syntactic modifications of 2b, we can observe an instance of positional fixation of the complement of the adjective in the main clause, resulting in bringing the copula and the subject complement back to back (*biþ iliche*), as well as an instance of Object-Verb > Verb-Object reordering in the subordinate clause.

Structures like Example 3 exhibit individual responses by the scribes marking small beginnings of another major Late Middle English syntactic development – early instances of the abolishment of the verb-second rule:

(3)   a.   *þurh cristes menniscnysse <u>wurdon men alysde</u> fram deofles þeowte*
            (Clemoes 1997: 362.206–207)

        Through Christ.GEN.SG incarnation.ACC.SG became.3.PL.IND men.NOM.PL delivered.NOM.PL from devil.GEN.SG bondage.DAT.SG

    b.   *þuruh cristes menniscnesse <u>men weren alesde</u> from deofles þeowdome*
            (Morris 1867–1868: 99.8–9)

        'through Christ's incarnation men were redeemed from the devil's bondage'

In contrast to 3b, the Updated version in 4b introduces a verb-second structure upon inserting the initial adverbial *þa* into the first clause. This modification illustrates the amount of variation in the Updated texts, implying that the verb-second rule was an option that was still widely available (as it began to decline only from the late fourteenth century onwards). Another syntactic modification in 4b comes in the second clause, where the updating scribe resorts to an Object-Subject-Verb > Subject-Verb-Object reordering:

(4)   a.   *<u>heo feoll</u> þærrihte and gewat. and <u>hi man bebyrigde</u> to hire were*
            (Clemoes 1997: 358.99–100)

        she.NOM.SG fell.3.SG.IND at once and died.3.SG.IND, and her.ACC.SG one buried.3.SG.IND with her husband.DAT.SG

        'she fell at once and died, and they buried her with her husband'

---

display the sensitivity of the Updated Old (and Early Middle) English word-structure to consonant clusters and combinations – at a time when the word-structure appeared to be striving for a shape that contains fewer morphemes and less allomorphy. The point needs much further elaboration but this sensitivity appears to be in accordance with Skalička's (1964) typological observation that the progression of a language from synthesis (fusion) to analysis (isolation) favours an increasingly smaller functional load of consonant groups.

b.   *þa feol heo þer adun and iwat and me buriede heo mid hire fere*
(Morris 1868: 93.6)

Then fell.3.SG.IND she.NOM.SG down and died.3.SG.IND, and one
buried.3.SG.IND her.ACC.SG with her husband.DAT.SG

'Then she fell down and died, and they buried her with her husband'

A configuration of archaic features alongside novel ones is apparent also from
Example 5:

(5)   a.   *ac he gæð of þam fæder and of ðan suna gelice*
(Clemoes 1997: 179.19–20)

but he.NOM.SG comes.3.SG.IND of the.DAT.SG father.DAT.SG and of
the.DAT.SG son.DAT.SG likewise

b.   *ac he geð of þe fader and of þe sune gelice*   (Morris 1868: 219.8)
'but he comes of the Father and of the Son alike'

In 5b, the lack of case marking on the determiners in *of þe fader and of þe sune* as an
innovative modification is counterbalanced by the archaizing preservation of the
mutated finite verb form *geð*. This is a high-frequency item, but elsewhere in the
textual sample forms displaying i-mutation tend to be replaced by non-mutated
ones (cf. dat. sg. *modor*, rather than *meder*, as e.g., in Warner 1917: 46.4–5, updating on Clemoes 1997: 435.170). Occasionally, the preservation of an archaizing
mutated form results in grammatical ambiguity, as in the ambiguously marked
category of number in 6b. There the scribe chose to do away with inflection on the
determiner and the modifier of the original noun phrase (*ænigum wisan men*), but
kept the mutated nominal form *men*.

(6)   a.   *þær bið yfel to wunienne ænigum wisan men*   (Morris 1868: 304.2–3)
there shall_be.3.SG.IND hard.NOM.SG to dwell any.DAT.SG wise.DAT.SG
man.DAT.SG

b.   *þere bið uuel to wunienne eni wise men*   (Morris 1868: 117.24)[7]
'there shall it be hard for any wise man to dwell'

The levels of grammatical marking in the Updated noun phrases suggest that
though the inflectional endings were in retreat this was a gradual and orderly
movement rather than a sudden and confused one. In a number of instances,
deflexion proceeds by deliberate steps aimed at maintaining functional contrasts,

---

7.   The inflected infinitive *wunienne* is another archaizing feature of 6b. It came to be
"half-petrified" by Early Middle English as part of the construction featuring the infinitive of
obligation (Möhlig-Falke 2012: 10).

mainly the central category of number.[8] This is the case in 7b, where – in a context that shows little updating otherwise – the editing scribe adds an analogous, historically inauthentic –*n* to *sawle* in an attempt to formally reinforce the plural reference (as a parallel example, cf. *ehtan* in Example 1 above).

> (7)   a.   *se hælend us gewissige to hys wyllan symble þæt ure <u>sawla</u> moton siðian eft to him*   (Morris 1868: 304.31)
>
>   the.NOM.SG Saviour.NOM.SG us.ACC.PL direct.3.SG.SBJV to his will.DAT.SG ever, so that our.NOM.PL souls.NOM.PL may.3.PL.SBJV return again to him.DAT.SG
>
>   b.   *se Hælend us gewissige to his wille symle þæt ure <u>sawlen</u> moten siðigen eft to him*   (Warner 1917: 16.23)
>
>   'may the Saviour direct us ever to his will, so that our souls may return again to him'

Example (8) features a structural change in word-formation:

> (8)   a.   *underfoð steore þy læs þe god <u>yrsige</u> wið eow*   (Morris 1868: 304.5–6)
>
>   receive.IMP.PL correction.ACC.SG lest GOD.NOM.SG be_angry.3.SG.SBJV with you.ACC.PL
>
>   b.   *vnderfoð steore þi les ðe god <u>iwurðe wrað</u> wið eou*
>   (Morris 1868: 117.28–29)
>
>   'receive correction lest God be angry with you'

The substitution of Old English *yrsian* ('to be angry') may, at a first sight, look like a lexical replacement that is similar to the case of *gescead > wisdom* in Example 1 above. Indeed, like *gescead*, *yrsien* appears attested in the *MED* only very marginally. The sporadic occurrence of this verb solely in texts of the late twelfth and early thirteenth century suggests it was obsolescent by then. Yet, its moribund status may have been due not only to lexical reasons, but also to structural ones – namely its obsolescent morphology. The OE verb *yrsian* was derived from the adjective *yrre* ('angry'), itself a word of only very marginal lexical status around the year 1200, by means of an unproductive suffix –*s*–. Its lack of productivity – as well as the fact that the verb in 8b came to be replaced by an analytical combination of copula+adjective – may have been caused at least partially by the fact that the language at this time preferred syllabic derivational suffixes of an

---

8.   Cf. Baechler's (2019) analysis of the *Lambeth Homilies* where she shows that the loss of inflection was not a linear process: new systems could emerge and the number distinction was – along with the distinction of feminine from non-feminine and that of possessive from non-possessive – the crucial one.

agglutinating nature.[9] In general, structural substitutions of this kind were related to the incipient transition in derivation from the root- and stem-based principle to word-based derivational strategies.[10] In most general terms, these tendencies demonstrate profound diachronic linking between inflectional and derivational morphology in the fusional type of language structure.

The verb *yrsien* was then clearly on its way out of use, not least because of its obsolescent derivational pattern, but not all of the replacements of vocabulary by the updating scribes indicate lexical obsolescence.[11] Those replacements that do not are representations of lexico-stylistic variation, substitutions of words by (near-)synonyms, like the pair of *God* and *drihten* in Example 1 above. On the whole, scribes who edited the Updated texts appear to manifest a sure way with words along these lines so that the collection of more lexical data from the updatings and alterations they made is likely to provide invaluable new material for historical dictionaries.

3. The story of the impersonal construction

For reasons of space, an account of the history of the impersonal construction in early English can be presented here only in a nutshell, drawing primarily on Möhlig-Falke (2012) and Allen (1995). Though a well-established theme in literature, this history continues to pose intriguing research questions. This is mainly because the demise of the construction was such a slow process, with the bulk of change consisting mainly in a gradual shift from non-nominative to nominative experiencers situated in the fourteenth century.

Old English used a well-developed system of grammatical marking to encode the roles of the experiencer and source in the impersonal construction. The construction was centred around a fairly sizeable class of semantically rather heterogeneous verbs, with a varying degree of impersonal prototypicality. The verbs

---

9. Other examples of the kind from Updated Old English texts include the OE verb *ge-un-rot-s-ian* ('to become troubled, discontented') which the updating scribes render in two ways – as *sorg-ian* and as *ben sari*, and the OE noun *þeow-et* ('service', 'servitude'), replaced by *þeow-dom* in Example 3 above.

10. Other significant structural changes in word-formation were related to the peripheralization of formations based on i-mutation as well as on ablaut. They too were conditioned typologically as they represented the demise of the introflexional principle in Early Middle English word-formation (for typological introflexion, cf. Sgall 1999).

11. For a useful typology of lexical replacements, cf. Faulkner (2012: 193f.).

featured principally in two formal patterns, the impersonal-dative/accusative pattern and the zero-impersonal pattern. From early on, the latter structure was paralleled by a pattern featuring dummy *hit* ('it'). At the same time, impersonal structures existed alongside personal ones, with many verbs inhabiting both orbits (Möhlig-Falke 2012: 59, 237ff.; cf. also Allen 1995: 72–73).

In Middle English, the system continued showing signs of only a slow loss of productivity. There was a significant temporal gap between the deflexion whose most relevant morphological changes were complete by the middle of the thirteenth century in most parts of the country[12] and the introduction of nominative experiencers with many impersonal verbs in the early fourteenth century (Allen 1995: 442). Some of the Old English impersonal verbs died out, but between c. 1250 and 1400 the lexical stock came to be replenished by several dozens of verbs that were newly capable of impersonal use based mostly on semantic analogy (Miura 2015: 8; Allen 1995: 446). Some were inherited ones, now extending their functional and formal scope, some newly coined, and some borrowed from Old French and Old Norse (cf. Möhlig-Falke 2012: 15, 209–11; Allen 1995: 224).

This lengthy story of the 'gradual decline' (Allen 1995: 451) of the impersonal construction in Middle English was probably due to a variety of reasons. Among the most important of these was the slow grammaticalization of word order, best interpreted as a situation of competition between underlying orders (Los & van Kemenade 2012: 1485). This kept in play the verb-second rule, which in its turn maintained object-fronted word orders as available for topicalization, and was one of the factors allowing for preposed dative experiencers to continue functioning as subjects. Another important reason was that the change from the impersonal to the personal uses was a lexically implemented syntactic change (Allen 1995: 287, 450–451) that came to be slowed down by continual lexical replenishment of the impersonal stock and by analogical extension of the impersonal-dative/accusative pattern. The timing of the loss of this pattern, which came to be largely unproductive by c. 1500 (Allen 1995: 286, 441), closely paralleled the timing of the demise of verb-second and of object-fronted word orders (Los 2009: 121 and 2009: 112, respectively). Around this time, it was no longer acceptable to encode the unmarked topic by an argument that was a grammatical and semantic object. The category of subject widened its semantic scope by including more and more non-agentive unmarked topics, which extended the functional scope of the personal transitive construction (Möhlig-Falke 2012: 271).

---

12.   The loss of morphological case played only an indirect role in the loss of the impersonal construction by contributing to the decrease of its frequency (Allen 1995: 12; 17), and by "making speakers more inclined to using non-morphological means of signalling grammatical and semantic roles" (Allen 1995: 451).

The shift to the personal structure, in compensation for the loss of the impersonal-dative/accusative pattern, appears to have taken three major structural paths and was highly verb-specific (Möhlig-Falke 2012: 19) – as long as the respective lexical pivots remained part of the lexis. The first path was that of substitution of the pattern by a nominative subject. The second path led by way of *it*-extraposition, and the third one encoded the argument of person as direct object. Individual impersonal expressions have survived as lexicalized or grammaticalized units.

4. Analysis

4.1 Lexico-semantic characteristics of the impersonal verbs in the sample

Given the big picture story of impersonal constructions, no spectacular changes affecting them in the Updated Old English period are to be observed. On the other hand, total indifference by the updating scribes should not be expected either. It is therefore worthwhile asking what processes of maintenance and variation relate to the diachronic trajectory of the impersonal constructions in a sample body of texts whose twelfth-century editors were, as the reader will recall, sensitive to variation and change in the linguistic usage of their day and prepared to reflect it, albeit unevenly, in their practice. Before we discuss several of these processes in some detail it is necessary to present an overall picture of the impersonal verbs in the sample.

The instances of impersonal verbs were extracted from the sample using the two central criteria applied by Möhlig-Falke (2012: 12): (1) the predicate verb is invariably marked for third-person singular; and (2) a noun phrase or pronoun in the nominative singular that could formally control verbal agreement is absent. For reasons discussed above, regional/dialectal characteristics of the impersonal verbs and of the texts that contain them were acknowledged as certainly involved, but not selected for tracing.[13]

In manual collation of the Updated Old English texts to their Old English predecessors, the sample was searched for impersonal uses generally as well as for novel impersonal uses featuring native or borrowed verbs. The search yielded the following twenty verbs attested impersonally in sixty-six occurrences altogether:

1. *behōfian* 'to need, require, want'
2. *dafenian* (*gedafenian*) 'to beseem, befit, be right'

---

13. Cf. e.g., Möhlig-Falke (2012: 236) about the possibility of an early loss of impersonal constructions in the northern areas of Middle English.

3. *gebyrian* 'to happen, take place; befit; concern'
4. *ge(h)rīsan (be(h)rīsan)* 'to befit, be appropriate'
5. *getīdan* 'to betide, happen'
6. *geweorðan* 'to become, be, happen, befall'
7. *hyngrian* 'to feel hunger, be hungry'
8. *līcian (gelīcian)* 'to please, be pleased'
9. *limpan (belimpan; gelimpan)* 'to happen, befall; befit; concern'
10. *lystan* 'cause pleasure or desire'
11. *mislīcian* 'to be displeased'
12. *oflīcian* 'to be displeased'
13. *ofþyncean*, 'to give offence, insult, weary, displease'
14. *onhagian* 'to suit, please, be comfortable'
15. *sceamian (gesceamian)* 'to be ashamed; rue, repent; cause shame'
16. *tīmian (getīmian)* 'to happen, befall'
17. *tōsǣlan (gesǣlan)* 'to happen, succeed'
18. *twēonian* 'to doubt'
19. *þyncean (geþyncean)*, 'to seem, appear'
20. *þyrstan* 'to feel thirst, be thirsty'

They are listed in their Old English forms and meanings, with prefixed forms listed separately only when the simple form is attested or in those cases where the prefix radically changes meaning (as in e.g., *þyncan* – *ofþyncean*), otherwise only in the brackets.

These twenty verbs represent 42.5% of the set collected for Old English proper by Möhlig-Falke, who lists forty-seven verbs altogether (including potential prefixed derivatives) as being capable of occurring in impersonal constructions before c. 1150 (2012: 83). Except for *behōfian*, mentioned at the very beginning of this chapter and discussed below, all of the Updated impersonal verbs were found to preserve their Old English meanings. Seventeen out of these twenty verbs were recorded in variable argument structures both in impersonal and personal uses in Old English generally. The three remaining verbs were *onhagian* and *tōsǣlan*, available only impersonally in Old English, and *behōfian*, a verb that was only starting to develop its impersonal uses in very late Old English. No newly arrived verbs of either a native or a borrowed status that would be employed in impersonal constructions were found in the Updated sample.

Using the semantic classification established by Möhlig-Falke (in descending order of categories according to the frequency of impersonal constructions in Old English texts, with the bottom three ones represented only marginally; Möhlig-Falke 2012: 113), the twenty Updated impersonal verbs were found to be distributed across the semantic categories as follows:

1. Emotion: *līcian*; *mislīcian*; *oflīcian*; *lystan*; *ofþyncean*; *sceamian*; *twēonian*
2. Cognition: *þyncean*
3. Ownership/Appropriateness: *gebyrian*; *dafenian*; *ge(h)rīsan*
4. Existential experience: *getīdan*; *limpan*; *tōsǣlan*; *tīmian*; *geweorðan*
5. Physical sensation: *hyngrian*, *þyrstan*
6. Motion: *onhagian*[14]
7. Benefaction: none
8. (Non)availability: *behōfian*

Given the fact that the Updated sample was gleaned from texts of a predominantly homiletic nature, semantic preferences of the impersonal verbs appear predictable – the more so that the category of Emotion in homiletic and hortatory texts borders on the expressing of moral judgement, close to senses associated with the Ownership/Appropriateness category. In comparison to the Old English impersonal verbs, the categorial spread of the Updated items corresponds, although in qualitative terms only, to Möhlig-Falke's order of the frequency of appearance, with the three bottom orbits close to empty: as *behōfian* starts moving towards the Ownership/Appropriateness category, *onhagian* remains their solitary inhabitant.[15] The only semantic domains underrepresented in comparison to the distribution of impersonal verbs in Old English are those of Physical sensation and Cognition. This difference is probably due again to the generic characteristic of the Updated textual sample.

In terms of pattern distribution, only three of the sixty-six instances of the impersonal construction represented the zero-impersonal structure. The remaining sixty-three were of the impersonal-dative/accusative pattern. Except for three cases, there was no transition between the personal and impersonal orbits of the verbs: two instances of *behoven* and one instance featuring *limpen* documented a change of the Old English personal usage into an Updated impersonal usage, but, surprisingly, no instance of a passage in the opposite direction was found. Alterations in the record of the impersonal construction appear to reflect neither the regional provenance of the manuscripts nor, even more importantly, general levels of deflexion in a given text.

---

14. Listed without those prefixed forms that do not exhibit a change of meaning.

15. Though Möhlig-Falke duly notes that *onhagian* expresses an emotional event in all its uses recorded in Old English, she nevertheless places this verb in the category of Motion because its argument structure differs from that of the other emotion verbs, and "this difference can be explained only on the basis of its original, non-metaphorical meaning as a verb of motion" (2012: 100).

4.2   Alterations in the record of the impersonal constructions in the sample

The levels of continuity of the impersonal construction from Old English to Updated Old English are reflected in the healthy state of its marking. As its status was not directly affected by the ongoing deflexion, the updating scribes generally had little reason to make modifications in their rendering of the impersonal constructions. As discussed below, scribal alterations were mostly minor, reflecting variation rather than change and being motivated by efforts to maintain the formal clarity of the constructions.

First of all, the Updated texts contain modifications that reinforce uses that were marginal in Old English or that were not to have lasting effects in Middle English. Both types of alteration are exemplified by Example 9, the former type by Example 10 below.

(9)   a.   *gemune þu, hu <u>hit gelamp</u> be Dathan*   (Assmann 1889: 132.525)
             remember.IMP.SG thou how it went.3.SG.IND with Dathan.DAT.SG

       b.   *Gemun þu, hu <u>lamp</u> daþan*   (Assmann 1889: 131.513–514)
             remember.IMP.SG thou how went.3.SG.IND Dathan.DAT.SG
             'remember how it went with Dathan'

This example demonstrates a change that consists in employment of the zero-impersonal pattern. The updating scribe's intervention here appears to reflect archaizing usage as the use of the zero-impersonal pattern has been reported to be on the decrease in the late Old English period and, in Middle English, it is found only sparsely in records up to 1400 and becomes lost afterwards (Möhlig-Falke 2012: 14).

(10) a.   *Seo meniu þe eode beforan þam hælende ciddon þam blindan. & heton
             þæt he stille wære. Seo meniu getacnað: ure unlustas & leahtras þe us
             hremmað. & ure heortan ofsittað þæt we ne magon us swa geornlice
             gebiddan swa <u>we behofedon</u>.*   (Clemoes 1979: 260.68–69)

             The.NOM.SG crowd.NOM.SG that was_going.3.SG.IND in front of
             the.DAT.SG Saviour.DAT.SG rebuked.3.PL.IND the.DAT.SG blind.DAT.
             SG and commanded.3.PL.IND that he.NOM.SG. quiet.NOM.SG be.3.SG.
             SBJV. The.NOM.SG crowd.NOM.SG betokens.3.SG.IND our.ACC.PL
             evil_pleasures.ACC.PL and vices.ACC.PL that us.ACC.PL afflict.3.PL.IND
             and our.ACC.PL hearts.ACC.PL oppress.3.PL.IND so that we.NOM.PL. not
             can.1.PL.IND as eagerly pray as (lit.) we.NOM.PL. behove.1.PL.SBJV.

       b.   *Seo mænige þe eode beforen þan Hælende cidden þan blinde, and heten
             þæt he stille wære. Seo geferræden getacned unlustes and lehtres þe us
             hefegiged, and ure heorte ofsitted, þæt we ne mugen us swa geornlice
             gebidden, swa <u>us behofede</u>.*   (Warner 1917: 149.14–17)

             'The crowd that was going in front of the Saviour rebuked the blind
             one, commanding him that he be quiet. The crowd betokens our evil
             pleasures and vices that afflict us and oppress our hearts so that we
             cannot pray as eagerly as would behove us.'

This is a case of the Updated b-version's substituting a dative form (*us behofede*) for the Old English nominative experiencer (*we behofeden*). The shift fosters an impersonal use of this verb, in Old English attested only late and marginally; Möhlig-Falke finds only 9.8% of impersonal uses with this verb in Old English (2012: 115). At the same time, the new impersonal use encapsulates the semantic change in the verb from "as we need" to "as is appropriate for us", placing *behōfian/behoven* in the Ownership/Appropriateness category. The semantic shift is documented by updated cases when *behōfian* replaces another verb in the context of moral obligation, as e.g., *dafenian* in the personal pattern of Example 11:

(11)   a.   *Swa swa ðam ealdan gedafeniað dugende þeawas and geripod*
           syfernyss...   (Morris 1868: 300.2–3)

           Just as the.DAT.SG old.DAT.SG befit.3.PL.IND kind.NOM.PL manners.NOM.
           PL and ripened.NOM.SG moderation.NOM.SG...

       b.   *Swa swa þan alden bihouað dugende ðewas and triwe treofestnesse...*
                                                                 (Morris 1868: 109.23–24)

           'just as kind manners and ripened moderation befit the old one'

Two mechanisms in particular appear to have been used to foster uninterrupted functionality of the impersonal constructions in the Updated texts: the one was by replacement of lexical pivots, the other was by addition of morphological support. These mechanisms are exemplified below by Examples (12) and (13), respectively.

(12)   *Gif þu bearn hæbbe, lær þa cræftas, þæt hie mægen be þon libban; uncuð hu*
       him æt æhtum gesæle.   (Cox 1972: 7.18)

       If you.2.SG children.ACC.PL have.2.SG.SBJV, teach.2.SG.IMP the.ACC.PL
       crafts.ACC.PL so that they.NOM.PL. can.3.PL.SBJV by them.DAT.PL live;
       unknown.NOM.SG how them.DAT.PL in property.DAT.PL happen.3.SG.SBJV.

       Gyf þu bearn habbe, lær heo þa cræftes, þæt heo mugen beo þan libben.
       Uncuð, hwu heom æt æhte getide.   (Warner 1917: 4.15–16)

       'If you have children, teach them craft so that they can live by it. Unknown
       it is how they will fare materially.'

Here, in an Updated text that is generally very conservative, the impersonal verb *gesǣlan* is replaced by another of the same semantic category (Existential experience) – *getīdan*. The scribal motive was to keep the impersonal construction in play by the removal of *gesǣlan*, an obsolescent verb that does not resurface in post-Conquest texts any longer. In the collected Updated verbal sample, another five verbs (i.e., six out of the twenty altogether) shared the destiny of *gesǣlan*, testifying to the high levels of word obsolescence and the urgent need for lexical replacement in the twelfth century: *dafenian, ge(h)rīsan, oflīcian, onhagian* and *twēonian*. Our lexicographic and textual evidence permitting, they do not reappear at all or else do so only very briefly, such as the *dafenen* replaced by *behoven* in Example 11 above. Some verbs of the Updated sample may be short-lived in some of their senses only: *geweorðan* is replaced in the sense 'to happen', in which it is attested only until the early thirteenth century (Möhlig-Falke 2012: 207).[16] Some of these losses may have been structural rather than lexical, as was the prosody-conditioned loss of *oflīcian* to *mislīcian* in a competition of prefixed impersonal verbs. However, systemic connection between lexical mortality and levels of impersonal use seems not to have existed. The six verbs from within the sample that are lost in the post-Conquest period differ widely as to how frequently they appeared in Old English impersonal constructions, from 97.3% (*onhagian*) to 24.8% (*oflīcian*), even though all of them exceeded the average levels of occurrence (set at 22.7% by Möhlig-Falke, 2012: 115).

The other mechanism in the formal reinforcement of the impersonal construction was added morphological support, as in Example 13:

(13)   a.   <u>*Geleaffullum*</u> *gedafenað þæt hi wuldrian on gedrefednyssum.*
                                                        (Clemoes 1997: 495.262)

Believing.DAT.PL /ones/ befits.3.SG.IND that they.NOM.PL. glorify.3.PL. SBJV in afflictions.DAT.PL.

   b.   <u>*Geleaffulle mannen*</u> *gedafeneð þæt heo wuldrigen on gedrofednysse.*
                                                        (Warner 1917: 76.9–10)

'It befits the believing (men) that they should glorify /God/ in affliction.'

In cases like this one, the noun phrase consisting of a strong adjective used as head is updated by insertion of a noun (of a general sense, like *men*) to disambiguate grammatical marking, potentially threatened by ongoing sound changes in unstressed syllables and by changes in grammar. Such removals of the absolute use of adjectives are frequent in the Updated texts.[17] They reflect a systemic link between the inflectional and derivational morphologies of the waning fusional type of language structure in the post-Conquest period as the recession of nominalized weak adjectival forms was associated with the marginalization of the agentive nominal suffix *-a* (e.g., Old English *cuma*, 'visitor, stranger, guest'). Both the adjectival and nominal forms tended to be replaced by syntactic combinations (which is the case in Example 13) or lexically (by native or borrowed synonyms).

Strong morphological support for the continued functionality of the Updated impersonal construction also came from the high incidence of tenacious and distinct

---

16.   An example of such a replacement, resulting in a substitution of *geweorðan* by *gelimpan*, is available from Warner (1917: 4.35–36) as compared to Cox (1972: 9.30).

17.   Faulkner (2012: 175) reports a similar situation in the texts of alterations.

dative forms of personal pronouns (cf. Examples (10b) and (12) above).[18] Structures that featured pronominal datives may, then, have played a significant role in syntactic analogy, helping, as cognitive models, maintain dative forms of nouns.

In order to provide a balanced picture of the overall status of the impersonal construction in the Updated sample, this section is concluded with an example that illustrates its disappearance:

(14)   a.   *ða þa he bebyrged wæs þa com his wif saphira and nyste <u>hu hyre were</u>*
          <u>gelumpen wæs</u>   (Clemoes 1997: 357.95–96)

         when he.NOM.SG buried was.3.SG.IND then came.3.SG.IND his wife.NOM. SG Saphira and not knew.3.SG.IND how her husband.DAT.SG befallen was.3.SG.IND

         'when he was buried, then came his wife Sapphira and did not know (lit.) how had befallen her husband'

   b.   *þa he iburied was. þa com his wif saphira and nuste <u>hwet hire were</u>*
          <u>ilumpen wes</u>   (Morris 1868: 93.3–4)

         when he buried was.3.SG.IND then came.3.SG.IND his wife.NOM.SG Saphira and not knew.3.SG.IND what.NOM.SG her husband.DAT.SG befallen was.3.SG.IND

         'when he was buried, then came his wife Sapphira and did not know what had befallen her husband'

This example constitutes a mirror image to Example 9, the first one in Section 4.2. In 14b, the updating scribe removed the impersonal construction by changing the structure of the nominal content interrogative clause. However, such instances documenting dissolution of the impersonal constructions are only very marginal in the Updated sample.

5. Discussion and concluding remarks

The eventual loss of the construction is a paradigm case of loss in the history of English, but the data considered here shows the perseverance of the construction at this early stage. Reacting indirectly, as most Middle English syntactic changes do, to developments in the phonology of non-tonic syllables and to deflexion (itself gradual and fairly orderly), the gradual loss of the impersonal construction had not only its internal, syntactic conditioning (linked primarily to the demise of the verb-second and object-fronted word-orders as part of the word-order

---

18.   This is a point made generally by Allen (1995).

grammaticalization), but also a lexical dimension (based on the continual replacement of obsolescing lexical pivots[19]).

In the period documented by Updated Old English texts, the impersonal construction is fully functional. Against the background of widespread though unsystematic updating at all levels of linguistic structure in the texts, the scribes make alterations in the record of the construction only very occasionally. If they do, their motivation clearly is to preserve the functionality of the construction by adding disambiguating morphological support or by changing an obsolescent impersonal verb as the constructional pivot. This scribal programme of maintenance is a universal one: there appears to be no significant difference between the scribes' treatment of the zero-impersonal and the impersonal-dative/accusative patterns. Likewise, the scribes maintain the record of the construction regardless both of the regional provenance of the manuscript and of the amount and distribution of deflexion in the given text.

Apart from the other levels of the language, there is, then, clear evidence that the updating scribes could and did change the syntax also of their originals, even though the resulting updating is bound to be – as much as at the other levels of language structure – a mixture of archaic and innovative features. However, syntactic variation in Updated Old English is less conspicuous compared to morphology and lexis. This is no doubt due also to the fact that this was the domain where the scribes naturally felt most hindered as updaters – much more than when it came to capturing the sound of an outgoing inflectional ending or excising an obsolescent word.

But there were more relevant reasons than just methodological ones for the sparse and uneven presence of syntactic variation in the Updated texts. The principal syntactic changes of Middle English gather momentum only in the late centuries because syntax is, in general, slowly reactive to change that comes primarily from the lower levels: possibly first from sound developments (cf. the transition from morphological to lexical stress and its impact on unstressed syllables), and subsequently from morphology, which follows in a gradual and fairly orderly retreat (cf. e.g., economy of grammatical marking and lack of category confusion in the deflexion; tendency to remove paradigmatic allomorphy; systemic links between inflectional and derivational morphology).

The Updated Old English texts thus present a useful vantage point for the study of losses in the history of English. Manifest though complex cases of loss in the twelfth and early thirteenth century, particularly at the levels of phonology, morphology and lexis, can be studied there in their interaction (as, for example, the interaction of receding derivational patterns and lexical obsolescence). Other,

---

19.   Cf. Möhlig-Falke (2012: 203–213).

less dramatic or more resistant instances of loss in the history of English display resilience, featuring renewal and replenishment in the Updated texts (as eminently exemplified by the relation between the resolution of lexical loss and syntactic retention in the case of the impersonal construction itself).

Despite the serious methodological challenges it poses, Updated Old English material represents a valid new source of data on the history of early English. The process of updating no doubt involved an enormous number of determinants, both structural and sociolinguistic, interconnected in intricate ways, but manual collation only allows for tracing a theme of limited scope, one story at a time. The creation of a stronger empirical basis – corpora of Updated Old English, corpora of corresponding Old English texts arranged by genre and text type, a corpus of twelfth-century textual alterations, and a corpus of original vernacular texts of the twelfth and early thirteenth centuries – will make possible a systematic overall assessment of the Updated Old English language and style. Linguists and philologists will then be much better placed to distinguish inadvertent archaism and conscious belatedness from spontaneous innovation, and to piece together individual microscopic variations in order to see and understand tendencies in a bigger picture – one that will hopefully also encompass refined chronologies, dialectal affiliations and paths of textual transmission.

Acknowledgements

This work was supported by the European Regional Development Fund project "Creativity and Adaptability as Conditions of the Success of Europe in an Interrelated World" (reg. no.: CZ.02 .1.01/0.0/0.0/16_019/0000734) and by the Charles University Project Progress Q07, Centre for the Study of the Middle Ages.

References

Allen, Cynthia L. 1995. *Case Marking and Reanalysis. Grammatical Relations from Old to Early Modern English*. Oxford: OUP.

Allen, Cynthia L. 1997. The development of an 'impersonal' verb in Middle English: The case of behove. In *Studies in Middle English Linguistics* [Trends in Linguistics: Studies and Monographs 103], Jacek Fisiak (ed.), 1–21. Berlin: Mouton de Gruyter. https://doi.org/10.1515/9783110814194.1

Allen, Cynthia L. 2006. Case syncretism and word order change. In *The Handbook of the History of English*, Ans van Kemenade & Bettelou Los (eds), 200–223. Oxford: Wiley-Blackwell. https://doi.org/10.1002/9780470757048.ch9

Allen, Cynthia L. 2011. Obsolescence and sudden death in syntax: The decline of verb-final order in Early Middle English. In *Generative Theory and Corpus Studies. A Dialogue from 10 ICEHL*, Ricardo Bermudez-Otero, David Denison, Richard M. Hogg & Chris B. McCully (eds), 3–26. Berlin: De Gruyter.

Allen, Cynthia L. 2016. Typological change: Investigating loss of inflection in early English. In *The Cambridge Handbook of English Historical Linguistics*, Merja Kytö & Päivi Pahta (eds), 444–459. Cambridge: CUP. https://doi.org/10.1017/CBO9781139600231.027

Assmann, Bruno. 1889. *Angelsächsische Homilien und Heiligenleben* [Bibliothek der angelsächsischen Prosa 3]. Kassel: Georg H. Wigand.

Baechler, Raffaela. 2019. Analogy, reanalysis and exaptation in Early Middle English: The emergence of a new inflectional system. *English Language and Linguistics* 23: 1–30.

Belfour, Algernon O. 1909. *Twelfth-Century Homilies in MS. Bodley 343* [Early English Text Society o.s. 137]. London: OUP.

Bosworth, Joseph. 2010. *An Anglo-Saxon Dictionary Online*, Thomas Northcote Toller and Others (eds), Sean Christ & Ondřej Tichý (comp). Prague: Faculty of Arts, Charles University. <bosworthtoller.com> (17 April 2019).

Clayton, Mary. 2013. *Two Ælfric Texts: The Twelve Abuses and the Vices and Virtues* [Anglo-Saxon Texts 11]. Cambridge: D. S. Brewer.

Clemoes, Peter. 1997. *Ælfric's Catholic Homilies: The First Series: Text* [Early English Text Society s.s. 17]. London: OUP.

Conti, Aidan. 2007. The circulation of the Old English homily in the twelfth century: New evidence from Oxford, Bodleian Library, MS Bodley 343. In *The Old English Homily: Precedent, Practice, and Appropriation*, Aaron J. Kleist (ed.), 365–402. Turnhout: Brepols. https://doi.org/10.1484/M.SEM-EB.3.3784

Cox, Robert S. 1972. The Old English dicts of Cato. *Anglia: Zeitschrift für englische Philologie* 90: 1–42. https://doi.org/10.1515/angl.1972.1972.90.1

Crawford, Samuel J. 1969. *The Old English Version of the Heptateuch, Ælfric's Treatise on the Old and New Testament and his Preface to Genesis*, with the text of two additional manuscripts transcribed by N. R. Ker, repr. with the text of two additional manuscripts [Early English Text Society o.s. 160]. London: OUP.

Curzan, Anne. 2003. *Gender Shifts in the History of English*. Cambridge: CUP. https://doi.org/10.1017/CBO9780511486913

Dance, Richard. 2011. "Tomarʒan hit is awane": Words derived from Old Norse in four Lambeth homilies. In *Foreign Influences on Medieval English*, Jacek Fisiak & Magdalena Bator (eds), 77–127. Frankfurt: Peter Lang.

Dance, Richard. 2012. *Ealde æ, niwæ laʒe*: Two words for "law" in the twelfth century (with an appendix by Richard Dance & Aidan Conti). Special issue *Producing and Using English Manuscripts in the Post-Conquest Period*, Elaine Treharne, Orietta Da Rold & Mary Swan (eds). *New Medieval Literatures* 13: 149–182. https://doi.org/10.1484/J.NML.1.102443

Dance, Richard. 2014. Getting a word in: Contact, etymology and English vocabulary in the twelfth century. Sir Israel Gollancz Memorial Lecture read 26 November 2013. *Journal of the British Academy* 2: 153–211.

Da Rold, Orietta & Swan, Mary. 2012. Linguistic contiguities: English manuscripts 1060 to 1220. In *Conceptualizing Multilingualism in Medieval England c. 800–c. 1250*, Elizabeth M. Tyler (ed.), 255–270. Turnhout: Brepols.

DOEC = *Dictionary of Old English Web Corpus*. 2009. Antonette diPaolo Healey with John Price Wilkin & Xin Xiang (eds). Toronto: Pontifical Institute of Mediaeval Studies for the Dictionary of Old English Project. <http://tapor.library.utoronto.ca/doecorpus/> (19 March 2019).

Faulkner, Mark. 2012. Archaism, belatedness and modernisation: "Old" English in the twelfth century. *Review of English Studies, n.s.* 63: 179–203. https://doi.org/10.1093/res/hgr050

Fehr, Bernhard. 1966. *Die Hirtenbriefe Ælfrics, in altenglischer und lateinischer Fassung. Reprint with a supplement to the introduction by Peter Clemoes* [Bibliothek der angelsächsischen Prosa 9]. Darmstadt: Wissenschaftliche Buchgesellschaft.

Fischer, Andreas. 1996. The vocabulary of Very Late Old English. In *Studies in English Language and Literature: 'Doubt Wisely', Papers in Honour of E. G., Stanley*, 29–41, M. Jane Toswell & Elizabeth M. Tyler (eds). London: Routledge.

Godden, Malcolm. 1979. *Ælfric's Catholic Homilies, The Second Series. Text* [Early English Text Society s.s. 5]. London: OUP.

Irvine, Susan. 1993. *Old English Homilies from MS Bodley 343* [Early English Text Society o.s. 302]. Oxford: OUP.

Kitson, Peter. 1992. Old English dialects and the stages of the transition to Middle English. *Folia Linguistica Historica* 11: 27–87.

Kitson, Peter. 1997. When did Middle English begin? Later than you think! In *Studies in Middle English Linguistics* [Trends in Linguistics, Studies and Monographs 103], Jacek Fisiak (ed.), 221–269. Berlin: Mouton de Gruyter. https://doi.org/10.1515/9783110814194.221

Los, Bettelou. 2009. The consequences of the loss of verb-second in English: Information structure and syntax in interaction. *English Language and Linguistics* 13: 97–125. https://doi.org/10.1017/S1360674308002876

Los, Bettelou & van Kemenade, Ans. 2012. Information structure and syntax in the history of English. In *English Historical Linguistics. An International Handbook,* Vol. 2, Alexander Bergs & Laurel L. Brinton (eds), 1475–1490. Berlin: De Gruyter Mouton.

McColl Millar, Robert & Nicholls, Alex. 1997. Ælfric's *De Initio Creaturae* and London, British Library, Cotton Vespasian A.xxii: Omission, addition, retention and innovation. In *The Preservation and Transmission of Anglo-Saxon Culture*, Paul C. Szarmach & Joel T. Rosenthal (eds), 431–464. Kalamazoo MI: Publications of the Center for Medieval Studies.

MED = *Middle English Dictionary*. 1956–2011. Hans Kurath, Sherman M. Kuhn & Robert E. Lewis (eds). Ann Arbor MI: University of Michigan Press. <https://quod.lib.umich.edu/m/middle-english-dictionary/dictionary> (17 April 2019).

Miura, Ayumi. 2015. *Middle English Verbs of Emotion and Impersonal Constructions*. Oxford: OUP.

Möhlig-Falke, Ruth. 2012. *The Early English Impersonal Construction: An Analysis of Verbal and Constructional Meaning* [Oxford Studies in the History of English]. Oxford: OUP. https://doi.org/10.1093/acprof:oso/9780199777723.001.0001

Morris, Richard. 1868. *Old English Homilies and Homiletic Treatises (Sawles Warde, and Þe Wohunge of Ure Lauerd: Ureisuns of Ure Louerd and of Ure Lefdi, &c.) of the Twelfth and Thirteenth Centuries, Edited from MSS. In the British Museum, Lambeth, and Bodleian Libraries* [Early English Text Society o.s. 29 and 34]. London: Trübner.

OED = *The Oxford English Dictionary* (first published as A New English Dictionary on Historical Principles), James A. Murray, Henry Bradley, W. A. Craigie & C. T. Onions (eds). Oxford: Clarendon Press, 1928; 2nd edn prepared by John A. Simpson & Edmund S. C. Weiner, 1989; 3rd edn. in progress. <http://www. oed.com/< (19 March 2019).

Pope, John C. 1967–1968. *Homilies of Ælfric: A Supplementary Collection* [Early English Text Society o.s. 259, 260]. London: OUP.

The Production and Use of English Manuscripts 1060 to 1220, Orietta Da Rold, Takako Kato, Mary Swan & Elaine Treharne (eds). Leicester: University of Leicester, 2010; last update 2013). <http://www.le.ac.uk/ee/em1060to1220> (5 November 2020).

Scragg, Donald G. 1992. *The Vercelli Homilies and Related Texts* [Early English Text Society o.s. 300]. Oxford: OUP.

Sgall, Petr. 1999. Prague School. In *Approaches to Language Typology*, Masayoshi Shibatani & Theodora Bynon (eds), 49–84. Oxford: OUP.

Skalička, Vladimír. 1964. Konsonantenkombinationen und linguistische Typologie. *Travaux Linguistiques de Prague* 1: 111–114.

Skeat, Walter W. 1881–1900. *Ælfric's Lives of Saints* [Early English Text Society o.s. 76, 82, 94, 114]. London: N. Trübner.

Swan, Mary. 1997. Old English Made New: One Catholic Homily and Its Reuses. *Leeds Studies in English, n.s.* 28: 1–18.

Swan, Mary & Treharne, Elaine. 2000. *Rewriting Old English in the Twelfth Century* [Cambridge Studies in Anglo-Saxon England 30]. Cambridge: CUP.

Swan, Mary. 2006. Old English textual activity in the reign of Henry II. In *Writers of the Reign of Henry II*, Ruth Kennedy & Simon Meecham-Jones (eds), 151–168. London: Palgrave. https://doi.org/10.1007/978-1-137-08855-0_7

Swan, Mary. 2007. Preaching past the conquest: Lambeth Palace 487 and Cotton Vespasian A. XXII. In *The Old English Homily. Precedent, Practice, and Appropriation*, Aaron J. Kleist (ed.), 403–423. Turnhout: Brepols. https://doi.org/10.1484/M.SEM-EB.3.3785

Thorpe, Benjamin. 1844–1846. *The Sermones Catholici or Homilies of Ælfric*. London: Ælfric Society.

Treharne, Elaine. 2006. The life and times of Old English homilies for the first Sunday in Lent. In *The Power of Words. Anglo-Saxon Studies Presented to Donald G. Scragg on his Seventieth Birthday*, Hugh Magennis & Jonathan Wilcox (eds), 205–242. Morgantown WV: West Virginia University Press.

Warner, Rubie D. N. 1917. *Early English Homilies from the Twelfth-Century* MS. Vespasian D.XIV. [Early English Text Society o.s. 152]. London: Kegan Paul.

CHAPTER 4

Corpus driven identification of lexical bundle obsolescence in Late Modern English

Ondřej Tichý
Charles University

This chapter explores a new methodology for extracting multi-word units that were once common but have since become obsolete from large corpora (esp. from the Google ngrams dataset of the Google Books project). It complements a modified frequency-based methodology previously used for detecting lexical obsolescence (Tichý 2018) with a bottom up approach to calculating association measures in multi-word sequences inspired by Wahl & Gries (2019). The analytical part examines expressions identified as potentially obsolete on their way from Late Modern to Present-day English. Conditions, circumstances and consequences of the loss of such expressions are considered with a focus on the competing forms expressing similar functions that may be recognized as supplanting the old forms.

Keywords: lexicology, corpus linguistics, diachronic linguistics, obsolescence, ngrams, lexical bundles, multi-word expressions, Late Modern English, Google Books

1. Introduction

Lexical obsolescence, like other topics covered in this volume, is a relatively under-studied field[1], and obsolescence of lexical bundles has been explored even less. This fact is evidenced in the fuzziness (in the field of corpus linguistics) of the

---

[1] Few studies on the topic have been published, cf. Trench (1871), Němec (1968), Maixner (1970) or Coleman (1990). The only general corpus-based study so far seems to be Petersen, Tenenbaum, Havlin & Stanley (2012), which, however, focuses on overall trends of lexical mortality and word-birth, while the most recent study by Rudnicka (2019) focuses on a specific type of grammatical obsolescence.

https://doi.org/10.1075/slcs.218.04tic
© 2021 John Benjamins Publishing Company

keywords of this chapter, "obsolescence", but also of "lexical bundles" that will need to be further explored in the following section.

As to the period under scrutiny here – Late Modern English (LModE, here 1700–present), it is usually not associated with large-scale obsolescence, except, perhaps, for the loss in variation (as much as standardisation can be understood as loss of variation). Traditionally, lexical and even structural loss in English has been regarded as largely restricted to the transition from Old to Middle English.

Why then study lexical bundle obsolescence in LModE? In order to facilitate the identification and analysis of so far unnoticed losses in semantic and structural expressivity, I have previously developed a corpus driven methodology for identifying obsolescence in lexical units (Tichý 2018). But as Biber notes "[in] English, there are many multi-word expressions that function as a structural or semantic unit" (Biber et al. 2000: 988) while Wahl and Gries (2019) notice that "L1 speakers produce *strong coffee* but not *powerful coffee*" and "crucially, note that *strong coffee* appears decomposable into individual semantic units and thus does not seem to be an idiom expected to be stored in memory". Multi-word sequences therefore form semantic, but not necessarily idiomatic units. Similar to *strong coffee*, L1 speakers today produce *a straight line*, rather than *a right line* (272 vs. 0 hits in the *The British National Corpus*, 2001), but as I show below, the situation used to be reversed, in other words, *a right line* has become obsolete as a lexical bundle (and was replaced by *a straight line*). It seems therefore highly desirable to extend the methodology for identifying lexical obsolescence to lexical bundles.

My previous research has also focused on LModE, because, as will become apparent later, studying obsolescence requires large amounts of data. And while LModE may not be a period typical for loss of linguistic means, it is, together with the already mentioned standardisation, a period of previously unparalleled book production. In other words, it is a period with an abundance of material that is relatively easy to analyse using computer technology. Specifically, the LModE printed texts yield fairly well to optical character recognition (OCR), and the orthographic standardisation, hand in hand with an almost present-day morphology and syntax, allow for the use of natural language processing tools developed for Present-day English (PDE) necessary for handling big data.

In general then, this chapter will focus on formulating and extending a methodology for corpus driven identification of obsolescence in the largest available corpus of English texts: the Google Books project, specifically its Google Ngrams (GN) dataset. More precisely, it will attempt to better define the statistical parameters necessary for such identification. This will be achieved partly by studying the frequency distribution of lexical bundles in the given corpus and partly by analysing examples of presumably obsolete units. While the quantitative identification itself is the focus of this chapter, the final section will shift to qualitative analysis of some of the examples identified by this methodology, especially as concerns their types and the causes of their loss between LModE and PDE.

2. Material

As noted above, the corpus used for this study is the Google Ngram dataset derived from the Google Books project. The reason for using this corpus is simply its size and while the need for such a large dataset will only be explained in the following section that discusses the methodology itself, to understand this discussion it is important to describe the nature of the dataset.

According to the authors of the dataset (Michel et al. 2011): "The corpus has emerged from Google's effort to digitize books. Most books were drawn from over 40 university libraries around the world. Each page was scanned with custom equipment, and the text was digitized by means of optical character recognition (OCR). Additional volumes, both physical and digital, were contributed by publishers. Metadata describing the date and place of publication were provided by the libraries and publishers and supplemented with bibliographic databases. Over 15 million books have been digitized [~12% of all books ever published]. We selected a subset of over 5 million books for analysis on the basis of the quality of their OCR and metadata ... The resulting corpus contains over 500 billion words, in English (361 billion)". To most corpus linguists, some of the limitations of this corpus will be evident immediately.

One of them stems from the composition of the corpus. It is obvious that the corpus is non-representative: it only covers published book production, the coverage in later periods is up to a thousand fold of the coverage of earlier periods (see Figure 1 for token distribution by decade) and the genre of the books is vastly divergent between the periods covered.

Another limitation is that dating in Google Books and therefore the years assigned to ngrams in GN are not particularly reliable, since publication dates are often very different from the actual time of composition of the texts, esp. in case of reprints or re-editions that often introduce hundreds of years old texts as new.

The third problem is the quality of the OCR. Although only the best third of the results of the recognition process were used, as will be apparent later, the present methodology tends to bring up those types of OCR errors where the results of the recognition markedly decline in quality with age of the texts – and there are plenty of those errors in the data. This is e.g., the case of the long s (ſ), which appears predominantly in earlier texts and is often wrongly recognized as the letter f. Words with long s wrongly recognized as f (e.g., beſt for best) are therefore often misidentified as candidates for obsolescence.

The last major flaw, for my purposes, is the form of the dataset – it is not so much a traditional corpus, but rather a part-of-speech (POS) tagged list of ngrams (1- to 5-grams) with their frequency in a given year and a number of books these were found in. Therefore, the range of statistics that can be calculated over the data is limited and the limited access to the data also means that there is no concordance line for GN and therefore almost no way to double-check how the statistics correspond to actual texts. It is possible to look up individual occurrences in Google Books (I used this for the examples below), but this is severely limited and unreliable (mostly for copyright reasons).

Clearly, both the form and the composition of the corpus have great impact on how the data can be processed, analysed and interpreted. The problems discussed above may seem to indicate that this dataset is simply not fit for linguistic research. The next section will attempt to explain the decision to use the corpus anyway, while the technical aspects of the processing of the dataset will be discussed in Section 4.

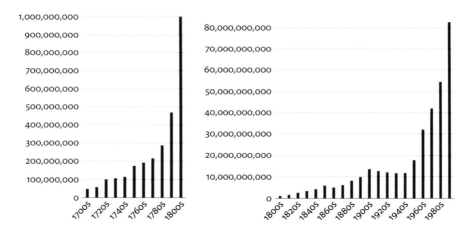

Figure 1. Token distribution by decade (divided into two cut-outs because of the vast difference between early and later decades)

3.   Methodology

Lexical bundles are here understood to be similar to Biber's lexical bundles (Biber et al. 2000), but note that different quantitative parameters for their identification will be used in this study.

Obsolescence, or at least the adjective *obsolete*, is a term of long-standing (if hazy definition) in lexicography, but its definition in corpus linguistics is difficult, especially if applied to units other than lexemes, such as lexical bundles.

What are then obsolete lexical bundles? Since being obsolete is a result of a process, rather than just a state of paucity per se, I will focus on expressions that at one point used to be *common* but later became *lost* (note that this is a different type of obsolescence compared to Rudnicka's approach in her chapter of this volume, where she focuses on items that have "never made it to the mainstream"). The inherent problem lies therefore in what *common* and *lost* or *obsolete* actually mean in terms of corpus linguistics. The basic idea of the proposed methodology is to identify high frequency items that later became low frequency items. Therefore, before the details of the identification/selection process are explained in subsection 3.2, the following subsection will establish the thresholds for the high frequency (common) items and the low frequency (potentially obsolete) items that are crucial in applying the methodology on any data. It is also worth noting that while being obsolete is indeed understood here to be a result of a process, I do not follow Rudnicka's otherwise highly useful distinction of *obsolete* as a state and *obsolescent* as a process leading to it (that she observes in her chapter of the present volume).

3.1   Thresholds

In my previous research, I attempted to link frequency and an intuitive understanding of these terms based on the notion that common words are those understood (if not actively used) by most of the linguistic community, while lost words are not only generally unknown by the community, but are also beyond the scope of most general dictionaries. It is not difficult to establish a frequency span that covers a certain number of most frequent words/types and therefore corresponds to a notion of an average speaker's passive vocabulary – though there is of course a wide variety of opinions on how extensive such vocabulary is (Aitchison 2012; Kilgarriff 2015; Milton & Donzelli 2013 and others). Similarly, if you think of the headwords in large general dictionaries as comprising all of the current vocabulary, it is not difficult to derive a corpus frequency of the least common dictionary words and then the frequency of lexical "trash" or "non-words" (like misspelled words or Old English words in PDE texts). This way a relatively intuitive frequency thresholds, defining on the one hand common and on the other potentially obsolete items, can be set (Tichý 2018).

The same line of thought is, however, impossible to follow with lexical bundles where the matter is complicated by the variable length of these expressions. Going back to Biber's treatment of multi-word sequences, he defines "sequences of word forms that commonly go together in natural discourse" as lexical bundles and both specifically and quite arbitrarily sets the threshold for their minimum frequency in a corpus to 10 ppm.[2] But recognizing that longer lexical bundles are also less

---

2.   parts per million.

frequent, he employs this threshold only for 3- to 4-grams and, in case of 5- to 6-grams, sets the threshold lower: to 5 ppm instead (Biber et al. 2000: 990, 992–3).

Interestingly, Biber lists examples of the lexical bundles he identified by several frequency ranges. When these bundles were sampled and compared with their frequencies in the corpus used for this research, their frequencies came up consistently lower than the average of their respective frequency range (as reported by Biber). Biber also notices that lexical bundles are less frequent in a corpus of academic texts compared to a corpus of conversations (see Biber et al. 2000: 28 for the composition and character of their corpus); but when only the examples from academic texts were sampled, they were still from 1.1 to 30 times more frequent and on average 8.5 times more frequent than in the GN dataset (composed, as noted above, of published books only). The GN frequencies are based on the dataset I downloaded, processed and queried using the BigQuery tool as described in Section 4. In Tichý (2018: 88) a similar process was used, but the dataset was based on the public data available directly to Google Cloud apps.[3]

In Tichý (2018: 88), lexical items considered to be common are defined as the 40 thousand most frequent types of the GN dataset for the period in question, and the corresponding lower frequency threshold of this group of words is set to ca. 1 ppm. According to the *Oxford English Dictionary's Key to frequency* (2019), which is also based on GN, this frequency is at the lower threshold of their frequency Band 5 (out of 8, where 8 is the band with the most frequent words). Band 5 is characterized by the OED as composed of "literate vocabulary associated with educated discourse, although such words may still be familiar within the context of that discourse" (among the examples given for individual word classes are *surveillance, conditional, appropriate* or *markedly*). These items still intuitively seem like words that would be known to most native speakers of English, unlike perhaps some of the examples in Band 4 (e.g., *embouchure* or *egregious*). OED also states that Bands 8–5 make up only a bit over 5% of all headwords in the dictionary. When compared to the data in GN, the top 40 thousand lexical items make up only about 0.64% of all types in the dataset, but this difference is perhaps best explained by the presence of "trash" items in the dataset that are obviously not present in the OED.

Lexical items considered to be lost, on the other hand, are defined as those that have a frequency comparable to or lower than words that are well known to be lost (such as Old English *habban* or *drihten* that can only be used in PDE as a metalanguage) or that are obvious "trash", such as misspellings. The upper frequency thresh-

---

3. Note that the frequencies in GN can be also reviewed through the public GN interface, but the units used there are in percentages rather than in ppm.

old for such words was set to 0.03 ppm, which is at the lower end of OED's frequency Band 4 but should mostly contain words from Bands 1–3. While the three bands with the least frequent words make up over 80% of OED's headwords and over 95% types in the GN, they only represent less than 1.5% of all the tokens in the same dataset. In other words, the dataset conforms to Zipf's law: an overwhelming part of the data consists of only a small number of high-frequency words.

As we have little intuition about how many distinct lexical bundles of variable length constitute common items or "trash", we may compare their distribution in GN with the distribution of individual words as described above. Such comparison shows not only that the longer the unit, the lower its frequency (as reported by Biber), but also that overall, there are fewer tokens in the dataset[4] and perhaps most importantly, that their frequency distribution is markedly different. In contrast to individual words (or 1-grams), as far as longer ngrams are concerned, most of the dataset text is made up of low frequency items. If we again consider the 0.64% of the most frequent types that make up over 95% of the 1-gram data, the same percentage of the most frequent respective ngrams only makes up about 75% of the 2-gram data, less than 50% of the 3-gram data, about 30% of the 4-gram data and less than 20% of the 5-gram data. See Figure 2 for the number of ngram types and their corresponding frequencies on logarithmic scales for the different lengths of lexical bundles (in the GN dataset) and Figure 3 for the overall composition of the dataset in percentages of all tokens covered by types of different frequencies.

This difference in frequency distribution clearly shows that the thresholds will need to be based on the length of the lexical bundles. For the upper threshold (common lexical bundles), I have considered the actual frequency of Biber's examples of lexical bundles in GN and set the threshold for 3-grams at 1 ppm, decreasing/increasing it by the ratio of 2 per every increase/decrease in the length of the ngram. This may seem surprisingly low when compared to the frequencies reported in Rudnicka's chapter in this volume. Afterall, she considers a much higher frequency of one of her sequences at 4.7 ppm to beg the question: "does this mean that the construction is on the way out?". However, while her construction is also a 3-gram in sense of number of words, it is defined using variable POS labels as a *so*-adj-a sequence and is therefore not an invariable ngram, but a grammatical

---

4. This is probably due to the way the GN dataset was restricted. Michel et al. (2011: 176) report that the data were limited "to n-grams occurring at least 40 times in the corpus", though the Google Ngram Viewer website claims that only ngrams appearing in at least 40 books were considered. In any case, due to their lower frequency, this limits the number of longer ngrams more severely than the number of shorter ngrams. Moreover, all ngrams spanning sentence boundaries were excluded from this research, which again means fewer longer ngrams.

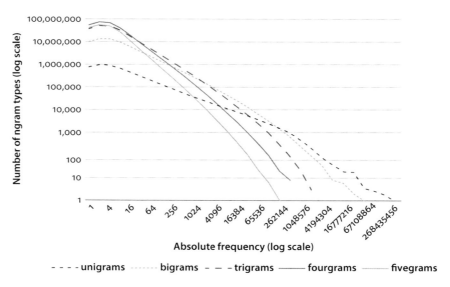

Figure 2. Number of 1- to 5-gram types per their absolute frequencies (illustration of Zipf's law)

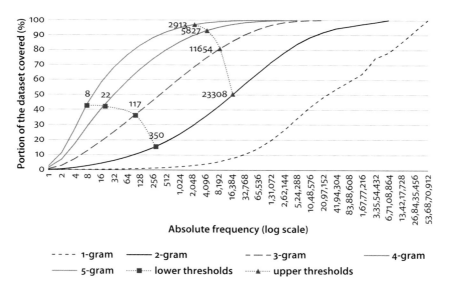

Figure 3. Percentages of all tokens covered by types of different frequencies and the thresholds defined in this section

construction with variable lexical realisations being naturally more frequent than the invariable lexical bundles considered here.

In the case of the lower threshold, I have set it to 7×10^{-4} ppm for 5-grams, and this value is roughly tripled with every decrease in the length of the ngram (see Table 1 for all the threshold values). I have arrived at this value partly by exploring 5-grams of different frequencies, and partly by deciding to always keep the presumably "trash" expressions in a frequency band that comprises less than half the dataset text even for the longest ngrams considered (5-grams). These, as noted above, consist overwhelmingly of low frequency items. While it may seem overly bold – How can almost half of the data be made up of lost/trash items? – it is important to note that lexical bundles are much more variable than lexemes in their internal composition (i.e., the choice and order of letters in a word compared to the choice and order of words in a lexical bundle) resulting in the observed differences in frequency. To better imagine this difference, consider that the least frequent items comprising only 1% of the 1-gram data may have the absolute frequency of as much as 500 tokens in the 1940s data,[5] while the least frequent 5-grams comprising almost 50% of the 5-gram data never appear more than ca. 10 times.

Table 1. Threshold values of common lexical bundles (maximum ppm and absolute freq), "trash" (last period ppm and absolute freq), Obsolescence Index (OI) and LogDice of the same period in which maximum ppm occurred. OI and LogDice are explained in subsection 3.2.

ngram length	maximum ppm >	maximum freq >	last period ppm <	last period freq <	OI <	LogDice of max period >
2-grams	2	23308	0.03	350	5	4
3-grams	1	11654	0.01	117	4	4
4-grams	0.5	5827	0.0019	22	3	4
5-grams	0.25	2913	0.0007	8	2	4

This observation highlights the initial difficulty in setting a "trash" frequency band for lexical bundles: in terms of lexicon, we are used to speaking about high-frequency (common) items, low-frequency (rare) items and "trash" that is composed of "non-words", words with an impossible (misspelled) order of graphemes or words that are not part of the vocabulary of the variety under consideration (however difficult its precise definition might be). But with lexical bundles the option is only binary – frequent, common or recurrent lexical bundles on one hand

---

5. This decade was used here for technical reasons explained in section 4.

and less common lexical bundles on the other. There are no lexical bundles with an impossible order of constituent elements, unless we consider syntactic principles of a given language. There are lexical bundles containing misspelled words, but these are surprisingly frequent. For example, the 3-gram e.g., *the existance of* reaches at times the frequency of 0.08 ppm, which is eight times above the lower threshold for 3-grams.[6] Considering all this, it should be noted that, as in Biber's case, the thresholds are in the end to some degree arbitrary.

3.2   Selection

Even if we were to filter out only the lexical bundles that at one point exceeded the upper threshold for common items and later dipped below the lower threshold of the potentially lost items, there would still remain a huge amount of data – beyond the scope of manual analysis. Two additional parameters were therefore applied to filter out and sort best candidates for manual analysis.

The first parameter is an association measure. Biber (2000: 40) uses Pointwise Mutual Information for select cases in his study and so did I in the initial stages of this study, but later I decided to switch to LogDice as a more reliable collocational measure that does not over-evaluate low- or high-frequency items.[7] Collocational measures, however, work (by design) with collocations, that is 2-grams, and not necessarily with longer ngrams. I have therefore adopted and modified a recursive algorithm called MERGE (by Wahl & Gries 2019) that combines adjacent 2-grams into progressively longer sequences calculating the collocation measure for each combined pair. Using this algorithm, I calculated LogDice for all combinations of adjacent ngrams in the dataset and later only considered such lexical bundles that at one time reached a LogDice value of at least four. Additionally, I used the change in the LogDice over time for further analysis of the examples below. The technical aspect of applying the MERGE algorithm and calculating the LogDice on the dataset are discussed in the following section, but note that according to Rychlý (2008), positive LogDice value means that there is a statistically significant collocation and while the theoretical maximum is 14 (absolute co-occurrence), usually its value is less than 10.

The second parameter is the Obsolescence Index (OI) based on Tichý (2018), which takes the average relative frequency over a segment of time in which the

---

6.   See section 5.1 for more details.

7.   See Rychlý (2008) for both the definition of LogDice and its comparison to MI and other collocational measures.

item reached its maximum (here the period is five decades)[8] and multiplies it by an inverse logarithm of the item's relative frequency in the final segment of the period in question (here the final decade). See Figure 4 for the actual formula.[9]

$$OI = \frac{f_{i-2} + \cdots + f_{i+2}}{5} * \log(\frac{1}{lf})$$

Figure 4. OI formula, where f=relative frequency; i=the period of maximum relative frequency; lf=relative frequency in the last period

This way, the greater the difference between the item's maximum and its final frequency, the greater the OI. The average prevents undue influence of spikes and flukes in the data, and the logarithm alleviates the influence of extremely low frequencies in the final segment: it should not make a great difference here whether the final frequency is 10^{-5} or 10^{-6}, it is enough that it is very low (see again Table 1 for thresholds based on OI). It should be stressed that OI is therefore not as much a degree of obsolescence (as a state) as the degree of its drop in frequency over time. In general and by itself, OI is not very useful as an absolute value. While higher value means greater potential obsolescence, and a negative value should be understood as signalling no chance of obsolescence, it has no meaningful upper or lower limits. Its use here is in highlighting better candidates of obsolescence and its threshold was selected after examining individual examples.

Therefore, before the analysis, all items that conformed to all the thresholds were sorted by decreasing OI and the analysis proceeded from the items with the highest OI (i.e., from the most likely candidates for obsolescence).

As already noted above, the dataset was chosen based on my previous research and due to its size. When dealing with obsolescence, a large dataset is crucial, especially in the final period which is used to verify that an item has dropped below the threshold that identifies it as potentially lost. Basically, the problem is of demonstrating the evidence of absence, which, famously, is not the same thing as

---

8. Note that if the dataset does not include the two decades preceding or following the period of maximum relative frequency, the average is calculated from fewer decades.

9. Unlike in Tichý (2018), simple relative frequencies are used in this study for calculation of the OI rather than relative frequency adjusted by the distribution of items in the corpus, since the only information on distribution in the corpus is the number of books/volumes a particular ngram appeared in for a given year. But there is no way of identifying which books these were and when upper and lowercase forms are conflated, this type of information is no longer valid (and given the status of capitalization in 18th century English, collapsing the case felt as more vital for this analysis).

simply demonstrating the absence of evidence. We need a corpus where we can be confident that any data missing from it would appear below our lower frequency threshold in a different (even larger) corpus of the same composition. Or in other words, we need to be confident that anything that does not appear in our data set is by our definition obsolete. Using Cvrček's (2019) brand new *Corpus Confidence Calculator Online*, it is possible to calculate the minimal size of a corpus needed to include items of a specific frequency with certain statistical confidence. In our case, we need a corpus of at least 6 billion tokens (in the final period alone), because in such a corpus, relative frequency of 7×10^{-4} (our lower threshold) translates to an absolute frequency of four (i.e., items on our lower threshold should typically appear 4 times) and with that frequency in a 6 billion corpus, we have more than 95% confidence that items of similar or higher frequency will appear in the corpus at least once (the confidence calculation is based on Cvrček 2019). Likewise, anything that does not appear in the data is, with similarly constructed confidence interval, below the threshold. Or in other words, with a corpus of this size, we have a 95% confidence that anything that does not appear in our data is below our lower threshold and therefore by our definition obsolete.

The requirements in terms of size mean that while GN displays a number of deficiencies in terms of corpus linguistic research, as noted in the previous section, it is so far the only large enough diachronic corpus covering a substantially long period. Potentially, a large corpus could be used that only covers the final period, while the once common items (their maximum frequencies) could be derived from a smaller diachronic corpus. In fact, there are large enough synchronic web-based corpora that cover ca. a decade of PDE – like the News on the Web (NOW) corpus currently running at over 7 billion tokens – but to use two corpora of such different genre composition (historical texts vs. web) seems to be problematic from the outset. It should be noted here that although the dataset and therefore the results are from a linguistic point of view suspect, this chapter is focused on establishing the methodology rather than on the description of the obsolescence in the given period. If the methodology is found to be successful, it may be applied to more linguistically reliable data in the future.[10]

4.   Technical aspects

The size of the dataset presents a considerable technical obstacle. The whole dataset is composed of over 361 billion tokens, which translates to ca. 20 terabytes of data.

---

10.   A study applying the present methodology on the data of the Early English Books Online is currently underway and it will be interesting to see how the smaller size but higher quality of the data influences its results.

It is currently unfeasible to process such an amount of data on a PC, and even the virtual machine (32 CPUs & 192 GB RAM) available to the Czech National Corpus Institute in Prague (kindly made available to me) would take several months to process it. The only feasible solution was to use Google's own cloud infrastructure, specifically its Dremel based BigQuery database engine that can query data of this size in a matter of seconds or minutes.[11] However, while the public GN dataset and the BigQuery engine are both hosted by Google, there is no other way to move the data into BigQuery than to download and upload them again.[12] Uploading all this data even on a gigabit internet connection, however, would again take over a month at least. I have therefore decided to limit the dataset and process it in stages.

First, I decided to use data only from the 18th century to identify the common items. This decision is based on the experience from Tichý (2018), where, although the whole period 1700–2000 was considered, the maximum frequency of all items identified as potentially obsolete and analysed occurred in the 18th century (i.e., obsolescence is more probable and more profound over a longer period, which is to be expected). Moreover, I decided to limit the last period, in which the items are identified as potentially lost, to the 1940s. The decision to process data by decades is arbitrary; the decision to choose the 1940s as the final decade is based on the size of the data – after this decade, the size of the data grows dramatically (see again Figure 1). With the dataset limited to 1700–1800 and 1940–1949, it was possible to pre-process the data on the virtual server, which took about four days. At this stage, all punctuation, non-alphabetic ngrams and all ngrams spanning sentence boundaries were removed and the data was formatted for import into Google Cloud. The resulting dataset of 274 GB was ca. 100 times smaller than the original one and the upload thus took less than a day.

Second, separately for each length of the ngrams, the data was lowercased; summed up by decades; relative frequencies, OI and LogDice were calculated and the data was formatted into a pivot table for export. As noted above, the LogDice calculation was inspired by Wahl and Gries (2019): the association measure was calculated for each continuous 2-gram and in the case of longer ngrams, the first two words were merged for the purposes of this calculation and the association of this temporary 1-gram with the following word was calculated. This procedure was repeated until all continuous combinations had a LogDice value calculated.

---

11.   Note that the queries were made using SQL (Structured Query Language) which is a standard for most databases today, but the BigQuery tool uses a variety different from most other database engines.

12.   Google Cloud offers a subset of the GN for test purposes, but it only contains trigram data and it does not seem to be identical to either the 2009 or 2012 version of the dataset officially published by Google and may easily change or be removed at any point (and it is therefore inadvisable to be used for research).

Unlike Wahl and Gries (2019), I processed all continuous combinations and kept all of them in the resulting dataset. For example, the 3-gram "end + and + design" has two LogDice values calculated, one for "end_and + design" and one for "end + and_design)". Next, the top twenty thousand ngrams sorted by their frequency maximum and with OI > 2 were exported for each length of the ngrams, resulting in a table of eighty thousand ngrams (with an equal number of ngrams for each length) for further analysis.

Third, the thresholds (see again Table 1) were applied and the ca. four thousand ngrams were sorted by OI (from highest to lowest) for manual analysis.

5.   Analysis

The analysis proceeded from "better" candidates (higher OI) until all items that satisfied the threshold requirements were exhausted. However, since the OI and LogDice thresholds in particular are quite arbitrary, the analysis could have easily continued with more examples. In fact, during the initial analysis, before the thresholds were applied, a number of interesting examples cropped up,[13] but analysing more than almost four thousand lexical bundles by hand was beyond the scope of this mostly methodological probe.

Each lexical bundle was first quickly reviewed and assigned one or more of the following labels: the obsolete lexical bundles themselves, OCR errors, POS errors, foreign language, proper nouns, spelling changes, morphological changes, lexical obsolescence and parts of other lexical bundles. Only the actual obsolete lexical bundles were further analysed and categorised (see subsection 5.2), the rest is, from the perspective of this chapter, trash.

5.1   Trash

An unfortunate effect of applying the proposed methodology to a relatively low quality dataset like GN, is that the trash comprises an overwhelming majority (ca. 95%) of its output. Considering Table 1 it is, however, evident that most of the trash is composed of OCR errors and spelling changes. The first may be avoided by using a better dataset and both could be mitigated by tweaking the methodology to allow for small graphemic differences by comparing the edit distance of sharply declining and rising units. For example, the sharply declining *of my self* and the sharply rising *of myself* would be merged and no longer identified as possibly obsolete.

---

13.   E.g., *there needs no* as in *"For where no sacrifice is, there needs no priest."* signaling perhaps the decline in impersonal constructions in the overall typological transformation of English.

Table 2. Composition of trash results

OCR errors	71.8%
spelling change	17.3%
POS errors	2.8%
parts of other bundles	2.8%
proper nouns	2.5%
foreign language	2.0%
morphological change	0.6%
lexical	0.1%

- The most numerous of the trash results were the OCR errors and among them, the most common was the already mentioned *long s* wrongly recognized as the letter *f* (e.g., *beft* instead of *best*). The OCR is evidently much more accurate with 20th century texts than with the texts from the 18th century.
- The POS errors are not simply errors in the POS tagging, but specifically those errors that contributed to the analysed items being identified as potential candidates for obsolescence. Those are especially the cases where one and the same ngram is systematically tagged differently in the early periods than in the latter periods (creating a false impression of a rapid decline, since differently tagged ngrams are treated separately). In some cases, the errors are easy to understand, e.g., converted words or border case assignments of word class (such as nominal modifiers being tagged first as nouns and later as adjectives; or participles being tagged at first as verbs and later as adjectives), but sometimes the tagging is more difficult to explain, such as *salvation* tagged as a verb or *realm* as an adjective.[14]
- Lexical bundles composed of one or more non-English (especially Latin) words and proper nouns are, due to their frequency distribution over time, prime candidates for obsolescence but are not particularly interesting for linguistic analysis.
- Misspellings as well as spelling and morphological changes, while certainly linguistically interesting, are also not the focus of this chapter. Suffice it to say that the changes to spelling are mostly connected to the changing status of compounds (e.g., *my self* > *myself*) or to the changes in spelling individual constituent words (e.g., *catholick* > *catholic*).[15]

---

14.   The POS tagger is reportedly "a state-of-the-art Conditional Random Field (CRF) based tagger" with 97.22% accuracy (Michel et al. 2011).

15.   There is of course the difficulty of deciding what is an OCR error, misspelling, alternative spelling or change of spelling (if there even is a difference between the last three from a

- Morphological changes concern mostly variation in verbal class membership (e.g., *shew*).
- Lexical obsolescence is often a cause of the obsolescence of the whole lexical bundle. It is sometimes difficult to separate the two or to say how much the decline of each element has contributed to the loss of the whole expression, but I have attempted to discard those cases, where the influence of one part was obviously greater than of the expression as a whole (e.g., *is to the fluxion of*).
- The items analysed as parts of other ngrams are those lexical bundles that, while interesting for further analysis, appear either as parts of a longer ngram or are extended versions of shorter ngrams where the other version is more salient (mostly due to its higher maximum LogDice).

5.2   Results

All the remaining candidates for obsolescence were again analysed: their diachronic frequency profiles were checked using the online Google Ngrams Viewer[16] and the possible reasons for their obsolescence were considered. See Table 3 (in the Appendix) for a selective list of prototypical examples with the statistics used to identify them and examples of their usage. The examples were grouped into nine mostly semantic categories that emerged from the analysis. What follows are examples seen as especially illustrative of those categories.

From a formal point of view, Biber's (2000: 992) characterization of lexical bundles applies here quite well: the 2-grams are typical collocations, often terminological and mostly equivalent to one word expressions. 3-grams are often "extended collocations" or binomials, while 4-grams and 5-grams are either more complex extensions of shorter ngrams or phrasal in their composition.

---

diachronic perspective) considering the limited access to the original texts, but for my purposes, these distinctions were not especially important since the focus of the study is on the obsolescence of multi-word units rather than on changes of orthography. It was therefore safe to assume any of these lexical bundles are "trash".

16.   While the dataset used to identify candidates for obsolescence only employs data up to the 1940s, Figures 5 & 6 here extend until the 2000s since the GN Viewer was used to retrieve them (and the percentages used in the online version were converted to ppm). The frequencies may also differ a bit from those in Table 3 due to the processing described in the methodological section. In all examples here, the frequency in the 2000s was checked to confirm that the decrease in relative frequency continued beyond the 1940s.

5.2.1 Terminology

The first category consists of scientific terminology, and most of the lexical bundles belonging to the category are 2-grams or binomials that function as one-word units.[17] Due to their function, it is usually easy to see how these items became obsolete: by relatively straightforward replacement by a different term. The replacement does not happen at once, there is usually a period of competition, often of more than one term. This is especially typical for sciences that are, in the 18th century, establishing their English nomenclature – such as chemistry and geology, but there are also examples from physics and geometry. Some representative examples are:

(1)   *vitriolic acid* – also *vitriol*, replaced by *sulphuric/sulfuric acid* (see Figure 5)

(2)   *volatile alkali* – replaced by *ammonia*

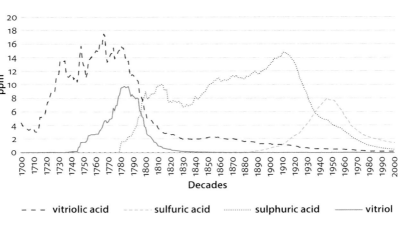

Figure 5. Replacement of vitriolic acid by sulfuric/sulphuric acid and variation with vitriol (Example 1)

Both Examples (1) & (2) may also be replaced by a single word synonym.

(3)   *nitrous air* – replaced by *nitrous oxide*

(4)   *spirit of salt* – replaced by *hydrochloric acid*

Notice that while these terms function as one-word units, they would not have been identified without extending the methodology to lexical bundles and espe-

---

17.   These forms have been also called Multi-word Terms, though the term is mostly used in the field of information retrieval (Farradne, Poulton & Datta 1965).

cially with ngrams where one or more words are very common (like Example 3 & Example 4), the loss in the semantic field of that word (i.e., *air* meaning *oxide*) would not have been detected either.

(5)   *calcareous earth* – partly replaced by *calcareous soil/rock/sediment* and *limestone*

In Example 5, the replacement is less straightforward, and it seems that the more specific term *calcareous* is giving way to a more general *limestone* – separately and in its collocations.

(6)   *right line* – replaced by *straight line*

(7)   *rectangle contained between*: "…but the square of AB and BC, considered as one line, exceeds the two squares of AB and BC, by twice the *rectangle contained between*."[18]

The two examples from geometry, Examples (6) & (7), show different circumstances of obsolescence. While Example 6 is a straightforward replacement (perhaps due to semantic shift in *right*), Example 7 represents a term that starts as a very specific translation in Euclid's *Elements of Geometry*, but is, in later translations and expositions, rephrased by less condensed expressions such as "a rectangle contained by the segments".

5.2.2   *"Quasi" terminology*

The second category is similar, but most items it contains are not exactly scientific terminology, being either more vague or originating in other genres. Some representative examples are:

(8)   *immediate Revelation*[19] – replaced by *direct revelation*

(9)   *Primitive Fathers* – replaced by *Early Church Fathers* and similar

(10)   *End and Design* – replaced by various expressions like *purpose, aim, goal, objective*

(11)   *(God's)*[20] *Grace and Assistance*

---

18.   Examples whose meaning may not be obvious are illustrated by quotations directly, the rest is illustrated in Table 33.

19.   Capitalization in the examples is used for readability and to represent typical instances found in Google Books, but the actual dataset was lowercased and is therefore case insensitive.

20.   Implied elements are included in brackets for ease of understanding – though these are common collocations of the lexical bundles in question, they are not part of the automatically identified pattern itself.

Where the interpretation of the circumstances of the decline of Examples (8) & (9) seems very similar to the examples of scientific terminology, Examples (10) and especially 11 are more difficult. In Example 10, it is possible to identify a number of words or expressions that replace it, but in Example 11, without recourse to theology, it is not quite clear what happened to the expression beyond the possibility that it is more general than the others and was therefore perhaps not an essential term of its genre, and disappeared without an obvious replacement.

It is also important to note here that there is a large proportion of religious and specifically Christian expressions among the potentially obsolete items and only a smaller proportion of scientific and legal/administrative terminology. While with religious discourse, it is safe to imagine that the English linguistic community has become less religious or less concerned with religion since the 18th century, and has therefore been naturally producing less text on the topic, this will not hold for science and law. The obvious decline in the terminology of these two genres shows an important bias of the whole dataset that skews the results perceptibly. Firstly, especially in terms of science, the GN dataset records a number of magazines and journals of the 18th and 19th century that together with the scientific monographs comprise most of the scientific publishing of the time. However, scientific journals of the 20th century, the most important vehicle of natural sciences, are mostly unrecorded. Secondly, the huge increase in other genres (fiction etc.) side-lines the previously dominant genres and makes their terminology more prone to be identified as potentially obsolete. In general, this problem highlights the fact that, in most cases, the circumstances of the obsolescence are complex and motivated by a number of factors, often also including genre decline. It also emphasizes the problem of representativeness in the data.

(12) *body of forces:* "In consequence of this Edward immediately sent Sir Anthony Lacy, with a considerable *body of forces*, to repel the insurgents." – rephrased by various forms

(13) *the Stomach and Guts:* "The lower Spleen seated between *the Stomach and Guts*" – replaced by *gastrointestinal tract*

Example 13 is interesting for two reasons. First it shows that sometimes a shorter/longer part of a lexical bundle is identified by this methodology rather than the part that seems more salient. And in fact, the 3-gram *Stomach and Guts* (without the article) has a slightly higher LogDice than the 4-gram presented above. But at the same time, the final frequency of the 3-gram goes slightly above the minimum threshold and was not, therefore, identified as potentially obsolete. Should we in such cases follow the stronger association of the 3-gram and ignore the threshold, or remove even this example that passes all the thresholds? In any case, the second interesting point here is illustrated by Figure 6. While the replacement is evident, compared to Figure 5, there is a marked lag between the disappearance of the first and the rise of the second expression. The decline of Example 13 is probably connected with the disuse of *guts* as a technical medical term, but what exactly was used to express the meaning of Example 13 during the 19th century is not quite clear (possibly some other construction with *intestine* or *stomach*).

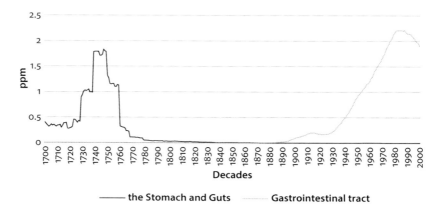

Figure 6. Replacement of *the Stomach and Guts* by *Gastrointestinal tract* (Example 13)

(14)   *gives fire with steel*: "Gray iron ore has a shining metallic appearance, and commonly *gives fire with steel*." – replaced by *pyrophoric*

Example 14 demonstrates an almost complete clause (used as a scientific term describing pyrophoric properties of materials) replaced by a one-word form.

5.2.3   *Appellations*

(15)   *His Czarish Majesty*: replaced by *His Majesty the Czar/Tzar/Tsar*

(16)   *Lords the States (General of United Provinces)*

(17)   *right trusty and right welbeloved (cousin and councillor)*

All the Examples 15–17 represent expressions of appellation whose potential obsolescence is directly caused by extralinguistic factors. Example 15 declines with the death of the last Tsar; the decline of Example 16 follows the political changes in the Netherlands, where the members of the States General are no longer referred to as *Lords*; Example 17 reflects the decrease in importance of the Privy Council and the estates of the realm (and the representation of the texts concerning it in the dataset), whose members have been styled this way.

5.2.4   *Legal/administrative phrases*

Examples (18) and (19) in fact usually follow each other as in "And wee doe also by these Presents authorize and impower you our said Comissioners or any seaven or more of you..." and both decline with changes of expression in (and smaller representation of) parliamentary papers.

(18)   *you,*[21] *Our said Commissioners*

(19)   *(or two/three or more) of you, as aforesaid*

(20)   *(prosecuted/sued/decreed) in the exchequer for*

Example 20 is similar to the examples in the previous category in that it has direct extralinguistic cause for obsolescence since the Exchequer was dissolved as a judicial body in 1880.

5.2.5   *Dating*

A small and very specific category comprises the expressions of time, as in:

(21)   *(in) the Year before Christ (number)* – replaced by simple number and BC/CE or *in the year* number *BC*.

(22)   *(in the Xth) year of Edward the Third* – replaced by *(in the Xth) of the reign of Edward the Third/ of Edward the Third's reign*

Example 22 is interesting in terms of this methodology, because it shows the need of extending it to "skipgrams" (ngrams with some constituents variable or skipped), since probably the most salient part of this expression is *in the Xth year of*, but the *Xth* is too variable to garner enough frequency at any time (unlike the names of important rulers who are relatively few in number).

5.2.6   *Pragmatic markers*

(23)   I proceed now

(24)   and thus I have done (esp. *concerning myself*): "*And thus I have done* with these idle politick Visions"

(25)   *what meant by it*: "Heresy, *what meant by it* in Scripture, Vol. II. p. 51"

---

21.   Punctuation is added for readability in the examples and represents the common form in Google Books examples, but was removed from the actual dataset.

(26)   *Upon which Account:* "*...*not by the conformity of their sentiments to divine revelation, but by their implicit assent to the established creeds; *upon which account,* those who are zealous for the honour of divine revelation, cannot fail."

Examples (23–26) represent expressions that organize or structure the discourse, though Example 26 could be also seen as a complex relativizer. The ultimate causes for the decline of each individual example here are difficult to specify, but perhaps in Example 23 and Example 24, the general shift away from subjective narration in the scientific genre may play some role, in Example 24 it is perhaps exacerbated by the decline of *thus.* Example 25 can be partly explained by the decline of the passive form and by standardization of referencing in technical texts. Example 26 is more difficult to assess, perhaps in addition to the decline of *upon* and *which* (partly replaced by *that*), the tendency for condensation or clarity could have played some part. A trend of decreasing popularity of elaborate subordinators noted in Rudnicka's chapter of this volume may also be worth noting here, since subordinators, relativizers and pragmatic markers are all text-hierarchy indicators.

5.2.7   *Replacement in collocations*
The following two examples are difficult to categorize, but in both there is a very specific expression that replaces them. Moreover, both collocations only have one element replaced in them that is, however, by itself not becoming obsolete. In 28, there is the semantic shift in *crave* away from "to ask for" to "to long for". Nevertheless, the cause for the change especially in 27 is far from obvious to me.

(27)   *continued uniformly* – replaced by *continued steadily*

(28)   *crave leave to* – replaced by *asked leave/permission to*

5.2.8   *Countability and accommodation*
While Examples (29) and (30) look similar, i.e., one of the elements of the ngram changes its expression of number, each represents a different case. Example 29 shows a genuine change in number, or rather in countability (i.e., transition from uncountable to countable, as suggested by Denison 1998: 96), Example 30 represents naturalization of foreign structure with the plural marking on both elements into a native form with a plural noun and its post-modification (that takes no plural ending). Both can be also analysed as changes in morphology and therefore left out of the data as per the section 5.1, but since in both cases the change seems to affect the whole lexical bundle, I decided to keep them in.

(29)   *dangerous consequence:* "And yet, notwithstanding those great apprehensions of what *dangerous consequence* it might be" – replaced by *dangerous consequences*

(30)   *letters patents* – replaced by *letters patent*

5.2.9 *Complex verb phrase*

(31) *if we be not wanting:* "My opinion is, that *if we be not wanting* in trouble and time, as artful a piece may be produced, as what has been hitherto done" – replaced by *if we are not wanting, if we are not deficient in* etc.

(32) *be made appear:* "which fact, as also a reasonable endeavour to obtain such evidence, shall *be made appear* to the satisfaction of the court" – replaced by *be made to appear* or other expressions like *be shown* or *make apparent*

In many ways, the two final examples are the most intriguing, since they reflect changes in LModE grammar rather than in lexis or semantics. Example 31 is perhaps an example of the continuing loss of the subjunctive, here possibly exacerbated by a complex verb phrase that makes the whole structure more difficult to parse. In Example 32, the tendency to use more explicit structures may be apparent as well, but it is interesting to notice that while this causative construction in passive using the verb *have* takes here the verb in the bare infinitive and requires the *to* infinitive in PDE, the opposite is true of the active constructions of this kind (see Iyeiri 2018: 154). Probably, like other variation throughout LModE, the variation of the two forms of infinitives is being resolved here into their specific uses – a process also noted (as "the rise of the to-infinitive") by Rudnicka in her chapter of this volume. In this, the verb *appear* seems to lag behind other verbs, since a quick test in GN Viewer shows that verbs *do* or *make* seem to have already lost the bare infinitives in passive by 1700.

6. Discussion

Given the functional and formal variety of the examples presented in the previous section, it seems the proposed methodology is successful in the identification of candidates for obsolescence from across the given corpus. Analysing the character of the examples also shows that they are relatively representative of the processes at work in the LModE – on all the levels, in fact, proposed by Rudnicka's Section 4 and especially Figure 7 in her chapter of this volume: Namely the establishment of scientific nomenclature in English, continuing accommodation of foreign (French & Latin) expressions in legal/administrative texts, decreasing influence of religious language, morphological changes not only in verbal classes, but also in the relatively new category of countability and various minute shifts in complex verb phrases. And even the grammatical processes, while in itself not profound or surprising, can actually show in the data. This seems to be in agreement with Denison (1998: 93): "relatively few categorical losses or innovations have occurred in the last two centuries, syntactic change has more often been statistical in nature". It is encouraging therefore that the statistical nature of the losses yields even to a corpus-driven methodology based on lexical bundles, and not only to a premeditated search for particular grammatical constructions.

7. Conclusions

Several problems remain, however, with this methodology. Some have to do with the process of identification of the potentially obsolete lexical bundles, some with the data used here.

While the dataset is not part of the methodology per se, the methodology needs to be adjusted to it and it seems the non-representative character of the data could be a problem, but there is not much that can be done. The only obvious solution to prevent genres that are overrepresented in the early periods and under-represented in the latter periods from dominating the obsolescence charts seems to be the tweaking of the thresholds to allow more potential candidates for manual analyses, even from other genres. It could also be worthwhile to apply the method-ology to a dataset that is either more representative or that is annotated for genre.

Similarly, the results might benefit from information on the distribution of the data, since currently, items that appear frequently in a small number of books (e.g., Example 25) may reach an undue prominence in the early periods of the dataset. While the number of books in which an expression appears is problematic after lowercasing the data, it may be possible to use the maximum and minimum of this value as a guide for minimum and maximum distribution and adjust the OI accordingly. Another improvement to the methodology could be the accom-modation of skipgrams and/or POSgrams that would account for ngrams con-taining a highly variable element (like the number in Example 22, but perhaps more importantly a variable lexical element as in Example 20). The methodology should also be more sophisticated when processing lexical bundles that are subsets of, or that contain other lexical bundles, so that the most salient expressions are always selected as candidates for obsolescence rather than less salient extensions of these expressions that happen to better fulfil the thresholds of obsolescence (like Example 13). On the other hand, the methodology is currently only a tool for detecting potential items, and the final analysis and interpretation needs to be the work of a linguist that can easily take this into account. If OI were to be used as an absolute parameter of obsolescence, it would need to include the other measures used here as well as be tweaked to have some meaningful limits that would allow it to be easily interpreted when standing alone.

Finally, the use of association measure throughout the study also merits some attention. In all our examples (see Table 3 in the Appendix) the decrease in fre-quency is accompanied by a dramatic decrease in LogDice – after all, LogDice is based on frequency. Are not the statistics therefore redundant here? First, note that the difference between the maximum and final LogDice varies largely among the examples. It is greatest with Example 14 and lowest with Example 28. Second, there are even examples in the data of increase in LogDice, e.g., *the lord hath* increases LogDice from 7.7 (in the decade of its frequency maximum) to 7.9 in the 1940s while at the same time dropping in relative frequency from 5.5 to 0.4. Looking at these examples closely, Example 14 is a lexical bundle composed of common words that used to form a set expression. And while the expression is now lost, the words are still common. Example 28 contains the verb *crave*, which of itself decreases in frequency more than tenfold but the expression, while perhaps obsolete, is still one of its collocations. And *the lord hath* contains the verb form *hath* which used to be common in the 18th century, but became restricted to specific uses and genres, as exemplified in this very expression. Therefore, if both frequency and LogDice decrease, the expression itself is becoming obsolete – but interestingly not its constituents (though they may have shifted in meaning as in Example 3). LogDice is therefore very useful in combination with OI, especially for the analysis into the causes of obsolescence.

It is my hope that while the methodology relies on less accessible big data sources, it can, in the future, be used more widely and for other periods as well, either by restricting the timespan using the GN dataset (e.g., 19th & 20th centuries) or by using a different corpus for the early periods.

Acknowledgements

This work was supported by the European Regional Development Fund project "Creativity and Adaptability as Conditions of the Success of Europe in an Interrelated World" (reg. no.: CZ.02. 1.01/0.0/0.0/16_019/0000734).

References

Aitchison, Jean. 2012. *Words in the Mind: An Introduction to the Mental Lexicon*. Oxford: Wiley-Blackwell.

Biber, Douglas, Johansson, Stig, Leech, Geoffrey, Conrad, Susan & Finegan, Edward. 2000. *Longman Grammar of Spoken and Written English*. London: Longman. https://doi.org/10.2307/3587792

Coleman, Robert. 1990. The assessment of lexical mortality and replacement between Old and Modern English. In *Papers from the 5th International Conference on English Historical Linguistics [Current Issues in Linguistic Theory 65]*, Sylvia M. Adamson, Vivien A. Law, Nigel Vincent & Susan Wright (eds), 69–86. Amsterdam: John Benjamins. https://doi.org/10.1075/cilt.65

Cvrček, Václav. n.d. Corpus Confidence Calculator. <https://jupyter.korpus.cz/shiny/cvrcek/calc/> (27 April 2019).

Denison, David. 1998. Syntax. In *The Cambridge History of the English Language*, Vol. 4: 1776–1997, Suzanne Romaine (ed.). Cambridge: CUP.

Farradne, J., Poulton, R.K & Datta, M. S. 1965. Problems in analysis and terminology for information retrieval. *Journal of Documentation* 21(4): 287–90. https://doi.org/10.1108/eb026380

Iyeiri, Yoko. 2018. Causative *make* and its infinitival complements in Early Modern English. In *Explorations in English Historical Syntax [Studies in Langage Companion Series 198]*, Hubert Cuyckens, Hendrik De Smet, Liesbet Heyvaert & Charlotte Maekelberghe (eds), 139–58. Amsterdam: John Benjamins. https://doi.org/10.1075/slcs.198.06iye

Kilgarriff, Adam. 2015. How many words are there? In *The Oxford Handbook of the Word*, John R. Taylor (ed.), 29–37. Oxford: OUP.

Maixner, Vítězslav. 1970. Zánik Slov v Nové Angličtině.

Michel, Jean-Baptiste, Kui Shen, Yuan, Presser Aiden, Aviva, Veres, Adrian, Gray, Matthew K., The Google Books Google Books Team, Pickett, Joseph P. 2011. Quantitative analysis of culture using millions of digitized books. *Science* 331(6014): 176–182. https://doi.org/10.1126/science.1199644

Milton, James & Donzelli, Giovanna. 2013. The lexicon. In *The Cambridge Handbook of Second Language Acquisition*, Julia Herschensohn & Martha Young-Scholten (eds), 441–60. Cambridge: CUP. https://doi.org/10.1017/CBO9781139051729.027

Němec, Igor. 1968. Strukturní předpoklady zániku slov. *Slovo a Slovesnost* 29(2): 152–58. <http://sas.ujc.cas.cz/archiv.php?art=1617> (5 November 2020).

Oxford English Dictionary. n.d. Key to frequency. Oxford: OUP. <https://public.oed.com/how-to-use-the-oed/key-to-frequency/> (22 April 2019).

Petersen, Alexander M., Tenenbaum, Joel, Havlin, Shlomo & Stanley, H. Eugene. 2012. Statistical laws governing fluctuations in word use from word birth to word death. *Scientific Reports 2 (March)*: 313. https://doi.org/10.1038/srep00313

Rudnicka, Karolina. 2019. *The statistics of obsolescence: Purpose subordinators in Late Modern English*. Basel: NIHIN. https://doi.org/10.6094/978-3-928969-75-8

Rychlý, Pavel. 2008. A lexicographer-friendly association score. *RASLAN 2008*, 6–9. Brno: Masarykova Univerzita.

The British National Corpus, Version 2 (BNC World). 2001. Praha: Distributed by Oxford University Computing Services on behalf of the BNC Consortium. *Ústav Českého národního korpusu FF UK*. <http://www.korpus.cz>

Tichý, Ondřej. 2018. Lexical obsolescence and loss in English: 1700–2000. In *Applications of Pattern-Driven Methods in Corpus Linguistics* [Studies in Corpus Linguistics 82], Joanna Kopaczyk & Jukka Tyrkkö (eds), 81–103. Amsterdam: John Benjamins. https://doi.org/10.1075/scl.82.04tic. 10.1075/scl.82.04tic

Trench, Richard Chenevix. 1871. *English. Past and Present.*, New York, NY: Charles Scribner and Co.

Wahl, Alexander & Gries, Stefan T. 2019. Computational extraction of formulaic sequences from corpora: Two case studies of a new extraction algorithm. In *Computational Phraseology* [IVITRA Research in Linguistics and Literature 24], Gloria Corpas Pastor & Jean-Pierre Colson (eds), 84–110. Amsterdam: John Benjamins. https://doi.org/10.1075/ivitra.24.05wah

Appendix

Table 3.   Examples – max. ppm. is the highest ppm, LogDice of max is the LogDice reached in the same decade

n.	lexical bundle	OI	max ppm	final ppm	LogDice of max	final LogDice	samples of use (Google Books 1700–1800)
1	*vitriolic acid*	10.3	11.7	9.9E-3	11.9	1.5	we noticed that gentleman's unfavourable opinion of the *vitriolic acid*
2	*volatile alkali*	5.2	6.1	1.0E-2	12.1	4.5	in which the quantity of *volatile alkali* produced is very remarkable
3	*nitrous air*	7.4	10.2	1.6E-2	10.0	0.8	In about one day, and without any heat, about one-third of a given quantity of *nitrous air* was imbibed by liver of sulphur.
4	*spirit of salt*	4.5	4.2	8.2E-3	9.6	1.5	For many hearing what great succes, my *Spirit of Salt* hath had
5	*calcareous earth*	5.9	6.1	9.7E-3	9.8	1.3	Argillaceous earth mixed with a variable quantity of pyrites, a little magnesia, and *calcareous earth*
6	*right line*	10.4	6.1	1.8E-3	9.0	-2.8	Through a given point A, draw a *right line* parallel to a given right line BC
7	*rectangle contained between*	25.0	5.0	0	12.4	-	but the square of AB and BC, considered as one line, exceeds the two squares of AB and BC, by twice the *rectangle contained between.*
8	*immediate Revelation*	9.9	15.8	2.6E-2	11.7	3.4	the light of self-knowledge was hid from his Eyes; except by *immediate Revelation*
9	*Primitive Fathers*	5.1	4.0	6.5E-3	9.6	1.8	But after All, let the Authority of the *Primitive Fathers* be what it will, and even as Great as you yourself suppose it
10	*End and Design*	7.5	5.5	8.3E-3	9.6	1.8	Eternal Salvation the only *End and Design* of Religion
11	*Grace and Assistance*	5.6	4.9	3.4E-3	10.3	1.2	But then we cannot effect this without supernatural *grace and assistance.*
12	*body of forces*	4.5	3.3	8.2E-3	8.9	0.6	These were the principal actions after raising the Siege of Limerick, till the arrival of a *body of Forces* from England

(Continued)

Table 3. (*Continued*)

n.	lexical bundle	OI	max ppm	final ppm	LogDice of max	final LogDice	samples of use (Google Books 1700–1800)
13	the Stomach and Guts	3.0	2.2	5.2E-4	12.0	2.5	Fluids mixed in *the Stomach and Guts*, will dissolve the Bodies in them, raise Steam, & c.
14	gives fire with steel	4.6	1.1	8.6E-5	11.0	−5.2	It freely *gives fire with steel*. In its purer state, it makes no effervescence with Aqua Fortis
15	His Czarish Majesty	4.1	3.5	8.6E-4	8.5	0.3	His Danish Majesty did not condescend thereto but merely out of Regard to *his Czarish Majesty*
16	Lords the States	9.7	10.7	5.1E-3	10.9	−1.6	at the assembly of the *Lords the States* General
17	right trusty and right welbeloved	5.1	1.7	0	12.6	-	And to our *right trusty and right welbeloved* Cousin and Councillor, Robert Earle of Roxburgh
18	you, Our said Commissioners	4.7	4.4	2.6E-4	6.2	−7.7	And we do hereby authorize and empower *you Our said Commissioners*
19	of you, as aforesaid	4.1	2.4	0	11.2	-	willing, commanding, and authorizing you, or any five or more *of you, as aforesaid*
20	in the exchequer for	3.0	4.9	1.0E-3	4.6	−7.7	and he produced a decree *in the Exchequer for* an account of all small tithes
21	the Year before Christ	3.7	4.6	1.3E-3	8.9	−0.8	Mainus his younger Nephew succeeded, *the Year before Christ* 290
22	year of Edward the Third	3.6	3.2	0	7.8	-	More than twenty dispatches, in the eighth *year of Edward the Third*, bear date at this place

23	*I proceed now*	4.8	3.2	9.3E-3	4.3	-3.5	This being all You are pleased to say, in justification of your Doctrine: *I proceed now* to consider, what You urge
24	*and thus I have done*	2.9	1.7	3.4E-4	6.8	-4.5	*And thus I have* done concerning myself
25	*what meant by it*	4.1	2.4	0	11.2		Heresy, *what meant by it* in Scripture, Vol. II. p. 51
26	*Upon which Account*	6.5	3.8	6.9E-3	10.0	2.4	and strike all Things out of themselves, or at least, by Collision, from each other: *Upon which Account*, we think it highly reasonable to produce our great Forgetfulness, as an Argument unanswerable
27	*continued uniformly*	6.3	7.7	3.6E-3	10.6	-0.1	and this conduct they *continued uniformly* to pursue, till the dismal accounts of the tortures to which protestants were subjected in France
28	*crave leave to*	6.0	4.0	9.0E-3	11.3	6.1	My Lord, I humbly *crave leave to* speak but one Word
29	*dangerous consequence*	6.3	4.7	2.7E-2	9.7	3.5	notwithstanding those great apprehensions of what *dangerous consequence* it might be, it is now universally received. ... as an undoubted truth
30	*letters patents*	9.7	13.2	2.7E-2	11.2	3.0	to discharge such Sallaries ... attending the Execution of these our *Letters Patents*; and the Powers and Directions herein contained
31	*be made appear*	4.3	2.5	9.4E-3	7.8	0.3	which fact, as also a reasonable endeavour to obtain such evidence, shall *be made appear* to the satisfaction of the court
32	*if we be not wanting*	2.6	0.9	0	9.2	-	My opinion is, that *if we be not wanting* in trouble and time, as artful a piece may be produced, as what has been hitherto done

A constructional account of the loss of the adverse avertive schema in Mandarin Chinese

Yueh Hsin Kuo
The University of Edinburgh

This study defines the kind of loss under investigation as schema loss in diachronic construction grammar and proposes that schema loss may be related to change in prototypicality. Using the adverse avertive schema in Chinese as an example, it is shown that while older prototypical members of the schema motivated its composition, newer members demotivated it, because their semantics and pragmatics were not a good match with the form and meaning of the schema. The analysis emphasises that loss, like gain, is multidimensional in that both schematic and substantive patterns need to be considered.

Keywords: diachronic construction grammar, prototype, schema loss, *chadian*, bleaching

1. Introduction

There is a growing literature on diachronic construction grammar (e.g., Traugott & Trousdale 2013; Hilpert 2015; Barðdal & Gildea 2015), but most studies focus on gain, not loss. Some constructional studies on loss in English include Trousdale (2008) on the impersonal construction, Petré (2010) on *weorðan* 'become', Noël (2019) on deontic constructions such as *be obliged to* and Kranich (this volume), who examines modal constructions such as *may* and *must* and particularly a subtype of the *may* construction, *we + may + verb of speaking/reasoning*. Outside English, Colleman and Noël (2012) look into the Dutch evidential construction, parallel to *be said to* in English, and Rosemeyer (2014) investigates the decline of the Spanish auxiliary construction *ser + past participle*. Other studies that look at phenomena closely associated with loss include Van de Velde (2014) on 'degeneracy' and Norde and Trousdale (2016) on 'exaptation', both of which examine Germanic languages such as English and Dutch. Similar to these studies, this study

https://doi.org/10.1075/slcs.218.05kuo
© 2021 John Benjamins Publishing Company

focuses on schematic patterns (to be defined below), but examines an adverbial adjunct schema in Mandarin Chinese, the adverse avertive schema. Exemplified by *chāyīxiēr bù* in (1), the schema can be characterised by the paraphrase 'almost did something adverse' and the form [ADVERB (NEG) VP] in which the negator slot, filled by *bù* in (1), actually does not negate the truth value of the proposition.[1]

(1)   争些兒不殺了一個人
      zhēngxiēr bù   shā le   yī   gē   rén
      AA   NEG kill PFV one CLF person
      'almost killed someone.'   張協狀元 *Zhāngxié zhuàngyuán* (late 13th c.)

Building on Goldberg's (2006) proposal that the most prototypical member of a schema motivates the formal and functional composition of the schema, this paper proposes that it can be extended to obsolescence as well: schema loss can be related to change in prototypicality. Using the adverse avertive schema as an example, it is shown that its older prototypical members motivated it, but newer ones demotivated it, leading to schema loss, because the newer ones had a different lexical origin and pragmatics.

This paper is organised as follows. Section 2 defines the scope of investigation as schema loss. Section 3 discusses construction grammar and prototypicality. Section 4 introduces the adverse avertive schema and describes its history. Section 5 analyses its loss in terms of change in prototypicality. Section 6 briefly compares this case study to loss-related processes such as 'renewal', 'degeneracy' and 'exaptation'. Section 7 concludes.

2.   Constructions and loss characterised

Section 2.1 characterises the concept of 'construction' in construction grammar and Section 2.2 defines loss as schema loss.

2.1   Constructions

Constructions in construction grammar as conceived by Goldberg have been defined differently in her key publications (1995, 2006, 2019). The constant over the years is that constructions are mental entities that combine both conventionalised linguistic form and meaning. The original 1995 definition requires there

---

1.   Abbreviations: 1SG= 1st person singular, 3SG= 3rd person singular, AA= adverse avertive adverb, CLF= classifier, CONJ= conjunctive, NEG= negation, PFV= perfective, POSS= possessive, PRS= present, PTCL= particle, REFL= reflexive

to be non-compositionality: "C is a CONSTRUCTION iff$_{def}$ C is a form-meaning pair < F$_i$, S$_i$> such that some aspect of F$_i$ or some aspect of S$_i$ is not strictly predictable from C's component parts or from other previously established constructions" (Goldberg 1995: 4), where F and S stand for form and sense/meaning. Subsequently this definition has been relaxed, but the most restricted, 1995 definition will be used in this study.

Construction grammar proposes that users form generalisations over specific expressions at different levels of 'schematicity' and associations between them, thus creating a network of interrelated constructions. For example, Goldberg (1995, 2006) has shown that users have an abstract mental representation of the ditransitive, which has the schematic meaning of [X causes Y to receive Z] and form of [Subj V Obj$_1$ Obj$_2$]. Depending on the verb in the V slot, the meaning of the ditransitive may be an extension of the schematic meaning (e.g., a ditransitive construction with a verb of refusal, i.e., *refuse/deny someone something*, means 'cause someone not to receive something'). Schematicity is a gradient concept (Langacker 1987): under a schematic, high-level construction, we can also posit lower-level constructions that are less schematic, or more substantive; that is, constructions whose form and meaning are more specified (e.g., [Subj *deny* Obj$_1$ Obj$_2$] is more substantive than [Subj V Obj$_1$ Obj$_2$]).

2.2   Loss as schema loss

As construction grammar focuses on both form and meaning, when it comes to loss, attention can be paid to both formal and functional sides. Given this principle, loss can be approached from various perspectives, as it may occur at multiple levels of schematicity and to multiple members and/or aspects of a construction. For example, Kranich (this volume) shows that members of the *may* modal construction (particularly *we + may + verb of saying/reasoning*) decline at different rates. Some studies have highlighted that declining constructions are often restricted to particular genres and/or social niches (Traugott & Trousdale 2013: 67–68; Hundt 2014; see also Hundt, Kempf, Kranich and Schweinberger, this volume). That is, fine-grained functional aspects of a construction may be restructured during loss.

The kind of loss under investigation is defined here as schema loss, which is found in cases where higher-level generalisations about lower-level form-meaning pairings are lost. More specifically, this study investigates the loss of the adverse avertive schema, i.e., the pattern [ADVERB (NEG) VP] that means roughly 'almost did something adverse'. The specific functional properties of its members, except for their pragmatics, do not figure as prominently here as in other construction-based studies (nevertheless, this should not be taken to downplay the importance of fine-grained functional properties; see Kranich, this volume).

Focusing on schemas (as opposed to individual, more substantive constructions) has some advantages. First, it does not oblige us to explain idiomatic expressions that are instances of previously productive schemas. For example, *methinks* is a relic of the English impersonal (for a constructional account, see Trousdale 2008; Čermák this volume). Despite its obvious (for historical linguists) connection with the impersonal schema, there is no productive impersonal schema sanctioning it now. Therefore, we need not concern ourselves with the synchronic status of 'relics' like *methinks*, if our focus is on schema loss. Second, because schemas are built on lower-level constructions and users' experience with language, focusing on schemas requires us to keep track of what happens under a schema during loss as well (e.g., what members of the schema and their tokens of use are undergoing). This allows us to recognise that there may be different processes of change at different levels. For example, members of a schema may develop into new constructions, while the schema itself is undergoing loss, as this study will show.[2] It has been observed that loss and gain are often intertwined, in terms of meaning: Smirnova (2015a, b) sees the expansion of a new construction into new contexts as 'loss of contextual constraints', and loss of lexical meaning, or 'bleaching', can lead to growth of grammatical meaning (Sweetser 1988; Brems 2011; Traugott & Trousdale 2013). This study therefore suggests that loss and gain may also be interrelated in terms of form-meaning pairings.

3.   Prototypicality, construction grammar and diachronic construction grammar

Categorisation in Prototype Theory is not absolute, but graded: organised around the 'prototype', members of a category can be more or less representative of the category. Their frequency of use tends to differ, too: what is more prototypical tends to be more frequent. This is true not only in conceptual categories represented by substantive items such as *furniture* and *bird*, but also schematic grammatical patterns (e.g., Langacker 1987; Geeraerts 2006; Goldberg 2006). The section reviews and generalises the relationship between a schema and the most prototypical member that instantiates it, as discussed in Goldberg (2006: Ch. 4) regarding argument structure constructions (ASCs).

---

2.   A parallel can be found in Smirnova (2015a), who shows that *würde* 'would' + *infinitive* in German was originally a member of the construction *werden* 'become' + *infinitive*, but *würde* + *infinitive* developed into a construction on its own and *werden* + *infinitive* underwent further change.

Section 3.1 introduces Goldberg's proposal that the most prototypical member of an ASC guides users' acquisition. Section 3.2 extends the idea to adjunct constructions in diachrony and describes 'the most prototypical member' as 'constructional meaning supplier': the member that scaffolds the learning of the schema and upholds its composition. Section 3.3 introduces basic notions in diachronic construction grammar.

3.1 Prototypicality in ASCs

Goldberg (2006: Ch. 4) notes that in child-directed speech, there is only one verb that is highly frequent in each of the ASCs listed below. She describes such verbs as 'general-purpose'. For example, *go* in the intransitive motion, *put* in the caused motion, *give* in the ditransitive are much more frequent than any other verbs. Table 1, adopted from Goldberg (2006: Tables 4.1 and 4.3), outlines the form and meaning of each construction and general-purpose verb.

Table 1. General-purpose verbs and their respective constructions' forms and meanings

verb	construction label	form	meaning
go	Intransitive motion	Subj V Obl$_{path/loc}$	X moves Y$_{path/loc}$
put	Caused motion	Subj V Obj Obl$_{path/loc}$	X causes Y to move Z$_{path/loc}$
give	Ditransitive	Subj V Obj Obj$_2$	X causes Y to receive Z

Goldberg proposes that in acquisition, "patterns are learned on the basis of generalizing over particular instances" (2016: 79) and that general-purpose verbs are what children generalise over to learn ASCs. Goldberg draws her explanations from Prototype Theory. General-purpose verbs are prototypes in their respective ASCs: quantitatively they are the most frequent and qualitatively their properties correspond to ASCs to such an extent that they can help predict and acquire ASCs' form and meaning.[3]

The proposal that general-purpose verbs encode, or at least correlate with ASCs' form and meaning has also been made independently (see Casenheiser & Goldberg 2005; Goldberg 2006 for reviews). For example, Goldberg's (1995) analysis of the ditransitive relies on *give*. Just like *give*'s semantics, the ditransitive prototypically means 'agent successfully causes recipient to receive patient'. Other ditransitive patterns are analysed as extensions from this prototypical sense. For example, verbs of future transfer in the ditransitive mean 'agent acts to cause

---

3.　ASCs are less likely to help predict and acquire general-purpose verbs, as child language acquisition is item-based (Goldberg 2006: Chapter 3).

recipient to receive patient at some future point in time', as in *leave someone something* (see Goldberg 2006: Ch. 2).

Goldberg et. al (2004) and Casenheiser and Goldberg (2005) further demonstrate the role of prototypes in schema-learning with experimental results. If a schema in an artificial language had a prototypical organisation in terms of frequency like the ASCs, learning was more successful. That is, if there was one particularly frequent member in a schema, it was easier to learn than a condition where members were more or less equally frequent. These results align with literature on non-linguistic categorisation: category learning is more successful if frequency of input is skewed around a particular instance, i.e., the prototype (general-purpose verbs, in the case of ASCs).[4] The cognitive explanation for the connection between prototypicality and learning is that prototypes provide 'cognitive anchoring': they serve as a reference point that guides learning because they are the most frequent and representative (Goldberg 2006: 89).

In sum, general-purpose verbs are prototypes in their respective ASCs and play an important role in acquisition because children learn ASCs by generalising over tokens of general-purpose verbs: they help predict ASCs' form and meaning by providing cognitive anchoring. Section 3.2 generalises this relationship between general-purpose verbs and ASCs to adverbs and adjunct constructions in diachrony.

3.2   Extending prototypicality in ASCs

Goldberg (2006: 89) notes "in the case of other constructions, relevant skewing of the input could be around a noun, adjective, or complementiser". That is, a prototypical organisation could be found within non-ASC constructions. It is thus not controversial to extend the findings regarding ASCs to adjunct constructions such as the adverse avertive, with the following caveats.

First, in order to generalise the notion of 'general-purpose verb', 'the most prototypical member of a schema' will be used, or more succinctly, 'constructional meaning supplier'. Since users build up schemas around their respective prototypes, in a way prototypes supply schemas with meaning, just like how an ASC's meaning can be 'read off' from its general-purpose verb because the latter is the basis of generalisation for the former (e.g., the ditransitive's meaning of 'cause to receive' is read off from *give*, and the caused motion's 'cause to move' from *put*). Second, as frequency strongly correlates with prototypicality, in the absence of

---

4.   Frequency is not the only factor that determines prototypicality, despite "a strong correlation between the frequency with which a token occurs and the likelihood it will be considered a prototype by the learner" (Goldberg 2006: 85). Meaning plays a role too (Geeraerts 2006).

native speakers to consult, frequency can be used inferentially as a (partial) indicator of prototypicality in diachronic studies. This makes the prediction that whichever member is the most frequent is the prototype and thus supplies the schema with meaning. The decision to use frequency as a proxy for prototypicality risks putting the cart before the horse: something could be the most frequent *because* it is the most prototypical, not the other way around (see also Geeraerts 2006: Chapter 2.5). However, frequency will not be the sole measure; functional evidence will also be used to determine prototypicality.

This study will show that the demise of the adverse avertive schema, an adjunct schema with an adverbial function, is related to change in constructional meaning supply. While older suppliers' meaning motivated the schema's form and meaning, newer ones could not, as they did not have a comparable meaning supply that could sustain the survival of the schema.

3.3   Diachronic construction grammar

Three heuristic labels for different levels of generalisation are proposed by Traugott and Trousdale (2013) in their constructional framework: 'micro-construction', 'subschema', and 'schema', while 'construct' refer to utterances produced in actual usage events. These labels are also adopted here.

Unlike traditional grammaticalisation studies with a 'monostratal' or 'linear' view on language (see Fischer 2018; Traugott 2018), diachronic construction grammar, particularly Traugott and Trousdale (2013), has recognised three gradient concepts relevant to the multidimensional nature of change: schematicity, compositionality and productivity. Schematicity and compositionality have already been introduced above, while productivity can be determined by type and/or token frequency (see also Hilpert 2015; Barðdal & Gildea 2015). According to Traugott and Trousdale (2013), in 'constructionalisation', the creation of new constructions, schematicity and productivity increase while compositionality decreases. Increases in schematicity and productivity can be interrelated because increases in token frequency may allow generalisation to happen, leading to increases in type frequency and schematicity.[5] Compositionality decreases in constructionalisation

---

5.   However, as with prototypicality (footnote 4), frequency does not always uniquely predict productivity or schematicity. Goldberg (2019) shows that semantic and phonological variability between members of a construction interacts with its productivity in various ways. For example, a construction with low variability and high type frequency is less productive than one with high variability and low type frequency. See Barðdal and Gildea (2015) for a related concept, coherence, "the internal consistency found between members of a construction", which also predicts productivity.

because new patterns, being 'new', are not 'fully' predictable from pre-existing constructions. During schema loss, schematicity and productivity decrease by definition: a schema becomes less general and sanctions fewer constructs. Compositionality also decreases because the connections between the schema and its component part(s) or other schemas grow opaque and the obsolescent schema becomes more and more isolated.

There has been growing interest in 'horizontal links' in diachronic construction grammar (Traugott 2016, 2018); that is, 'sibling' constructions on the same level of schematicity. Previously, vertical links, or 'parent' constructions were typically the main focus, such as how the ditransitive schema motivates micro-constructions such as *deny* or *leave someone something*, but not how ditransitive *deny* or *leave* are related. However, as Traugott (2018) points out, horizontal links can enrich our understanding of the network of constructions. For example, Van de Velde (2014) also demonstrates how they can shed light on change: one of the two horizontally-linked constructions may take over the function of the other when it goes through obsolescence. The adverse avertive schema has several sub-schemas, horizontally linked to each other. However, rather than 'supporting' the declining members, the surviving one in the adverse avertive schema might be described as encroaching on its own siblings and in the process, obliterating the schema. That is, competition emerged from within the schema, which ultimately affected the schema's organisation and broke it up, to be detailed in Sections 4–5.

4.   The adverse avertive schema in Chinese

Section 4.1 starts with a brief discussion of data sources. Sections 4.2–4.3 describe the whole schema and its component parts. As a long history is involved, Sections 4.2–4.3 are necessarily an idealised 'snapshot' description of the schema.

4.1   Data sources

The following description drew most of its data from two corpora: the Center for Chinese Linguistics (CCL) Corpus at Peking University and the Academia Sinica (AS) Corpus of Modern Chinese. The CCL Corpus contains data from most periods of written Chinese, while the AS Corpus represents Present-Day Chinese (PDC). The two corpora use different styles of characters; all characters used in this study have been converted into Traditional Chinees characters.

The CCL Corpus is not tagged. All queries in it have been manually examined and counted. Its periodisation is dynasty-based; therefore, each subsection is labelled with only dynasty names, but not precise dates. The subsections utilised include all the dynasties from the *Yuán* Dynasty (1271–1368) to the Republic of China (ROC) Era, established in 1912. Data from the ROC Era are subdivided into two periods: *Mínguó* (lit. 'republic') and *Xiàndài* (lit. 'modern'). The corpus does not specify when the former ends or the latter begins, but that the latter includes data from before 1949 (when the communist People's Republic of China was established and ousted the ROC). In this study, the corpus' periodisation is retained, but the two ROC periods will be referred to as 'Early Republic' and 'Pre-1949 Republic'. Specific dates, if available, will be provided with each example. As the *Yuán* Dynasty subsection is much smaller than the other subsections, data from a genre subsection, *Yuánqǔ*, a genre specific to the *Yuán* Dynasty, were also included.[6]

The AS Corpus is tagged and divided into genres, topics, text types, etc. It was chosen over the CCL Corpus to represent PDC because the latter's PDC section (labelled *Dāngdài*, 'contemporary') has a lot of 'noise': sampling errors, repetitions and even linguistic essays that analyse the adverse avertive. There is a gap in coverage between the AS Corpus and the Pre-1949 Republic section of the CCL Corpus: the former contains only data from 1981 to 2007. However, choosing the CCL Corpus for PDC would not solve this issue. Apart from the noise, the CCL Corpus's PDC section provides no specific dates that assure us of the temporal continuity between its pre-1949 and PDC sections. Instead of combing through the CCL's PDC section yet still struggling to properly reconstruct the post-1949 history of the adverse avertive, continuity between the Pre-1949 Republic section and the AS Corpus has been assumed.

4.2 Overview of the schema

The adverse avertive schema is an adjunct construction with an adverbial function and the following form: [ADVERB (NEG) VP]. The ADVERB slot is typically filled by items of verbal or adjectival origins, while the optional NEG slot is filled by negators. The semantic function of the NEG slot is 'expletive' (or 'pleonastic') in the sense that the negator in it does not negate the truth value of the proposition denoted by the VP, even though outside the schema the negator typically does. The meaning of the schema can be paraphrased as 'almost did something adverse', or 'something adverse almost happened', and decomposed into four functional features: pastness, imminence, counterfactuality, and adversity. A construct of the schema with a filled NEG slot is (1), reproduced as (2):

6.　The number of characters in each section: 961,884 in *Yuán*, 21,038,301 in *Míng*, 48,109,077 in *Qīng*, 35,371,339 in Early Republic and 15,250,163 in Pre-1949 Republic. Data from *Yuánqǔ* and *Yuán* have a combined total of 6,713,739.

(2) 爭些兒不殺了一個人

　　zhēngxiēr bù   shā   le   yī   gē   rén
　　AA   NEG   kill   PFV   one CLF   person
　　'almost killed someone.'   張協狀元 *Zhāngxié zhuàngyuán* (late 13th c.)

The schema is not compositional in that items filling in the ADVERB or NEG slot do not fully predict the form or meaning of the schema. That is, the schema's four functional features (pastness, imminence, counterfactuality, and adversity) and expletive negation cannot be fully attributed to the individual parts that make up the schema, qualifying it as a construction in Goldberg's (1995) sense.

The first three descriptive functional features, pastness, imminence and counterfactuality, are inspired by Kuteva (2001), while adversity is inspired by Heine and Miyashita (2008). Kuteva (2001) assigns the label 'avertive' to a crosslinguistic category that describes a 'past' action that was about to happen ('imminence'), but did not ('counterfactuality'). For example, Bulgarian expresses it using the construction [*štjax + da* + V].[7]

(3) Šteše   da   se   poreže
　　want.3SG.IPFV   CONJ.PTCL REFL   cut.3SG.PRS
　　'She/he nearly cut her/himself.'   Kuteva (2001: 88)

The label 'adverse' is used by Heine and Miyashita (2008) to describe 'threaten' verbs that are similar functionally in various European languages. The precise characterisation of such verbs varies, on which there has been much research (see Heine & Miyashita 2008 for a review). For Traugott, *threaten* in English is epistemic and expresses that "the speaker views the proposition as likely, and evaluates it negatively" (1993: 350):

(4) I am sometimes frightened with the dangers that threaten to diminish it.
                                                    (c 1780; Traugott 1993: 350)

However, for Heine and Miyashita (2008), such verbs signal the proximative aspect (e.g., 'be about to' or 'imminence' in Kuteva's terminology) and adversity, so that they can be paraphrased as "something undesirable is about to happen" (2008: 56).

(5) Mein Mann   droht   krank zu warden
　　my   husband   threatens   sick   to become
　　'My husband threatens falling ill.'   (Heine & Miyashita 2008: 56)

The adverse avertive in Chinese resembles both the avertive and *threaten*-verbs in that it describes an imminent, past action that would have negatively affected

---

7. The avertive can be found in several languages, French *avoir failli* + *infinitive* being one of them (see Kuteva 2001: 78–85 for a survey).

someone, typically participant(s) of the action, the topic or speaker, but did not. A close English equivalent might be *was/were in danger of Ving*. For example, (2) shows that the subject would have been negatively affected by (unintentionally) committing homicide, or the object 'someone' would have been killed, while (6) shows that the topic *Sītúlǎng*, not the subject *yǎnlèi* 'tear(s)', would have been negatively affected (the distinction between 'topic' and 'subject' follows that of Li & Thompson 1981).

(6) 司徒朗一回頭看了看賀豹，眼淚差點流下來

Sītúlǎng yī   huí   tóu   kàn le   kàn
Sītúlǎng as.soon.as turn head look PFV   look

Hèbào, yǎnlèi chādiǎn liú   xiàlái
Hèbào tear   AA   drip   down

'As soon as *Sītúlǎng* turned around to take a look at *Hèbào*, his tears almost fell down.'   雍正劍俠圖 *Yōngzhèng jiànxiá tú* (ca. 1928–1943)

Given the Principle of No Synonymy (Goldberg 1995: 67), the schema's two variants [ADVERB VP] and [ADVERB NEG VP] are expected to differ semantically or pragmatically. Drawing on crosslinguistic data, Ziegeler (2016: 19) hypothesises that expletive negation in expressions similar to the adverse avertive is 'intersubjective' in that it signals that "the speaker is aware of the emotional impact on the addressee of uttering a statement about closeness to misfortune". Following her hypothesis, [ADVERB NEG VP] is taken to be pragmatically different from [ADVERB VP] in being more intersubjective.

The existence of [ADVERB NEG VP] does not prohibit [ADVERB VP] from combining with a canonical negator. Therefore, (7) is also grammatical and instantiates the schema as well— the negator does not instantiate the NEG slot within the schema, but the canonical negation pattern within which the negator actually negates. This can be contrasted with (2) or (8), where the negator is expletive.

(7) 我姓名險些不保

wǒ   xìngmìng xiǎnxiē bù   bǎo
1SG   life   AA   NEG   keep

'I almost did not retain my life (I almost lost it)'

三國志平話 *Sānguózhì pínghuà* (c. 1320)

(8) 險些兒不送了楊謝祖的性命

xiǎnxiēr bu song le   Yáng Xièzǐ di   xìngmìng
AA   EN cost PFV Yáng Xièzǐ POSS life

'It almost cost *Yáng Xièzǔ*'s life.'   by 王仲文 *Wáng Zhòngwén* (1273–1347)

Given a filled ADVERB slot, the sequence 'negator + VP' may be ambiguous in that the negator can be either expletive or canonical. As many researchers have pointed out since Zhu (1959), adversity constrains the interpretation of negation (see Li 1976; Peyraube 1979; Biq 1989). Because the sequence 'negator + VP' must be adverse, the negator is expletive if VP conveys adversity, e.g., 'cost *Yáng Xièzǔ*'s life' in (8). The negator is canonical if VP alone conveys no adversity, e.g., *bǎo (xìngmìng)* 'keep (one's life)' in (7), because logically a non-adverse VP would be adverse when negated (see Kuo 2016b for a review).

4.3   Slots in the schema

Only a few kinds of items occur in the ADVERB slot in the schema, such as *wéi, xiǎnxiē, zhēngxiē, chādiǎn*, most of which can be used as adjectival or verbal predicates outside the schema. Items in the ADVERB slot can be categorised into two subtypes, 'danger' and 'proximity' adverbs, based on their lexical origins. The 'danger' subtype includes *wéi* and *xiǎnxiē*, as *wéi* and *xiǎn* literally mean 'danger; dangerous; threaten', while the 'proximity' subtype contains *zhēngxiē* and *chādiǎn*, as they literally mean 'come close to; differ little from' (Shuai 2014; for a detailed description, see Kuo 2016b).

Wéi is the oldest item in the slot and not contemporaneous with the youngest items *zhēngxiē*, and *xiǎnxiē* (for more precising dating, see Kuo 2016b). As far as the corpora show, *wéi* has no variant form. For example,

(9)   五聘絕域危不脫

    wǔ   pìn   juéyù   wēi bù   tuō

    five serve.as.envoy remote.place AA NEG escape

    'He served as an envoy in far-flung places five times. He almost could not escape.'

                                           新唐書 *Xīntángshū* (1060)

Xiǎnxiē's and *chādiǎn*'s variants vary on the basis of what degree modifiers follow *xiǎn* and *chā*, but *xiǎn* alone can also appear in the ADVERB slot. The modifiers, meaning 'slightly; a bit', are *(yī)xiē* and *(yī)diǎn*, both of which can take the diminutive suffix –*r*, while only *(yī)xiē* may take a general classifier *ge* 'one counting unit' that functions like a diminutive suffix. *Xiē* in *zhēngxiē* is the same modifier as *(yī)xiē*. Even though taking no *yī*, *zhēngxiē* takes –*r* or *ge* optionally. The degree modifiers, –*r* and *ge* do not drastically alter the meaning; they emphasise the 'imminence' meaning component, signalling that the event 'nearly' happened. Following are two examples, *chāyīxiēr* and *xiǎnyīdiǎnr*, a paraphrase of which may be 'came *this* close to…':

(10)   差一些兒不曾壓死

     chāyīxiēr bù   céng yā   sǐ

     AA   not   ever   crush die

     'almost crushed (her) to death.'

                    醒世姻緣傳 *Xǐngshì yīnyuán zhuàn* (mid–late 17th c.)

(11) 險一點兒喊出來
xiǎnyīdiǎnr hǎn chūlái
AA shout out
'almost shouted out.' 雍正劍俠圖 *Yōngzhèng jiànxiá tú* (ca. 1928–1943)

Exactly how these degree modifiers, –*r* and *ge* became part of the adverbs and differences between the variants lie outside our focus.[8] The variants will be described as 'micro-constructions' of the adverse avertive schema, while the labels *xiǎnxiē*, *zhēngxiē* and *chādiǎn*, corresponding to the most frequent variants, represent 'subschemas', i.e., abstractions over micro-constructions. The following table summarises the subschemas and micro-constructions attested in the corpora (there is no *wéi* subschema, as there is no level of abstraction above that of the *wéi* micro-construction).

Table 2. The adverse avertive subschemas and micro-constructions

subschema	lexical meaning	micro-construction(s)
xiǎnxiē	'danger; dangerous; threaten'	*wéi*
		xiǎn, xiǎnxiē, xiǎnxiēr, xiǎnxiēge, xiǎnyīxiē, xiǎnyīxiēr, xiǎnyīdiǎn, xiǎnyīdiǎnr
zhēngxiē	'come close to; differ little from'	*zhēngxiē, zhēngxiēr, zhēngxiēge*
chādiǎn		*chādiǎn, chādiǎnr, chāyīdiǎn, chāyīdiǎnr, chāyīxiēr*

The two lexical meanings, 'danger' and 'proximity', represent two alternative ways of expressing the adverse avertive meaning. *Wéi* and *xiǎnxiē* focus on the event as something *dangerous* (similar to *be in danger of Ving*), while *zhēngxiē* and *chādiǎn* construe it as something *close* to happening (similar to *be on the verge of/close to Ving*). The three schemas may be viewed as horizontally linked to each other because they are on the same level of schematicity (see Section 3.3): below the level of the schema, they represent the three most schematic abstractions of formal and functional properties (*wéi* is not contemporaneous with the three subschemas; therefore it is not considered in detail here).

Negators that can fill the NEG slot are, in chronological order: *bù* 'not', *bù céng* 'not ever', *méi* and *méiyǒu* 'have not'. Of all the negators, *méi* and *méiyǒu* are the 'best fit' for the schema. The event referred to by the schema is typically associated with perfectivity: being on the verge of doing something adverse entails a certain

---

8. See Kuo's (2016b) account of the adverse avertive's history, Kuo (2018) for degree modifiers *dian* and *xie*, and Kuo (2020) for a brief discussion of *xie + ge*.

endpoint beyond which something adverse will be done. *Méi* and *méiyǒu* typically negate perfective predicates (i.e., they deny more specifically the endpoint of an event), so they are more compatible with the schema semantically. On the other hand, *bù* typically denies imperfective predicates and may be vague with respect to the completion of an event (Li & Thompson 1981: Chapter 12); therefore, it is less compatible with the schema (for more on incompatibility between adverse avertive expressions and *bù* in PDC, see Ziegeler 2006: 191). When *bù* in the schema was first attested (ca. 7th c.; see 12), *méi* and *méiyǒu* had not begun being used as negators; according to Xu (2003) they entered the standard negation system in the 13th century. However, even after *méi* and *méiyǒu* became widely used, the NEG slot still retained the possibility of being filled by *bù* and *bù céng* (Shuai 2014; Kuo 2016b). This again indicates the schema's non-compositionality and the fact that users must have had an independent mental representation of the schema: the schema did not immediately respond to wider systematic change in negation by incorporating the negators that are in hindsight, the 'best fit'.[9]

Possible functional nuances have been overlooked here (e.g., genre-specific or dialectal preferences, discourse properties, etc). One might ask how the micro-constructions differ from each other functionally, or whether they prefer any particular negator and why. Unfortunately, these questions cannot be addressed for reasons of space. As outlined in Section 2, the focus is on schema loss (i.e., the loss of [ADVERB (NEG) VP]), and it is proposed here that to provide one possible interpretation of the schema's obsolescence, we can look at subschemas such as *xiǎnxiē*, *zhēngxiē*, and *chādiǎn* and their semantics and pragmatics, which abstract over functional nuances in micro-constructions (nevertheless, this approach does not rule out alternative interpretations).

5.   The demise of the adverse avertive schema

The schema has been lost in PDC. Section 5.1 considers qualitative criteria. Section 5.2 focuses on reduction in frequency. Section 5.3 proposes that the demise of the schema can be related to the change in 'prototypicality', or 'constructional meaning supply'—the older supplier, *xiǎnxiē*, was a good match with the schema's form and meaning, while the new one, *chādiǎn*, was not, in terms of semantics and pragmatics. Therefore, it was unable to maintain the schema's composition properly. Section 5.4 summarises by visualising the process.

---

9.   See Jiang (2008) for expletive negation in Chinese, including the adverse avertive, or Kuo (2016b) for a review.

5.1 Qualitative aspects

The schema's schematicity has reduced to almost nil: *chādiǎn* is arguably the sole surviving 'descendant' (not 'member') of the schema. The function of expletive negation in the schema has also become so opaque in PDC that it has inspired quite some discussion (Kuo 2016b), i.e., its compositionality has decreased. Section 5.2 discusses productivity in more detail.

As described in Section 4.2, the status of the negator can be distinguished by whether the following VP is adverse or not. However, this distinction only holds diachronically. Biq (1989) demonstrates with the following two examples that no adversity is necessarily associated with the adverse avertive synchronically.

(12)   tā   gāoxìngde chāyīdiǎn méi bǎ tā   mǔqīn bào qǐlái
        3SG happily   AA   EN BA 3SG mother hug up
        'He was so happy that he almost lifted his mother up'

(13)   chāyīdiǎn méi gēn tā wò   shǒu
        AA   EN with 3SG shake hand
        '(I) almost shook hands with her (Princess Diana)'
                                          abridged from Biq (1989: 79)

Furthermore, Zhou (2003) shows that the sequence *chādiǎn + méi(yǒu)* is inherently ambiguous: in PDC *méi(yǒu)* can be either an expletive or canonical negator, regardless of the following VP. This suggests that PDC no longer has the adverse avertive schema. While the adversity feature previously constrained the interpretation of the negator (see 7 and 8), its loss creates ambiguity in the PDC sequence *chādiǎn + méi(yǒu)*.

Kuo (2016a) proposes that (12) and (13) are possible in PDC because, first, the adversity feature has been lost due to bleaching, and second, *chādiǎn + méi(yǒu)* have fused together (but *chādiǎn* remains a possible variant). This bleaching is also a case of generalisation, whereby the number of characteristic features that constrain a construction's functional range is reduced.[10] The fusion, or boundary loss, is a kind of decrease in compositionality (cf. *a lot of* > *a lotta*; Traugott & Trousdale 2013). Kuo's evidence comes from the fact that *chādiǎn* tended to be used hyperbolically in Pre-PDC (63% of the time), downplaying the adversity feature with its 'tongue-in-cheek' contextual meaning, and *chādiǎn + méi(yǒu)* co-occurred more frequently (51%, cf. *xiǎnxiē + méi(yǒu)*'s 7%), encouraging them to fuse into *chādiǎnméi(yǒu)*. Examples where *chādiǎn + méi(yǒu)* was used

---

10.   This bleaching/generalisation of adversity widens the range of *chādian*'s pragmatic contexts. There are thus both loss and gain (Sweetser 1988; Brems 2011).

hyperbolically typically modify extreme events involving 'death' (48%) and 'physical harm' (15%).[11]

The loss of adversity is not unique. The Chinese passive *bèi* was used only when adversity was involved, but this constraint has been lifted (e.g., Chao 1968; see Chappell 1986 for different views). The comparable *threaten*-verb in Spanish, *amenazar*, has also shown signs of 'bleaching': Cornillie (2004: 27) observes that it "may also defocus the evaluation dimension" (i.e., the adversity meaning). For example,

(14)   … una tenue brisa amenazaba con convertirse en un viento más ligero
       'a persistent breeze threatened to become a lighter wind.' (Cornillie 2004: 28)

Looking into the wider context of (14), he notes that in the example "two birds are swimming in a strong stream; in the background a breeze is about to change to a lighter wind, which cannot be viewed as negative" (Cornillie 2004: 28).

Henceforth, with respect to their synchronic statuses, *chādiǎn* and *chādiǎnméi(yǒu)* will be referred to as *chādiǎnméi(yǒu)*, while *chādiǎn* is used to label the pre-PDC adverse avertive subschema. *Chādiǎnméi(yǒu)* is not an instance of the adverse avertive schema, as neither its adversity feature nor the NEG slot has survived in it. *Chādiǎnméi(yǒu)* is a new construction, more general than *chādiǎn* (as *chādiǎnméi(yǒu)* need not be associated with adversity). Note that this may evoke the Sorites Paradox: how many grains of sand have to be removed from a heap before it is no longer a heap? Or, how different does a construction have to be in order to be considered as a dead (or new) construction?[12] This study's position is that the adversity feature no longer characterises *chādiǎnméi(yǒu)* and its NEG slot is non-existent— *méi(yǒu)* in *chādiǎnméi(yǒu)* is fixed and fused— so it has form and meaning different from its ancestor *chādiǎn*, despite shared genealogy. It is also 'extended grammaticalisation' in Breban's (2015) terms: the structural relation between *chādiǎnméi(yǒu)* and other linguistic units remains the same; it is still adverbial and preverbal, but not as pragmatically constrained/specialised as *chādiǎn*.

---

11.   Kuo (2016a) only collects data from the *Yuán* Dynasty to the Early Republic Era (labelled 'Premodern Chinese'). He only counts *chā(yī)dian(r)*, but not any other variants, which is justified partially by the fact that *chā(yī)dian(r)* is the most frequent by far.

12.   This is a general issue about change: it can be difficult to determine precisely when one thing ends and another begins. Börjars et al. (2015) and Hilpert (2015) raise the Sorites Paradox with respect to Traugott and Trousdale's (2013) distinction between constructionalisation and constructional change. See also Joseph (2014) for 'counting' grammaticalisation and Breban and Kranich (2015) for 'secondary grammaticalisation'.

5.2   Quantitative aspects

Type productivity of the schema has been severely reduced: neither *wéi* nor *zhēngxiē* exists in PDC. In the AS Corpus, all 24 instances of the subschema *xiǎnxiē* are confined to written language, none of which occurs with any negator, expletive or canonical. This also suggests that the NEG slot and the schema have become defunct. Users presumably do not have a mental representation of the schema; they might not even recognise *chādiǎnméi(yǒu)* and *xiǎnxiē* as related. *Xiǎnxiē* therefore resembles *methinks* in that both are historical relics from previously productive schemas. Productivity at a lower level has also reduced: while there was a wide range of micro-constructions (see Table 2), in PDC only *chā(yī)diǎn(r)* is attested while there are 23 constructs of *xiǎnxiē* and one of *xiǎndiǎn*.

To describe the overall trajectory, Figure 1 visualises the frequency of the schema, represented by the subschemas *xiǎnxiē*, *zhēngxiē* and *chādiǎn* from the *Yuán* Dynasty (1271–1368) to the Republic Era (1911–1949) in the CCL Corpus. *Wéi* was rare by *Yuán*, so it is not included in any frequency count here.

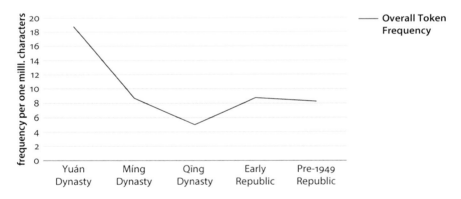

Figure 1. Relativised token frequency of the schema per one million characters

Figure 1 is puzzling: it looks like the schema has not plunged to its death, but rose and plateaued after the *Qīng* Dynasty. However, if we look at the individual subschemas, a different story emerges. Figure 2 represents the frequency of each subschema making up Figure 1.

Figure 2 shows that *zhēngxiē* flat-lined after the *Míng* Dynasty, *xiǎnxiē* has been nowhere near its peak, and *chādiǎn* started gaining ground on *xiǎnxiē* after the *Qīng* Dynasty and has been rising. The 'plateau' in Figure 1 could be attributed to *chādiǎn's* rise. Figure 2 also reveals an important fact: before *chādiǎn* 'usurped' the unique status of being the most frequent schema member, *xiǎnxiē* was the most frequent one. This begs the question: 'what kind of impact did it have on the schema'?

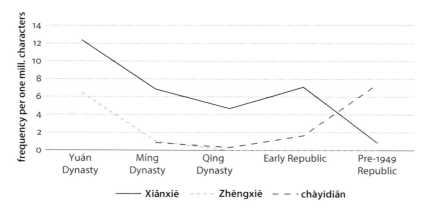

Figure 2. Relativised frequency of the adverbs per one million characters

Additionally, even though by PDC the schema has become obsolete, *chādiǎn*'s descendant in PDC, *chādiǎnméi(yǒu)* is thriving, as Figure 3 shows:

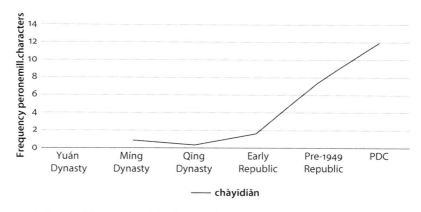

Figure 3. Relativised frequency of *chādiǎn/chādiǎnméi(yǒu)* per one million characters

Figure 3 poses the question 'why does *chādiǎn/chādiǎnméi(yǒu)* seem to have an overall upward trajectory while in PDC its form and function warrants a different constructional status and the schema is obsolete'? Section 5.3 attempts to provide some answers.

5.3   The demise of the schema: from 'danger' to 'proximity'

In Section 4.3 the adverbs in the schema are categorised into two subtypes on the basis of their original semantics: *wéi* and *xiǎnxiē* are the 'danger' subtype and *zhēngxiē* and *chādiǎn* are the 'proximity' subtype. Building on the role that the most prototypical member plays in a schema (Section 3.2), this section proposes that the erosion of the schema can be related to its change in 'prototypicality' or 'constructional meaning supply', from 'danger' to 'proximity', as the former motivated the schema but the latter demotivated it.

The 'danger' subtype has a natural association with the schema. *Wéi*, literally 'danger; dangerous; threaten', established the schema and *xiǎnxiē*, with a similar semantics, emerged after *wéi*. In terms of meaning, *wéi* and *xiǎnxiē*, like *threaten*-verbs, encode adversity, which is directly related to their original lexical semantics. In terms of form, the crosslinguistic use of expletive negation in proximative expressions has been hypothesised to be motivated by adversity as well, such as in Spanish, Portuguese, Bulgarian and Polish (see Ziegeler 2016 for an overview). That is, the form and meaning of the schema are motivated by the lexical semantics of *wéi* and *xiǎnxiē* because it encodes notions of 'danger'. They are good 'cognitive anchors' that guide users to learn the schema.

The original semantics of the 'proximity' subtype such as *zhēngxiē* and *chādiǎn*, 'come close to; differ little from', however, is not directly related to 'danger' and does not 'cue' the form and function of the schema as easily. That is, the lexical source of the 'proximity' subtype is not a good fit, but more opaque with respect to the schema, whereas the schema's meaning could be easily 'read off' from the 'danger' subtype, which also motivates its formal feature of expletive negation.[13]

Therefore, hearing a 'danger' adverb construct may strengthen the mental representation of the schema or prime the schema, as 'danger' has a strong association with it, while hearing a 'proximity' adverb construct may not strengthen or prime it as much. Assuming that frequency may determine the source of 'prototypicality' or 'meaning supply' in a schema, in Pre-1949 Republic Era, the constructional meaning supply of the schema changed: previously the 'danger' subtype, represented by *xiǎnxiē*, had been the source but then the 'proximity' subtype, represented by *chādiǎn*, took over. This change motivated the breakdown of the schema: while the supply provided by the 'danger' subtype could easily maintain the schema by encouraging associations between 'danger' and both the meaning of 'adversity' and the form of 'expletive negation' in the schema, the supply from the 'proximity' subtype was not as capable of maintaining such associations. Even though frequency and prototypicality might not align perfectly, the hindsight from *chādiǎnméi(yǒu)* justifies positing *chayidian* to be the younger meaning supplier and *xiǎnxiē* to be the older one: the fact that *chādiǎnméi(yǒu)* has been bleached suggests that the schema's adversity meaning constraint must have been loosening, as *xiǎnxiē* receded and *chādiǎn* started to bleach in its absence.

---

13. This assumes that users recognise the adverbs' lexical sources. This is highly likely, given that the adverbs and their lexical sources are not distinguished orthographically or phonologically.

However, the demotivating effect *chādiǎn*'s original semantics had on the schema should not be the only factor. In fact, despite the imperfect match between *chādiǎn* and the schema, in principle *chādiǎn* should still be able to express adversity as its constructional meaning after it became the meaning supplier. After all, *chādiǎn* and *zhēngxiē*, though not transparently related to 'danger', were historically members of the schema and could express adversity. In addition, it is not necessary that everything in the schema should hinge upon the adverb; as described above, crosslinguistically expletive negation can 'cue' adversity. In short, the question is: to what extent can we 'blame' the schema's obsolescence on the lack of adversity in *chādiǎn*'s original semantics, given that it was actually an instance of the schema for much of its history and expletive negation could be regarded as a source of supply of adversity as well?

The original lexical semantics of *chādiǎn* is a more abstract generalisation, but it is also important to consider its usages in context. After all, from the perspective of a usage-based framework like diachronic construction grammar, change must originate in constructs. As described in Section 5.1, *chādiǎn* tended to be used hyperbolically, which is a significant deviation from the schema's meaning of adversity. Once the construct-level tendency towards hyperbole became entrenched and recognised as a pragmatic aspect of the subschema *chādiǎn*, the association between *chādiǎn* and the schema deteriorated. The looser connection between the schema and the 'proximity' subtype's semantics already does not encourage strongly the latter to be categorised as an instance of the former, so the hyperbolic pragmatics of *chādiǎn* further discourages such a categorisation. That is, the original lexical semantics of *chādiǎn* alone did not seal the schema's fate; its pragmatics was also complicit. Both *chādiǎn*'s semantics and pragmatics resulted in a constructional meaning supply that provided no proper 'cognitive anchoring' with respect to the schema. Nevertheless, the semantics must have also motivated its pragmatics: the lack of inherent adversity lent it easily to hyperbole.

Having interpreted the obsolescence of the schema in terms of constructional meaning supply, we can consider the second question raised in Section 5.2: why *chādiǎn/chādiǎnméi(yǒu)* has been on the rise, while the schema has obsoleted. The hyperbolic tendency of *chādiǎn* probably encouraged its use and crowded out *xiǎnxiē*. That is, there was schema-internal competition between them. It was very likely a scenario similar to Haspelmath's (1999) 'extravagance' account of grammaticalisation: *chādiǎn* was more attention-grabbing than *xiǎnxiē*. The sharp increase in *chādiǎn*'s frequency and the steep decline of *xiǎnxiē* in Pre-1949 Republic Era might reflect this: *chādiǎn* reached a critical point where it quickly gained ground on *xiǎnxiē*, on the strength of its much more sensational contextual meaning. Assuming that expletive negation is more 'intersubjective' (see Section 4.2; Ziegeler 2016), the higher co-occurrence rate of *chādiǎn* + *méi(yǒu)* (51%) than that of *xiǎnxiē* + *méi(yǒu)* (7%), reported by Kuo (2016a), also suggests that *chādiǎn* is more 'extravagant'.[14] *Chādiǎn*, or rather its extension, *chādiǎnméi(yǒu)*, probably also owes much of its growth to its sensational nature and versatility, unconstrained by any constructional adversity feature. This 'in-fight' between sibling subschemas *chādiǎn* and *xiǎnxiē* is likely to have had a hand in the declining vitality of the parent schema, too: with *xiǎnxiē* deteriorating, the likelihood of any association between the schema and 'danger', thus adversity and expletive negation, dwindled.

5.4 A visual summary

Before 1949, both frequency and functional evidence suggest that the 'danger' subtype was the constructional meaning supplier: it was the most frequent and its meaning closely corresponded to the schema's (Sections 3.1–3.2). The schema's form (the NEG slot) and meaning were motivated by the supplier's semantics of 'danger' and a 'good fit' can be observed between the schema and supplier. The 'proximity' subtype, such as *zhēngxiē* and *chādiǎn* also emerged; the adversity it expressed was attributed to the constructional meaning of the schema, as its semantics, unlike 'danger', did not directly motivate adversity. This initial stage is represented in Figure 4, where CM, LS and EN stands for 'constructional meaning', 'lexical semantics' and 'expletive negation' respectively. The boxes representing the schema and *xiǎnxiē* are coloured grey to symbolise that the latter supplies the former with meaning.

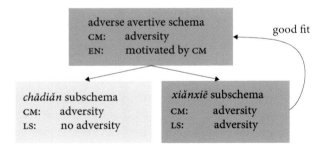

Figure 4. Initial stage

The lack of inherent adversity in the proximity subtype such as *chādiǎn* encouraged it to be used hyperbolically and begin being disassociated from the constructional meaning of adversity. However, the supply of 'danger' constrained the disassociation. *Xiǎnxiē* reined in *chādiǎn*'s extension to non-adverse contexts in

---

14.   Micro-constructions such as *xianyīdianr* and *chāyīxiēr* (Section 4.2) also suggest that the schema may be used extravagantly because these micro-constructions seem more 'emphatic' or even 'sensational' than their much shorter counterparts (e.g., *xiǎn* and *chāxiē*).

that it imposed the adversity meaning on the schema and its members. This is represented in Figure 5, where *chādiǎn*'s lexical semantics motivates hyperbolic uses.

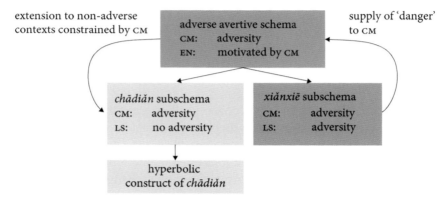

Figure 5. Hyperbolic uses of *chādiǎn*

Repeated hyperbolic uses led to the incorporation of hyperbolic pragmatics into *chādiǎn*. That *chādiǎn* was inherently adversity-free and gravitated toward hyperbole further encouraged its frequent uses, thus gradually ousting the reigning 'danger' adverb, *xiǎnxiē* in an 'extravagance'-style competition. As *xiǎnxiē* decreased in frequency and lost the status of meaning supplier to *chādiǎn*, the adversity constraint, or the association between the schema and adversity, eroded. Users oriented themselves towards *chādiǎn* in building up the schema, but the meaning supply or cognitive anchoring it provided was different from *xiǎnxiē*'s in terms of both semantics and pragmatics. That is, there was a 'bad fit' between *chādiǎn* and the schema because the former's semantics and pragmatics did not motivate the latter's adversity feature and expletive negation. This is represented in Figure 6, where PG stands for 'pragmatics' and the question mark symbolises that the adversity feature was eroding. The dashed lines suggest disassociations between *xiǎnxiē* and the schema.

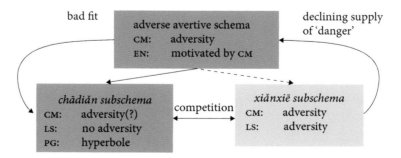

Figure 6. Bad fit between the schema and chādiǎn

The analysis presented here can be refined or falsified by collostructional analysis that measures attraction between constructions (Gries & Stefanowitsch 2004). If it is correct, it is predicted that 'danger' adverbs are more attracted to the schema than 'proximity' adverbs for most of the schema's history. Furthermore, if as constructional meaning suppliers 'danger' adverbs strengthen associations with the schema more than 'proximity' adverbs do, they should also prime the schema more (see Rosemeyer 2014 and Torres Cacoullos 2015 for using priming in historical studies; see also Schweinberger this volume;). This means that it should be more likely to find constructs of the schema (whether the 'danger' or 'proximity' kind) following 'danger' adverbs than following 'proximity' adverbs. However, in PDC, if the schema is really obsolete, *xiǎnxiē* and *chādiǎnméi(yǒu)* should not prime each other, or at least not as strongly.

6.   Generalisation as loss

A brief comparison is made here to suggest that generalisation can be associated with loss. In diachronic construction grammar, as well as historical linguistics in general, at least three loss-related processes have been recognised. First, renewal (Hopper & Traugott 2003), whereby a newer construction comes to express the meaning of an obsolescent construction. Periphrastic future replacing morphological future is one commonly cited example (Rosemeyer 2014; see also Barðdal & Gildea 2015: 38–41 for renewal in diachronic construction grammar and Reinöhl & Himmelmann 2017 for a critique). Second, 'degeneracy' (Van de Velde 2014), which happens when a pre-existing construction (not a 'new' construction', as in renewal) comes to express the meaning of an obsolescent construction. For example, the English impersonal, typically used to signal the Experiencer construction, has come to be coded by the transitive construction, which co-existed with the impersonal but has taken over its function (see Trousdale 2008). 'Exaptation', or 'refunctionalisation' (Norde & Trousdale 2016) describes the process by which an obsolescent construction is recruited to a different schema and expresses novel meaning. For example, Norde and Trousdale (2016) argue that the genitive -*s* in Swedish, previously restricted to certain declensions of nouns, is now sanctioned by the determiner schema.

The history of the adverse avertive involves generalisation (the bleaching of adversity) and loss, but not any of the three processes. Chinese has had no comparable schema with the same bundle of functional features used to characterise the schema in Section 4.2, so there is no renewal (no new construction expressing the adverse avertive meaning), or degeneracy (no pre-existing construction taking on the adverse avertive meaning). There is also no exaptation: the descendent *chādiǎnméi(yǒu)* is not aligned to a different schema, nor does it express 'novel' meaning. It is still sanctioned by an adjunct schema that can be described using 'imminence', 'counterfactuality' and 'pastness' (see also 'extended grammaticalisation' in Section 4.3). Thus, *chādiǎnméi(yǒu)* has become more like adverbial expressions such as *jīhū* 'close to; almost' in that both *chādiǎnméi(yǒu)* and *jīhū* are not characterised by 'adversity' (for differences and similarities between *jīhū* and *chādiǎnméi(yǒu)*, see Kuo 2016b; Shuai 2014; Peyraube 1979). This suggests that 'generalisation', without 'renewal', 'degeneracy' or 'exaptation' can be associated with loss as well.

It should be noted that even though there is no construction conventionalised for the expression of the adverse avertive, this does not mean that PDC speakers cannot express the adverse avertive meaning. Instead, 'conventionalised' is the operative word here: users may still express the same meaning, not through *one conventionalised construction*, but *multiple constructions* that are not conventionalised for the function, or they may leave it to be derived contextually. For example, *chādiǎnméi(yǒu)* can still imply adversity; it just no longer has a conventionalised adversity feature. Similarly, if the number category 'dual' has been lost in a language, it does not mean that its users have no access to the expression or mental representation of 'two entities'; they may still express it lexically, using the numeral for 'two' or a quantifying construction like *a pair of*, or let it be inferred.

7.   Conclusion

The kind of loss under investigation was defined as 'schema loss' in diachronic construction grammar. The analysis of the demise of the adverse avertive schema drew on the construction grammar proposal that the most prototypical member of a schema motivates the schema's formation, or supplies it with meaning. It was proposed that change in prototypicality, or constructional meaning supply, in the adverse avertive schema demotivated the schema, leading to its loss. The meaning supply from the newer most prototypical member, *chādiǎn*, differed from its predecessor *xiǎnxiē* in that its lexical semantics and pragmatics are not transparently 'adverse'. *Chādiǎn* thus provided a supply that did not help maintain the schema. Future research using collostructional analysis or priming may refine or falsify the analysis. Finally, it was suggested that generalisation can be associated with loss, independently of other loss-related processes widely recognised in the literature.

This study has highlighted that loss can be multidimensional: the substantive (e.g., constructs of *chādiǎn*) and partially schematic (the subschemas *xiǎnxiē* and *chādiǎn*) interact with the schematic (both the whole and parts, e.g., the schema and the NEG slot). Moreover, members of an obsolescent schema may have different histories. Some may meet their end (e.g., *xiǎnxiē*), but others may find life after death (e.g., *chādiǎn*). Finally, this study also complements that of Kranich (this volume); both show that loss can be considered at different levels of schematicity in diachronic construction grammar.

Acknowledgement

I would like to thank the editors, two anonymous reviewers, audiences at the Lost in Change workshop and my supervisors Nikolas Gisborne and Graeme Trousdale for their helpful comments. All remaining errors are my own.

References

Barðdal, Jóhanna & Gildea, Spike. 2015. Diachronic Construction Grammar: Epistemological context, basic assumptions and historical implications. In *Diachronic Construction Grammar*, [Constructional Approaches to Language 18], Jóhanna Barðdal, Elena Smirnova, Lotte Sommerer & Spike Gildea (eds), 1–50. Amsterdam: John Benjamins. https://doi.org/10.1075/cal.18.01bar

Biq, Yung-O. 1989. Metalinguistic negation in Mandarin. *Journal of Chinese Linguistics* 7(1): 75–94.

Börjars, Kersti, Vincent, Nigel & Walkden, George. 2015. On constructing a theory of grammatical change. *Transactions of the Philological Society* 113(3): 363–382. https://doi.org/10.1111/1467-968X.12068

Breban, Tine. 2015. Refining secondary grammaticalization by looking at subprocesses of change. *Language Sciences* 47(b): 161–171. https://doi.org/10.1016/j.langsci.2014.07.002

Breban, Tine & Kranich, Svenja. 2015. What happens after grammaticalizationǎ Secondary grammaticalization and other late stage processes. *Language Sciences* 47(b): 129–228. https://doi.org/10.1016/j.langsci.2014.09.001

Brems, Lieselotte. 2011. *Layering of Size and Type Noun Constructions in English*. Berlin: Mouton de Gruyter. https://doi.org/10.1515/9783110252927

Casenhiser, Devin & Goldberg, Adele E. 2005. Fast mapping of a phrasal form and meaning. *Developmental Science* 8(6): 500–508. https://doi.org/10.1111/j.1467-7687.2005.00441.x

Chao, Yuen Ren. 1968. *A Grammar of Spoken Chinese*. Berkeley CA: University of California Press.

Chappel, Hilary. 1986. Formal and colloquial adversity passives in Standard Chinese. *Linguistics* 24: 1025–1052. https://doi.org/10.1515/ling.1986.24.6.1025

Colleman, Timothy & Noël, Dirk. 2012. The Dutch evidential NCI: A case of constructional attrition. *Journal of Historical Pragmatics* 13(1): 1–28. https://doi.org/10.1075/jhp.13.1.01col

Cornillie, Bert. 2004. The shift from lexical to subjective readings of Spanish *prometer* 'to promise' and *amenazar* 'to threaten': A corpus-based account. *Pragmatics* 14(1): 1–30. https://doi.org/10.1075/prag.14.1.04cor

Fischer, Olga. 2018. Analogy: Its role in language learning, categorisation, and in models of language change such as grammaticalisation and constructionalisation. In *New Trends in Grammaticalization and Language Change* [Studies in Language Companion Series 202], Sylvie Hancil, Tine Breban & José Vicente Lozano (eds), 75–104. Amsterdam: John Benjamins. https://doi.org/10.1075/slcs.202.04fis

Geeraerts, Dirk. 2006. *Words and Other Wonders*. Berlin: Mouton de Gruyter. https://doi.org/10.1515/9783110219128

Goldberg, Adele E. 1995. *Constructions: A Construction Grammar Approach to Argument Structure*. Chicago IL: Chicago University Press.

Goldberg, Adele E. 2006. *Constructions at Work: The Nature of Generalization in Language*. Oxford: OUP.

Goldberg, Adele E. 2019. *Explain me This: Creativity, Competition and the Partial Productivity of Constructions*. Princeton NJ: Princeton University Press.

Goldberg, Adele E., Casenhiser, Devin & Sethuraman, Nitya. 2004. Learning argument structure generalizations. *Cognitive Linguistics* 14(3): 289–316.

Gries, Stefan T. & Stefanowitsch, Anatol. 2004. Extending collostructional analysis: A corpus-based perspective on 'alternations'. *International Journal of Corpus Linguistics* 9(1): 97–129. https://doi.org/10.1075/ijcl.9.1.06gri

Haspelmath, Martin. 1999. Why is grammaticalization irreversible? *Linguistics* 37(6): 1043–1068.

Heine, Bernd & Miyashita, Hiroyuki. 2008. Accounting for a functional category: German *drohen* 'to threaten'. *Language Sciences* 30: 53–101. https://doi.org/10.1016/j.langsci.2007.05.003

Hilpert, Martin. 2015. From hand-carved to computer-based: Noun-participle compounding and the upward strengthening hypothesis. *Cognitive Linguistics* 26(1): 113–147. https://doi.org/10.1515/cog-2014-0001

Hopper, Paul & Traugott, Elizabeth Closs. 2003. *Grammaticalization*. Cambridge: CUP. https://doi.org/10.1017/CBO9781139165525

Hundt, Marianne. 2014. The demise of the *being to V* construction. *Transactions of the Philological Society* 112(2): 167–187. https://doi.org/10.1111/1467-968X.12035

Jiang, Lansheng. 2008. Semantic accumulation and constructional integration: An explanation on the asymmetry between affirmation and negation. *Zhōngguó Yǔwén* 6: 483–497.

Joseph, Brian D. 2014. What counts as (an instance of) grammaticalization? *Folia Linguistica* 48(2): 1–23.

Kuo, Yueh Hsin. 2016a. A diachronic pragmatic account of *chādiǎn's* ambiguity and development. *The Proceedings of the 18th Annual Conference of Pragmatics Society of Japan*, 155–162.

Kuo, Yueh Hsin. 2016b. A Diachronic Constructional Investigation into the Adverse Avertive Schema in Chinese. *MSc by Research dissertation*, University of Edinburgh.

Kuo, Yueh Hsin. 2018. The development of three classifier constructions into degree adverbs in Chinese. In *New Trends on Grammaticalization and Language Change* [Studies in Language Companion Series 202], Sylvie Hancil, Tine Breban, & José Vicente Lozano (eds), 315–331. Amsterdam: John Benjamins. https://doi.org/10.1075/slcs.202.13kuo

Kuo, Yueh Hsin. 2020. Reinforcement by realignment in diachronic construction grammar: The case of classifier *xiē* in Mandarin Chinese. *Constructions and Frames* 12(2): 239–271. https://doi.org/10.1075/cf.00040.kuo

Kuteva, Tania. 2001. *Auxiliation: An Enquiry into the Nature of Grammaticalization*. Oxford: OUP.

Langacker, Ronald. 1987. *Foundations of Cognitive Grammar,* Vol. I: Theoretical Prerequisites. Stanford CA: Stanford University Press.

Li, Charles N. 1976. A functional explanation for an unexpected case of ambiguity (S or -S). In *Linguistic Studies Offered to Joseph Greenberg on the Occasion of his Sixtieth Birthday,* Alphones Juilland (ed.), 527–535. Saratoga CA: Anma Libri.

Li, Charles N. & Thompson, Sandra A. 1981. *Mandarin Chinese: A Functional Reference Grammar.* Berkeley CA: University of California Press.

Noël, Dirk. 2019. The decline of the Deontic NCI construction in Late Modern English: Towards a radically usage-based perspective on constructional attrition. *Cognitive Linguistics Studies* 6(1): 22–57. https://doi.org/10.1075/cogls.00029.noe

Norde, Muriel & Trousdale, Graeme. 2016. Exaptation from the perspective of construction morphology. In *Exaptation and Language Change* [Current Issues in Linguistic Theory 336], Muriel Norde & Freek Van de Velde (eds), 163–195. Amsterdam: John Benjamins. https://doi.org/10.1075/cilt.336.06nor

Petré, Peter. 2010. The functions of *weorðan* and its loss in the past tense in Old and Middle English. *English Language and Linguistics* 14(3): 457–484. https://doi.org/10.1017/S1360674310000158

Peyraube, Alain. 1979. Les "approximatifs" Chinois: *Chàbuduō, jīhū, chàyidiǎnr. Cahiers de Linguistique Asie Orientale* 6: 49–62.

Reinöhl, Uta & Himmelmann, Nikolaus. P. Renewal: A figure of speech or process sui generis? *Language* 93(2): 381–413.

Rosemeyer, Malte. 2014. *Auxiliary Selection in Spanish: Gradience, Gradualness, and Conservation* [Studies in Language Companion Series 155]. Amsterdam: John Benjamins. https://doi.org/10.1075/slcs.155

Shuai, Zhisong. 2014. The evolution of *'chādiǎn'r mei'* from the perspective of lexical semantic information. *Yǔyán kēxué* 13(6): 615–631.

Smirnova, E. 2015a. When secondary grammaticalization starts: A look from the constructional perspective. *Language Sciences* 47(b): 215–228. https://doi.org/10.1016/j.langsci.2014.07.009

Smirnova, Elena. 2015b. Constructionalization and constructional change: The role of context in the development of constructions. In *Diachronic Construction Grammar* [Constructional Approaches to Language 18], Jóhanna Barðdal, Elena Smirnova, Lotte Sommerer & Spike Gildea (eds), 81–106. Amsterdam: John Benjamins. https://doi.org/10.1075/cal.18.03smi

Sweetser, Eve E. 1988. Grammaticalization and semantic bleaching. In *The Proceedings of the Fourteenth Annual Meeting of the Berkeley Linguistics Society,* Shelley Axmaker & Helen Singmaster (eds), 389–405. Berkeley CA: BLS.

Torres Cacoullos, Rena. 2015. Gradual loss of analyzability: Diachronic priming effects. In *Variation in Language: System-and Usage-based Approaches,* Aria Adli, Marco García García & Göz Kaufmann (eds), 265–288. Berlin: Mouton de Gruyter. https://doi.org/10.1515/9783110346855-011

Traugott, Elizabeth Closs. 1993. The conflict promises/threatens to escalate into war. In *The Proceedings of the Nineteenth Annual Meeting of the Berkeley Linguistics Society,* Joshua S. Guenter, Barabara A. Kaiser & Cheryll C. Zoll (eds), 348–358. Berkeley CA: BLS.

Traugott, Elizabeth Closs. 2016. Do semantic modal maps have a role in a constructionalization approach to modals? *Constructions and Frames* 8(1): 97–124.

Traugott, Elizabeth Closs. 2018. Modelling language change with constructional networks. In *Beyond Grammaticalization and Discourse Markers*, Salvador Pons Bordería & Óscar Loureda Lamas (eds), 17–50. Leiden: Brill.

Traugott, Elizabeth Closs & Trousdale, Graeme. 2013. *Constructionalization and Constructional Changes*. Oxford: OUP. https://doi.org/10.1093/acprof:oso/9780199679898.001.0001

Trousdale, Graeme. 2008. Words and constructions in grammaticalization: The end of the English impersonal construction. In *Studies in the History of the English Language, IV: Empirical and Analytical Advances in the Study of English Language Change*, Susan Fitzmaurice & Donka Minkova (eds), 301–326. Berlin: Mouton de Gruyter. https://doi.org/10.1515/9783110211801.301

Van de Velde, Freek. 2014. Degeneracy: The maintenance of constructional networks. In *Extending the Scope of Construction Grammar*, Ronny Boogaart, Timothy Colleman & Gijsbert Rutten (eds), 141–179. Berlin: Mouton de Gruyter.

Xu, Shi-yi. 2003. On the evolution of the negative *mei* and *meiyou*. *Journal of Huzhou Teachers College* 25: 1–6.

Zhou, Yiming. 2003. *Cha dian er mei* VP Sentences in Pekingese. *Yŭyán jiàoxué yŭ yánjiū* 6: 24–30.

Zhu, Dexi. 1959. Shuō *chàyīdiǎn*. *Zhongguo Yuwen* 9: 435.

Ziegeler, Debra. 2006. *Interfaces with English Aspect: Diachronic and Empirical Studies* [Studies in Language Companion Series 82]. Amsterdam: John Benjamins. https://doi.org/10.1075/slcs.82

Ziegeler, Debra. 2016. Intersubjectivity and the diachronic development of counterfactual *almost*. *Journal of Historical Pragmatics* 17(1): 1–25. https://doi.org/10.1075/jhp.17.1.01zie

PART II

Motivations and explanations for loss: Language-internal and external factors

CHAPTER 6

Loss or variation? Functional load in morpho-syntax – Three case studies

Alexandra Rehn
University of Konstanz

In order to get a better understanding of the circumstances under which elements can get lost in the course of their diachronic development, three phenomena of German non-standard varieties will be compared: loss of adnominal genitive, optional realization of adjectival inflection and variation in the choice of relative clause introducers. It will be shown that on the one hand, a substitutional strategy to compensate for the function of the element that undergoes loss is required but that this alone does not necessarily lead to loss. Depending on the functional load of the individual items and the options the syntax provides the availability of a substitutional strategy may result in loss, optionality or variation.

Keywords: dialectal variation, functional load, adjectival inflection, adnominal genitive, RCIs

1. Introduction

The loss of categories can be observed repeatedly in the course of the diachronic development of German as well as other languages. At the beginning of the 20th century, von der Gabelentz (1901: 256) already notes that two forces seem to be at play in language change. On the one hand the "Bequemlichkeitstrieb" (laziness) leads to loss of elements, however, at the same time the "Deutlichkeitstrieb" (desire to be explicit) prevents that loss leads to the *destruction* of language - a dichotomy that is indeed relevant when investigating loss.

Within more formal approaches to language change, loss is assumed to be the last stage in developments that are described as grammaticalisation, e.g., Lehmann (1995) or van Gelderen (2011) in a minimalist approach to language change. This view implies that (i) language change is unidirectional and (ii) that in the process of grammaticalisation, variation is generally reduced. However, not all elements

https://doi.org/10.1075/slcs.218.06reh
© 2021 John Benjamins Publishing Company

undergo all grammaticalisation steps and it is thus not entirely clear, which factors allow for an element to disappear from a language at some point and which factors prevent such a development.

One example for loss in German is nominal inflection. It is a well-known fact that nouns in German only show remnants of case inflection whereas in Old High German, a rather rich inflectional paradigm existed. There are different explanations regarding this fact. On the one hand, it is sometimes assumed that the loss of nominal inflection triggered the development of the article to compensate for it, as noted in Oubouzar (1992). On the other hand it is equally plausible that the emergence of the article led to the loss of nominal inflection as case and number were now marked on the article and nominal inflection became redundant (cf. Oubouzar 1992). Either way: the loss of nominal inflection was compensated for by the article and case as well as phi-feature marking was retained. Similarly, the loss of the adnominal genitive in colloquial and non-standard varieties of German is compensated for by substitution strategies that are able to express the relations the adnominal genitive used to mark (cf. Kasper 2014; Kiefer 1910), a scenario that will be discussed in detail in Section 3. These two examples of loss have thus one thing in common: the original function is retained and compensated for by another element or strategy.

Thus, the availability of a substitution strategy might seem to be sufficient, not only necessary, for an element to undergo loss. However, this is not the case. In some German dialects there are in fact three ways to introduce relative clauses. In (1) the relative clause introducer (RCI) is a d-pronoun, in (2) it is the particle *wo* and in (3) we have the combination of both. These strategies co-exist and instead of loss, we have variation.

(1)   *Das Haus, **das***
      The house that

(2)   *Das Haus, **wo***
      The house, PRT

(3)   *Das Haus, **das wo***
      The house that PRT

This means that besides an alternative strategy there must be additional requirements that trigger or prevent loss.

In order to identify possible conditions of loss, I will compare three phenomena: (i) a case of loss, namely the adnominal genitive in non-standard German, (ii) a case of optionality, which is adjectival inflection in Alemannic (a southern German dialect) and (iii) variation in the case of relative clause introducers in Alemannic as briefly presented above.

Based on the case studies discussed, three factors are identified that have an impact on loss: the functional load of an element, the presence of a substitution strategy, and the underlying syntactic structure. It will be shown that for the cases discussed, loss is possible when the functional load of an element is low. Low functional load in morpho-syntax is understood in the sense that an element is restricted to a specific morpho-syntactic context, whereas high functional load means that one and the same element appears in different morpho-syntactic contexts, hence it is multifunctional. The latter case, as will be shown, has an impact on loss in the sense that high functional load may sometimes prevent loss.

2. Background

2.1 The Alemannic dialect

As the paper focusses in most parts on the Alemannic dialect, I will first give some background information on this language followed by some notes on the theoretical framework used in the remainder of the paper. Alemannic is a southern German dialect that is itself divided into five varieties: Highest, High, Middle, Low Alemannic and Swabian. The areas, in which these varieties are spoken are given in Map 1 showing the classical dialect map by Wiesinger (1983). The region in which Alemannic is spoken is quite large and several political borders run through it. Alemannic is spoken in Switzerland, Alsace in France, parts of southern Germany, Vorarlberg in Austria and Liechtenstein. To locate the Alemannic region, a map marking the political borders giving the same snippet Wiesinger's map shows is displayed below it to make it easier to locate the area. Unfortunately, this map does not include Alsace, in which Low Alemannic is spoken.

Alemannic is ideal for linguistic investigations for several reasons. It still has many speakers and since the area is large and political borders of different countries run through it, it makes an ideal testing ground for (microsyntactic) variation. Furthermore, Alemannic is well documented as there are Alemannic grammars and dictionaries available (e.g., Birlinger 1868, Staedele 1927). There are also texts available from different stages of German, including Old High German, Middle High German and Early New High German, which allows the investigation of language change.

Characteristic linguistic features of Alemannic are numerous and I will only list some here. Alemannic, with the exception of the Swabian variety, has not undergone diphthongization (e.g., *Wii* instead of *Wein* for wine) in Middle High German, which is one of its prominent phonological features. Furthermore, Alemannic speakers productively use the so called double perfect construction as in (4) and, as already mentioned in the introduction, there are three ways to introduce a relative clause as shown in (1) to (3). Furthermore, as already noted in Birlinger (1868), a characteristic feature of the Alemannic language is the use of uninflected adjectives, a phenomenon that will be discussed in detail in Section 4.

Map 1. Southern Germany and its dialects (maps created with the REDE SprachGIS[1])

---

1.   The REDE SprachGis is a free tool developed and provided on www.regionalsprache.de by Schmidt, Herrgen & Kehrein (2008).

(4) *I ha' mei Brill verlore ghet* (Swabian)
     I have my glasses lost had
     'I had lost my glasses'

The empirical study in which a large amount of data was collected, was part of the project SynALM (Syntax of Alemannic[2]), a project that aimed at a deeper understanding of syntactic phenomena by collecting a large amount of data and analyzing them within a generative framework, which is what I will also pursue in this paper. In the following, some basic concepts of the framework will thus be given.

2.2 Theoretical background: Loss from a generative perspective

Most generative frameworks have the assumption in common that the basic make up of sentences and noun phrases is very similar. This means that there is a lexical layer consisting of the noun or the verb. Above this, there is a functional layer in which inflectional material and hence also agreement is located. On the sentence level this is normally T(ense)P(hrase) and on the noun phrase level this projection is often labelled AgrP (agreement phrase) and it is the position in which adjectives are realized. Above these projections, there is the highest functional layer, which provides the connection to the discourse. This is CP on the sentence level, determining the sentence type (e.g., question). In noun phrases, this is the DP, which is the locus of article elements and which is responsible for the referentiality of the whole noun phrase. Crucially, the interpretation of relevant morpho-syntactic features like tense, person or number is assumed to be tied to a specific position, thus it is not variable. In other words, if the relevant features are marked on different elements, sometimes movement must take place so the relevant features appear in the designated position in the structure. These assumptions have an impact on the way change is modelled. Change may be triggered by the need for feature specification in a certain position as the original element is no longer available. This situation can be observed e.g., in nominal concord. Before the article system was in place, nouns as well as adjectives showed obligatory inflection for phi-features (number and gender) and case. Nominal inflection was lost due to the *Auslautgesetze* (cf. Braune & Heidermanns 2018) and features had to be marked by another element compensating for this loss, which was the article (or another determiner element). Another important aspect in the framework is that complementary distribution is a diagnostic for determining whether two elements share the same position in the syntax which is in turn connected to fulfilling a particular (morpho)syntactic function. Articles and possessive pronouns for example cannot

---

2. The SynALM project was a DFG funded project (2013 to 2016) led by Ellen Brandner.

co-occur in German, whereas they do in Italian. In German, they are thus both analyzed to be of the category D occupying the same structural position - a diagnostic that will become relevant when discussing relative clause introducers. The d-pronoun and the particle *wo* can co-occur, as already mentioned in the introduction, hence they are not in complementary distribution and must therefore be in different structural positions. Likewise, since *so* and *wo* are particles, they are heads and since both are or in the former case used to be relative clause introducers their structural position is (or was) the same. When Kempf (this volume) thus observers that the relative pronouns *d-* and *welch-* and the particle *so* were not in competition, this is attributed to their different status (head vs phrase) and thus their occupying different positions in the structure in the framework used in this paper. There is some consensus that change generally takes place in the process of language acquisition as within this process syntactic rules are deduced through the input (cf. Roberts & Roussou 2003). The trigger for change can thus be an ambiguity in the input or the competition of two elements that share the same function and position in the syntax. This means that the framework chosen may also have an impact on how loss is understood and modelled (cf. Kuo (this volume) for an approach within construction grammar). Nevertheless, the empirical side is theory independent and in a broad sense, loss is understood as the absence of a feature or element (maybe only in a particular context) that used to be part of the system.

3.   The loss of the adnominal genitive in some varieties of German

The adnominal genitive presents a case of loss, as there is a discrepancy in productivity when comparing Modern Standard German (MStG) to colloquial German or dialects. While the adnominal genitive is still productive in MStG, occurring in a variety of semantic patterns, it is no longer used in most non-standard varieties (cf. Fleischer & Schallert 2011; Hentschel 1993; Kasper 2014: 58). In the following, I will thus briefly introduce the constructions, in which the adnominal genitive occurs in MStG and the alternative strategies that are used in non-standard varieties focusing on Alemannic.

In (5) to (8), four examples of the use of the adnominal genitive in MStG are given, illustrating the patterns that will be part of the discussion in this paper. I only present four constructions, because even though the semantic patterns are quite different, the constructions in (5) to (7) can be subsumed under the cover term genitivus thematicus (Lindauer 1998: 109). Example (8) is a partitive construction, which differs in its properties from the genitivus thematicus, however shares with it that the genitive DP occurs postnominally (the genitive may only be prenominal in constructions with proper names) and that two DPs are involved that are in a dependency relation. This means that the genitive in (5) to (8) can be analyzed as a 'connector' between two DPs (Kiefer 1910; Pittner 2014; Weinrich 2005). Such a connector is necessary as its absence leads to ungrammaticality (cf. the man's hat vs *the man hat). As stressed in Weinrich (2005: 706) the adnominal genitive in the examples given has thus only one function, namely to link two DPs that are in an asymmetric relation. This means that the adnominal genitive marks a dependency relation between two DPs.

(5)   Possessives: *d-ie Tasche d-es Kind-es*
                      The-NOM bag the-GEN child-GEN
                      The child's bag
                      Peter-s Hund
                      Peter's dog

(6)   Property: *d-er Geruch frisch-en Brot-es*
                  The-NOM smell fresh-WK[3] bread-GEN

(7)   Part-whole   *d-as Dach d-es Auto-s*
                   the-NOM roof the-GEN car-GEN

(8)   Partitives: *ein Teil dies-es Buch-es*
                    a part this-GEN book-GEN
                    a part of the book

In some cases, the preposition *von* is used instead of a genitive construction, but this is very restricted in MStG. It occurs when no article (or adjective) bears genitive inflection as in (9) a. The PP-strategy with *von* may also be used when an adjective could serve as a host for genitive inflection, so in some cases, two strategies are available in MStG to express the same relation (Gallmann 2018; Weinrich 2005: 704–705).

(9)   a.   *d-er Verkauf von Äpfel-n*
            the-NOM selling of apple-DAT.PL.

      b.   *d-ie Einfuhr spanisch-er Aprikosen*
            the-NOM import Spanish-GEN apricots

      c.   *d-ie Einfuhr von spanisch-en Aprikosen*
            the-NOM import of Spanish-DAT.PL apricots

In addition to the constructions above, which all involve two DPs, the genitive also occurs in so called measure phrases and pseudo partitives. The difference to the constructions above is that only one DP is involved and the noun, which is a mass

---

3.   WK stands for weak inflection.

or collective noun, is preceded by a container or count expression. The restrictions on genitive marking in these constructions as given in Gallmann (2018: 164) are listed in (10), as the construction with genitive "competes with a juxtaposed phrasal construction" (Gallmann 2018: 163), which often dominates as the version with genitive is considered marked (Gallmann 2018: 163, cf. also Hentschel (1993) focusing on variation in juxtaposition). The construction in (10) a., which is marked as ungrammatical was productive up to the 19th century but alternative strategies are generally used in contemporary German.

(10)   a.   *mit ein-em Glas Wasser-s

     b.   ?mit ein-em Glas kühl-en Wasser-s

     c.   mit ein-em Glas Wasser

     d.   mit ein-em Glas kühl-em Wasser
        with a-DAT glass (cold-WK/DAT) water-(GEN)

Shifting our focus from MStG to non-standard varieties, the picture is quite different as the adnominal genitive is no longer productive. In the contexts in (5) to (10) above, alternative strategies are used that replace the function of the genitive, a development that Kiefer (1910) has already described in detail (but see also Fleischer & Schallert (2011) and Kasper (2014) with focus on possession). In all of the examples above, except for the ones in (10), a PP is a possible alternative (cf. Example (11) a., d. and e.). In possessive constructions with animate possessors the so-called possessive dative is also a possible alternative, as illustrated in (11) b. and c. Measure phrases as in (10) are generally realized by juxtaposition of the involved noun phrases as given in (11) f. and g. The data stem from the SynALM project, except for (11) e., f. and g., which are translations of a native speaker of Alemannic who did not participate in the questionnaire studies. This means that despite the fact that the adnominal genitive is productive in MStG and alternative strategies are very restricted, it nevertheless presents a case of loss of a category as it is no longer productive in colloquial German or any of the German dialects (Kasper 2014: 58).

(11)   a.   d-es Rad vu d-er Lena
        the-NOM bike of the-DAT Lena

     b.   d-er Lena ihr Rad
        the-DAT Lena her bike

     c.   d-em Vater sin Platz
        the-DAT father his seat

     d.   d-er Platz vu-m Vadder
        the-NOM seat of-the.DAT father

     e.   en Teil vu d-em Buech
        a part of the-DAT book.

> f.   *mit e-m Glas kalt-e Wasser*
>   with a-DAT glass cold-WK water
>
> g.   *mit e-m Glas kalt-em Wasser*
>   with a-DAT glass cold-DAT water

As already said, these substitution strategies - even though presented in Alemannic - are not specific to a certain dialect and the observation of the replacement of the adnominal genitive raises the following general questions:

1. how is loss possible even though the genitive occurs/used to occur in a variety of patterns
2. what does the loss of the genitive tell us about general conditions of loss

In order to investigate the questions given above, I will briefly look at the diachronic development of the adnominal genitive and its substitution before I discuss the conditions that led to the decline of the adnominal genitive in non-standard German varieties.

3.1   The decline of the adnominal genitive

The previous section gave a brief overview of the constructions, in which the adnominal genitive is still productive in MStG and the substitution strategies used in non-standard German. For understanding the loss of the adnominal genitive in the latter, the diachronic development of these substitution strategies will briefly be considered.

The adnominal genitive in MHG expresses the same semantic relations as in MStG (cf. Paul 2007: 245f). The main difference to MStG lies in the possible ordering variations regarding the two involved DPs and the article, because the genitive can also occur prenominally as in (12) a. and b., whereas in MStG it generally occurs postnominally (with the exception of proper names). The genitive attribute can also occur prenominally preceded by the article belonging to the DP it modifies as in (12) d. and e., a construction mainly found in the 12th century (Paul 2007: 330).

> (12)   a.   *d-er riesen spileman*
>   the-GEN giants minstrel
>
>   b.   *min-er tohter tocke*
>   my-GEN daughter bonnet
>
>   c.   *ein boten guot-es willen*
>   a messenger good-GEN will
>
>   d.   *d-en got-es engelen*
>   the-DAT god-GEN angels
>
>   e.   *d-er ware got-es sun*
>   the-NOM true god-GEN son

MHG is also the period of time, for which substitution strategies are already attested according to Kiefer (1910). He thoroughly investigated the beginning of the loss of the adnominal genitive and shows that the PP strategy and the possessive dative are attested from the 12th century onwards (Kiefer 1910: 52, 66). Fleischer and Schallert (2011: 94f.) point out, though, that an exact dating is difficult as most constructions are ambiguous and can be interpreted as one DP with a PP complement or as two separate arguments to the verb (cf. (13) and (14) below), a point to which I will return. It may thus be the case that genitive substitution dates back to the OHG period. Juxtaposition as in (10) c. or (11) f. above can be found from the 15th century onwards (Kiefer 1910: 83–84). Kiefer notes that it is safe to assume that in spoken language, the process began much earlier and that genitive loss was probably well advanced in spoken compared to written German. The discrepancy may be attributed to normative pressure, a fact that is reflected in the difference between MStG and colloquial/dialectal varieties, as normative grammar does – in most cases – not consider the substitution strategies for e.g., possessive correct but requires the use of an adnominal genitive. This means that actual language usage and prescriptive rules clearly differ in this case. Furthermore, Kiefer (1910: 53) points out that the Swiss poet Albrecht von Haller changed the PP-construction back to the 'more correct' genitive in the third edition of his work in 1743 – a time in which the standardization process had undergone much progress (cf. Polenz (1994) or Jellinek (1914) for an overview on this topic). Kiefer thus sees a connection in normative pressure and the 'stagnation' or even decline of genitive substitution in written works of the time. It may thus be argued that normative pressure plays a role in the 'preservation' of the genitive in MStG, as the varieties that are not regulated by normative grammar have progressed in the replacement of the adnominal genitive much further. However, this may explain the difference between standard and non-standard varieties, but it does not explain the conditions that led the adnominal genitive to disappear from the latter.

3.2   The loss of the adnominal Genitive

As pointed out above, for the adnominal genitive constructions in (5) to (8), the role of the genitive can be reduced to one specific function, namely that of a linker between two DPs in a dependency relation. The observation that despite the various semantic patterns in which the adnominal genitive occurs, its actual function in terms of morpho-syntax is very limited is crucial. If Kiefer (1910) is correct, the PP construction is in place before the possessive dative. Both constructions have originated from a reanalysis of a phrasal boundary. This means that they resulted from a reanalysis of ambiguous examples like the ones in (13) and (14), cited from Fleischer & Schallert (2011: 95). The bracketing in the examples in (13) a. and (14)

a. illustrate that the PP as well as the phrase containing the possessive pronoun are analyzed as two separate arguments of the verb. The bracketing in (13b) and (14b) illustrates that a second reading is available, in which the two phrases are interpreted as a single argument of the verb.

(13)   a.   *da erging [ein Gebot] [von Kaiser Augustus]*

      b.   *da erging [ein Gebot von Kaiser Augustus]*
          there emanated an order from emperor Augustus
          'there was a commandment from emperor Augustus'

(14)   a.   *ich habe [d-em Mann] [sein-en Hut] genommen*

      b.   *ich habe [d-em Mann sein-en Hut] genommen*
          I have the-DAT man his-ACC hat taken
          I have taken the man's hat/ I have taken the hat from the man

The relevant point is that once the PP-construction in (13b) is productive and the preposition *von* was able to serve as a 'connective' between two DPs as defined in Section 3, the core function of the adnominal genitive could be fulfilled by a second strategy. Since the functional load of the adnominal genitive is limited (in the sense that it only appears in a specific morpho-syntactic context compared to multifunctional elements, cf. Section 1), the genitive could be substituted in most contexts within the nominal domain. This phenomenon resembles the well known effect of blocking, which is common e.g., in morphology but also in syntactic constructions (cf. Kroch 1994: 5). We thus have two important prerequisites for loss that play a role here: a "doublet", using Kroch's (1994) term, and low functional load (i.e., the restriction to a very specific morpho-syntactic context).

The PP is a competing strategy to the adnominal genitive (unlike the possessive dative) because it is a true 'doublet' construction. The PP in the contexts discussed (i) expresses the same semantic relations the adnominal genitive realizes and (ii) it occurs in the same structural position. Both the PP and the genitive DP are realized as complements[4] to the noun. This is illustrated in Figure 1, which shows that the genitive DP and the PP are in the same structural position w.r.t. the head noun *Dach* (roof), the corresponding example is given in (15). When two elements fulfilling the same function occur in the same syntactic position,

---

4.   It may be questioned whether the DP/PP are indeed realized as complements to the noun as this involves selection and since the noun *Dach* (roof) is not relational, this is not straightforward. This issue has been investigated in Barker (2019) who points out that there clearly is a relation between the two nouns in examples like (14) above and he shows that such relations can be explained with type-shifting.

they either occur in complementary distribution or one of the two is lost, due to competition (cf. Kroch 1994).

(15)   a.   *d-as Dach d-es Haus-es*
            the-NOM roof the-GEN house-GEN

       b.   *d-as Dach von d-em Haus*
            the-NOM roof of the-DAT house

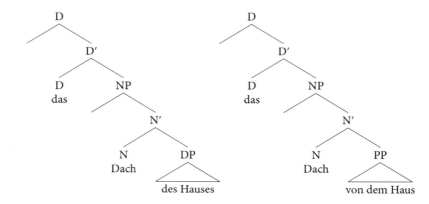

Figure 1. Adnominal genitive and PP as complements to N

As noted above, in addition to the PP strategy, a second means of expressing possession is the possessive dative given in (11) b. and c., which may have occurred after or parallel to the PP-strategy. The question to be answered thus is: how is it possible that one element is replaced by two different constructions, which both 'survive'? The PP, as noted above, is a true 'doublet' to the adnominal genitive construction, however, the possessive dative is neither a doublet of the adnominal genitive nor of the PP-constructions. The reason is that the possessive dative is restricted to animate possessors and the presence of the two substitution strategies thus allows a distinction between animate and inanimate possessors. Therefore, PP and possessive dative are not in competition but 'co-exist' and provide a means to make the animate-inanimate distinction of possessors overt. The origin of the possessive dative construction as well as its syntactic properties are a recurring topic in linguistic research that I will not discuss in more detail here but see e.g., Ramat (1986), Olsen (1996), Weiß (2012), or Kasper (2014).

       For adnominal genitive constructions, the 'connective function' was focused on. The second context, in which the genitive occurs in noun phrases are measure phrases as in (9). These constructions also provide a very limited pattern, because the head noun must be a mass noun and it is preceded by a container noun. The general function of case, as noted in Gallmann (2018), is the marking of syntactic relations. In measure phrases, however, the function of the genitive is rather that of marking the notion of 'a portion of'. The container expression preceding the head noun makes this 'portion' explicit (e.g., a glass of milk). Thus, in addition to the genitive, there already is another means within the same noun phrase fulfilling a similar function. With the loss of the genitive in this context, its function is already compensated for and no further substitution strategy is implemented.

Returning to the questions in 1. and 2. in Section 3 above, we can now make the following (preliminary) statements: the functional load of the adnominal genitive is low in the sense that its primary role is to mark the dependency between two DPs. The fact that an alternative strategy became available serving the very same function was able to trigger the loss of the adnominal genitive within the nominal domain. The question at this point is of course, what these observations on the adnominal genitive may tell us about the conditions of loss in general. In order to place this phenomenon in the 'bigger picture' it must be compared to other phenomena, which is the goal of the next sections. It will be argued that the combination of a limited functional load in connection with available substitution strategies allows for the loss of an element – the presence of the latter alone is not sufficient.

4. German adjectival inflection – A case of optionality

In Section 2 we have seen that the adnominal genitive is no longer productive in non-standard varieties of German, but that the function it used to fulfill is retained. In all contexts, in which the adnominal genitive used to occur an alternative strategy is now available maintaining the original relation. In this section, adjectival inflection with focus on Alemannic is investigated in detail. It can provide relevant insights regarding conditions of loss, because in Alemannic, adjectival inflection is optional, as will be demonstrated below. This means that the element under discussion can but does not have to be realized – nevertheless, the inflection does not disappear.

First, the features that MStG and non-standard German varieties share when it comes to adjectival inflection will be identified. In both MStG as well as dialects, there are two inflectional paradigms – traditionally called strong and weak after Grimm (1822) – and the distribution is driven by the inflectional properties of the preceding article. When phi-features[5] and case are realized on an article, the adjective bears weak inflection. When these features are not realized on an article, the adjective bears strong inflection as illustrated in Table 1 (cf. Rehn 2017: 2).

---

5.   Phi-features generally include number, gender and person and thus those features that are involved in agreement relations within the noun phrase but also in subject verb agreement.

This distribution is known as *morpho-syntactic distribution*. In addition, attributive adjectives in MStG must always inflect (setting aside a few exceptions here).

(16)   *Ein groß-*(er) Hund*
       a big-NOM.MASC.SG dog

Table 1. The morpho-syntactic distribution of adjectival inflection in German

The Distribution of Adjectival Inflection in German	
Strong paradigm Article-Ø Adjective-φ Ø Adjective-φ	**Weak paradigm** Article-φ Adjective-WK
⇩	⇩
ein-Ø klein-er *Hund* a small-NOM.MASC.SG dog	*d-er* *klein-e Hund* the-NOM.MASC.SG small-WK dog
Ø gut-er *Wein ist teuer* Ø good-NOM.MASC.SG wine is expensive	*mit ein-em* *klein-en Hund* with a-DAT.MASC.SG small-WK dog

It has already been noted that Alemannic is a southern German dialect that consists of Highest, High, Middle, Low Alemannic and Swabian (cf. Wiesinger 1983). In the following, I will not refer to these varieties as the results of the study hold across the Alemannic area covered, but when necessary, I will refer to the political areas as they formed the basis of the empirical study.

In Alemannic, there is also the strong-weak-distinction and it follows the same distribution as in MStG. Unless specified otherwise, all Alemannic examples in this section stem from the questionnaires of the SynALM project, which was already introduced above. Unlike in MStG, attributive adjectives can also appear uninflected as illustrated in examples (17) to (19), which are given in Swabian. The examples were part of the questionnaire study on adjectival inflection, which is introduced in more detail below. The realization of uninflected adjectives is independent of the inflectional properties of the preceding article.[6]

(17)   *d-es lang-(e) Soil*
       the-NOM.SG long-(WK) rope

(18)   *a guat-(r) Wei*
       a good-(NOM.MASC.SG) wine

---

6.   This option is not a peculiarity of Alemannic but it is also present in other dialects as e.g., discussed in Rowley (1991) for a Bavarian variety and in Schirmunski (1962) for various dialects including Low German varieties, which shows that uninflected adjectives are not restricted to southern German dialects.

(19)   *mit d-em alt-(a) Waga*
     with the-DAT.SG old-(WK) car

The observation of uninflected attributive adjectives in Alemannic raises a number of questions, which are connected to the main purpose of this paper, namely to identify conditions of loss of a category:

1.   Is the uninflected variant a remnant of an earlier stage of German?
2.   Do uninflected adjectives follow a certain distribution?
3.   Is adjectival inflection in Alemannic in the process of being lost?

To find out whether uninflected adjectives are a remnant of an earlier stage of German, we need to look at some data from Old, Middle and Early New High German. Up to Old High German (OHG) the two inflectional paradigms were distributed dependent on the definiteness status of the whole DP (cf. Braune & Heidermanns 2018; Demske 2001; Kovari 1984). As Table 2 illustrates, the strong inflection occurred in indefinite and the weak inflection in definite DPs. All examples given are late OHG examples from Notker, so the dialect is also Alemannic. The examples are taken from the *Referenzkorpus Altdeutsch*[7] accessed via the ANNIS platform (Krause & Zeldes 2016). It is important to note that there used to be two variants of the strong inflection: the pronominal and the nominal inflection. The nominal inflection in OHG was zero but these zero-inflected adjectives are not considered to be uninflected as they followed the described distribution and only occurred in indefinite DPs (Braune & Heidermanns 2018; Klein 2007; Paul 2007), which means they are considered to be paradigmatic. The relevant point for the discussion in this section is, that at some point their distribution becomes wider and it is no longer feasible to consider them a paradigmatic variant of the inflectional paradigm of adjectives.

Table 2. The semantic distribution in Old High German

Strong inflection	Weak inflection
mit **éinemo** rôtemo with a-DAT.NEUT.SG red-DAT.NEUT.SG tûoche cloth	mít sînero uuîziglich-**ûn** with his-DAT.SG.FEM prophetic-wk gérto stick-DAT.SG
éines scônis a-GEN.NEUT.SG pretty-GEN.NEUT.SG chíndes child-GEN.SG	temo gláseuáreuu-**en** mére the-DAT.SG transparent-wk sea
ein heilig-Ø keist a holy spirit	

---

7.   Accessed online via <https://korpling.german.hu-berlin.de/annis3/ddd>

In Middle High German (MHG) the distribution of the two paradigms was already morpho-syntactically determined (Klein 2007). In addition there are also genuinely uninflected adjectives as Klein (2007) points out, as they appear in both definite and indefinite DPs. This means that the weak ending can be dropped, which was not the case up to OHG. In MHG certain morpho-syntactic features restrict uninflected adjectives. They only appear in nominative singular DPs for all genders and in accusative singular only with neuter nouns. A similar observation can be made for the distribution of adjectival inflection in Early New High German (EarlNHG) as Solms and Wegera (1991) note and which is confirmed by a small corpus study, which was also based on the same corpus (the *Bonner Frühneuhochdeutschkorpus*) in Rehn (2017). The distribution of EarlNHG and MHG uninflected adjectives is summarized in Table 3.[8]

Table 3. Uninflected adjectives in MHG and EarlNHG. Table reproduced from Rehn (2017: 103).

Distribution of uninflected adjectives in MHG and ENHG					
	Masc	Fem	Neut	Sing	Pl
NOM	(✓)	(✓)	(✓)	(✓)	✗
ACC	(✗)	(✗)	(✓)	(✓)	✗
DAT	(✗)	(✗)	(✗)	(✗)	(✗)

In order to answer the question whether uninflected adjectives in Alemannic are a remnant of an earlier stage of German we need to test whether they are subject to the same morpho-syntactic restrictions or if they are even more restricted in their distribution. An even greater restriction is expected in this case because,

---

8.   The brackets in the accusative line mark a difference between MHG and EarlNHG. For MHG, Paul (2007: 200) illustrates that uninflected adjectives in nominative occurred with all genders, in the accusative only with neuter nouns. Solms and Wegera (1991) do not mention this restriction for EarlNHG.

The brackets in the dative line indicate that uninflected adjectives are mentioned as exceptions in dative plural in Solms & Wegera (1991). In addition, I found some examples of uninflected adjectives in dative singular in the corpus they used but only in definite DPs and less frequent than with Nom and Acc:

> *der heilig-Ø kron*
> the.DAT.FEM.SG. holy crown
>
> *dem gemain-Ø Tisch*
> the.DAT.MASC.SG. common table

if uninflected adjectives are a remnant of EarlNHG, it is expected that the further diachronic development results in the inflectional properties that we have in MStG, namely obligatory inflection.[9]

The distribution of uninflected adjectives was investigated in detail in an empirical study across the Alemannic area. The following regions were included: The German county Baden-Württemberg, Alsace in France, the Swiss German areas and Vorarlberg in Austria. All places to which questionnaires were sent out within this area are marked on Map 2. The northernmost parts of Baden-Württemberg were also included in the study even though other dialects are spoken there (eastern Franconian and a Palatinate variety). The advantage of including these areas is that it can be tested whether the results of the study can be extended to varieties other than Alemannic.

In the study, I tested the influence of *case, gender, number* and *definiteness* on the acceptance/rejection of uninflected adjectives, because these variables used to have an impact on the occurrence of uninflected adjectives in the past. Questionnaires containing sentences with inflected and uninflected adjectives were sent out to the regions displayed in Map 2. In these questionnaires, participants rated sentences from 1 (natural) to 5 (not possible) that were given in the Alemannic variety they speak, as illustrated in Figure 2. The corresponding example is given in (20).

(20)   *D' Anna het e neu Fahrrad*
       the Anna has a new bike
       'Anna has a new bike.'

Table 4 below summarizes the main results. For definite and indefinite DPs in Nom/Acc I give the results for the German and the Swiss regions separately to illustrate that there is no considerable difference between the two regions. This is of particular importance because in Switzerland the dialect is the dominant variety in all areas of everyday life, whereas outside of Switzerland it is not, which may have an impact. Regarding the results, it is obvious that there are considerable differences w.r.t. acceptance/rejection for the variables tested. However, these

---

9.   A reviewer notes that there are examples of uninflected adjectives even in MStG. This is correct however, uninflected adjectives are very restricted and the constructions can be analyzed as lexicalized expressions. In some cases, absence or presence of inflection also reflects a semantic difference, which is not the case for the Alemannic data. The reviewer listed the following examples:

   gut-(es) Ding will Weile haben*
   good thing wants time have
   'good things need time'

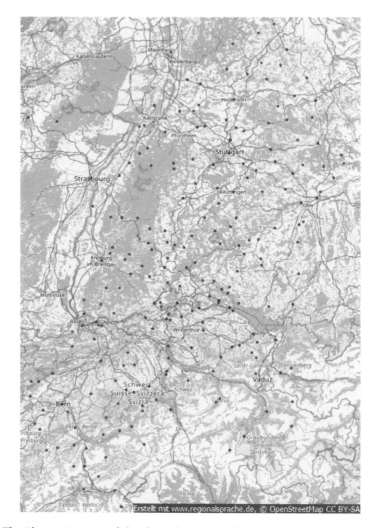

Map 2. The Almeannic area and the places that were included in the study

	natürlich				geht nicht
	1	2	3	4	5
D' Anna het e **neu** Fahrrad.	○	○	○	○	○

Figure 2. Judgement task from the questionnaire study

differences reflect the former restrictions on the realization of uninflected adjectives. The highest acceptance is with singular neuter and masculine nouns. With feminine nouns, uninflected adjectives receive lower acceptance rates but they are not prohibited in this context. Uninflected adjectives also receive lower acceptance rates with dative compared to nominative and accusative. This difference, however, reflects the former restriction on dative, as uninflected adjectives did not frequently occur in oblique DPs (Mausser 1933; Solms & Wegera 1991; Walch & Häckel 1988). The same observation can be made for plural. Uninflected adjectives were – with some exceptions – restricted to singular DPs but in modern Alemannic they can also occur in plural DPs, showing lower acceptance rates though. It is thus not the case that one of the variables clearly triggers or prohibits uninflected adjectives. The results from the study show that the former morpho-syntactic restrictions on uninflected adjectives do no longer hold. Uninflected adjectives have actually spread to contexts from which they were formerly excluded.

The observation that uninflected adjectives have a wider distribution in modern Alemannic compared to MHG and EarlNHG provides the answer for 2) and 3) above: Uninflected adjectives are not a remnant of an earlier stage of German, in the sense that they do not constitute a preserved archaic stage but rather present a case of (ongoing) change. This is evident in the fact that their distribution is less restricted in current varieties compared to e.g., MHG or EarlNHG. In fact there is no longer a particular distribution to be observed – neither a regional nor a morpho-syntactic one.[10]

It might therefore be the case that in German dialects – or at least in Alemannic – adjectival inflection is in the process of being lost. However, this is not the case as the data from the questionnaire prove. For each sentence with an uninflected adjective, I also tested inflected ones, which received very high acceptance throughout. High acceptance means 60% (indef. oblique) to 80% (indef. Nom/Acc and def. oblique) of the sentences were rated with 1 or 2. In addition, the adjectives *rosa* (pink) and *lila* (purple), which occur uninflected in MStG, can occur both in uninflected and inflected form in Alemannic as illustrated in (21) and (22). This means that for all contexts, in which uninflected adjectives appear, inflection is also always possible.

---

10.   It must be noted though that uninflected adjectives are excluded from DPs without articles. In Rehn (2017) it is argued that this restriction can be explained by obligatory number marking in DPs without articles when a modifier is present. It is further argued that the inflection that appears on the adjective is actually realized higher up in the structure and the adjective moves for convergence at PF. Therefore, these results do not pose a counter example to the general observation of optionality here.

(21)   a.   *Ein rosa Rock*
              a pink skirt

       b.   *Ein lila Pullover*
              a purple jumper

(22)   a.   *A rosaner Rock*
              a pink-STR skirt

       b.   *A lilaner Pulli*
              a purple-STR jumper

Table 4. Results of the questionnaire study

	Uninflected Adjectives in Alemannic					
Judgement	1	2	3	4	5	x
Singular						
n=10598	26.89	22.16	17.31	13.41	13.5	6.73
Indefinite NPs (Nom & Acc)						
D (n=2510)	25.98	21.43	20.24	13.07	11.2	8.09
CH (n=1140)	18.68	18.6	14.74	17.11	23.77	7.11
Definite NPs (Nom & Acc)						
D (n=2510)	37.21	27.5	15.06	10.16	5.7	4.38
CH (n=1140)	33.42	24.74	15.44	9.3	12.11	5
Gender (Nom & Acc, def & indef)						
Fem (n=1514)	23.51	23.18	18.03	13.87	14.93	6.47
Masc (n=1293)	27.22	22.12	15.93	12.68	18.17	3.9
Neut (n=1293)	40.84	23.28	11.76	7.58	12.61	3.94
Oblique case						
Def (n=1514)	18.69	20.34	18.36	16.11	18.3	8.19
Indef (n=1514)	20.08	18.03	18.96	17.44	18.1	7.4
Plural:						
n=2733	19.72	12.62	14.45	17.78	30.44	4.98

Question 1 above can therefore be answered with 'no': Adjectival inflection is not in a process of loss. What we observe is a case of optionality. For all contexts given, it is possible to drop inflection but it is also possible to realize the inflectional ending without any interpretive effect.

The question at this point is: Why does adjectival inflection not disappear, if it obviously does no longer fulfill a particular function? In the next section it will be shown that the answer to this question lies in the elements themselves, to be more precise, it lies in their multifunctional nature.

4.1   Why optionality and not loss?

In order to understand why adjectival inflection has become optional instead of being lost we need to have a closer look at the inflectional elements themselves. As shown above, we have two paradigms, the strong and the weak one. The strong paradigm is also called pronominal as the very same ending can be found on different functional elements: it combines with *d-* forming the definite determiner, demonstrative or relative pronoun and it also combines with the indefinite article or possessives to build their pronominal counter parts. It even appears in isolation, functioning as personal pronoun as Wiltschko (1998) convincingly argues. The different contexts, in which the pronominal paradigm appears, are illustrated in Table 5.[11]

Table 5. The pronominal paradigm

adj.	th-	one-	my	he, it, she
adj.	d-	ein-	mein-	er
adj.	d-	ein-	mein-	es
adj.	d-	ein-	mein-	(s)(i)e

The weak paradigm in its function as adjectival inflection is in fact younger than the pronominal one whereas the element itself is also very old as it used to be a so called stem suffix. The origin of this element is already investigated in detail in Osthoff (1876). Of main interest for our purposes are the functions this element still has in our language. The weak paradigm used to be a very productive word formation morpheme in the Germanic period (Wessén 1914) and in modern German varieties it is still present as an inflectional ending on so called weak masculine nouns. Furthermore, Los (2005) and Wessén (1914) note that the infinitive ending on German verbs may also be the very same element. The contexts in which the weak ending appears in modern German are summarized in Table 6.

---

11.   The origin of the s- on the feminine form is not clear, as pointed out in Wiltschko (1998: 150). Regarding spelling: The standard German variant of the feminine personal pronoun is *sie* but in colloquial German as well as in the dialects it is often pronounced as *se*.

Table 6. Weak inflection in different contexts

	Weak masc. nouns	Weak adjectival inflection	Infinitive
	Bauer (farmer)	*gut (good)*	*machen (to make)*
Nom.	Bauer	gut-e	mache-en
Acc.	Bauer-n	gut-en	
Dat.	Bauer-n	gut-en	
Gen.	Bauer-n	gut-en	

Weak and strong paradigm have thus in common that neither of them does exclusively function as adjectival inflection. Both paradigms occur in different contexts, in which they fulfill different functions, corresponding to the notion of high functional load as introduced in Section 1. The consequence of this observation is that these elements must remain available in the lexicon and cannot be subject to loss. In other words, they cannot disappear because they are multifunctional. It may be objected that despite its high functional load, the pronominal paradigm was lost in English. English, as is well known, has undergone quite different developments compared to the rest of the Germanic languages, which may be due to language contact rather than language internal developments (McWhorter 2002). Thus, additional factors besides (or instead of) the ones discussed in this paper must have led to extensive loss in the English language. The connection between functional load and loss that is made in this paper should thus not be understood as a single factor that always has the same effect of triggering or preventing loss in different languages. In most cases more than one factor is probably involved, which may in turn affect the impact high or low functional load can have (cf. e.g., the role of register in the loss of *so* relatives as discussed by Kempf (this volume)). This also means that findings that hold for one language may not automatically hold in others, thus raising the question whether there is indeed a general principle that is always involved in loss – a question that is beyond the scope of the paper, which can only provide a language-specific contribution to this question.

Returning to adjectival inflection, the observations made above do not answer the question why the two paradigms still appear on adjectives without any particular function in this context. Even though the two inflectional paradigms cannot disappear completely they could still disappear from the adjectival context. In order to understand the observed optionality we need to have a closer look at the syntactic structure of modified DPs.

Regarding the syntax of modified DPs, I follow the general assumption that adjectives are merged in the specifier of a designated projection (Cinque 2010; Gallmann 1996; Julien 2005; Kester 1996) which I call Mod(ifier) P(hrase) corresponding to the AgrP as mentioned in Section 2.1, but the actual label is of minor relevance. The important point is that adjectival inflection is not placed inside the AP but heads this functional projection as illustrated in Figure 3. This assumption is based on the diachronic development of the category adjective and its inflection as worked out in detail in Rehn (2017), a point I will not elaborate further here.

The relevant aspect for our purposes is that whenever an adjective is merged in SpecModP the head-position is of course also available. Furthermore, as was argued above, the inflectional elements that appear as adjectival inflection are also always available. Therefore, the presence of the two paradigms in the lexicon together with the availability of a slot in the syntactic structure make the optional realization of adjectival inflection in Alemannic possible. They always can but never have to be merged in Mod°. At the same time, loss of the elements functioning as adjectival inflection is prevented – or at least seems to be affected – in Alemannic by their multifunctional nature as was already noted above. Furthermore, the position in the structure, in which the pronominal or weak paradigm are merged, also determines how they are interpreted. I follow Borer (2005) in assuming that the structure under which an element is embedded is responsible for its interpretation. The lexical element *walk* for example, is not categorially specified as noun or verb, but it is interpreted as noun when embedded under DP and as verb when embedded under TP.[12] For the inflectional endings this means that despite their multifunctional nature, ambiguity does never arise, a point that is also stressed in Hachem (2015). The reason is that e.g. the pronominal paradigm fulfills a different function when merged in the DP-layer (as inflection on the demonstrative for example) than in ModP. Since the syntactic contexts are different the interpretation is necessarily also different. In Figure 3 we can see that the pronominal paradigm can be merged in Mod° where it does not fulfill a particular function besides the phonetic realization of concord, which is optional. The same element can also appear in the D-layer (the highest portion of the noun phrase, in which articles are realized and thus corresponding to the leftmost position linearly) as inflection on the definite article. In this case it is obligatory as it makes case and phi-features visible in the highest projection of the DP. This is of relevance as the features must be visible for further syntactic processes (e.g., subject verb agreement).

The same holds for the weak inflection as well as other multifunctional elements as we will see in the next section and which is investigated and in detail in Hachem (2015) for German and Dutch d- and w-pronouns.

---

12.   Since D is the locus of determiners (cf. section 2.1), a functional element only found in noun phrases, and T is associated with tense, a property of verbs, these projections determine the categorial status of the lexical elements, which are embedded under them.

(23)   a.   *ein gut-(es) Buch*

     b.   *das gut-(e) Buch*

       a/the good book

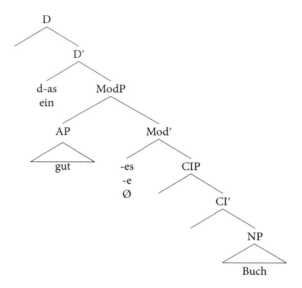

Figure 3. Optional inflection in Mod°

In the next section, I will discuss relative clause introducers (RCI) in German dialects. In the case of RCIs, the availability of different strategies does not lead to the loss of one of the elements (unlike in the case of the adnominal genitive), but we can observe variation. I will again attribute this fact to the multifunctional nature of German RCIs.

5.   Relative clauses

Relative clauses are generally introduced with a d-pronoun in MStG as in (24). This means that in StG there is only one strategy[13] available to introduce relative clauses, namely the *pronoun-strategy.*

---

13.   When I say 'one' strategy, I mean the use of a pronoun as an RCI but besides the d-pronoun there is of course also the option of using *welch-* as an RCI. This element also falls under the 'pronoun strategy', which is why I do not list it as a separate strategy to introduce RCs in Standard German.

(24)   *Der Nachbar, **d-er**...*   (Standard German)
       The neighbor, the-NOM.MASC.SG

In Alemannic (as well as other dialects) there are three different strategies to introduce relative clauses. Like in MStG, the d-pronoun can be used as in (25). In addition, the particle *wo* is a common RCI, illustrated in (26). As a third option, the
d-pronoun can be combined with the particle as in (27).

(25)   *Der Nochbr, **d-er**...*   (Alemannic)
       The neighbor, the-NOM.MASC.SG

(26)   *Der Nochbr, **wo**...*
       The neighbor, PRT

(27)   *Der Nochbr, **d-er wo**...*
       The neighbor, the-NOM.MASC.SG PRT...
       'The neighbor, who...'

Regarding Alemannic, several questions arise in connection to the variation in
(24) to (26):

1. Is there a dominant strategy?
2. If there is a dominant strategy, is the other one declining?
3. If the strategies are equally accepted, what exactly prevents loss?

"Han ihr net/it g'hört, dass er grad erscht Arbeiter entlassen het müsse."		
5.5 Sogar an Schreiner	**der** ☐ **der wo** ☐ **wo** ☐	bei ihm scho 15 Jahr g'schafft hot!

Figure 4. Questionnaire task choice of RCI

Let us consider the first of the three questions. Bräuning (2017) undertook a very
detailed empirical study on RCIs in Alemannic, which was also set within the Syn-
ALM project already mentioned above. The area is thus the same as for the study
on adjectival inflection displayed in Map 2 and I will also refer to the political areas
when necessary. The method was slightly different though. Instead of judgement
tasks, the participants of the questionnaire study had to fill in the preferred RCI in
a given sentence. This is illustrated in Figure 4, which is part of the questionnaire
undertaken previous to the one on adjectival inflection.

The results of Bräuning's study show that there are regional differences regarding the choice of the RCI. In the Alemannic areas in Germany and Austria there is
no clear dominant strategy. All three options listed in (25) to (27) can occur and
none is dominant. In the Swiss and French Alemannic areas, however, there is a

clear preference for the particle strategy. The other two options are only marginally realized as Bräuning's results show.

Since there are three different strategies available, it may be the case that the choice of strategy is determined by morpho-syntactic factors. Fleischer (2006) as well as Salzmann (2006) investigated this assumption in some detail. The basic idea is, that in relative clauses the indirect object must always be case-marked overtly. This assumption is plausible as it corresponds to the *Accessibility Hierarchy* proposed in Keenan and Comrie (1977), stating, that arguments that are higher up in this hierarchy are easier to access and thus might not require overt case marking. In this hierarchy the subject (SU) and direct object (DO) are higher than the Indirect Object (IO). Fleischer (2004, 2006) takes this observation as a starting point to investigate whether this hierarchy has an impact regarding case marking in relative clauses. The expectation is that SU and DO do not require case marking, hence the particle strategy should be available, whereas the IO does. Therefore IO should require the presence of the d-pronoun. In the German and Austrian Alemannic regions this strategy is available, however, it is absent in Swiss Alemannic. Therefore, a resumptive is expected to occur in this context. The expected grammatical and ungrammatical patterns are illustrated in (28) to (31). Examples (28) to (30) are taken from Salzmann (2006: 18) and are all Alemannic. Example (31) is a Bavarian example quoted from Fleischer (2006: 230):

(28)   *D Frau, wo (*si) immer z spat chunt*   (SU)
        The woman, PRT (she) always too late comes
        'the woman who is always late'

(29)   *es Bild, wo niemert (*s) cha zale*   (DO)
        a picture, PRT nobody (it) can pay
        'a picture that nobody can afford'

(30)   *De Bueb, wo mer *(em) es Velo versproche hand*   (IO)
        The boy, PRT we (he.DAT) a bike promised have
        'the boy we promised a bike'

(31)   *deà Mo, *(dem) wo dees keàd*   (IO)
        [the man]$_{Nom}$ d-DAT PRT that belongs
        'the man this belongs to'

Fleischer (2006) points out that across the German dialects he investigated based on various grammars, there is no clear regional pattern to be observed. There is a great amount of variability, as some dialects seem to correspond directly to the above restriction on IO-marking, including Swiss German, whereas others do not.

Bräuning (2017) investigated the choice of RCI and the presence vs absence of a resumptive pronoun to test the above made predictions in detail for Alemannic.

Unlike the assumptions and findings in Salzmann (2006, 2013) or Fleischer (2004, 2006) her study does not confirm obligatory case marking for IO – neither for the Alemannic dialects spoken in Switzerland nor for the Alemannic varieties of Austria or Germany. Bräuning also finds variability regarding the acceptance vs rejection of certain constructions but she can clearly show that neither resumptives nor the d-pronoun or doubling are obligatory in IO relative clauses. Table 7 and Table 8 show the results for the sentences in (32) (a judgement task similar to the one displayed in Figure 2).[14]

(32) a. resumptive:
          *Des isch der Maa, **wo** ma **em** de Hund klaut het*

      b. d-pronoun
          *Des isch der Maa, **dem** ma de Hund klaut het*

      c. doubling
          *Des isch der Maa, **dem wo** ma de Hund klaut het*

      d. particle
          *Des isch der Maa, **wo** ma de Hund klaut het*
          this is the man, RCI one the dog (resumptive) stolen has
          'This is the man whose dog was stolen'

Table 7. Results for sentence (32a) and (32b). These results are from a judgement task (scale from 1 (natural) to 5 (not possible)).

	Sentence (32a)				Sentence (32b)			
	BW	CH	VA	EL	BW	CH	VA	EL
	n=444	n=279	n=21	n=8	n=444	n=279	n=21	n=8
1	1.13%	7.53%	0%	12.5%	66.22%	29.03%	61.9%	25%
2	1.35%	8.6%	4.76%	12.5%	17.57%	28.32%	9.52%	50%
3	11.71%	17.56%	14.29%	12.5%	7.88%	15.05%	4.76%	25%
4	19.14%	20.07%	14.29%	12.5%	1.58%	11.47%	0%	0%
5	60.59%	42.65%	66.67%	37.5%	2.7%	13.26%	14.29%	0%
x	6.08%	3.58%	0%	12.5%	4.05%	2.87%	9.52%	0%

---

14. A reviewer noted that methodology might play a role regarding the results. It is of course ideal when different methods can be used for investigating a certain phenomenon, however, the method of questionnaires for collecting dialectal data is by now an established one and was used in several dialect projects (e.g., SAND or Syhd).

Table 8. Results for sentence (32c) and (32d). These results are from a judgement task (scale from 1 (natural) to 5 (not possible).

	Sentence (32c)				Sentence (32d)			
	BW	CH	VA	EL	BW	CH	VA	EL
	n=444	n=279	n=21	n=8	n=444	n=279	n=21	n=8
1	39.41%	19%	42.86%	25%	46.4%	67.74%	52.38%	37.5%
2	22.07%	23.3%	19.05%	12.5%	29.5%	15.77%	19.05%	37.5%
3	19.82%	17.2%	4.76%	25%	13.29%	7.17%	4.76%	0%
4	6.53%	11.11%	4.76%	0%	3.83%	2.51%	9.52%	12.5%
5	6.98%	26.52%	23.81%	25%	3.83%	4.3%	9.52%	12.5%
x	5.18%	2.87%	4.76%	12.5%	3.15%	2.51%	4.76%	0%

The acceptance of resumptives is slightly higher for the Alemannic variety spoken in Switzerland compared to the other Alemannic regions, however, the results show that they are clearly not obligatory. The results above show a rather low acceptance for sentence (32a) even for Swiss Alemannic, however, rejection is lower as more people were undecided and rated the sentence with 3. Acceptance rates are higher for other IO-sentences (around 40% acceptance[15]) but still lower than expected if a resumptive was indeed obligatory (see Bräuning (2017) for discussion of this point).

Again, we are faced with the question: Why do we have variation instead of substitution/loss? When different elements are available that fulfill the same function the expected outcome is complementary distribution or the development of a dominant strategy and at the same time decline and at some point loss of the others. In the case of RCIs in Alemannic neither is the case. The three available strategies seem to be in free variation in the Alemannic varieties spoken in Germany and Austria. In order to understand the source of this type of variation, we need to investigate the RCIs themselves in more detail.

5.1   The Origin of the Alemannic RCIs

In the following, it will be shown that the elements themselves will again provide the answer. Let us first look at the relative pronoun in some detail. The d-element discussed here can appear in three contexts: as an RCI as in (33), as a definite article as in (34), and as a demonstrative as in (35):

---

15.   Acceptance means a rating with 1 or 2 on a scale from 1 (natural) to 5 (not possible).

(33)   *Das ist der Hund, **der** gestern abgehauen ist.*
       This is the dog, which yesterday away-ran is
       'This is the dog, which ran away yesterday.'

(34)   *Ist das **der** Hund aus dem Tierheim?*
       Is this the dog from the animal shelter?

(35)   *Das ist nicht der Hund aus dem Tierheim, sondern **DER** Hund*
       This is not the dog from the animal shelter but that dog

       dort ist es.
       there is it

       'This is not the dog from the animal shelter but it is that dog over there.'

The three contexts above show that the d-element is multifunctional just like the inflectional paradigms that were discussed in the previous section and is thus also an element that shows high functional load. It occurs in various contexts with different functions. Therefore, the d-element itself cannot disappear.[16] However, we must again ask why it remains available as an RCI since a second strategy is available. Furthermore, the option of combining particle and pronoun strategy must also be explained – but before doing so, the particle *wo* as an RCI is investigated in more detail.

There are four different scenarios regarding the origin of *wo* as an RCI:

1.   *wo* has its origin in the locative adverb (Bidese, Padovan & Tomaselli 2012; Fiorentino 2007),
2.   *wo* has its origin in the split R-pronoun construction (Staedele (1927),
3.   *wo*-relative clauses are related to free relative clauses that used to be introduce by a w-element that was preceded and followed by *so* in Old High German (sô (h)wâr sô) (cf. Braune & Heidermanns (2018: 346) or Grimm[17]),
4.   the particle *wo* is directly related to the equative element *so,* which used to be an RCI, too (Brandner & Bräuning 2013).

As a locative adverb *wo* is the wh-counterpart of *da* (there/here) as in (36). The split-pronoun construction is illustrated in (37). A free relative clause is given in (38). In (40) a *so*-relative (quoted from Brandner & Bräuning (2013: 132)) is given and an equative construction in (39) to illustrate the basis for Brandner and Bräuning's (2013) analysis.

---

16.   An alternative analysis would of course be to assume three different lexicon entries for *der*. I will not address this as an option here but see Hachem (2015) for discussion.

17.   Source is the online version of Grimm's dictionary accessed via: <http://dwb.uni-trier .de/de> (25 March 2019).

(36)　*Wo ist das Telefon? - Da steht es.*　　(locative adverb)
　　　Where is the phone? - It is over there.

(37)　*Wo hast nichts **von** gehört*　　(split pronoun)
　　　Where have you nothing of heard?
　　　'What did you hear nothing about?'

(38)　*Die Kinder essen, was auf den Tisch kommt.*　　(free relative)
　　　The children eat what on the table comes
　　　'The children eat whatever is on the table.'

(39)　*Peter ist **so** groß wie Maria*　　(equative)
　　　Peter is as tall as Maria

(40)　*hier das Geld **so** ich neulich (…)*　　(so relative clause)
　　　here the money **so** I recently
　　　'Here is the money that I recently (…)'

At first glance, relating the particle *wo* to the locative adverb seems the most intuitive scenario. However, as Brandner and Bräuning (2013) argue, the distribution of the particle *wo* does not resemble the distribution of its locative counterpart, which makes a relation between the two questionable. Furthermore, there are no other w-elements in spoken language used as an RCI (an observation that is also true for other Germanic languages as Fiorentino (2007) notes). Regarding the split R-pronoun as the origin of the particle, it is noted that a rather unusual process would have taken place. In this scenario, we have a complex pronoun; however, in the process of grammaticalization into an RCI, only one part is grammaticalized whereas the other one does not play a role. Furthermore, split R-pronouns are attested in Alemannic but are not highly productive, because the construction is restricted to the preposition *mit* (with), whereas in other dialects, this restriction cannot be observed (Brandner & Bräuning 2013; Fleischer 2002: 123–124). For this reason they are an unlikely basis for *wo* as an RCI. Free relative clauses as origin of *wo*-relative clauses are also argued against because of their different semantics and syntax. In addition, if free relatives were the source of *wo*-relatives it remains unclear why w-pronouns do not generally occur as RCIs in German (Brandner & Bräuning 2013: 146). These are only some of the points mentioned in Brandner and Bräuning regarding scenarios 1. to 3. and I will not go into the criticism in more detail.

　　They propose an alternative approach, in which they relate the particle *wo* to the equative element *so*. The main idea is that *wo* as an RCI is directly connected to relative clauses introduced by *so* as in (39) above. These *so*-relative clauses are attested up to the 19th century (see also Kempf (this volume) on the loss of *so*-relative clauses) and can even be found in current Alemannic as in the empirical study undertaken by Bräuning, in which a translation task was given and some participants translated the standard German relative clauses using *so* as RCI. It is convincingly argued that *so*-relative clauses – and thus the element *so* – is the origin of *wo* as an RCI. This scenario is very likely for two main reasons:

a. the two elements are particles occupying C° and *wo*-relatives are simply a continuation of a former particle strategy
b. the semantics of RCs and equative constructions is similar (involving a conjunction).

The point in a. is explained in (40) and (41). The latter illustrates how the RC must be paraphrased to reveal the equative semantics.

(41) *des Buech, wo ich g'lese ha*
      the book PRT I have read

(42) x is a book <u>and</u>
      I read something (=y)
      whereby *so/wo* states that x=y   (Brandner & Bräuning 2013:148)

The important point for our purpose is that *so* as an equative element is not an exclusive RCI (see (39) above, which is just one example) and neither is *wo*. Besides *wo*, it is argued in Brandner and Bräuning (2013: 150), *so* is also the origin of *wie,* because the equative marker now realized as *wie* was actually realized as *so* in OHG. Both *wie* and *wo* are complementizers introducing temporal clauses (in MStG they are introduced by *als* as in (43) c. The choice of element depends on the dialects as is illustrated with the examples given in (42).

(43) a. *Wo er hom gloffe isch…*   (Alemannic)
      b. *Wia ar heim glauffen is…*   (Bavarian)
      c. *Als er heimlief…*   (Standard German)
          'When he walked home…'   (Brandner & Bräuning 2013: 153)

The relevant point for our discussion is that *wo*, just like its earlier form *so*, does not exclusively occur in relative clauses. Again, the element fulfills different functions in different contexts, a fact that can be attributed to the etymological connection between *wo* and *so*. This means that again we have an element that is multifunctional and thus cannot disappear from the lexicon. Crucially, the main observation of *wo* being a multifunctional element does not only hold when adopting Brandner and Bräuning's approach but also when adopting one of the other approaches listed in 1. to 4. above.

This observation does not explain, however, why both – particle and pronoun strategy – are kept in the context of relative clauses. From a purely syntactic point of view, there are a number of different analyses, which I will not address here as they are not relevant to the point I want to make, but see e.g., Alexiadou, Law, Meinunger & Wilder (2000) or Boef (2013) for an overview.

We nevertheless must have a closer look at the basic syntactic structure of relative clauses and the position in which pronoun and particle are merged, which is illustrated in Figure 5, an adapted version of the structure given in Bräuning (2017: 275). The pronoun is a phrase and thus merged in specifier-position, namely in SpecCP (this is put down as *Pron* in Figure 5), which is the leftmost position in the relative clause. The pronoun is not based in this position but it moves to SpecCP from its position in the verb phrase, a point, which I will not address in more detail here. The particle is a head and it is merged in C° (it is put down as PRT in Figure 5). The relevant point is that the two elements are realized in different positions in the syntactic structure, and thus the combination of pronoun and particle strategy is a variant of doubly filled comp (cf. Bayer 1984). As pronoun and particle occupy different structural positions, they cannot be in complementary distribution. In addition, since both elements do not only function as RCIs, they must remain available in the lexicon and cannot disappear. Therefore, variation is possible as well as the co-occurrence of both RCIs. The preference for the particle strategy in the Swiss-Alemannic parts must have independent reasons. It would of course be desirable to understand the origin of this particular regional distribution better, but I leave this point for future research (but see Bräuning (2017) for discussion and also Section 5 on the analysis of variation in terms of multiple grammars).

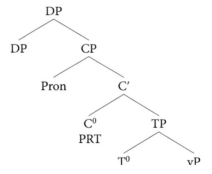

Figure 5. Simplified structure of an RC adapted from Bräuning (2017: 275)

Having investigated three rather different phenomena, I will discuss them again in the next section focusing on the question, which conditions allow or prevent loss in a language.

6.   Discussion

In the previous sections three different constructions have been investigated, in order to understand the conditions of loss of a category better. I looked at the adnominal genitive as an instance of loss, adjectival inflection as an example for optionality and RCIs illustrating (free) variation. All three phenomena have in common that an alternative element or strategy is able to fulfill the function the elements under discussion have or used to have. The main question thus is: what are the conditions allowing or preventing loss?

The adnominal genitive, as was shown, has the core function of being a connective between two DPs in a dependency relation. In this function, the adnominal genitive is retained in MStG but has been replaced by various substitution strategies in colloquial German and German dialects. The important observation regarding the adnominal genitive is the fact that it almost solely appears in one specific morpho-syntactic context unlike adjectival inflection or the RCIs that were investigated. Therefore, the limited functional load of the adnominal genitive in combination with the available substitution strategies was taken as a condition for loss. This assumption was then underpinned by comparing the loss of the adnominal genitive with other phenomena. It was shown that the two German adjectival paradigms show 'high functional load' in the sense that they appear in a variety of contexts, in which they fulfill different functions. So despite the fact that adjectival inflection is optional in Alemannic the element is not lost due to its multifunctionality. The fact that adjectival inflection does not disappear from the context of attributive adjectives either – despite its being optional in this position – is connected to the fact that the syntax provides a slot in which the two paradigms can always be merged. Adjectives are merged in the specifier of a designated functional projection headed by the pronominal or weak inflection. Since this head-position is always available whenever an adjective is merged, optional realization of adjectival inflection is possible.

Regarding variation in RCIs, it was illustrated that the German RCIs are also multifunctional, just like adjectival inflection. In addition, they are merged in different structural positions (SpecCP and C), which makes not only their co-occurrence possible but it also explains the observed variation regarding the choice of RCI. Furthermore, the general observation that multifunctionality does not lead to ambiguity (Hachem 2015) also holds for RCIs as well as adjectival inflection. As noted above, the syntactic environment determines the interpretation of an element, which also explains the (syntactic) possibility of multifuncitonality.

We can thus conclude that loss – at least in the varieties discussed – seems to require two things:

1. the functional load of the element undergoing loss must be limited and
2. an alternative strategy must be available.

This means that even though individual elements or constructions may at some point disappear from a language, their function does not. In other words: languages do not lose the option to express certain relations by losing a certain category (but see Kuo (this volume) on the loss of a whole construction rather than an individual element).

Since in the paper different varieties were compared, another open question is whether the morpho-syntactic differences between these varieties may be analyzed in terms of multiple grammars (cf. Anttila 2007; Kroch 1989). This would mean that the adnominal genitive in non-standard varieties is not lost but the difference between MStG and non-standard varieties can be attributed to multiple grammars among which speakers choose one or the other depending on the sociolinguistic context. Even if one would like to explain the difference between these varieties by attributing it to the existence of multiple grammars, this would not affect the conclusion of the paper. The reason is that synchronic variation may be analyzed by assuming multiple grammars, however, the diachronic development of Alemannic nevertheless involves loss of the adnominal genitive as it used to be productive in earlier stages of German. This means that within this variety a process of loss must have taken place that allows us to investigate the difference between Alemannic (or other dialects) and MStG. More generally: for the specific constructions that were discussed (modified DPs and RCs), the assumption is that the underlying syntactic structure is the same in all German varieties (including MStG). The observed variation does therefore not reflect a syntactic difference. The reason why one variety makes use of all options the syntax provides whereas others do not is an independent question.

For the purpose of this paper I investigated three phenomena focusing on the southern German dialect Alemannic, leading to the conclusions given in 1. and 2. above. In order to find out whether this correlation can be generalized, a cross-linguistic investigation of similar phenomena in languages other than German would be necessary. It would be particularly interesting to investigate loss of similar elements in languages that do not belong to the Germanic language family. Nevertheless, despite the limited set of varieties that were investigated there is independent evidence that functional load may be a constraint on loss, because functional load has already been shown to have an impact on loss in phonemic contrasts, for which its definition is of course different (cf. Wedel, Kaplan & Jackson 2013).

Acknowledgements

I thank Ellen Brandner and Yvonne Viesel for valuable feedback on the topic as well as two anonymous reviewers, the editors and the audience of the Lost in Change Workshop. Any remaining errors are my own.

References

Alexiadou, Artemis, Law, Paul, Meinunger, André & Wilder, Chris. 2000. *The Syntax of Relative Clauses* [Linguistik Aktuell/Linguistics Today 32]. Amsterdam: John Benjamins. https://doi.org/10.1075/la.32

Anttila, Arto. 2007. Variation and optionality. In *The Cambridge Handbook of Phonology*, Paul de Lacy (ed.), 519–536. Cambridge: CUP. https://doi.org/10.1017/CBO9780511486371.023

Barker, Chris. 2019. Possessives and relational nouns. In *Semantics-Noun Phrases and Verb Phrases*, Paul Hortner, Klaus von Heusinger & Claudia Maienborn (eds), 177–203. Berlin: De Gruyter Mouton. https://doi.org/10.1515/9783110589443-006

Bayer, Josef. 1984. COMP in Bavarian syntax. *The Linguistic Review* 3 (3): 209–274. https://doi.org/10.1515/tlir.1984.3.3.209

Bidese, Ermenegildo, Padovan, Andrea & Tomaselli, Alessandra. 2012. A binary system of complementizers in Cimbrian relative clauses. *Working Papers in Scandinavian Syntax* 90: 1–21.

Birlinger, Anton. 1868. *Die Alemannische Sprache Rechts des Rheins seit dem XIII.* Jahrhundert. Berlin: Ferd. Dümmler's Verlagsbuchhandlung.

Boef, Eefje. 2013. Doubling in Relative Clauses: Aspects of Morphosyntactic Microvariation in Dutch. PhD dissertation, Utrecht University.

Borer, Hagit. 2005. *In Name Only, Vol. 1*. Oxford: OUP.

Brandner, Ellen & Bräuning, Iris. 2013. Relative wo in Alemannic: Only a complementizer? *Linguistische Berichte 2013* (234): 131–169.

Braune, Wilhelm & Heidermanns, Frank. 2018. *Althochdeutsche Grammatik I*. Berlin: De Gruyter. https://doi.org/10.1515/9783110515114

Bräuning, Iris. 2017. Relativsatzstrategien im Alemannischen. PhD dissertation, University of Konstanz.

Cinque, Guglielmo. 2010. *The Syntax of Adjectives. A Comparative Study* [Linguistic Inquiry Monographs 57]. Cambridge MA: The MIT Press. https://doi.org/10.7551/mitpress/9780262014168.001.0001

Demske, Ulrike. 2001. *Merkmale und Relationen. Diachrone Studien zur Nominalphrase des Deutschen* [Studia Germanica Linguistica 56]. Berlin: Walter de Gruyter. https://doi.org/10.1515/9783110811353

Fiorentino, Giuliana. 2007. European relative clauses and the uniqueness of the relative pronoun type. *Italian Journal of Linguistics* 19 (2): 263–291.

Fleischer, Jürg. 2002. Preposition stranding in German dialects. In *Syntactic Microvariation. Online Proceedings - Workshop on Syntactic Microvariation* Sjef Barbiers, Leonie Cornips & Susanne van der Kleij (eds.), 116–151. <https://www.meertens.knaw.nl/books/synmic/> (6 November 2020).

Fleischer, Jürg. 2004. A typology of relative clauses in German dialects. *In Dialectology meets Typology. Dialect Grammar from a Cross-linguistic Perspective*, Walter Bisang, Hans Henrich Hock & Werner Winter (eds), 211–243. Berlin: Mouton de Gruyter.

Fleischer, Jürg. 2006. Dative and indirect object in German dialects. In *Datives and Other Cases. Between Argument Structure and Event Structure* [Studies in Language Companion Series 75], Daniel Hole, André Meinunger & Werner Abraham (eds), 213–238. Amsterdam: John Benjamins. https://doi.org/10.1075/slcs.75.10fle

Fleischer, Jürg & Schallert, Oliver. 2011. *Historische Syntax des Deutschen. Eine Einführung*. Tübingen: Gunter Narr.

von der Gabelentz, Georg. 1901. *Die Sprachwissenschaft. Ihre Aufgaben, Methoden und bisherigen Ergebnisse*, 2 edn. Leipzig: Chr. Herm. Tauchnitz.

Gallmann, Peter. 1996. Die Steuerung der Flexion in der DP. *Linguistische Berichte* 164: 283–314.

Gallmann, Peter. 2018. The genitive rule and its background. In *Germanic Genitives* [Studies in Language Companion Series 193], Tanja Ackermann, Horst J. Simon & Christian Zimmer (eds), 149–188. Amsterdam: John Benjamins. https://doi.org/10.1075/slcs.193.07gal

van Gelderen, Elly. 2011. *The Linguistic Cycle. Language Change and the Language Faculty*. Oxford: OUP.

Grimm, Jacob. 1822. *Deutsche Grammatik*, 4 Vols, Vol. 2. Göttingen: Dietrich.

Hachem, Mirjam. 2015. *Multifunctionality. The Internal and External Syntax of D-and W-Items in German and Dutch*. Utrecht: LOT.

Hentschel, Elke. 1993. Flexionsverfall im Deutschen? Die Kasusmarkierung bei partitiven Genetiv-Attributen/A decay of inflectional endings in German? The case marking of partitive genitive attributes. *Zeitschrift für germanistische Linguistik* 21: 320–333.

Jellinek, Max-Hermann. 1914. *Geschichte der neuhochdeutschen Grammatik II. Von den Anfängen bis auf Adelung*, Vol. Zweiter Halbband. Heidelberg: Carl Winter's Universitätsbuchhandlung.

Julien, Marit. 2005. *Nominal Phrases from a Scandinavian Perspective* [Linguistik Aktuell/Linguistics Today 87]. Amsterdam: John Benjamins. https://doi.org/10.1075/la.87

Kasper, Simon. 2014. Linking syntax and semantics of adnominal possession in the history of German. In *Language Change at the Syntax-Semantics Interface* [Trends in Linguistics. Studies and Monographs 278], Chiara Gianollo, Agnes Jäger & Doris Penka (eds), 57–99. Berlin: Walter de Gruyter.

Keenan, Edward L. & Comrie, Bernard. 1977. Noun phrase accessibility and universal grammar. *Linguistic Inquiry* 8 (1): 63–99.

Kester, Ellen-Petra. 1996. Adjectival inflection and the licensing of empty categories in DP. *Journal of Linguistics* 32 (1): 57–78. https://doi.org/10.1017/S0022226700000761

Kiefer, Heinrich. 1910. Der Ersatz des adnominalen Genitivs im Deutschen. PhD dissertation, Hessische Ludwigs University, Giessen.

Klein, Thomas. 2007. Von der semantischen zur morphologischen Steuerung. In *Beiträge zur Morphologie. Germanisch, Baltisch, Ostseefinnisch*, Hans Fix (ed.), 193–225. Odense: University Press of Southern Denmark.

Kovari, Geoffrey. 1984. *Studien zum germanischen Artikel. Entstehung und Verwendung des Artikels im Gotischen* [Wiener Arbeiten zur germanischen Altertumskunde und Philologie 26]. Wien: Halosar.

Krause, Thomas & Zeldes, Amir. 2016. ANNIS3: A new architecture for generic corpus query and visualization. *Digital Scholarship in the Humanities* 31 (1): 118–139. https://doi.org/10.1093/llc/fqu057

Kroch, Anthony. 1994. Morphosyntactic variation. In *Papers from the 30th Regional Meeting of the Chicago Linguistics Society. Parasession on Variation and Linguistic Theory 2*, Katherine Beals (ed.), 180–201. Chicago IL: CLS.

Kroch, Anthony S. 1989. Reflexes of grammar in patterns of language change. *Language Variation and Change* 1 (3): 199–244. https://doi.org/10.1017/S0954394500000168

Lehmann, Christian. 1995. *Thoughts on Grammaticalization*. Munich: Lincom.

Lindauer, Thomas. 1998. Attributive genitive constructions in German. In *Possessors, Predicates and Movement in the Determiner Phrase* [Linguistik Aktuell/Linguistics Today 22], Artemis Alexiadou & Chris Wilder (eds), 109–140. John Benjamins: Amsterdam. https://doi.org/10.1075/la.22.06lin

Los, Bettelou. 2005. *The Rise of the To-infinitive*. Oxford: OUP.
https://doi.org/10.1093/acprof:oso/9780199274765.001.0001

Mausser, Otto Ernst. 1933. *Mittelhochdeutsche Grammatik, III Teil. Laut-u. Formenlehre nebst Syntax*, Vol. 1. Munich: Max Hueber.

McWhorter, John. 2002. What happened to English? *Diachronica* 19 (2): 217–272.
https://doi.org/10.1075/dia.19.2.02wha

Olsen, Susan. 1996. Dem Possessivum seine Eigentümlichkeit. In *Die Struktur der Nominalphrase* [Wuppertaler Arbeitpapiere zur Sprachwissenschaft 12], Hans Thilo Tappe & Elisabeth Löbel (eds), 112–143. Wuppertal: Bergische Universität-Gesamthochschule.

Osthoff, Hermann. 1876. *Zur geschichte des schwachen deutschen adjectivums*. Jena: Hermann Costenoble.

Oubouzar, Erika. 1992. Zur Ausbildung des bestimmten Artikels im Althochdeutschen. In *Althochdeutsch. Syntax und Semantik. Akten des Lyonner Kolloquiums zur Syntax und Semantik des Althochdeutschen*, Vol. 3, Yvon Desportes (ed.), 69–87. Lyon: Université Jean Moulin.

Paul, Hermann. 2007. *Mittelhochdeutsche Grammatik*, 25th edn. Tübingen: Max Niemeyer.

Pittner, Karin. 2014. Ist der Dativ dem Genitiv sein Tod? Funktionen und Konkurrenzformen von Genitiv-NPs im heutigen Deutsch. In *Linguistische und sprachdidaktische Aspekte germanistischer Forschung Chinesisch-Deutsch*, Corinna Reuter & Ann-Kathrin Schlief (eds), 41–56. Frankfurt: Peter Lang.

von Polenz, Peter. 1994. *Deutsche Sprachgeschichte vom Spätmittelalter bis zur Gegenwart, Bd. 2: 17. und 18 Jahrhundert*. Berlin: De Gruyter.

Ramat, Paolo. 1986. The Germanic possessive type dem Vater sein Haus. In *Linguistics across Historical and Geographical Boundaries*, Vol. 1, Dieter Kastovsky & Aleksander Szwedek (eds), 579–590. Berlin: De Gruyter.

Rehn, Alexandra. 2019. Adjectives and the Syntax of German(ic) DPs. PhD dissertation, University of Konstanz.

Roberts, Ian & Roussou, Anna. 2003. *Syntactic Change. A Minimalist Approach to Grammaticalization* [Cambridge Studies in Linguistics 100]. Cambridge: CUP.
https://doi.org/10.1017/CBO9780511486326

Rowley, Anthony R. 1991. Die Adjektivflexion der Dialekte Nordostbayerns: Morphologische Staffelung in einem ostfränkisch-bairischen Kontaminationsraum. *Zeitschrift für Dialektologie und Linguistik* 58 (1): 1–23.

Salzmann, Martin. 2006. Resumptive pronouns and matching effects in Zurich German relative clauses as distributed deletion. *Leiden Papers in Linguistics* 3 (1): 17–50.

Salzmann, Martin. 2013. On three types of variation in resumption: Evidence in favor of violable and ranked constraints. In *Linguistic Derivations and Filtering. Minimalism and Optimality Theory*, Hans Broekhuis & Ralf Vogel (eds), 76–108. Sheffield: Equinox.

Schirmunski, Viktor M. 1962. *Deutsche Mundartkunde (Vergleichende Laut-und Formenlehre der deutschen Mundarten. Berlin)*. Berlin: Akademie-Verlag.

Schmidt, Jürgen Erich, Herrgen, Joachim & Kehrein, Roland. 2008. Regionalsprache.de (REDE).

Solms, Hans-Joachim & Wegera, Klaus-Peter. 1991. *Flexion der Adjektive* [Grammatik des Frühneuhochdeutschen: Beiträge zur Laut-und Formenlehre 6]. Heidelberg: Winter.

Staedele, Alfons. 1927. Syntax der Mundart von Stahringen. Br. dissertation. Albert-Ludwigs-University of Freiburg.

Walch, Maria & Häckel, Susanne. 1988. *Grammatik des Frühneuhochdeutschen, Band 7: Flexion der Pronomina und Numeralia*. Heidelberg: Winter.

Wedel, Andrew, Kaplan, Abby & Jackson, Scott. 2013. High functional load inhibits phonological contrast loss: A corpus study. *Cognition* 128 (2): 179–186.
https://doi.org/10.1016/j.cognition.2013.03.002

Weinrich, Harald. 2005. *Textgrammatik der deutschen Sprache, dritte revidierte Auflage.* Hildesheim: Georg Olms.

Weiß, Helmut. 2012. The rise of DP-internal possessors: On the relationship of dialectal synchrony to diachrony. In *The Dialect Laboratory. Dialects as a Testing Ground for Theories of Language Change,* [Studies in Language Companion Series 128], Gunther De Vogelaer & Guido Seiler (eds), 271–294. Amsterdam: John Benjamins.
https://doi.org/10.1075/slcs.128.12wei

Wessén, Elias. 1914. *Zur Geschichte der germanischen n-Deklination.* Uppsala: Akademische buchdruckerei.

Wiesinger, Peter. 1983. Die Einteilung der deutschen Dialekte. In *Dialektologie. Ein Handbuch zur deutschen und allgemeinen Dialekforschung,* Vol. 2, Werner Besch, Ulrich Knoop, Wolfgang Putschke & Herbert Ernst Wiegand (eds), 807–900. Berlin: Walter de Gruyter.

Wiltschko, Martina. 1998. On the syntax and semantics of (relative) pronouns and determiners. *The Journal of Comparative Germanic Linguistics* 2 (2): 143–181.
https://doi.org/10.1023/A:1009719229992

"The next Morning I got a Warrant for the Man and his Wife, but he was fled"

Did sociolinguistic factors play a role in the loss of the BE-perfect?*

Marianne Hundt
University of Zürich

This chapter uses data from the Old Bailey Corpus to study the demise of the English BE-perfect between the 1720s and 1910s. The corpus provides ample evidence on the development in the period that saw the transition from BE to HAVE as perfect auxiliary in constructions with mutative verbs (i.e., intransitive verbs referring to a change of state or place); it also makes it possible to gauge the relative importance that social factors (such as speaker SEX, speaker ROLE or socio-economic background) may have played in the loss of one of the perfect variants. The stages for the development are derived from the data in a bottom-up approach using Variability-based Neighbour Clustering (VNC). In a second step, random forests and conditional inference trees are fitted to the data for each stage. The former provide information on the overall relative importance of predictor variables and the latter on interaction of predictor variables. It turns out that while, overall, social predictors play a far less important role in the process of loss than the predictor lexical VERB, they do show significant interaction with this language-internal variable. The speech-based socio-historical data thus add important details to previous studies on the loss of the BE-perfect, not least by lending support to the fact that this change happened largely below the level of speakers' awareness.

Keywords: BE:HAVE-perfect alternation, loss of BE-perfect, socio-historical variationist analysis

---

* I gratefully acknowledge the useful comments I received from two anonymous reviewers on an earlier version of this paper. Thanks are also due to Carlos Hartmann for retrieving the initial data set and excluding all instances of simple past and transitive uses.

1. Introduction

Like other languages – such as German and French – English used to have two perfect auxiliaries, namely HAVE and BE, whose use depended on the transitivity of the verb (see e.g., McFadden & Alexiadou 2006). Roughly speaking, HAVE is initially used only with transitives before it starts spreading to intransitives, whereas BE is used with intransitives until it is replaced by HAVE in these contexts in the late Modern period.[1] Auxiliary BE, moreover, is particularly common with so-called 'mutative' verbs, i.e., intransitives expressing a change of place or state whereas intransitives that denote action (e.g., *laugh*) are attested with *have* from the Old English period. As Los (2015: 75–76) points out, this is in accordance with Sorace's (2000) cross-linguistic Auxiliary Selection Hierarchy, which postulates a gradient from intransitives denoting controlled processes, through uncontrolled processes and stative intransitives to change of state and motion verbs. The following examples from the speech-based[2] *Old Bailey Corpus* (OBC)[3] of court proceedings illustrate variation with the motion verb *flee*.

(1) Do you remember your telling any person you had left your master, and
     he was fled to Holland for a rape?   (OBC, t17570420-42)

(2) Did you know that he *had fled* from his bail?   (OBC, t18520202-261)

The chronology of changes in auxiliary use with perfect constructions that previous research reconstructs depends somewhat on the definition of the phenomenon and the different measures applied, i.e., whether the spread of the HAVE-perfect is viewed generally (i.e., in terms of its text frequency) or only in relation to those

---

1. Jespersen (1931: 34) gives some examples of *go* with *have* as early as Old English (e.g., from *Beowulf* and *Judith*). Conversely, sporadic use of BE with transitive uses of motion verbs (e.g., *flee NP*) are attested in Middle English, according to Mustanoja (1960: 500–1); for a critical discussion of this evidence, see Denison (1993: 363). McFadden and Alexiadou (2006: 240) provide frequency information on *come* as an unambiguous case of a motion verb; according to their evidence, the first instance of the HAVE-perfect with the verb dates back to the early Middle English period. Huber (2019) is a recent study with a focus on semantic aspects of the verb in Middle English, which shows that counterfactuality is a more important predictor in the early stage of the competition than aktionsart.

2. The term is borrowed from Culpeper & Kytö (2010), who distinguish speech-based historical texts from speech-like (e.g., letters, diaries) and speech-purposed (e.g., drama) writing.

3. Examples from the corpus are quoted throughout with trial ID, of which the first four digits indicate the year of the trial.

contexts where it is in variation with BE as perfect auxiliary (see e.g., Kytö 1997 vs. Smith 2007). Variability between the BE- and HAVE-perfect continues well into the nineteenth century with certain verbs (particularly those denoting change of place, such as *go* and *come*), but in Present-Day English, it is limited to a few set phrases, such as *They are/have gone* or *The sun is/has set,* or formal registers, as in *Christ is risen* (see e.g., Rydén 1991 or Anderwald 2014).[4]

The demise of the BE-perfect has been studied quite extensively. Few studies, however, have looked at sociolinguistic variables. One of them is Kytö's (1997) longitudinal study. According to her evidence, women's usage is conservative in the period when HAVE finally wins out as the dominant auxiliary (Kytö, 1997: 51). The present study adds to previous research by looking at sociolinguistic factors in more detail. Suitable speech-based evidence for this study comes from a corpus of Late-Modern English court proceedings, the OBC (Huber 2007). Section 3 provides additional background information on the corpus, data retrieval and the definition of the variable. The analysis includes speakers' background data (gender, socio-economic background) and socio-pragmatic information, i.e., speaker ROLE in the courtroom, to evaluate whether social variables played a role in the loss of the BE-perfect in Late Modern (British) English. Prior to the analysis of external, sociolinguistic predictor variables, the relevant diachronic stages for the development are determined in a data-driven, bottom-up fashion using Variability-based Neighbour Clustering (see 3.3.1). The statistical approach chosen allows me to model not only the relative importance of the predictor variables but also potential interaction of external predictors with two language-internal predictors, the lexical verb in the construction and the morphology of the auxiliary.

2.   Previous research

2.1   The loss of the BE-perfect

Various qualitative and quantitative corpus-based studies have looked into the demise of the BE-perfect or the 'regularization' (Jespersen, 1931: 30) of HAVE to all contexts. Brinton (1994: 158–59) provides a succinct overview of the reasons that have been advanced in qualitative research to explain the (near) loss of BE-perfects. These include the ambiguity of contracted 's as a form of *has* or *is*, the

---

4.   Interestingly, Visser gives quite a number of examples of *become* (1973: 2047), *grow* (1973: 2048–49) and *arrive* (1973: 2055) with perfect auxiliary BE from twentieth-century sources, in addition to the attestations of *come* (1973: 2057) and *go* (1973: 2063), indicating that the use of BE-perfects enjoyed a limited productivity even in the twentieth century.

functional overload of BE as auxiliary for passive, perfect and progressive, prescriptive grammarians' attack on the BE-perfect in the eighteenth century and loss
of the dynamic meaning of BE.[5] For the nineteenth century, Anderwald (2014)
convincingly argues that continuing prescriptive criticism of the BE-perfect
(a grammatical 'blind-spot') was the result of erroneous functional analysis on the
part of the grammarians, which, in turn, was influenced by traditional grammars
of Latin. More importantly, Anderwald's (2014, 2016) systematic comparison
of prescriptive comments with usage data does not provide evidence of a direct
(causative) link between the loss of the construction and (prescriptive) grammar
writing. This indicates that the demise of the BE-perfect is likely to have been a
change below speakers' awareness.

The first systematic corpus-based study of auxiliary choice in the perfect construction is Rydén & Brorström (1987), summarized in Rydén (1991).[6] They use
letters and plays to trace the development between 1500 and 1900. Their study of
variable contexts shows that HAVE becomes the dominant auxiliary between 1800
and 1850. Kytö's (1997) investigation of historical reference corpora such as the *Helsinki Corpus* for Middle and Early Modern English and ARCHER (*A Representative Corpus of Historical English Registers*) for Late Modern English shows HAVE to
become the dominant auxiliary a little earlier, i.e., in the second half of the eighteenth
century, with American English somewhat ahead of British English. In Anderwald's
(2016) study of the *Corpus of Historical American English* (COHA), the BE-perfect is
already below 50% at the beginning of the nineteenth century and declines rapidly
to frequencies below 25% in the course of a few decades (2016: 135).

McFadden and Alexiadou (2010) and McFadden (2017) tell a slightly different
story on the basis of the parsed *Penn* corpora and a differently defined variable:
they look at the development of intransitive BE- and HAVE-perfects per number
of clauses, showing that the initial spread of the HAVE-perfect can be attributed
to a broadening of the HAVE-perfect's scope to experiential perfects. According to
McFadden (2017: 165), BE-perfects exhibit a relatively stable use per clause until
the beginning of the nineteenth century and a rapid decline only in the period
after 1810. In other words, they do not focus on semantic differences between the
two perfect constructions and thus treat the trajectories as separately motivated
developments. Importantly for this study, their bottom-up retrieval approach
from a parsed corpus rather than one relying on a pre-defined set of variable verbs
also shows the early nineteenth century as the decisive period in the decline of

---

5.   Examples of prescriptive criticism are quoted in Visser (1973: 2043–44).

6.   Jespersen (1931: 31) reports of a study based on a single work of fiction (i.e., *Robinson
Crusoe*), which found a preference for the BE over the HAVE-perfect.

BE-perfects, thus lending further support to Kytö's (1997) and Anderwald's (2014) dating of the change.[7]

As is the case in many instances of syntactic loss, the construction that once was a fully productive pattern may survive in a – typically lexically restricted – functional niche or in nonstandard varieties of the language (see e.g., Hundt 2004, 2014). Recent corpus-based studies by Seoane and Suárez-Gómez (2013) and Werner (2016) show that BE-perfects in World Englishes are not only attested in institutionalised second-language varieties but also continue to be used as relic forms in varieties of English as a first language. Moreover, Werner's evidence indicates that they are even extended to transitive verbs in institutionalised second-language varieties. Data from the *Freiburg English Dialect* (FRED) corpus[8] (see examples (3)–(8)) show that in non-standard varieties of English in the British Isles, BE-perfects are also occasionally attested with transitive verbs.[9] This means that dialect input in historical ESL varieties could have fostered extension to transitive verbs.

(3) They*'re finished* work at — say five o'clock … (FRED, HEB_028)[10]

(4) … and then you assembled them, you*'re done* the straps (FRED, WIL_005)

(5) You have to wait 'til you*'m catched* him. (FRED, SOM_005)

(6) … he put all around her, then you*'m had* the ones who'm rucking all this here off, you know. (FRED, SOM_028)

---

7. Smith (2007) looks at overall frequency developments of the two perfect constructions, including those with transitive verbs. According to this evidence, BE-perfects are a minority variant throughout the history of the language. They show a marked decline in his data already towards the Early Modern Period (from 11% to 4% of all perfect constructions). Seeing that he does not restrict his study to potentially variable contexts, the results do not easily lend themselves to comparison with other corpus-based research.

8. See Hernández (2006) or <http://www2.anglistik.uni-freiburg.de/institut/lskortmann/FRED/>

9. Note that occurrences in the Suffolk part of the corpus such as "And I*'re seen* a bloke with a chopper chop the rope" (SFK_002) are, in fact, instances of East Anglian smoothing of *have* to *are* (Hundt 2016a: 53). Interestingly, transitive BE-perfects in FRED include instances of generalised *am* (see examples (5)–(8)), a structural option that came to my attention through John McWhorter's *Lexicon Valley* Podcast (19 March 2019).

10. Note that this is different from the pseudo-passive construction of intransitives possible in standard English, which combine with prepositional phrases rather than bare NP objects, as in *I'm finished with the data retrieval for this paper* (see Quirk et al., 1985: 170).

(7)   You'm a young liar you'*m pushed* him down   (FRED, SEL_023)

(8)   so he've had yours afore you'*m said* anything to I.   (FRED, SOM_005.txt)

Other studies that have looked at residual use of BE-perfects are Yerastrov (2015), who provides an analysis of BE-perfects of the type BE *done* NP and BE *finished* NP in Canadian English and US dialects, and Hundt (2016a), who traces the historical and regional use of another low-frequency variant of the BE-perfect, i.e., BE *been*.

In standard English, however, the BE-perfect is a much more restricted optional variant today and can therefore be said to have been 'lost' as a productive syntactic pattern. The next section reviews previous research on the role of social factors in processes of constructional loss generally, i.e., not just with respect to variable auxiliary use in the perfect.

2.2   Syntactic loss and social factors

In historical sociolinguistics, the focus has often been on the role that social groups (different ranks, women or men) have played in the spread of morpho-syntactic innovation. However, 'innovation' does not necessarily mean that an entirely new pattern develops (as in grammaticalisation/constructionalisation). In fact, in various socio-historical linguistic studies, the topic of investigation has been the spread of a novel pattern at the expense of an older form, e.g., the spread of *you* as subject pronoun replacing older *ye* or the spread of third-person present-tense marking with {-s} ultimately ousting older {-th}. The disappearance of multiple negation from standard English, in turn, would be a genuine example of syntactic loss. Evidence from the Early Modern English *Corpus of Early English Correspondence* (Nevalainen & Raumolin-Brunberg, 2003) on the role of gender as a factor in morpho-syntactic developments of this type shows that women are often at the vanguard of change: they are early adopters of third-person {-s} and spearhead the change that replaces *mine* with *my, ye* with *you*, and relative adverbs such as *whereof* and *thereof* with periphrastic *of it*. The only syntactic loss that is led by male letter writers is the loss of multiple negation. Thus, women lead in more changes resulting in standard features than men; features that are spread by men are additionally associated with professional or educated usage. "They were favoured by the institutionally educated section of the male population in their private correspondence as well" (Nevalainen, 2002: 207).

With respect to socio-economic background, previous studies found that it was often the middle ranks that promoted change (e.g., for the adoption of third-person {-s}, subject *you* and the omission of multiple negation) rather than the nobility. Britain's (2012) survey of previous research shows that lawyers, in particular, are amongst the early adopters of change. He (2012: 458) also points to an open research question in this context:

> One question that arises from this apparently important innovating role for law-yers across these studies is whether this group really was sociolinguistically more innovative in general, or whether the finding stems from their important position in the written linguistic marketplace as language 'brokers,' having to routinely command a range of written styles addressed to a range of different audiences.

The data from OBC do not provide information on the earliest HAVE-perfects with verbs of motion and change of state since these date back to the early Middle English period (see footnote 1). Nevertheless, it will be interesting to see whether lawyers are indeed among the more advanced speakers in the growing use of the HAVE-perfect with this class of verb in the Late Modern period.

Against earlier sociolinguistic research that mostly provides evidence of the role that women play in morpho-syntactic innovation, Kytö's (1997) data indicate that women are conservative with respect to the loss of BE. Her findings corrobo-rate anecdotal observation of female conservatism in Rydén (1991: 351):

> In the texts examined for the study under discussion, the social stratification of the *be/have* paradigm is mirrored by way of individual preferences, as for exam-ple in Dickens's progressive uses and Jane Austen's conservative handling of the paradigm …, a trait Austen shares with some other female writers, for instance Charlotte Brontë, George Eliot and a group of late 18th century upper-class women letter-writers … .

The main aim of the present study is to verify whether data from Late Modern English court proceedings lend additional support to female conservatism in the loss of BE-perfects. The evidence also allows us to see whether additional social factors (such as occupation) play a role, and what the relative importance of such social factors may be against language-internal factors such as choice of lexical verb.

3. Data and methodology

Previous studies (with the exception of Anderwald 2014, 2016) have relied on relatively small corpora. In order to obtain large enough data sets with available sociolinguistic background information, this study is based on a large corpus of transcribed spoken use of Late Modern British English. The next section provides background information on the corpus. The approach used to retrieve variable contexts of BE- and HAVE-perfects is detailed in section 3.2, as is the definition of the response variable. The statistical approach used to derive information on relevant diachronic stages in the loss of the BE-perfect from the data as well as the methods used to determine predictor importance and interaction are described in Section 3.3.

3.1   The Old Bailey Corpus

Data for this study come from the *Old Bailey Corpus* of trial proceedings. The online version of the corpus provides data for the years between 1720 and 1913. Table 1a gives the word counts for the parts of the corpus which have information on speaker sex. Table 1b shows the amount of data available for the different speaker roles.[11] In order to fit the word counts into the tables, the numbers were added up across five decades. These are not the sub-periods that were subsequently used as break-off points for the statistical analyses (see Section 3.3.1).

Table 1a. Word counts per speaker SEX

	1720–1769	1770–1829	1830–1879	1880–1913	Total
Women	611,119	532,765	649,601	479,848	2,273,333
Men	2,316,599	3,163,302	3,105,030	2,846,773	11,431,704

Table 1b. Word counts per speaker ROLE

	1720–1769	1770–1829	1830–1879	1880–1913	Total
defendants	181,093	217,547	214,579	204,016	817,235
interpreters	741	4,022	13,338	24,644	42,745
judges	115,513	256,057	57,197	8,649	437,416
lawyers	193,927	453,781	104,335	14,230	766,273
victims	463,609	677,438	742,334	432,206	2,315,587
witnesses	1,106,999	1,415,530	2,561,961	2,621,291	7,705,781

As the tables show, there is ample evidence in the OBC for the time period when the BE-perfect was shown to decline rapidly in previous research. Moreover, the variable context is defined in such a way that different amounts of data available from the respective social groups does not pose a problem for the modelling.

3.2   Data retrieval and definition of the variable

Like previous research (Kytö 1997; Anderwald 2014, 2016), the present study makes use of a pre-defined set of intransitive verbs that are (frequently) attested

---

11.   The tables are based on the word counts provided on the corpus website <http://www1.uni-giessen.de/oldbaileycorpus/stats.html> (15 March 2019). Note that the totals from table 1a and 1b do not quite add up because additional information on speaker ROLE is not available for all speakers whose word counts are included in table 1a.

with the BE-perfect in earlier stages of the language and that still regularly form the perfect with auxiliary BE at the beginning of the eighteenth century. Specifically, it includes the following verbs: *arrive, become, begin, change, come, fall, flee, go, grow, pass, return* and *run*. The search made use of the PoS-annotation of the corpus and retrieved all instances of the past participle for each verb. The resulting concordances where then manually post-edited, false positives excluded, and the remaining instances annotated for choice of auxiliary verb.

While the primary motivation for the choice of verbs to be included was based on their text frequency and the fact that they still had to be variable at the beginning of the eighteenth century, it is interesting to see that they mostly fall into the two semantic groups of verbs, i.e., change of state (*become, change, grow*) and change of place/motion (*arrive, come, fall, flee, grow, pass, return, run*) that are highest on the gradient of verbs that are likely to select auxiliary BE (Sorace 2000: 863). The only verb that is not easily classified according to the Auxiliary Selection Hierarchy is *begin*, which is an inchoative verb that refers to the inception of a process and is thus relatively close in meaning to change of state verbs. The Auxiliary Selection Hierarchy would predict that HAVE takes over as auxiliary with change of state verbs, which are slightly lower on the hierarchy, earlier than with motion verbs, which are at the extreme end of the hierarchy.

The original concordances contained instances where BE was a copula rather than an auxiliary, with the participle functioning as part of a post-modifying phrase or clause, as in the following examples:

(9)   there *was* no pocket then *arrived* from the West-indies, nor no ship
(OBC, t17551022-26)

(10) "Yes, there *is* some gold *fallen*, which the officer picked up afterwards."
(OBC, t18360509-1265)

(11) … there *were* some men just *gone* up there …   (OBC, t17670603-43)

Such instances were not included in the analysis, as were cases where the participle had adjectival rather than verbal function, as in the following examples:

(12) I *was* pretty far *gone* in liquor;   (OBC, t17650710-27)

(13) the tissues of the mouth *were* far *gone* in decomposition, and eaten by maggots.   (OBC, t18601126-38)

(14) she *was* pregnant, and *gone* about six months.   (OBC, t18720923-695)

Other false positives are instances of transitive uses of some verbs, illustrated in (15) to (17), which are passive past tense rather than perfect constructions (including the rather unusual passive of the phrasal idiom *come to terms*); (18) is an active transitive HAVE-perfect which would not have a constructional variant with perfect BE, either.

(15)   a resolution *was passed* that there should be an independent valuation and
        that the vendors   (OBC, t19020721-562)

(16)   … that ledger *was* first *begun* to post up Mr. Chalmers's cash as far as
        possible.   (OBC, t18811212-116)

(17)   Terms *were* not *come to*, as Morris would not pay the rent asked.
                                                                    (OBC, t19130304-48)

(18)   tho' he *had changed* his Cloaths.   (OBC, t17320906-67)

Some intransitive verbs are polysemous and can be used with a different meaning from the one that allows for variable use of the perfect auxiliary. Therefore,
instances like the following use of *pass* in the sense of 'occur' were also removed
from the dataset.

(19)   Did you tell her what *had passed* between Lennard and you?
                                                                    (OBC, t17730707-2)

Similarly, idiomatic expressions where there is no variation between BE and HAVE
as auxiliaries were excluded (see, e.g., (20) and (21)).

(20)   … it was Williams's old shop; it had *changed hands*.   (OBC, t19100208-38)

(21)   however, sentence *was passed* upon him with the rest of the convicts
                                                                    (OBC, t17450911-27)

Instances where HAVE formed part of the modal idiom *had better,* as in (22) and
(23), also do not allow for variation between the two auxiliaries and were therefore
removed from the initial dataset.

(22)   The prisoner said she *had better* come herself …   (OBC, t18150111-60)

(23)   "You *had better* come before a Magistrate, and clear yourself?"
                                                                    (OBC, t18271206-249)

Finally, instances that were ambiguous between the BE- and the HAVE-perfect
because the form was indeterminate (i.e., variants with contracted 's, as in (24))
were not included in the dataset.

(24)   What's *become* of Grace now?   (OBC, t17370907-7)

Previous research (Hundt 2016a) has shown that BE also combines as auxiliary
with *been* (albeit at low frequencies) in the history of English. There is one instance
of this usage in combination with *gone out* (see Example (25)) in the OBC. However, since *gone* in this example is not unambiguously verbal, instances with *been*
were removed from the dataset, throughout.

(25)   The Deceas'd answered no, he *was been gone* out about an Hour;
                                                                    (OBC, t17261012-7)

The final dataset included in the analysis thus contained choice contexts for twelve verbs, illustrated with the following constructional variants with *arrive* as an example of a verb of motion and *grow* as a change-of-state verb:

(26)   They had advice of a cutter *being arrived* while they were at our house; …
                                                                (OBC, t17500711-31)

(27)   I am not aware of a registered letter *having arrived* half an hour before this test letter was sorted.   (OBC, t18601126-40)

(28)   *Are* these Gangs *grown* so notorious that the Country know them?
                                                                (OBC, t17471014-4)

(29)   … it *had grown* long again;   (OBC, t18271206-16)

As can be seen in Example (26), occurrences with non-finite auxiliaries were included.

3.3   Statistical modelling

The following statistical analysis will proceed in two steps. The first type of analysis aims to derive the relevant stages for the ongoing frequency changes in a bottom-up fashion rather than making use of pre-defined periodisation of the data. In a second step, multivariate approaches are used to determine (a) the relative importance of predictor variables for the choice of BE- over HAVE-perfects in the data and (b) any possible interaction of predictor variables. Establishing the relevant stages of the development in a bottom-up fashion, first, also allows for the annotation of randomized subsets of data from these stages, thus keeping the amount of data to be coded for the fine-grained analysis within manageable bounds.

3.3.1   *Bottom-up modelling of stages in diachronic change:*
Variability-based Neighbour Clustering (VNC)

Most diachronic research traces the development of grammatical constructions across pre-defined sub-periods in a given corpus. This is also the approach taken e.g., in Kytö (1997) and McFadden (2017). However, the trajectory of grammatical change – be it the birth or loss of a construction – might not necessarily be best described in relation to pre-existing periods that were used to sample a specific corpus. According to Gries and Hilpert (2008: 60), this approach "runs the risk of missing out on important generalisations: if the only division of the data that is assumed is the one that comes with the corpus data, then higher-level generalisations that only arise from grouping different temporal stages may be lost". They have therefore adapted hierarchical clustering to diachronic corpus studies and provided an algorithm that allows to model the periods relevant to a particular change in a bottom-up, exploratory fashion as it groups the data into periods on the basis of linguistic change rather than on the basis of pre-defined external periodisation. Essentially, the algorithm identifies cohesive groups in the data by merging similar observations into clusters while at the same time preserving the chronological order (see Gries & Hilpert 2008 and 2012 for details).[12] This study adopts the Variability-based Neighbour Clustering (VNC) approach to the variation between BE- and HAVE-perfects, i.e., it models the loss of the BE-perfect across time in relation to HAVE-perfects (see Section 4.2; for a similar application to variation in perfect auxiliaries in Spanish, see Rosemeyer 2014). In a second step, the relevant stages for the constructional change as they emerge from VNC are then used as the basis for modelling the potential role that social variables may have played in the loss of the BE-perfect (see Section 4.3).

3.3.2   *Modelling predictor variables: Random forests and conditional inference trees*

In order to model the relative importance of various social and two linguistic predictor variables in the demise of the BE-perfect, multivariate analysis was performed on a subset of the data for which information on three social variables (speaker SEX, ROLE and CLASS) was available.[13] There are various statistical approaches that have been used in sociolinguistic research to gauge the importance of social variables in ongoing variation and change (such as variable rule and other kinds of regression analysis). Tagliamonte and Baayen (2012) discuss advantages and problems inherent in such standard approaches to multivariate analysis. Most of these assume a normal distribution of the data which is, in fact, rarely the case. An inherent problem with standard linear regression analyses is that it provides information on the significance of predictor variables but not on their relative importance. Variable rule analysis provides information on the ranking of predictor variables but assumes that they are independent which, in fact, they typically are not. Following Tagliamonte and Baayen (2012), the present paper adopts random forest (RF) analysis as an alternative approach to gauging the relative importance of predictor variables. RF analysis is a type of permutation testing that does not rely on a normal distribution of the data but builds it by randomized resampling from the input. More specifically, the algorithm (see Strobl, Malley & Tutz 2009 or Strobl, Hothorn & Zeileis 2009) fits many regression

---

12.   A step-by-step guideline on how to apply the algorithm to data can be found online at   <http://global.oup.com/us/companion.websites/fdscontent/uscompanion/us/static/companion.websites/nevalainen/Gries-Hilpert_web_final/vnc.individual.html> (4 April 2019).

13.   Strictly speaking, one could argue that the label RANK would be more appropriate than CLASS for the socio-economic background of speakers, at least in the eighteenth century. The present paper follows the terminology used by the corpus compilers, who also use CLASS as the denominator for this variable.

tree models to random subsets of the data, resulting in a random forest. Variable importance is then estimated on the basis of this forest. In addition to avoiding the problem of non-normally distributed data, the RF analysis can also cope with correlated predictor variables (Tagliamonte & Baayen, 2012). In order to be able to model possible interaction between predictor variables, conditional inference trees (ctrees) usefully complement the RF analysis. This approach makes use of recursive partitioning and predicts outcomes on binary splits of the data (Hothorn et al. 2006). Single ctrees start off with the most important predictor variable at the topmost node and show how the other (significant) predictor variables in the model are selected at later stages, splitting the data into homogenous sets (with a minimum significance level of $\alpha = 0.05$). Partitioning of the data takes place until the subsets' homogeneity can be no longer increased significantly. The present paper thus follows the recommendation of Tagliamonte & Baayen (2012: 146) in that: "the kind of interactions that a (mixed-effects) generalized linear model can handle effectively may for some datasets be too restricted for the highly imbalanced cells typical of sociolinguistic data. As we shall see, this is where conditional inference trees and random forests provide a complementary technique that may provide insights that are sometimes difficult or impossible to obtain with the linear model."

This study makes use of three social predictor variables on which there is sufficient amounts of data in the OBC: the speaker's SEX (with the levels 'male' and 'female'), the speaker's socio-economic background or CLASS (with the levels given in Table 1 below) and the speaker's ROLE (with the levels 'defendant', 'interpreter', 'judge', 'lawyer', 'victim' and 'witness').[14]

Table 2. Classification of socio-economic background of speakers in the *Old Bailey Corpus*

level	description
hP	higher professionals
lP	lower professionals
sW	medium-skilled workers
wff	lower-skilled workers, farmers and fishers[15]
uW	unskilled workers, lower and unskilled farmers

---

14. The corpus also yielded one instance of a HAVE-perfect from 1892 with the speaker role given as 'policeman', a role that was not included in the list of speaker roles provided for the corpus in the table online (see <http://www1.uni-giessen.de/oldbaileycorpus/stats.html> (4 April 2019). The example was left in the dataset with the speaker role coded as in the original.

15. In the OBC original classification, farmers and fishers are classified separately from lower-skilled workers (classes 4 and 5, respectively).

In the original classification of socio-economic background provided by the OBC, unskilled workers are labelled as '6', lower und unskilled farmers as '7'; in addition, 'unspecified' workers are labelled as '6/7'. These are all relabelled as '5' for the purposes of this study.

The social variable ROLE allows us to test Britain's (2012) hypothesis that lawyers are among the early adopters of change, i.e., we would expect them to switch to auxiliary HAVE earlier than other speakers in the OBC. With respect to the other roles, predictions are less clear, but we might expect judges to behave in a similar way to lawyers (as members of the same profession). Speakers in a hierarchically subordinate role in the court context (i.e., victims, witnesses, defendants, interpreters) might be more conservative in their choice of auxiliary. Since the two social variables ROLE and CLASS are not entirely independent of each other (with lawyers and judges invariably being higher professionals, but not witnesses), the ctree analyses will be performed separately for these two predictors.

In addition to these social variables, two language-internal variables were included, namely VERB with the 12 lexical verbs (*arrive, become, begin, change, come, fall, flee, go, grow, pass, return* and *run*) providing the levels for this predictor, and the morphological properties of the auxiliary (MORPH) as the second linguistic predictor, with the levels 'present', 'past', 'base form' and 'participle'. The following examples illustrate the VP-internal constructional options that co-vary with the perfect.[16]

(30)   What *is become* of her now?   (OBC, t17550409-25) ['present']

(31)   What *was become* of your husband at this time? (OBC, t17800405-4) ['past']

(32)   Then on the 28th of August, the favourable opportunity *being come*, did you know Mr. Partridge was to go out of town that day?
                                        (OBC, t17620917-36) ['participle']

(33)   … supposing inflammation *to be begun* the use of aloes and gamboge would be unquestionably prejudicial …   (OBC, t18360404-906) ['base']

(34)   … Mr. Morris said that very likely he might *be gone* from Ilford, …
                                        (OBC, t17820605-1) ['base']

While previous research looked at a larger set of language-internal factors, the main aim of this study is to gauge the relative importance of social versus

---

16.   Readers familiar with the literature on the competition between BE and HAVE as perfect auxiliaries will notice that other factors (such as counterfactuality) were also found to have played a role in auxiliary choice (i.e., favouring HAVE). A more fine-grained analysis might therefore have been warranted.

language-internal predictors. Since the choice of the lexical item in a construction is often a powerful predictor in constructional variation and change (see e.g., Hundt 2016b, 2018), it is likely to be a useful language-internal predictor to compare with social variables. Similarly, the internal structure of the verb phrase was shown to be a strong predictor for the choice of auxiliary in previous research (Kytö 1997) and therefore will likely turn out to be an important factor in a model that includes social variables. Due to the amount of data to be coded, the second language-internal variable was coded for a randomized set of 300 instances from each stage of the development determined by the VNC (see 4.2).

4.   Results

The BE-perfect continues to be used into the 1910s in the OBC, with the last instances for which social background data is available stemming from 1912:

(35)   He said, "Do you know all the others *is gone* home?"   (OBC, t19120109-33)

(36)   … he would get into the house when everyone *was gone* to bed …
(OBC, t19120109-42)

Interestingly, one of them (35) is from a clearly non-standard context (by an unskilled worker in the role of victim), which fits in with previous observations that the BE-perfect survives longer in dialects than in standard English (Section 2.1). The other three, however, are all standard uses of *go* and *arrive*. The following sections provide information on the overall frequency development (4.1), the bottom-up modelling of the stages for the loss of the BE-perfect (Section 4.2) and the multifactorial analysis of the linguistic and social predictor variables for each stage (Section 4.3).

4.1   Summary statistics: Overall frequency development

As pointed out in Section 3.2, the data included in the analysis are intransitive HAVE- and BE-perfects of a set of 12 variable verbs of motion/change of state. Sociolinguistic background information on speaker SEX was available for a total of 7,776 instances of these verbs (3,593 BE- and 4,183 HAVE-perfects). These instances constitute the dataset used as a starting point for this study. Figure 1 plots the relative proportion of BE-perfects across decades. The graph (particularly the trend line) suggests a relatively continuous process with no obvious stages in the loss of the BE-perfect, which is still used at slightly over 80% in the 1720s and decreases to just a little above 5% in the 1910s. For the more fine-grained analysis of sociohistorical variables, stages in the development need to be identified. This is done with the help of VNC (see Section 3.3.1).

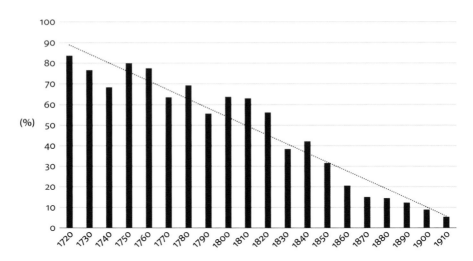

Figure 1. Proportion of BE-perfects per decade in the *Old Bailey Corpus*

4.2   Variability-based Neighbour Clustering (VNC)

The data shown in Figure 1 form the input for the VNC (the analysis was done using the relevant R package based on Gries and Hilpert's (2008) algorithm). The output of this analysis is given in Figure 2.

The dendogram on the left shows that the data is split into two major stages, i.e., between 1720s–1820s and 1830s-1910s. The scree plot, according to Perek and Hilpert (2017: 503),

> … indicate[s] how much dissimilarity between clusters (in the y-axis) is involved in the lowest-level merger every time a new cluster is added (in the x-axis). The appropriate number of clusters is reached when adding a cluster would result in a markedly less sharp decrease in dissimilarity, meaning that the merger involves items that are relatively similar to each other compared to the clusters identified so far. This breaking point or "elbow" can be visualized as a bend in the plot's curve.

The scree plot in Figure 2 provides evidence of an early breaking point, justifying an additional stage to be identified between the 1760s and 1770s; a further 'elbow' can be perceived between the 1860s and 1870s. The data for the investigation of the social predictor variables was therefore divided into the following four stages: 1720–1760, 1770–1820, 1830s–1850s and 1860s–1910s.[17]

---

17.   Thanks are due to Martin Hilpert (p.c.) for confirming my interpretation of the graphs in Figure 2.

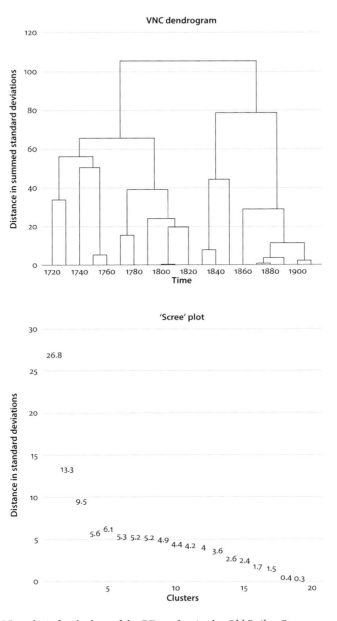

Figure 2. VNC analysis for the loss of the BE-perfect in the *Old Bailey Corpus*

4.3   Social variables

Figure 3 plots the distribution of the two perfect constructions by the social variable speaker SEX across the previously identified four stages in the development. Interestingly, the proportion of BE-perfects in the second stage (1770–1820) proves to be significantly lower for men than for women (p <.001 in a chi square test of contingency), suggesting that men are ahead of women at this stage in the loss of the BE-perfect. For all other stages, differences between men and women are below the level of statistical significance. The results thus lend some initial support to Kytö's (1997: 51) observation that men were leading the change in the Late Modern period, even though this might not be the most important, and certainly not the most pervasive, predictor for the loss of the BE-perfect. The predictor 'author's sex' proved only marginally significant in Kytö's (1997: 69) study once interaction with other factors was taken into account.

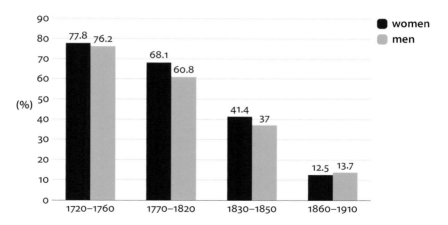

Figure 3. Proportion of BE-perfects by speaker SEX in the *Old Bailey Corpus*

Previous research suggests that lawyers are among the early adopters in ongoing change, and Britain (2012: 458) wondered whether this would translate into generally more innovative linguistic behaviour by this group of writers/speakers as 'brokers' in the linguistic marketplace. In order to test this (and allow for a multifactorial analysis of all speaker variables), the original dataset was reduced to those instances for which all sociolinguistic variables were known. This resulted in a total of 5,841 data points. Their distribution across the different stages is given in Table 3.

Figure 4 shows the proportion of BE-perfects used by lawyers and judges versus other speaker roles: it confirms that lawyers do, indeed, use the outgoing form proportionally less often than speakers with 'other' as role (defendants,

Table 3. Distribution of perfect constructions with full sociolinguistic background information

	1720–1760	1770–1820	1830–1850	1860–1910	total
BE-perfect	656	1265	496	299	2716
HAVE-perfect	154	677	670	1628	3125
% BE	81	65.1	42.7	15.5	

interpreters, victims, witnesses), significantly so at stages 1 and 2 (p <.001 in a chi square test of contingency). The comparison between lawyers and judges is somewhat less reliable seeing that the raw frequency for judges is overall much lower than for the other speaker groups (see Table A-1 in the Appendix); the more 'advanced' usage from the second half of the nineteenth century by judges may thus reflect a problem with data sparseness rather than a genuine difference between judges and lawyers.

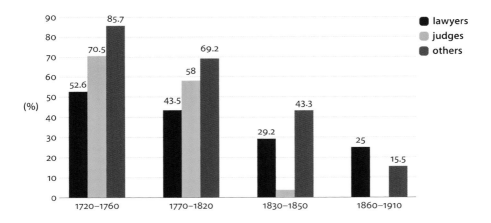

Figure 4. Proportion of BE-perfects by speaker ROLE in the *Old Bailey Corpus*

The multifactorial analysis also includes the predictor variables CLASS and ROLE as well as the linguistic variable VERB (for the lexical verb in the construction) and was conducted separately for all stages of the development, using the party package in R (Strobl, Hothorn & Zeileis 2009). Figures 5a–5d show the variable important plots as modelled in the RF analysis (with ntree=500 and mtry=2) for Stages 1–4, respectively. Model fit was evaluated with the help of Somers2, following Tagliamonte & Baayen (2012); the results are given in Table 5, showing that all RF analyses returned values for Somers2 > 0.5, i.e., throughout well above chance.

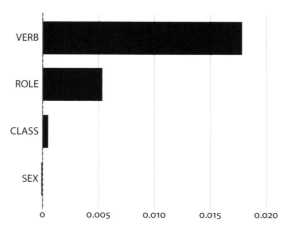

Figure 5a. Variable importance plot predicting BE as perfect auxiliary in the *OBC*, (1720–1760)

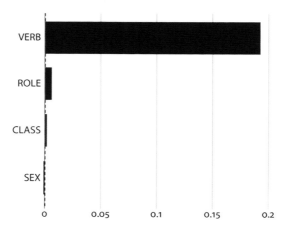

Figure 5b. Variable importance plot predicting BE as perfect auxiliary in the *OBC*, (1770–1820)

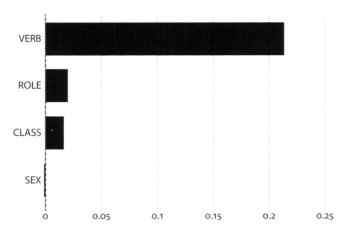

Figure 5c. Variable importance plot predicting BE as perfect auxiliary in the *OBC*, (1830–1850)

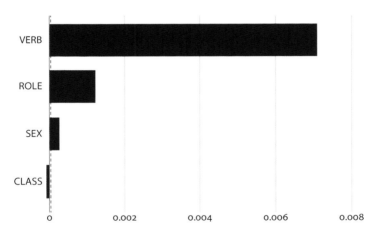

Figure 5d. Variable importance plot predicting BE as perfect auxiliary in the *OBC*, (1860–1910)

Table 5. Model fit for the RF analyses (Somers2)[18]

	1720–1760	1770–1820	1830–1850	1860–1910
C-statistic	0.795	0.846	0.865	0.789
Dxy	.589	.691	.730	0.579

The variable importance plots in Figure 4a-d reveal that the linguistic variable VERB is by far the most important predictor at all stages of the development, with speaker ROLE predicting choice of auxiliary far less strongly (and decreasingly so). CLASS as a predictor variable is even less important. Interestingly, speaker SEX does not emerge as a significant predictor at any of the four stages in the RF analyses. In other words, while men appeared to be leading the change in the second stage of the development when this social variable was considered in isolation, this speaker variable does not predict variation in the choice of the auxiliary very well if other factors are considered simultaneously.

Even though VERB turns out to be the most important predictor across time in the loss of the BE-perfect, it will be interesting to see how the other predictors (specifically ROLE and CLASS) interact with the linguistic predictor. Therefore, the partykit package in R (Hothorn et al. 2006) was used in a second step to fit ctrees to the data at the four stages of the development (with maxdepth=4, mincriterion=0.95). Since CLASS and ROLE are highly correlated in the data (i.e., lawyers, judges and interpreters belonging exclusively to the class 'higher professionals'), the ctrees were fit separately for the two predictors. In the following, only those ctrees will be presented where CLASS and ROLE were selected as significant variables. At stage one of the development, for instance, only ROLE is a relevant predictor for the choice of perfect auxiliary.

For the period 1720–1760, Figure 6a shows that, *become, flee, go* and *grow* are conservative in that they are most likely to select BE as perfect auxiliary. Interestingly, the language-internal predictor VERB does not show a clear split into motion and change-of-state verbs, as predicted by the Auxiliary Selection Hierarchy. With respect to social ROLE, witnesses and victims are slightly more conservative in their choice of auxiliary than the other speakers (cf. node 3 vs. nodes 5 and 6 in

---

18. Note that the C-statistic should be > .6 for a good model fit. In Tagliamonte & Baayen (2012), model fit improves with the inclusion of further predictor variables. However, seeing that model fit is already good and that the second language-internal predictor (MORPH), while improving model fit only slightly (see Table A-2 in the appendix), only serves to further diminish the importance of social variables but does not play out consistently across the different stages in the development.

the tree). Note, however, that speaker ROLE is not selected as a significant predictor for the verbs that already show a marked tendency towards selecting HAVE as their perfect auxiliary (see node 7).

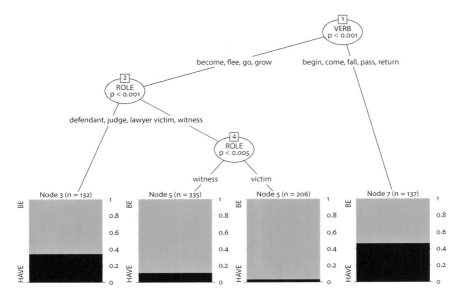

Figure 6a. ctree showing interaction between predictor variables for BE as perfect auxiliary (stage 1)

At stage 2 (1770–1820), *become, go, grow* and *change* still strongly favour the BE-perfect. It is interesting to note that at this stage, the verbs that lean clearly towards HAVE as auxiliary are all motion rather than change-of-state verbs, a finding that clearly goes against the prediction of the Auxiliary Selection Hierarchy.[19]

The interaction effects at the right hand side of the tree do not show a clear pattern with respect to speaker ROLE and conservative vs. innovative auxiliary choice (see Figure 6b), also because there is additional interaction between VERB and speaker ROLE for interpreters and victims (see nodes 10 and 11); the same goes for the ctree with social CLASS as a predictor variable (see nodes 8 and 9).

---

19.   Future research could look into more fine-grained distinctions between motion verbs, distinguishing between manner-of-motion verbs (not included here) and others, in order to test Los' (2015: 76–77) hypothesis of differences in aspectuality as a predictor for auxiliary selection.

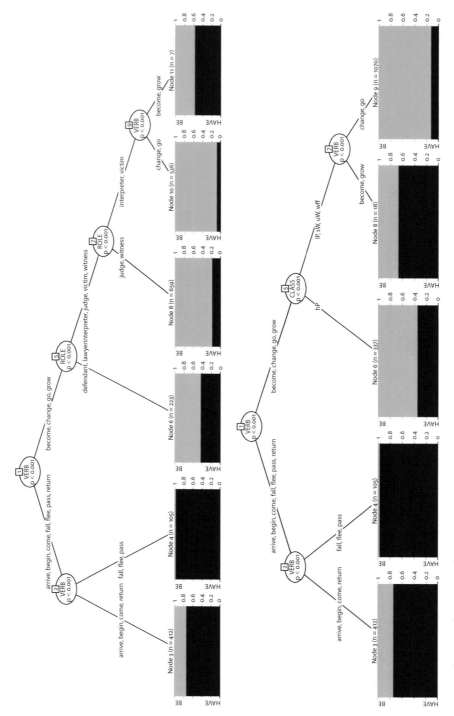

Figure 6b. ctrees for BE as perfect auxiliary (stage 2)

At stage 3 (1830–1850), *change* and *go* are the verbs that still regularly occur with BE as perfect auxiliary (see Figure 6c), providing additional evidence that the Auxiliary Selection Hierarchy might not merit a clear distinction between change-of-state and motion verbs in the final stages of loss. Note also that speaker SEX is chosen as a predictor in the single tree for stage 3 of the development. This may at first seem somewhat surprising seeing that it did not turn out to be significant in the RF analysis (see Figure 5c). It is interesting to see that women have a similar overall preference in their choice of auxiliary with *change* and *go* as victims (cf. nodes 5 and 9). The ctree thus reflects that men are over-represented among the lawyers and judges. The second ctree reveals that the predictor speaker SEX also interacts with social CLASS, with women among the lower professionals, workers and farmers being overall more conservative in their choice of auxiliary than their male peers (cf. nodes 6 and 7). Interestingly, the higher professionals (exclusively men) are more advanced in shifting towards HAVE as auxiliary with *change* and *go* at this stage in the development than speakers lower on the social scale (both men and women).

At the final stage in the OBC data (see Figure 6d), *change* and *go* continue to predict the choice of BE as perfect auxiliary more strongly than any of the other verbs, with *change* (overall) predicting the conservative auxiliary proportionally more often than *go* (see node 9); interpreters, lawyers and victims are more conservative in their choice of auxiliary with *go* than the other speakers at this stage (cf. nodes 7 and 8). Neither speaker SEX nor social CLASS produce significant splits in the ctree at this late stage in the development.

The RF analyses of the subsets that were also coded for the morphological properties of the auxiliary (MORPH) did not produce markedly different results with respect to the relative importance of predictor variables, with the exception of stage one, where speaker ROLE turned out to be more important than VERB in the more fine-grained analysis (see Figures A1–4 in the Appendix).[20] In other words, in the subsequent stages of loss, neither the additional linguistic predictor MORPH nor the social predictor gained in importance on the most important predictor variable, the lexical VERB. The ctrees (not reported here in detail) showed interaction between the inflectional properties of the verb (base vs. past, present, participle) with the type of verb in that auxiliaries in the base form strongly predict the choice of HAVE as auxiliary with those verbs that are generally conservative at the respective stages of development, i.e., otherwise would select BE, thus supporting previous research on the influence of verb morphology on the choice of auxiliary (e.g., Kytö, 1997: 69).

---

20. Note, however, that in this subsample of the 300 instances, 126 hits happened to be BE-perfects used by speakers with the role 'witness'.

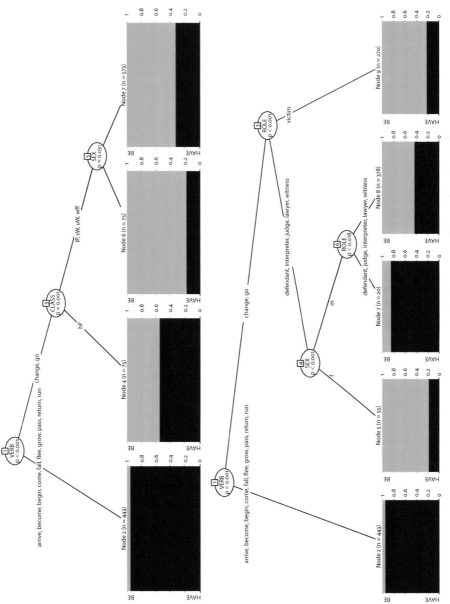

Figure 6c. ctrees showing interaction between predictor variables for BE as perfect auxiliary (stage 3)

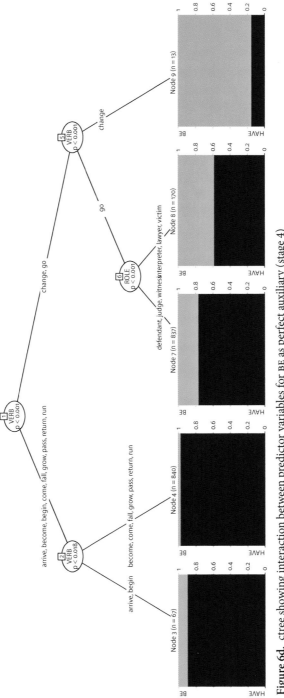

Figure 6d. ctree showing interaction between predictor variables for BE as perfect auxiliary (stage 4)

5.   Discussion

The data from the large corpus of speech-based Late Modern English analysed in this chapter have shown that the loss of the BE-perfect was certainly not caused or driven by any of the social factors investigated. Instead, the RF analyses revealed that the language-internal predictors VERB and TAM by far outweigh the importance of the social predictors in the loss of the construction (with TAM being somewhat weaker at stage 4). In other words, the demise of this perfect variant exhibits the opposite process of lexical diffusion, i.e., lexical attrition. Lexical attrition, in turn, is not a cause but a result of the factors that are likely to have initiated the loss of the BE-perfect, i.e., functional overload on BE as auxiliary and ambiguity of contracted third-person singular forms (see Section 2.1). According to the results of the ctree analyses, the two verbs that continue to select BE as auxiliary into the 1910s are *change* and *go*, i.e., prototypical mutative verbs that express 'change of state' and 'change of place' most clearly. The fact that the ctrees do not provide a clear trend with respect to the two types of mutative verb that are ranked separately on the Auxiliary Selection Hierarchy merits further research.

Let us now turn to a discussion of the social predictors and how we can interpret them. Evidence for this comes mostly from the ctrees and the interactions they show. There is some (albeit relatively weak) evidence that lawyers are initially at the vanguard of change, even though HAVE had started encroaching upon BE's territory as perfect auxiliary prior to the Late Modern English period, a time that is not covered by OBC evidence. At the initial stage in the OBC data, the data for the verbs that already tend slightly towards the HAVE-perfect do not show a significant split with respect to speaker ROLE (see Figure 6a); rather, lawyers are slightly less conservative than other speakers at the early stage of loss in that they already use a somewhat higher proportion of HAVE with the verbs that otherwise still strongly tend towards the BE-perfect (i.e., *become, go, grow, flee*). This can only be taken as rather weak evidence for Britain's (2012) hypothesis that lawyers, more generally, are brokers in the linguistic marketplace.

At stage 3 of the loss, the fact that the ctree analyses show interaction of the speaker variables SEX and speaker ROLE/social CLASS indicate that social predictors do play a role in the choice of auxiliary, with the general tendency being that higher class males tend towards more innovative usage in their choice of auxiliary with those verbs that, otherwise, still strongly select auxiliary BE. The present study thus lends further support to Ryden's (1991) and Kytö's (1997) findings on the role that men played in the loss of this syntactic option and the conservative role that female speakers played. This is unusual considering the general finding that women tend to be leading morpho-syntactic change. It might be explained by the fact that we are looking at an instance of syntactic loss (of a previously standard feature) here rather than at innovation. In Ryden's (1991) and Kytö's (1997) studies, data from higher class women was also included. It is therefore likely that, despite the fact that higher class women are underrepresented in the OBC corpus and the leading role of higher class males in the ongoing change is thus amplified, the innovative role of men and the conservative usage of women in this case of syntactic loss might not simply be a result of the necessarily skewed sampling of males and females in OBC.

With respect to the overall importance of language-internal vs. social predictor variables, the present study has shown that including an additional language-internal predictor did not boost the importance of any of the social predictor variables for those stages where BE was being replaced by HAVE. This indicates that future studies on the loss of the BE-perfect should focus more on modelling further language-internal predictors rather than social variables in this particular case of syntactic loss.

Why would social predictors play such a relatively marginal role in the loss of the BE-perfect? For this, it helps to return to Anderwald's (2014, 2016) comparison of prescriptive grammar writing with actual usage in nineteenth-century American English: her study already indicates that the loss of the BE-perfect must have been a change that happened below the level of speaker's awareness. It is thus not a linguistic variable that is likely to show strong sociolinguistic correlates in the process of loss. This fits well with the finding that, overall, the language-internal predictor variable VERB ranges far above the social predictors in the demise of the BE-perfect. Future studies might thus want to make use of the OBC's social background data in modelling the potential influence of social predictor variables in the loss of syntactic constructions that are likely to be changes from above speakers' awareness.

Corpora

FRED   *Freiburg English Dialect Corpus*
OBC   *Old Bailey Corpus*

References

Anderwald, Lieselotte. 2014. The decline of the *be*-perfect, linguistic relativity, and grammar writing in the nineteenth century. In *Late Modern English Syntax*, Marianne Hundt (ed.), 13–27. Cambridge: CUP. https://doi.org/10.1017/CBO9781139507226.004

Anderwald, Lieselotte. 2016. *Language between Description and Prescription. Verbs and Verb Categories in Nineteenth-Century Grammars of English*. Oxford: OUP. https://doi.org/10.1093/acprof:oso/9780190270674.001.0001

Brinton, Laurel J. 1994. The differentiation of statives and perfects in Early Modern English: The development of the conclusive perfect. In *Towards a Standard English, 1600–1800*, Dieter Stein & Ingrid Tieken-Boon van Ostade (eds), 135–170. Berlin: De Gruyter

Britain, David. 2012. Innovation diffusion in sociohistorical linguistics. In *The Handbook of Historical Sociolinguistics*, Juan Manuel Herández-Campoy & Juan Camilo Conde-Silvestre (eds), 451–464. Oxford: Blackwell. https://doi.org/10.1002/9781118257227.ch24

Culpeper, Jonathan & Kytö, Merja. 2010. *Early Modern English Dialogues: Spoken Interaction as Writing*. Cambridge: CUP.

Denison, David. 1993. *English Historical Syntax*. London: Longman.

Gries, Stefan T. & Hilpert, Martin. 2008. The identification of stages in diachronic data: variability-based neighbor clustering. *Corpora* 3 (1): 59–81. https://doi.org/10.3366/E1749503208000075

Gries, Stefan T. & Hilpert, Martin. 2012. Variability-based neighbor clustering. A bottom-up approach to periodization in historical linguistics. In *The Oxford Handbook of The History of English*, Terttu Nevalainen & Elizabeth Closs Traugott (eds), 134–144. Oxford: OUP.

Hernández, Nuria. 2006. User's Guide to FRED (Freiburg Corpus of English Dialects). Freiburg: Albert-Ludwigs-Universität.

Hothorn, Torsten, Hornik, Kurt & Zeileis, Achim. 2006. Unbiased recursive partitioning: A conditional inference framework. *Journal of Computational and Graphical Statistics* 15: 651–74. https://doi.org/10.1198/106186006X133933

Huber, Judith. 2019. Counterfactuality and aktionsart. Predictors for BE vs. HAVE + past participle in Middle English. In *Developments in English Historical Morpho-Syntax* [Current Issues in Linguistic Theory 346], Claudia Claridge & Birte Bös (eds), 149–173. Amsterdam: John Benjamins. https://doi.org/10.1075/cilt.346.08hub

Huber, Magnus. 2007. The Old Bailey Proceedings, 1674–1834. Evaluating and annotating a corpus of 18th- and 19th-century spoken English. In *Annotating Variation and Change* [Studies in Variation, Contacts and Change in English 1], Anneli Meurman-Solin and Arja Nurmi (eds). Helsinki: University of Helsinki. <www.helsinki.fi/varieng/series/volumes/01/huber/> (6 November 2020).

Hundt, Marianne. 2004. The passival and the progressive passive - A case study of layering in the English aspect and voice systems. In *Corpus Approaches to Grammaticalisation in English* [Studies in Corpus Linguistics 13], Hans Lindquist and Christian Mair (eds), 79–120. Amsterdam: John Benjamins. https://doi.org/10.1075/scl.13.06hun

Hundt, Marianne. 2014. The demise of the *being to V* construction. *Transactions of the Philological Society* 112 (2): 167–187. https://doi.org/10.1111/1467-968X.12035

Hundt, Marianne. 2016a. Error, feature, (incipient) change - Or something else altogether? On the role of low-frequency deviant patterns for the description of Englishes. In *World Englishes: New Theoretical and Methodological Considerations* [Varieties of English around the World G57], Elena Seoane & Cristina Suárez-Gómez (eds), 37–60. Amsterdam: John Benjamins. https://doi.org/10.1075/veaw.g57.03hun

Hundt, Marianne. 2016b. Who is the/a/ø professor at your university? A construction-grammar view on changing article use with single role predicates in American English. In *Corpus Linguistics on the Move: Exploring and Understanding English Through Corpora*, María José López Couso, Belèn Méndez Naya & Ignacio Palacios Martínez (eds), 227–258. Amsterdam: Brill.

Hundt, Marianne. 2018. It is time that this (should) be studied across a broader range of Englishes: A global trip around mandative subjunctives. In *Modeling World Englishes:*

Assessing the Interplay of Emancipation and Globalization of ESL Varieties [Varieties of English around the World G61], Sandra Dehors (ed.), 217–244. Amsterdam: John Benjamins. https://doi.org/10.1075/veaw.g61.09hun

Jespersen, Otto. 1931. *A Modern Grammar on Historical Principles*, Part IV, Vol 3: *Syntax*. London: Allen and Unwin.

Kytö, Merja. 1997. *Be/Have* + past participle: The choice of the auxiliary with intransitives from Late Middle to Modern English. In *English in Transition: Corpus-based Studies in Linguistic Variation and Genre Styles*, Matti Rissanen, Merja Kytö & KirsiHeikkone (eds), 16–85. Berlin: De Gruyter. https://doi.org/10.1515/9783110811148.17

Los, Bettelou. 2015. *A Historical Syntax of English*. Edinburgh: EUP.

McFadden, Thomas & Alexiadou, Artemis. 2006. Auxiliary selection and counterfactuality in the history of English and Germanic. In *Comparative Studies in Germanic Syntax: From Afrikaans to Zurich German* [Linguistik Aktuell/Linguistics Today 97], Jutta M. Hartmann & László Molnárfi (eds), 237–262. Amsterdam: John Benjamins. https://doi.org/10.1075/la.97.12mcf

McFadden, Thomas & Alexiadou, Artemis. 2010. Perfects, resultatives, and auxiliaries in Earlier English. *Linguistic Inquiry* 41 (3): 389–425. https://doi.org/10.1162/LING_a_00002

McFadden, Thomas. 2017. On the disappearance of the BE perfect in Late Modern English. *Acta Linguistica Hafniensia* 49 (2): 159–175. https://doi.org/10.1080/03740463.2017.1351845

Mustanoja, Tauno F. 1960. *A Middle English Syntax*. Helsinki: Société Néophilologique.

Nevalainen, Terttu & Raumolin-Brunberg, Helena. 2003. *Historical Sociolinguistics: Language Change in Tudor and Stuart England*. London: Longman.

Nevalainen, Terttu. 2002. Women's writings as evidence for linguistic continuity and change in Early Modern English. In *Alternative Histories of English*, Richard Watts & Peter Trudgill (eds), 191–209. London: Routledge.

Perek, Florent & Hilpert, Martin. 2017. A distributional semantic approach to the periodization of change in the productivity of constructions. *International Journal of Corpus Linguistics* 22 (4): 490–520. https://doi.org/10.1075/ijcl.16128.per

Quirk, Randolph, Greenbaum, Sidney, Leech, Geoffrey & SvartvikJan. 1985. *A Comprehensive Grammar of the English Language*. London: Longman.

R Core Team. 2016*R: A Language and Environment for Statistical computing*. Vienna, Austria: R Foundation for Statistical Computing. <https://www.r-project.org/> (6 November 2020).

Rosemeyer, Malte. 2014. *Auxiliary Selection in Spanish. Gradience, Gradualness and Conservatism* [Studies in Language Companion Series 155]. Amsterdam: John Benjamins. https://doi.org/10.1075/slcs.155

Rydén, Mats & Brorström, Sverker. 1987. *The Be/Have Variation with Intransitives in English. With Special Reference to the Late Modern Period*. Stockholm: Almqvist and Wiksell.

Rydén, Mats. 1991. The *be/have* variation in its crucial phases. In *Historical English Syntax*, Dieter Kastovsky (ed.), 343–354. Berlin: De Gruyter. https://doi.org/10.1515/9783110863314.343

Seoane, Elena & Suárez-Gómez, Cristina. 2013. The expression of the perfect in East and South-East Asian Englishes. *English World-Wide* 34 (1): 1–25. https://doi.org/10.1075/eww.34.1.01seo

Smith, K. Aaron. 2007. Language use and auxiliary selection in the perfect. In *Split Auxiliary Systems: A Cross-Linguistic Perspective* [Typological Studies in Language 69], Raúl Aranovich (ed.), 255–270. Amsterdam: John Benjamins. https://doi.org/10.1075/tsl.69.12smi

Sorace, Antonella. 2000. Gradients in auxiliary selection with intransitive verbs. *Language* 76 (4): 859–890. https://doi.org/10.2307/417202

Strobl, Carolin, Malley, James & Tutz, Gerhard. 2009. Introduction to recursive partitioning: Rationale, application, and characteristics of classification and regression trees, bagging and random forests. *Psychological Methods* 14 (4): 323–348. https://doi.org/10.1037/a0016973

Strobl, Carolin, Hothorn, Torsten & Zeileis, Achim. 2009. Party on! A new, conditional variable-important measure for random forests available in the party package. *The R Journal* 1 (2): 14–17. https://doi.org/10.32614/RJ-2009-013

Tagliamonte, Sali & Baayen, Harald. 2012. Models, forests, and trees of York English: Was/were variation as a case study for statistical practice. *Language Variation and Change* 24: 135–178. https://doi.org/10.1017/S0954394512000129

Visser, Fredericus Theodorus. 1973. *An Historical Syntax of the English Language, Part 3, Second Half: Syntactical Units with Two or More Verbs*. Leiden: Brill.

Werner, Valentin. 2016. Rise of the undead? BE-perfects in World Englishes. In *Re-assessing the Present Perfect. Corpus Studies and Beyond*, Valentin Werner, Elena Seoane & Cristina Suárez Gómez (eds), 259–294. Berlin: De Gruyter. https://doi.org/10.1515/9783110443530-012

Yerastov, Yuri. 2015. A construction grammar analysis of the transitive *be* perfect in present-day Canadian English. *English Language and Linguistics* 19 (1): 157–178. https://doi.org/10.1017/S1360674314000331

Appendix

Table A-1. Distribution of BE-perfects and HAVE-perfects (raw frequencies) by speaker ROLE across the four stages in the OBC

| | 1720–1760 | | 1770–1820 | | 1830–1850 | | 1860–1910 | |
	BE	HAVE	BE	HAVE	BE	HAVE	BE	HAVE
lawyer	50	45	121	157	7	17	5	15
judge	31	13	76	55	1	26	0	15
defendant	24	9	26	26	2	33	5	79
interpreter	0	0	2	0	6	5	5	16
policeman	0	0	0	0	0	0	0	1
victim	211	14	522	152	219	140	67	195
witness	340	73	518	297	261	460	217	1307
'other' overall	575	96	1068	475	488	638	294	1892

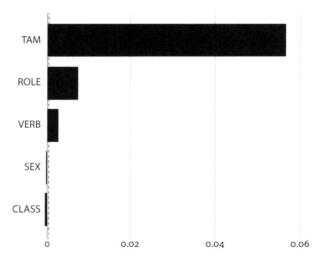

Figure A-1. Variable importance, MORPH included (stage 1)

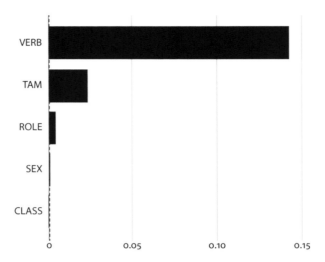

Figure A-2. Variable importance, MORPH included (stage 2)

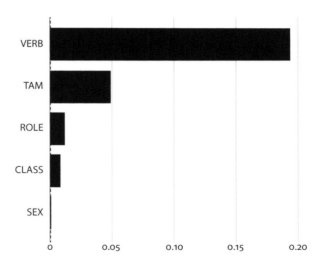

Figure A-3. Variable importance, MORPH included (stage 3)

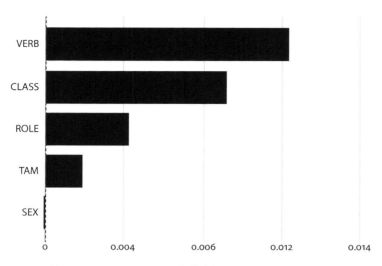

Figure A-4. Variable importance, MORPH included (stage 4)

Table A-2. Model fit for the RF analyses (Somers2), including inflection of the auxiliary as an additional predictor variable

	1720–1760	1770–1820	1830–1850	1860–1910
C-statistic	0.880	0.883	0.922	0.847
Dxy	.760	.766	.845	.693

CHAPTER 8

On the waning of forms – A corpus-based analysis of decline and loss in adjective amplification

Martin Schweinberger
The University of Queensland

This study takes a corpus-based approach to investigating the decline and near-loss of *very* as an adjective amplifier in spoken New Zealand English (NZE) based on *The Wellington Corpus of Spoken New Zealand English*. The paper analyzes the replacement of *very* as the dominant adjective amplifier across apparent time to provide insights into what factors correlate with and trigger the loss of formerly dominant variants from a variable context. While a wealth of studies has analyzed what causes innovative variants to become dominant, only relatively little attention has been placed on the process of waning. As a consequence, the expansion of innovative variants, e.g., the processes that underlie the expansion in use of *really*, is well understood; showing that the trajectory of change accompanying the increase of *really* follows a highly systematic and layered expansion in use. In contrast, questions as to whether the loss of *very* as a variant in spoken data is equally systematic remain unclear. The results of binomial mixed-effects regression models show that the decrease of *very* is remarkably uniform and does not parallel the highly systematic and step-wise trajectory of innovative incoming variants. This lack of an ordered heterogeneity that accompanies the retreat of *very* raises questions about the systematicity of loss as a linguistic phenomenon more broadly.

Keywords: adjective amplification, very, language change, New Zealand English, Mixed-Effects Model

1. Introduction

Variationist research over the past 50 or so years has produced a wealth of studies on language variation and change (Labov 1994, 2001, 2010), which have

https://doi.org/10.1075/slcs.218.08sch
© 2021 John Benjamins Publishing Company

contributed substantially to a detailed understanding of how innovative variants enter and come to dominate a variable context. However, despite this extensive body of research, comparatively little attention has been placed on variants which drop out of the variable context and, more specifically, the factors that this loss correlates with (a notable exception in this respect is D'Arcy 2015). Indeed, the replacement of a traditional form by an innovative rival is often considered a symmetrical process (Blythe 2016) during which incoming or generalizing forms "spread across semantic classes and types of adjectives, and across syntactic functions" (D'Arcy 2015: 470). However, replacement in terms of frequency is typically accompanied by a functional rearrangement of the changing system's grammar (D'Arcy 2015). As a consequence of this functional rearrangement, it is inaccurate to assume that one form simply takes the place of another form. Rather, during this process each form adapts and occupies new functional niches which emerge from the rearrangement. In other words, replacement in terms of frequency does not necessarily imply functional equivalence and the waxing of the innovative variant is thus not merely a mirror image of the waning of the traditionally dominant form.

Incoming variants enter new contexts typically in a very systematic manner during which constraints erode sequentially and contexts that the innovative form was previously barred from entering become available (Labov 1966). Such constraints encompass both language-internal as well as social and cognitive factors. Whether the process of waning of traditional variants, i.e., the dropping-out of variable contexts, proceeds in a similarly ordered and systematically step-wise manner is yet to be determined.

To address this issue, the present study takes a corpus-based approach to investigate the waning of *very* as an adjective amplifier in New Zealand English (NZE) (see (1) and (2)). The aim of this paper consists in providing a detailed analysis of how *very* drops out of the NZE amplifier system and to understand the mechanisms that underlie and condition this process.

(1)[1]   *very* as an adjective amplifier in attributive position

    a.   it's a *very important* indicator   (DGB036:Z2[2])

    b.   i'm a *very important* person   (DPC307:AT)

---

1.   All examples come from the WSC, are converted to lower case, and have been stripped of additional annotation such as symbols indicating overlap or pauses.

2.   In the identifier code the first three letters and three numbers before the colon identify the file while the letters and numbers after the colon identify the speaker so that "DGB036:Z2" informs the reader that the example was uttered by speaker Z2 in file DGB036, in the conversation part of the WSC.

    c.   it's a *very harsh* society really   (DGB004:Z1)

    d.   there were *very good* swimmers   (DGI160:AS)

(2)   *very* as an adjective amplifier in predicative position

    a.   it was *very extensive*   (DPC067:AN)

    b.   i'm *very nervous* about sunday   (DPF070:PM)

    c.   it's *very nice*   (DPC302:JO)

    d.   they were *very good*   (DGZ086:AN)

Amplification relates to the semantic category of degree and represents a subtype of intensification. Since intensifiers are prototypically recruited from the adverb class, adjective amplifiers are also referred to as adverbs of degree or degree adverbs (see, for instance, Biber et al. 2007: 554). Intensity ranges from very low (downtoning) to very high (amplification) (Quirk et al. 1985: 589–590). Within the amplifier category, Quirk et al. (1985: 589–590) differentiate between maximizers such as *completely* which are used to construe an upper extreme of a scale (Quirk et al. 1985: 590) and boosters such as *very* that construe a high degree or a high point on a scale. While maximizers form a more closed-class group, boosters form an open class that is known for adopting new members. Such new or "innovative" members replace forms which have lost their expressiveness due to overly frequent use (Quirk et al. 1985: 590). As the present study focuses on the decline of *very* as an adjective amplifier, other subtypes of intensification, such as downtoning which includes approximators such as *almost*, compromisers such as *more or less*, diminishers such as *partly*, and minimizers such as *hardly*, are disregarded.

Adjective amplifiers are particularly intriguing elements for investigating mechanisms of change because the amplifier domain has been deemed a domain of "fevered invention" (Bolinger 1972: 18) and an area of perpetual waxing and waning of forms that is characterized by continuous invention and renewal (D'Arcy 2015: 450). Because of this perpetual waxing and waning of forms, amplification lends itself to the analysis of conditioning factors of loss.

The current study tests whether the trajectory of change of a waning form exhibits a similar pattern of ordered heterogeneity observed in the trajectories of innovative variants (*really*) described in Canadian and New Zealand English (see Tagliamonte 2008 and D'Arcy 2015 respectively). In this respect, the analysis aims to add to our understanding of how waning variants drop out of adjective amplifier systems. In terms of hypothesized outcomes, the study tests two distinct pathways of loss: a systematic contraction of domains on the one hand and a uniform decline without systematic regression on the other. If the former were correct, the use of *very* would show substantial stratification along social and linguistic lines. In that case, the statistical analysis would report that the use of *very* correlated with various intra- as well as extra-linguistic factors, for example the gender, education level, and age of speakers, the syntactic function and semantic category of the adjective, its gradability as well as its emotionality. Furthermore, if correct, then the age of speakers, in particular, would interact with intra-linguistic factors. In contrast, if the near-loss of *very* did not follow a systematic regression and retreat from semantic domains as well as syntactic contexts, then we would expect *very* to correlate primarily with age and any other factors would show no or only marginal layering.

The next section provides an overview of findings from previous research with a special focus being placed on variationist research. Section 3 provides an overview of the data used in the current study and discusses issues relating to methodology, such as data processing and the statistical procedures applied to the data. Section 4 presents the results of the current study while Section 5 discusses these results in light of previous research and draws larger conclusions related to the loss of linguistic variants.

2. Previous research

Intensification has been subject of intense linguistic research for more than a century and various studies have been dedicated to historical changes in degree modification (for example Breban & Davidse 2016; Méndez-Naya 2003, 2008; Méndez-Naya & Pahta 2010; Nevalainen 2008; Nevalainen & Rissanen 2002; Paradis 1997, 2008; Peters 1992, 1993, 1994; Rissanen 2008). Due to the substantial amount of research, the developmental pathways of selected intensifier variants, in particular *so*, *really*, and *very* but also *wonder*, *pure*, *absolutely*, *completely*, *all*, and *totally*, are well documented (Aijmer 2011, 2018a, 2018b; Calle-Martín 2014; Macaulay 2006; Núñez-Pertejo & Palacios Martínez 2014; Rickford et al. 2007; Tao 2007). Furthermore, differences in amplifier use based on the age, gender, and social class of speakers are well understood as will be detailed in the following section, which surveys the main findings of previous research on the social stratification of amplifier use (Bauer & Bauer 2002; Fuchs 2017; Ito & Tagliamonte 2003; Macaulay 2002; Murphy 2010; Núñez-Pertejo & Palacios Martínez 2014; Palacios Martínez & Núñez-Pertejo 2012; Stenström 1999; Tagliamonte 2008; Tagliamonte & Denis 2014; Tagliamonte & Roberts 2005). The wealth of studies that have dedicated themselves to understanding the social meaning of amplifiers show that amplifiers play a crucial part in how speakers express themselves socially and emotionally (Labov 1985: 43; Ito & Tagliamonte 2003: 258; see also Murphy 2010). Thereby, intensifiers are part of an inventory on which speakers rely to create and mark their social identity (Tagliamonte 2012: 30). To elaborate, the use of *so* as an adjective amplifier encodes informality and youth while use of *very* as an adjective amplifier encodes formality and is associated with older or more learned speakers (Tagliamonte 2012: 30).

Various studies focusing on geographically distinct varieties of English found that in most of these varieties *very* is declining in apparent time while *really* is increasing (see Murphy 2010 for Irish English; D'Arcy 2015 for NZE; Ito & Tagliamonte 2003 and Barnfield & Buchstaller 2010 for North East British English; Tagliamonte 2008 and Tagliamonte & Denis 2014 for Toronto English; and Tagliamonte & Denis 2014 for South Eastern Ontario English). In addition, D'Arcy (2015), Ito and Tagliamonte (2003), Tagliamonte (2008), as well as Tagliamonte and Roberts (2005) show that change in intensifier systems does not proceed in a haphazard manner but that it is highly systematic. The systematicity of the observed changes is reflected by the fact that amplifier use is stratified along social and linguistic lines as will be discussed in the following section.

With respect to linguistic stratification, i.e., language-internal constraints, the syntactic function of the adjective that is amplified is one of the most consistent factors as collocation with adjectives in predicative function is commonly regarded as an indicator for a later stage of change (Mustanoja 1960: 326–327; Tagliamonte 2008: 373; Tagliamonte & Denis 2014: 116). In contrast, initial stages of change are typically associated with occurrence in attributive positions (D'Arcy 2015: 471–472; Mustanoja 1960: 326–327). This tendency has been explained as a symptom of grammaticalization processes and, specifically, delexicalization. As amplifier variants become progressively delexicalized, these forms increasingly enter syntactic contexts which these variants were previously barred from entering. Probably the best attested cline for this kind of delexicalization is the grammaticalization of *very* from descriptive modifier (*verry precious stones* 'genuine precious stones'), to noun-intensifier (*a verray sooth* 'a true truth'), focus marker (*the very feature* 'this exact feature'), adjective intensifier (*very frenshe* 'very French'), classifier (*very heyre* 'the rightful heir'), postdeterminer-intensifier (*the vereye same* 'the very same'), quantifier-intensifier (*verrie mony* 'very many') postdeterminer (*this very day*) (see Breban & Davidse 2016: 230–242). Based on this trajectory, modification of predicative adjectives has been deemed a sign of advanced delexicalization (Tagliamonte 2008: 373) while innovative variants typically occur with attributive adjectives first (Mustanoja 1960: 326–327) and only modify adjectives in predicative function during later stages (Tagliamonte 2008: 363).

With respect to its historical development in NZE, D'Arcy (2015: 474) reports that in the nineteenth century, *very* occurred predominantly in predicative contexts and, despite co-occurring across a range of semantic categories, "it was most used for adjectives of human emotion and propensities (*frightened, honest*)". During the first half of the twentieth century, *very* initially specialized on the subjective domains of human emotion and propensity before expanding across all semantic domains in the latter half of the twentieth century (D'Arcy 2015: 474). According to D'Arcy (2015), the move away from subjective domains indicates a loss of expressivity which accompanied or even triggered its decline: "Once this generalization was complete, and *very* no longer targeted selectively, its syntactic properties were jostled about as *very* waned and the system reorganized to accommodate the incoming, competing forms (*really, pretty, quite, so*)" (D'Arcy 2015: 476).

Another factor which accompanies changes in intensifier systems is the association of innovative variants with negative polarity items or emotional adjectives more generally (see, for example, Peters 1994). For instance, Tagliamonte and Roberts (2005: 289) found that the innovative intensifier *so* significantly collocates with emotional adjectives (particularly among female speakers) as does *really* among speakers between the ages of 20 and 29 in Toronto (Tagliamonte 2008: 383; Núñez-Pertejo & Martínez 2014: 230). Partington (1993: 184) argues that the reason for this tendency lies in the negative domain from which intensifiers are often recruited (*terrible, horrible*, etc.) and that these negative items must first undergo delexicalization before modifying positive polarity items such as *good* or *nice* (cf. also Lorenz 2002). In other words, during early stages of change, negative intensifiers tend to associate with semantically negative adjectives (*terribly bad*) and only during later stages, when the incoming forms have been bleached, do they collocate with positive adjectives as semantic restrictions erode (*terribly good*). Applied to the present case, this would suggest that *very* is unlikely to collocate with negative adjectives and that the emotionality of adjectives should maximally possess only a minor impact.

One of the most intriguing aspects that has been described in the respective literature relates to lexical restrictions on amplifier use. Tagliamonte (2008) found that innovative forms are restricted to a relatively small and fixed set of adjectives and that this set expands once a form becomes more frequent as collocational restrictions dissolve (cf. Tagliamonte 2008: 376 and Méndez-Naya 2003: 377).

Concerning extra-linguistic stratification, the situation is complex. Apparent time distributions as well as multivariate statistics confirm consistent trends for age – with younger speakers preferring *really* and other innovative forms such as *dead, fucking, pretty* or *so* whereas older speakers strongly prefer *very* (D'Arcy 2015; Ito & Tagliamonte 2003; Murphy 2010; Tagliamonte 2008). In contrast, findings for gender preferences are less coherent when it comes to adjective amplification. Fuchs (2017), for instance, found that intensification has increased from the 1990s to the 2010s and that men consistently use intensifiers less frequently than women – a trend confirmed for Irish English by Murphy (2010: 131–133) who also found that men amplify less frequently than women but use a wider variety of forms. Tagliamonte and D'Arcy (2009) also found a significant but weak gender difference which was, however, restricted to the use of the innovative amplifier *so* while D'Arcy (2015: 477) found that ongoing change in the amplifier system of NZE did not show significant gender differences (yet *really* was used significantly more by men in her data). Similarly, Ito and Tagliamonte (2003) as well as Tagliamonte (2008) did not find consistent gender differences and argue that such stratification interacts with the age of speakers because "the use of intensifiers by male and female speakers of different ages is intimately tied to the stages of intensifier renewal in the community grammar" (Tagliamonte 2008: 385). Finally, Xiao and Tao (2007) report that men prefer maximizers (for instance *completely*) in British English while women prefer boosters (for instance *very*).

After reviewing previous research on intensification, the next section presents the data used in the current study.

3.   Data and methodology

This section consists of three subsections: the first subsection describes the corpus data and details the data processing while the subsequent subsection provides an overview of the variables included in the statistical analysis. The third subsection explains the statistical procedures that were applied to the data.

3.1   Data sources and processing

The present study makes use of *The Wellington Corpus of Spoken New Zealand English* (WSC; Holmes, Vine & Johnson 1998). The WSC consists of 555 files and approximately 1,000,000 words representing formal speech/monologue (12%), semi-formal speech/elicited monologue (13%), and informal speech/dialogue (75%). All data was collected between 1988 and 1994 and represents speakers who lived in New Zealand since before age of 10 and who spent less than half their lifetime or a maximum of 10 years overseas.

To extract all adjectives, the corpus data was first split into turns, then metadata such as comments and non-linguistic tags (for instance <laughter>) were removed. Then, the cleaned turns were part-of-speech tagged in the programming environment R (R Development Core Team 2019) by implementing a maximum entropy tagger provided in the openNLP package (Hornik 2016). After part-of-speech-tagging, all adjectives (tag JJ) were extracted and it was determined for each adjective whether or not it was amplified and, if it was, which lexical form served as an amplifier (see Table 1). Next, if the same amplifier type had occurred within a span of three previous pre-adjectival slots, the respective instance of an amplifier was coded as being primed (Szmrecsanyi 2005, 2006; Tulving & Schacter

1990: 301). After coding for priming, negated adjectives, misclassified items, adjectives preceded by downtoners as well as comparative and superlative forms were removed from the analysis following common practice (see, for instance, D'Arcy 2015 or Tagliamonte 2008). Furthermore, adjectives that were never amplified, or which were not amplified by at least two different amplifier types, were removed from the analysis. This was done to remove lexicalized expressions, for example *right honorable*, from the analysis as the pre-adjectival slot in fixed expressions does not represent a variable context (as it does not allow for variation in amplifier use). Then, a Sentiment Analysis was applied to the adjectives in the data using the syuzhet package in R (Jockers 2017). The Sentiment Analysis was applied in order to determine whether a given adjective was associated with a positive emotion (as, for instance, *happy* or *nice*) or with a negative emotion (as, for instance, *sad* or *angry*) or with no emotion (e.g., *rusty* or *flat*). Next, all remaining adjectives were classified semantically based on the classification proposed by Dixon (1977, 2004; see also D'Arcy 2015; Ito & Tagliamonte 2003; Tagliamonte 2008; and Tagliamonte & Roberts 2005). The model diagnostics of a first minimal adequate model showed that an additional six data points had to be removed from the data set as these data points were too influential and thus skewed the results of the model. A tabulated summary of data during different stages of the data processing is provided below.

Table 1. Frequency of speakers, adjective slots, amplified adjective slots, and percentage of amplified slots during different stages of data processing.

Data	Speakers	Adj. slots (N)	Amp. Adj. slots (N)	Amplification (%)
Raw data	1,434	57,132	4589	8.0
After processing	531	11,285	1,715	15.2
Only amp. slots	441	1,715	1,715	100.0
After removing outliers (final data)	441	1,709	1,709	100.0

In a next step, all adjectives that were not amplified were removed and, finally, the data was manually cross-evaluated and socio-demographic information about the speakers (age, gender, etc.) was added.

3.2   Classification and coding of variables

The following section describes the coding of the variables in this study. The basis for the classification of the sociolinguistic variables is the WSC guide that accompanied the textual data and which provides socio-demographic information about the speakers and the corpus material itself.

very (*dependent variable*)

The dependent variable in the present study are instances of amplifying *very* in pre-adjectival slots. Each pre-adjectival slot was coded as 0 (an amplifier but not *very* occurred in the pre-adjectival slot) or as 1 (*very* is present in the pre-adjectival slot). The resulting factor has accordingly two levels (0, 1) and represents a nominal variable.

Adjective (*random effect*)

Adjective refers to the adjective type (type as opposed to token) and is included in the random effect structure of regression modeling. Each of the 261 adjective types in the final data set thus has an individual intercept and since Adjective is part of the random effect structure, it does not have a reference category.

Age

The very detailed age classification of the WSC which originally consisted of 16 age groups was condensed into six cohorts (16–19, 20–29, 30–39, 40–49, 50–59, 60+). Condensing age groups was necessary due to the moderate number of adjective slots in some of the original age groups. Relying on the original age groups would have decreased the reliability of the statistical analysis. The resulting variable has six levels of which '16-19' represents the reference category. Reference category refers to the level of a variable against which other levels are evaluated. This means that the regression model tests how the likelihood of *very* changes, if we switch from '16-19' (the reference category) to another age group while all other variables are held constant.

Gender

The classification of gender is based on the self-reported sex in the guide accompanying the WSC data. In the present study, gender is a nominal variable and represents a factor with two levels (*Man, Woman*).

Education

The classification of the education level of speakers in the WSC is based on the self-reported highest degree achieved by a speaker. The very detailed information was condensed into a variable with only two levels: *College* and *NoCollege*.

Function

Function refers to the syntactic position or function of the adjective and has two levels: *Attributive* as in (1) and *Predicative* as in (2). Function, therefore, represents a nominal variable of which *Attributive* represents the reference category.

Gradability

Gradability represents a semantic property of an adjective which encodes degrees of a characteristic (Biber et al. 2007: 521) and refers to a more or less compared to a base-line. Gradable adjectives can be marked to denote comparative or superlative forms either morphologically with <-er> or <-est> or periphrastically with 'more' or 'most'. The base forms of gradable adjectives do not have special marking. Certain adjectives only rarely form a comparative or superlative as, for example, *more dental* or **?most motionless*. Although amplifiers are not commonly used with such ungradable adjectives, they can be employed for pragmatic purposes, e.g., for emphasis. In addition, during its grammaticalization, *very* has spread from non-gradable to gradable adjectives (Adamson & González-Díaz 2004 cited in Tagliamonte 2008) indicating that an increase in the co-occurrence of a specific amplifier variant with non-gradable adjectives can be indicative of ongoing grammaticalization of that amplifier variant. This means that gradability represents a quantitative rather than a qualitative property of an adjective. To take this into account, gradability is operationalized as the logit of the probability of an adjective being used in a comparative role versus the overall rate of comparison among adjectives. As the WSC is insufficient in size to warrant such an operationalization, the gradability score was calculated based on the *Corpus of Contemporary American English* (COCA) (Davies 2010). Operationalized this way, a gradability value of 0 represents a neutral state where an adjective occurs with an average rate in comparative contexts while negative values indicate a tendency towards non-gradability (the adjective occurs less often in comparative contexts than the average adjective) and positive values indicate a tendency towards gradability (the adjective occurs more frequently in comparative contexts than the average adjective). For instance, the adjective *nice* occurs 5,675 times in the COCA and, of these occurrences, 334 appear in comparative contexts either as *nicer* or *nicest* or together with *more* and *most*. There are 5,302,538 adjectives in the COCA and 329,399 of these surface in comparative contexts. The gradability score for *nice* thus is -0.0576[3]. The fact that the value is negative indicates that, compared to the overall ratio of comparatives in the COCA, *nice* occurs (slightly) less often in comparative contexts than the average adjective and is thus less gradable than the average adjective.

Emotionality

As innovative amplifier variants have been reported to favor co-occurrence with emotional adjectives, the emotionality of adjectives was included as a predictor. The emotionality of an adjective was determined using a Sentiment Analysis

---

3.   logit((334*(5,302,538-329,399-(5,675-334))) / ((329,399-334)*(5,675-334)) / (1 + (334*(5,302,538-329,399-(5,675-334)))/((329,399-334)*(5,675-334))))).

based on the syuzhet package in R (Jockers 2017) which relies on the *Word-Emotion Association Lexicon* (Mohammad & Turney 2013; see also http://www.purl. org/net/NRCemotionlexicon). The *Word-Emotion Association Lexicon* contains 10,170 words and their emotionality scores that were gathered through the crowd-sourced Amazon Mechanical Turk service. To arrive at the emotionality scores, Turk service participants answered a sequence of questions for each word which were then fed into the emotion association rating (see Mohammad & Turney 2013). The rating encoded whether participants associated a given word with one of eight basic emotions (ANGER, ANTICIPATION, DISGUST, FEAR, JOY, SADNESS, SURPRISE, TRUST) (Plutchik 1980, 1994). The emotionality scores were derived from 38,726 ratings provided by 2,216 participants. Each term was rated by at least five different raters and for 85 percent of words at least four raters provided identical ratings. For example, the words *dark* or *tragic* are associated with SADNESS whereas *happy* or *beautiful* are associated with JOY and *cruel* or *outraged* are associate with ANGER. If an adjective had positive scores for ANGER, DISGUST, FEAR, or SADNESS, the adjective was classified as *Negative Emotional*. If an adjective was associated with ANTICIPATION, JOY, SURPRISE, or TRUST, the adjective was coded as *Positive Emotional*. If a word was not associated with any of the core emotions, that word was coded as *Non Emotional*.

Semantic Category

The semantic classification of adjectives uses the semantic categories advocated by Dixon (1977, 2004). Dixon (1977, 2004) proposed the categories *dimension* (e.g., *big, large, little, small*), *difficulty* (e.g., *difficult, simple*), *physical property* (e.g., *hard, soft, heavy, light*), *color* (e.g., *black, white, red*), *human propensity* (e.g., *jealous, happy, kind*), *age* (e.g,. *new, young, old*), *value* (e.g., *good, bad, proper*), *speed* (e.g., *fast, quick, slow*), *position* (e.g., *right, left, near*). All adjectives were rated independently by five linguistically trained coders, who were offered an additional option (other) if an adjective did not fit into any of the semantic categories proposed by Dixon (1977, 2004). The resulting categorical variable consists of the ten levels *Value* (733), *Human Propensity* (378), *Physical Property* (217), *Other* (143), *Dimension* (99), *Difficulty* (41), *Position* (36), *Age* (28), *Speed* (21), and *Color* (19) with *Other* being the reference category.

Frequency

Frequency represents a numeric variable and refers to the token frequency of adjective types by age. The grouping by age was necessary to prevent apparent time changes in adjective frequency to confound changes in the use of *very*. In addition, frequency was scaled so that the regression results show changes in the likelihood of *very* based on the mean value of frequency rather than based on a value of 0.

Priming

Priming refers to the re-use of material that was used in previous utterances (cf. Tulving & Schacter 1990: 301). The type of priming relevant for the current study is form or production priming (Szmrecsanyi 2005: 113) which is short-lived and disappears soon after exposure to a stimulus (Althaus & Kim 2006: 962). To account for the rapid decay of form or production priming, the current study operationalizes priming as spanning up to three pre-adjectival slots. This means that an instance of *very* was coded as being primed if another instance of *very* occurred in at least one of three previous pre-adjectival slots. Thus, priming is represented by a factor with two levels (*NoPrime, Prime*).

Statistical procedures

The study uses a two-fold two-step procedure meaning that the two steps described in the following were performed twice: the first model fitting process, i.e., the first fold, was used to arrive at a model that could be diagnosed to identify outliers. After the outliers were removed, the two step-procedure was repeated to arrive at a final minimal adequate model.

The first step of the analysis consisted of performing a Boruta analysis (Kursa & Rudnicki 2010). As Boruta is a variable selection procedure, it reports which variables have some non-random relationship with the dependent variable (*very*). However, Boruta does neither provide information about the direction of the effect nor about whether the variable affects the use of *very* as a main effect or as part of an interaction. As such, Boruta only serves to determine which variables to include in the regression modelling. In this second step, a mixed-effects binomial logistic regression model, which is a hierarchical multivariate analysis, was applied to the data to test how the variables suggested by the Boruta analysis affect the use of *very*.

To arrive at a final minimal adequate model, i.e., a model which explains a maximum of variance with a minimum number of predictors, this study used a step-wise step-up procedure (see Gries 2009; independent variables and interactions between them are added consecutively, i.e., the model is built up). After each addition of a predictor, an analysis of variance (ANOVA) was applied to the smaller and the more saturated model. The predictor was retained (i) if the ANOVA reported a significant improvement of model fit and (ii) if the variance inflation factors (vif) had values smaller than three for main effects (Zuur et al. 2010) and smaller than 30 for interactions[4], and (iii) if the inclusion of a

---

4. Variance inflation factors (vifs) measure collinearity and values higher than the thresholds would mean that the model provides unreliable results as the predictors in the model are correlated and thus collinear – interactions can have higher vifs because we expect interactions to correlate with the main effects that they consist of.

predictor did not cause an excessive inflation in the Bayesian Information Criterion (BIC). These restrictions are necessary as high vif indicate that variables are highly correlated (collinearity) which would lead to unreliable results. Similarly, an increase in BIC suggests that the model violates the principle of parsimony according to which models should explain a maximum of variance with a minimum number of predictors. In addition to including main effects, the statistical analyses tested all secondary or two-way interactions (interaction between two main effects).

To ascertain if the sample size of the present analysis was sufficient, an additional post-hoc power analysis was conducted following the procedure introduced by Green and MacLeod (2016). The common threshold for acceptable statistical power and thus a sufficient sample size, assumes that a medium effect (Cohen's $d = 0.5$ which represents an odds ratio of 3.47; see Chen, Cohen & Chen 2010) should be detected with an accuracy of 80 percent.

4. Results

The following section presents the results of the analysis starting with an overview of the final data set (Table 2) and continuing with a survey of the frequency of amplifier variants (Table 3).

Table 2. Frequency speakers, amplified adjective slots, instances of *very*, and percentage of *very* of all amplifiers by age and gender in the final, processed data set.

Age	Gender	Speakers	Adjective slots (N)	very (N)	%
16–19	Man	26	75	7	9.33
16–19	Woman	47	223	13	5.83
20–29	Man	74	295	39	13.22
20–29	Woman	124	573	56	9.77
30–39	Man	26	66	11	16.67
30–39	Woman	35	134	22	16.42
40–49	Man	19	52	21	40.38
40–49	Woman	34	100	36	36.00
50–59	Man	15	50	26	52.00
50–59	Woman	23	86	52	60.47
60+	Man	7	23	14	60.87
60+	Woman	11	32	16	50.00
Total		441	1,709	313	30.91

Table 2 shows that the final data set contains 441 speakers, 1,709 adjective tokens of which 313 are amplified by *very* which amounts to an average of 30.91 percent across age cohorts and genders. Table 3 displays the frequencies of adjective amplifiers in the WSC data.

Table 3. Frequency and percentages of amplifiers in the WSC.

Amplifier	Frequency (N)	Total (%)	Amplifiers (%)
Ø (not amplified)	9,570	84.8	
really	774	6.86	45.13
very	319	2.83	18.60
so	250	2.22	14.58
pretty	161	1.43	9.39
real	50	0.44	2.92
absolutely, bloody	19 (38)	0.17 (0.34)	1.11 (2.22)
totally	15	0.13	0.87
fucking	13	0.12	0.76
completely	11	0.1	0.64
incredibly	7	0.06	0.41
particularly	6	0.05	0.35
actually, perfectly	5 (10)	0.04 (0.08)	0.29 (0.58)
definitely, especially, much	4 (12)	0.04 (0.12)	0.23 (0.69)
amazingly, awful, enormously, exceedingly, true, ultra	3 (18)	0.03 (0.18)	0.17 (1.02)
entirely, extremely, seriously, terribly, wicked	2 (10)	0.02 (0.10)	0.12 (0.60)
awfully, considerably, crazy, dead, distinctly, exceptionally, excruciatingly, fully, highly, horrendously, hugely, immensely, mighty, obviously, purely, remarkably, shocking, specially, traditionally, truly, utterly	1 (21)	0.01 (0.21)	0.06 (1.26)
Total	11,285 (1,715)	100 (15.2)	100

Table 3 shows that *really* is the most frequent amplifier in the New Zealand data which contrasts with the findings for historical NZE by D'Arcy (2015: 468) who found *very* to be the most frequent adjective intensifier. Together, the three most frequent amplifier types *really*, *very*, and *so* account for 76.31 percent of all adjective amplification, leaving the remaining intensifiers a mere 23.69 percent.

To ascertain potential change in apparent time change, Figure 1 shows the percentages of *really*, *very* and all *other* amplifier types combined against the age of speakers from left (old; further removed in time) to right (young; more recent).

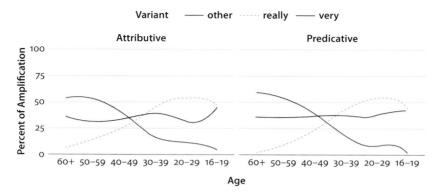

Figure 1. Loess-smoothed percentage of amplifier types in the WSC across apparent time by syntactic function.

Figure 2 provides the changes in relative frequencies of amplifier variants across apparent time to test if the trend that *really* has been replacing *very* according to the percentage values in Figure 1 also holds for frequencies. This additional visualization is necessary because a variant may decrease relative to other variants and would thus show a decrease in percentage values but remain stable in terms of relative frequency.

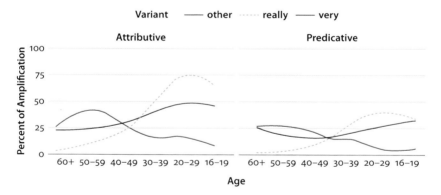

Figure 2. Loess-smoothed relative frequencies of amplifier types (per 1,000 words) in the WSC across apparent time by syntactic function.

Figure 1 and Figure 2 show a drastic decrease in the use of *very* across apparent time in both percentages and relative frequencies across attributive and predicative contexts. Thus, the figures strongly suggest that the formerly dominant adjective amplifier, *very*, has been replaced by *really* in terms of frequency. The distributions clearly follow an X-shaped distribution typical of lexical replacement. The trend emerging from Figures 1 and 2 thus mirrors trajectories observed in previous research on the NZE intensifier system. D'Arcy (2015) showed that *really* has replaced *very* in New Zealand English during the latter half of the twentieth century based on the *Origins of New Zealand English Corpus* (ONZE; cf. Gordon et al. 2007). We will now turn to the results of the statistical analysis.

4.1   Boruta

The Boruta variable selection procedure confirmed the variables gender, syntactic function, and education level as unimportant. The results of the final Boruta run which only contained variables which were deemed as being either important or at least tentatively important, i.e., having some kind of relationship with the use of *very*, are displayed in Figure 3.

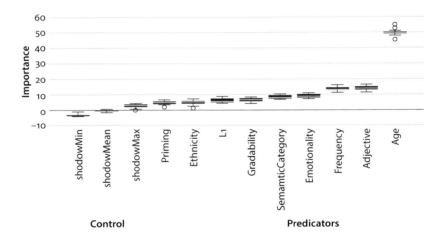

Figure 3.   Variable importance according to the Boruta variable selection procedure (the shadow variables to the left represent the effect size of the shuffled controls that variables have to outperform in order to be considered important).

The Boruta results suggest that the age of speakers is by far the most influential variable with respect to the use of *very*. The relatively marginal importance of both language-internal as well as social variables aside from age indicates that the decrease of *very* does not follow a systematic or step-wise progression and that the waning of *very* proceeds across all variable levels in a rather uniform manner. We will now turn to the results of the regression analysis to gain a more detailed understanding of this process.

4.2   Mixed-effects binomial logistic regression model

The results of the regression model in Table 4 confirm that the age of speakers and the emotionality of adjectives significantly correlate with the use of *very* as an adjective amplifier (see also Table 5 as well as Figures 5 and 6). Neither priming, the education level of speakers, the frequency, gradability, or semantic category of adjectives correlated significantly with the use of *very* and neither did any of the interactions between predictors.

Table 4. Results of the final minimal adequate mixed-effects binominal logistic regression model (ANOVA display).

	χ2	Df	Significance (Pr(>χ²))
(Intercept)	91.84	1	p<.001***
Age	190.14	5	p<.001***
Emotionality	17.52	2	p<.001***

As evident from the χ^2-value in Table 4 and the odds ratio value in Table 5, age is by far the factor that correlates most strongly with the use of *very*. Before turning to the main effects, it is advantageous to inspect the random effect structure of the mixed-effects model which confirms notable differences between adjective types in their association with *very* (Figure 4).

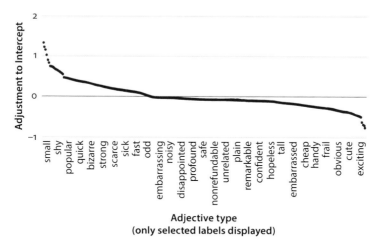

Figure 4. Adjustments to intercepts by adjective type.

Figure 4 only displays every 9th adjective type on the x-axis to render the labels readable. According to Figure 4, *very* co-occurs most frequently with and is thus "attracted" to adjectives such as *small* and *shy*, adjective types such as *profound* and *safe* are neutral and co-occur as frequently with *very* as would be expected by chance while adjective types such as *cute* and *exciting* prefer other amplifier variants.

Figure 5 shows the predicted probability of *very* across age groups and confirms that the use of *very* decreases dramatically across apparent time with speakers below an age of 30 using *very* significantly less often that speakers older than 50 among whom *very* remains the dominant adjective amplifier.

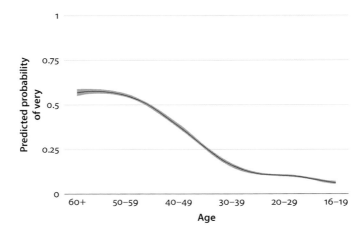

Figure 5. Predicted probability of very across age in the WSC.

Figure 6 shows that emotionally neutral and positive emotional adjectives such as *wooden, rusty* and *flat* or *happy, lucky* and *friendly* are significantly more likely to co-occur with *very* compared with negative emotional adjectives such as *sad* and *desperate*.

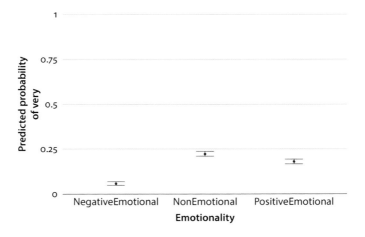

Figure 6. Predicted probability of very by emotionality of the amplified adjective.

The increasing odds ratios in Table 5 furthermore show that *very* correlates positively with age, i.e., the older a speaker, the more likely it is that they use *very* to

Table 5. Results[5] of the final minimal adequate mixed-effects binominal logistic regression model.

	Groups	Variance	Std. Dev.	L.R. χ2	DF	Pr(>|z|)	Significance
Random Effect(s)	Adjective	0.53	0.73	88.5	1	0.0000	p<.001***
Fixed Effect(s)	Estimate	VIF	Odds Ratio	Std. Error	z value	Pr(>|z|)	Significance
(Intercept)	−4.02		0.02	0.38	−10.49	.0000	p<.001***
Age:20–29	0.55	3.09	1.74	0.26	2.10	.0361	p<.05*
Age:30–39	1.02	2.09	2.78	0.31	3.24	.0012	p<.01**
Age:40–49	2.12	2.28	8.36	0.30	7.00	.0000	p<.001***
Age:50–59	2.81	2.17	16.62	0.31	9.10	.0000	p<.001***
Age:60+	2.95	1.54	19.14	0.39	7.56	.0000	p<.001***
Emotionality: NonEmotional	1.48	2.31	4.40	0.32	4.57	.0000	p<.001***
Emotionality: Negative Emotional	1.43	2.29	4.18	0.36	4.02	.0001	p<.001***
Model statistics				L.R. χ2	DF	Pr(>|z|)	Values
Number of Groups							261
Number of Cases in Model							1,709
Observed Successes							313
Residual Deviance							1,331.95
R2 marginal (conditional)							0.199 (0.308)
C							0.834
Somer's D$_{xy}$							0.667
AIC (BIC)							1,349.95 (1,398.95)
Prediction Accuracy							85.02%
Model Likelihood Ratio Test				295.47	8	0.0000	p<.001***

5. Explanations of the parameters reported in Table 5 are provided in Baayen (2008: 204) as well as Field, Miles, and Field (2012: 317–318).

amplify an adjective. Compared with the effect size of age, the effect size of emotionality is rather marginal.

The post-hoc power analysis confirmed that the sample size of the present study is more than sufficient as effects with a medium effect size (Cohen's $d = 0.5$ or an odds ratio of 3.47) were detected with 100 percent accuracy. The threshold of 80 percent accuracy was breached within the lower range of a small effect (odds ratio of 1.97). Small effects at the verge of noise (Cohen's $d = 0.2$ or an odds ratio of 1.68) were detected with an accuracy of 46 percent.

In sum, the regression modelling confirms that age is the most important factor determining the use of *very* while the absence of other significant predictors indicates a uniform process and an absence of a systematic, stepwise loss of *very*. If the waning of *very* had proceeded in a systematic, stepwise manner, then we would have observed more variables to correlate significantly with the use of *very*. As such, it is the absence of significant predictors that is the most important result of the regression modelling. The following section discusses these results in the context of previous research.

5. Discussion

The analysis of the waning and near-loss of *very* as an adjective amplifier in informal spoken conversation in NZE based on the WSC shows a steady decline in use of *very* as the dominant amplifier and its replacement by *really* in terms of frequency in informal private spoken discourse. The trend observed in the WSC thus confirms the pattern reported by D'Arcy (2015) and also aligns with the trend that has been described in various other varieties such as Toronto English (Tagliamonte 2008; Tagliamonte & Denis 2014), South Eastern Ontario (Tagliamonte & Denis 2014), North East British English (Barnfield & Buchstaller 2010; Ito & Tagliamonte 2003), and Irish English (Murphy 2010) where *very* is being replaced my more expressive, innovative variants (typically *really*).

The results strongly suggest that the waning of *very* does not follow a systematic regression whereby a waning variant disappears from the repertoire of one social cohort at a time – which would have represented the reverse of the pathway for incoming forms (Labov 1966, 2001, 2010; Tagliamonte 2012). In fact, *very* itself entered and expanded in use quite systematically by associating with subjective adjectives that denote human emotions and propensities before expanding to all semantic domains, including objective domains such as speed and dimension, during the first half of the twentieth century (D'Arcy 2015: 475). Thus, amplifying *very* initially exhibited a strong preference for attributive contexts before expansion to predicative contexts during the same period that it expanded semantically. In contrast to this, the present study shows that the retreat of *very* in spoken informal conversations is uniform and does not exhibit a comparable degree of stratification. Indeed, the regression results confirm this absence of social layering in the use of *very* – aside from a marked age stratification. This means that this process is not governed and thus independent of the social identity of speakers. The absence of a social meaning of *very* stands in stark contrast to the diffusion through speech communities by innovative variants which requires such variants to associate almost parasitically with social groups (see Labov 2001:308 for a more detailed discussion).The results presented here thus confirm the uniform trend described by D'Arcy (2015) who only found the age of speakers and the gradability of adjectives to be correlated with the use of *very* during its decline in NZE.

The lack of stratification is not restricted to social variables, e.g., the gender, ethnicity, L1, and education level of speakers, but also expresses itself in the absence of language-internal constraints based on the gradability, frequency, and semantic category of adjectives. However, the absence of specialization was to be expected given D'Arcy's (2015) findings according to which *very* had fully generalized across semantic domains and syntactic contexts during the latter half of the twentieth century. A minor difference between the results produced by D'Arcy (2015) and the results of the present study relate to the impact of gradability and emotionality. D'Arcy (2015: 480) found that during its retreat, *very* almost exclusively modified gradable adjectives, whereas the present study fails to substantiate this trend as the gradability of adjectives does not correlate with the use of *very* in any meaningful way in the WSC data. However, in the WSC data, *very* prefers positive emotional or neutral adjectives while disfavoring negative emotional adjectives - a trend which was not present in the ONZE data (Gordon et al. 2007) analyzed by D'Arcy (2015). A likely cause for the differences between the results relate to data processing: all adjective types that were not amplified by at least two distinct amplifier types were disregarded in the present study while this restriction was not applied in D'Arcy's (2015) study. Despite this minor difference, it is, however, remarkable how similar the results of the present study and the results produced by D'Arcy (2015) are – the convergence of both studies lends additional confidence to the findings presented in both studies and highlights the advantages of replication, which remains an underdeveloped practice in linguistics.

Another aspect of the current analysis which deserves additional attention relates to priming. While priming lacked a significant impact on the use of *very* in the present data, the inclusion of priming is still recommendable in variationist and sociolinguistic research as it safeguards from over-estimating the impact of social variables. Fortunately, studies that focus on alternations are increasingly incorporating priming as a predictor (e.g., Gries 2005; Gries & Hilpert 2010; Hilpert 2013; Schweinberger 2018, 2020; Szmrecsanyi 2005, 2006).

Finally, it is important to note that the waning of *very* described in this study is register specific and restricted to informal spoken private conversations. The trend described here cannot be generalized across registers as it is, indeed, highly unlikely that *very* as an adjective amplifier will disappear altogether – rather the analysis shows that it is waning in one specific genre. The waning in this informal spoken register is, however, so substantial that *very* is on the verge of loss in this specific context.

In conclusion, the results presented here add to our understanding of loss in the domain of adjective amplification by showing that waning follows a uniform and almost homogeneous trajectory, which stands in stark contrast to the trajectories of incoming variants. As such, the present study highlights the differences between the trajectories of incoming and waning variants and thereby calls the assumption of symmetries in language change processes, at least in this particular case, into question.

References

Adamson, Sylvia & González-Díaz, Victorina. 2004. Back to the very beginning: The development of intensifiers in Early Modern English. Paper presented at the Thirteenth International Conference on English Historical Linguistics (ICEHL XIII), Vienna.

Aijmer, Karin. 2011. Are you totally spy? A new intensifier in present-day American English. In *Marqueurs discursifs et subjectivité*, Sylvie Hancil (ed.), 155–172. Rouen: Universités de Rouen and Havre.

Aijmer, Karin. 2018a. That's well bad. Some new intensifiers in spoken British English. In *Corpus Approaches to Contemporary British English*, Vaclav Brezina, Robbie Love & Karin Aijmer (eds), 60–95. London: Routledge.

Aijmer, Karin. 2018b. Intensification with 'very', 'really' and 'so' in selected varieties of English. In *Corpora and Lexis*, Sebastian Hoffmann, Andrea Sand, Sabine Arndt-Lappe & Lisa Marie Dillmann (eds.), 106–139. Leiden: Brill.

Althaus, Scott L. & Kim, Young Mie. 2006. Priming effects in complex information environments: Reassessing the impact of news discourse on presidential approval. *Journal of Politics* 68 (4): 960–976. https://doi.org/10.1111/j.1468-2508.2006.00483.x

Baayen, R. Harald. 2008. *Analyzing Linguistic Data. A Practical Introduction to Statistics using R*. Cambridge: CUP.

Barnfield, Katie & Buchstaller, Isabelle. 2010. Intensifiers on Tyneside: Longitudinal developments and new trends. *English World-Wide* 31 (3): 252–287. https://doi.org/10.1075/eww.31.3.02bar

Bauer, Laurie & Bauer, Winifred. 2002. Adjective boosters in the English of young New Zealanders. *Journal of English Linguistics* 30 (3): 244–257. https://doi.org/10.1177/007542420203003002

Biber, Douglas, Johansson, Stig, Leech, Geoffrey, Conrad, Susan & Finegan, Edward. 2007. *Longman Grammar of Spoken and Written English*. London: Longman.

Blythe, Richard A. 2016. Symmetry and universality in language change. In *Creativity and Universality in Language*, Mirko Degli Esposti, Eduardo G. Altmann & François-David Pachet (eds), 43–57. Cham: Springer. https://doi.org/10.1007/978-3-319-24403-7_4

Bolinger, Dwight. 1972. *Degree Words*. The Hague: Mouton. https://doi.org/10.1515/9783110877786

Breban, Tine & Davidse, Kristin. 2016. The history of very: The directionality of functional shift and (inter)subjectification. *English Language and Linguistics* 20 (2): 221–249. https://doi.org/10.1017/S1360674315000428

Calle-Martín, Javier. 2014. On the history of the intensifier *wonder* in English. *Australian Journal of Linguistics* 34 (3): 399–419. https://doi.org/10.1080/07268602.2014.898224

Chen, Henian, Cohen, Patricia, & Chen, Sophie. 2010. How big is a big odds ratio? Interpreting the magnitudes of odds ratios in epidemiological studies. *Communications in Statistics-Simulation and Computation* 39 (4): 860–864. https://doi.org/10.1080/03610911003650383

D'Arcy, Alexandra F. 2015. Stability, stasis and change—The longue durée of intensification. *Diachronica* 32 (4): 449–493. https://doi.org/10.1075/dia.32.4.01dar

Dixon, Robert M.W. 1977. Where have all the adjectives gone? *Studies in Language* 1: 19–80.

Dixon, Robert M. W. 2004. Adjective classes in typological perspective. In *Adjective Classes. A Cross-linguistic Typology*, Robert M. W. Dixon & Alexandra Y. Aikhenvald (eds), 1–49. Oxford: OUP.

Field, Andy, Miles, Jeremy & Field, Zoë. 2012. *Discovering Statistics Using R*. London: Sage.

Fuchs, Robert. 2017. Do women (still) use more intensifiers than men? Recent change in the sociolinguistics of intensifiers in British English. *International Journal of Corpus Linguistics* 22 (3): 345–374. https://doi.org/10.1075/ijcl.22.3.03fuc

Gordon, Elizabeth, Hay, Jennifer & Maclagan, Margaret. 2007. The ONZE Corpus. In *Creating and Digitizing Language Corpora, Vol. 2: Diachronic Databases*, Joan C. Beal, Karen P. Corrigan & Hermann L. Moisl (eds.), 82–104. Houndmills: Palgrave Macmillan. https://doi.org/10.1057/9780230223202_4

Gries, Stefan T. 2005. Syntactic priming: A corpus-based approach. *Journal of Psycholinguistic Research* 34 (4): 365–399. https://doi.org/10.1007/s10936-005-6139-3

Gries, Stefan T. 2009. *Statistics for Linguists with R. A Practical Introduction*. Berlin: Mouton de Gruyter. https://doi.org/10.1515/9783110216042

Gries, Stefan T. & Hilpert, Martin. 2010. Modeling diachronic change in the third person singular: A multifactorial, verb-and author-specific exploratory approach. *English Language and Linguistics* 14 (3): 293–320. https://doi.org/10.1017/S1360674310000092

Hilpert, Martin. 2013. *Constructional Change in English: Developments in Allomorphy, Word Formation, and Syntax*. Cambridge: CUP. https://doi.org/10.1017/CBO9781139004206

Ito, Rika & Tagliamonte, Sali. 2003. *Well* weird, *right* dodgy, *very* strange, *really* cool: Layering and recycling in English intensifiers. *Language in Society* 32: 257–279. https://doi.org/10.1017/S0047404503322055

Kursa, Miron B. & Rudnicki, Witold R. 2010. Feature selection with the Boruta package. *Journal of Statistical Software* 36 (11): 1–13. https://doi.org/10.18637/jss.v036.i11

Labov, William. 1966. *The Social Stratification of English in New York City*. Washington DC: Center for Applied Linguistics.

Labov, William. 1985. Intensity. In *Meaning, Form and Use in Context: Linguistic Applications*, Deborah Schiffrin (ed.), 43–70. Washington DC: Georgetown University Press.

Labov, William. 1994. *Principles of Linguistic Change*, Vol. 1: *Internal Factors*. Oxford: Blackwell.

Labov, William. 2001. *Principles of Linguistic Change*, Vol. 2: *Social Factors*. Malden MA: Blackwell.

Labov, William. 2010. *Principles of Linguistic Change*, Vol. 3: *Cognitive and Cultural Factors*. Malden MA: Wiley-Blackwell.

Lorenz, Gunter R. 2002. Really worthwhile or not really significant: A Corpus-based approach to the delexicalisation and grammaticalisation of adverbial intensifiers in Modern English. In *New Reflections on Grammaticalization* [Typological Studies in Language 49], Ilse Wischer & Gabriele Diewald (eds), 143–161. Amsterdam: John Benjamins. https://doi.org/10.1075/tsl.49.11lor

Macaulay, Ronald. 2002. Extremely interesting, very interesting, or only quite interesting: Adverbs and social class. *Journal of Sociolinguistics* 6 (3): 398–417. https://doi.org/10.1111/1467-9481.00194

Macaulay, Ronald. 2006. Pure grammaticalization: The development of a teenage intensifier. *Language Variation and Change* 18 (3): 267–283. https://doi.org/10.1017/S0954394506060133

Méndez-Naya, Belén. 2003. On intensifiers and grammaticalization: The case of SWIÞE. *English Studies* 84 (4): 372–391. https://doi.org/10.1076/enst.84.4.372.17388

Méndez-Naya, Belén. 2008. On the history of downright. *English Language and Linguistics* 12 (2): 267–287. https://doi.org/10.1017/S1360674308002621

Méndez-Naya, Belén & Pahta, Päivi. 2010. Intensifiers in competition: The picture from early English medical writing. In *Early Modern English Medical Texts: Corpus Description and Studies*, Irma Taavitsainen & Päivi Pahta (eds), 191–214. Amsterdam: John Benjamins. https://doi.org/10.1075/z.160.08men

Mohammad, Saif M. & Turney, Peter D. 2013. Crowd sourcing a word-emotion association lexicon. *Computational Intelligence* 29 (3): 436–465. https://doi.org/10.1111/j.1467-8640.2012.00460.x

Murphy, Bróna. 2010. *Corpus and Sociolinguistics: Investigating Age and Gender in Female Talk* [Studies in Corpus Linguistics 38]. Amsterdam: John Benjamins. https://doi.org/10.1075/scl.38

Mustanoja, Tauno F. 1960. *A Middle English syntax*, Part 1: *Parts of speech*. Helsinki: Société Néophilologique.

Nevalainen, Terttu. 2008. Social variation in intensifier use: Constraint on - *ly* adverbialization in the past? *English Language and Linguistics* 12(2): 289–315.

Nevalainen, Terttu & Rissanen, Matti. 2002. Fairly pretty or pretty fair? On the development and grammaticalization of English downtoners. *Language Sciences* 24: 359–380. https://doi.org/10.1016/S0388-0001(01)00038-9

Núñez-Pertejo, Paloma & Palacios Martínez, Ignacio. 2014. *That's absolutely crap, totally rubbish*. The use of intensifiers *absolutely* and *totally* in the spoken language of British adults and teenagers. *Functions of Language* 21 (2): 210–237. https://doi.org/10.1075/fol.21.2.03pal

Palacios Martínez, Ignacio & Núñez-Pertejo, Paloma. 2012. *He's absolutely massive. It's a super day. Madonna, she is a wicked singer*. Youth language and intensification: A corpus-based study. *Text and Talk* 32(6): 773–796.

Paradis, Carita. 1997. *Degree Modifiers of Adjectives in Spoken British English*. Lund: Lund University Press.

Paradis, Carita. 2008. Configurations, construals and change: Expressions of degree. *English Language and Linguistics* 12 (2): 317–343. https://doi.org/10.1017/S1360674308002645

Partington, Alan. 1993. Corpus evidence of language change: The case of intensifiers. In *Text and Technology: In Honour of John Sinclair*, Mona Baker, Gill Francis & Elena Tognini-Bonelli (eds), 177–192. Amsterdam: John Benjamins. https://doi.org/10.1075/z.64.12par

Peters, Hans. 1992. English boosters: Some synchronic and diachronic aspects. In *Diachrony within Synchrony: Language History and Cognition*, Günter Kellermann & Michael D. Morrissey (eds), 529–545. Frankfurt: Peter Lang.

Peters, Hans. 1993. *Die englischen Gradadverbien der Kategorie booster*. Tübingen: Gunter Narr.

Peters, Hans. 1994. Degree adverbs in Early Modern English. In *Studies in Early Modern English*, Dieter Kastovsky (ed.), 269–288. Berlin: Mouton de Gruyter. https://doi.org/10.1515/9783110879599.269

Plutchik, Robert. 1980. A general psychoevolutionary theory of emotion. *Emotion: Theory, Research, and Experience* 1 (3): 3–33. https://doi.org/10.1016/B978-0-12-558701-3.50007-7

Plutchik, Robert. 1994. *The Psychology and Biology of Emotion*. New York NY: Harper Collins.

Quirk, Randolph, Greenbaum, Sydney, Leech, Geoffrey & Svartvik, Jan. 1985. *A Comprehensive Grammar of the English Language*. London: Longman.

Rickford, John, Wasow, Thomas, Zwicky, Arnold & Buchstaller, Isabelle. 2007. Intensive and quotative *all*: Something old, something new. *American Speech* 82 (1): 3–31. https://doi.org/10.1215/00031283-2007-001

Rissanen, Matti. 2008. From 'quickly' to 'fairly': On the history of *rather*. *English Language and Linguistics* 12 (2): 345–359. https://doi.org/10.1017/S1360674308002657

Schweinberger, Martin. 2018. The discourse particle *eh* in New Zealand English. *Australian Journal of Linguistics* 38 (3): 395–420. https://doi.org/10.1080/07268602.2018.1470458

Schweinberger, Martin. 2020. Speech-unit final *like* in Irish English. *English World-Wide* 41(1): 89–117. https://doi.org/10.1075/eww.00041.sch

Stenström, Anna-Brita. 1999. *He was really gormless - she's bloody crap*: Girls, boys and intensifiers. In *Out of Corpora: Studies in Honour of Stig Johansson*, Hilde Hasselgård & Signe Oksefjell (eds), 69–78. Amsterdam: Rodopi.

Szmrecsanyi, Benedikt. 2005. Language users as creatures of habit: A corpus-based analysis of persistence in spoken English. *Corpus Linguistics and Linguistic Theory* 1 (1): 113–150. https://doi.org/10.1515/cllt.2005.1.1.113

Szmrecsanyi, Benedikt. 2006. *Morphosyntactic Persistence in Spoken English: A Corpus Study at the Intersection of Variationist Sociolinguistics, Psycholinguistics, and Discourse Analysis*. Berlin: Walter de Gruyter. https://doi.org/10.1515/9783110197808

Tagliamonte, Sali A. 2008. So different and pretty cool! Recycling intensifiers in Toronto, Canada. *English Language & Linguistics* 12 (2): 361–394. https://doi.org/10.1017/S1360674308002669

Tagliamonte, Sali. 2012. *Variationist Sociolinguistics: Change, Observation, Interpretation*. Malden MA: Wiley-Blackwell.

Tagliamonte, Sali A. & D'Arcy, Alexandra. 2009. Peaks beyond phonology: Adolescence, incrementation, and language change. *Language* 85(1): 58–108. https://doi.org/10.1353/lan.0.0084

Tagliamonte, Sali A. & Denis, Derek. 2014. Expanding the transmission/diffusion dichotomy: Evidence from Canada. *Language* 90 (1): 90–136. https://doi.org/10.1353/lan.2014.0016

Tagliamonte, Sali & Roberts, Chris. 2005. So weird; so cool; so innovative: The use of intensifiers in the television series Friends. *American Speech* 80 (3): 280–300. https://doi.org/10.1215/00031283-80-3-280

Tao, Hongyin. 2007. A corpus-based investigation of *absolutely* and related phenomena in spoken American English. *Journal of English Linguistics* 35 (1): 5–29. https://doi.org/10.1177/0075424206296615

Tulving, Endel & Schacter, Daniel L. 1990. Priming and human memory systems. *Science* 247 (4940): 301–306. https://doi.org/10.1126/science.2296719

Xiao, Richard & Tao, Hongyn. 2007. A corpus-based sociolinguistic study of amplifiers in British English. *Sociolinguistic Studies* 1 (2): 241–273. https://doi.org/10.1558/sols.v1i2.241

Zuur, Alain F., Ieno, Elena N. & Elphick, Chris S. 2010. A protocol for data exploration to avoid common statistical problems. *Methods in Ecology and Evolution* 1 (1): 3–14. https://doi.org/10.1111/j.2041-210X.2009.00001.x

Corpora

Davies, Mark. 2010. *The Corpus of Historical American English: 400 million words, 1810–2009.* <http://corpus.byu.edu/coha/> (30 November 2019).

Holmes, Janet, Vine, Bernadette & Johnson, Gary. 1998. *The Wellington Corpus of Spoken New Zealand English.* Wellington: School of Linguistics and Applied Language Studies, Victoria University of Wellington.

Software

Hornik, Kurt. 2016. Package "OpenNLP" – Apache OpenNLP Tools Interface. <https://cran.r-project.org/web/packages/openNLP/openNLP.pdf> (4 November 2019).

Green, Peter & MacLeod, Catriona J. 2016. SIMR: An R package for power analysis of generalized linear mixed models by simulation. *Methods in Ecology and Evolution* 7: 493–498

Jockers, Matthew. 2017. syuzhet: Extracts Sentiment and Sentiment-Derived Plot Arcs from Text. Version 1.0.1. <https://github.com/mjockers/syuzhet> (4 November 2019).

R Development Core Team. 2019. R: A Language and Environment for Statistical Computing. *R Foundation for Statistical Computing*, Vienna, Austria. <http://www.R-project.org> (4 November 2019)

CHAPTER 9

Decline and loss in the modal domain in recent English[1]

Svenja Kranich
University of Bonn

Numerous corpus studies have firmly established that in recent English, most core modals (e.g., *must*) have been declining in frequency, while the semi-modals (e.g., *have to*) have been on the rise (cf. e.g., Krug 2000; Mair & Leech 2006; Leech & Smith 2006). The present paper follows the constructional approach to modal meaning taken by Cappelle and Depraetere (2016), who show that modals tend to occur in certain contexts with particular meaning. An investigation of a sample of *may* and *must* in COHA (1960s & 2000s) shows that the decline of the modals (and the foreshadowed loss of some) may be witnessed particularly in the demise of certain constructions. A close-up investigation shows the construction *we + may* + verb of speaking/reasoning is on its way to be lost. Relevant factors (genre, function, culture) are discussed and suggestions about the general implications of the loss of this particular construction will be presented.

Keywords: English modals, recent change, constructions, hedging, democratization

1. Introduction

There has been a considerable amount of research on the core modals (*can, may, must* etc.) and their competitors, the so-called semi-modals or quasi-modals (*have to, have got to, had better* etc.) and the changes they have undergone in Modern English in general (e.g., Krug 2000) and recent decades in particular (e.g., Leech

---

1. I would like to thank the two anonymous reviewers for their helpful suggestions and my team members Gaby Axer, Hanna Bruns, Kiana Kläs, and especially Katharina Scholz for their assistance with proof-reading, formatting, corpus searches, and statistical calculations for the paper. Should errors be found, these naturally remain my own responsibility.

https://doi.org/10.1075/slcs.218.09kra
© 2021 John Benjamins Publishing Company

2003, 2009, 2013; Mair & Leech 2006; Leech et al. 2009). There is clear evidence for the overall trend in frequency changes – the core modals have been declining, and the semi-modals have been rising ever since Late Modern English times. On first sight, this seems to present a neat picture: since semi-modals such as *have to* can be used instead of core modals such as *must*, it looks like the modals are simply replaced by semi-modals. Yet, the modals fulfill a much larger spectrum of modal functions than the semi-modals. While in recent times, one also finds the use of semi-modals for epistemic functions (e.g., *You've got to be kidding!*), they are still mostly restricted to non-epistemic functions (i.e., used for deontic functions e.g., *We'd better go now*, and dynamic functions, e.g., *We're not able to make it*) (cf. Collins 2009a). This restriction is even more clear-cut in earlier decades – which nevertheless already exhibited a rise of the semi-modals and a decline of the core modals (cf. Krug 2000 for Early Modern English).

Furthermore, previous studies (Leech 2013; Kranich & Gast 2015) have shown that the core modals are not replaced by other expressions in the epistemic domain, e.g., lexical expressions (such as *seem, there's a chance* etc.) or modal adjectives or adverbs. Since the modals as a class are, however, declining at a sharp rate (especially some modals such as *shall, must*, and *may*) we have reason to suspect that in some of their previous uses, they are simply not replaced by anything. That is, some modal constructions that used to be established in the language use of the 19th or earlier half of the 20th century are presumably getting, or have gotten, lost completely. The present paper sets out to investigate this hypothesis, focusing on *must* and *may* between the 1960s and recent use (2000–2009), i.e., a period of their clear decline. From the functional analysis of the two modals in the two time frames, one construction in particular stands out as being affected by (almost complete) loss, which we will call the 'we may say'-construction. This construction consists of the first person plural pronoun, the modal verb *may* and a lexical verb that expresses an act of saying, thinking, or reasoning. In the construction grammar framework, this would be recognized as a construction at the meso level (cf. Trousdale 2008: 43): it is a conventionalized form-meaning pair whose function is not fully predictable from its components, hence a construction (cf. Goldberg 1995: 4), and it is situated at the meso level, as it is partly lexically filled but fairly abstract in meaning, with the overall function of a hedge, i.e., a mitigating device. This construction will be investigated in a broader perspective in COHA (*Corpus of Historical American English*), using a variety of verbs likely to occur in it, and reasons for its demise will be presented.

Relevant theoretical background on modality and a summary of previous research on frequency changes and the factors that seem to influence them (e.g., genre) will be presented in Section 2. Section 3 reports first on the decline of the modals in general as evidenced in COHA and then on the development of uses of *may* and *must* in different functions and constructions, using data from the 1960s and the 2000s (3.1). It then homes in on the loss of the 'we may say'-construction in the course of the 20th century up to today (3.2). Section 4 brings together the insights from these studies and from previous research, and presents potential reasons for the decline of certain modals and particular modal constructions, especially the 'we may say'-construction. The paper ends by drawing attention to potential general conclusions on patterns of loss and an outlook on avenues for further research into loss in recent English.

2. Basic concepts and previous research

2.1 The functions of modal expressions

According to Palmer (2001: 1–4), the basic function of modal markers is to signal that the situation expressed in the proposition is not asserted, but only expressed to be potential, desirable, possible, etc. This is compatible with Declerck's (2009) approach, who identifies modality with non-factuality, since epistemic modal markers "refer to a hypothetical actualization (while speaking about it in different degrees of necessity or possibility)" (Declerck 2009: 50) and dynamic modal markers (expressing notions such as ability and willingness) and deontic modal markers (expressing obligation or permission) also mark "the actualization of the situation referred to by the infinitive clause following the auxiliary [as] non-factual" (Declerck 2009: 51).

While there are also other possible categorizations (cf. van der Auwera et al. 2005; Nuyts 2005), the present approach will work with a tripartite division into dynamic, deontic and epistemic modality. Dynamic modality is understood as expressions of physical possibility, ability and willingness, deontic modality as expressions of permission and obligation, and epistemic modality is understood as expressions of the speaker's judgement concerning the likelihood of the truth of the proposition (cf. Palmer 2001: 6–8). Examples of each type will be presented in Section 3 when illustrating the classification I used for the data.

2.2 Frequency changes in the modal domain in recent English

Modality in English has been a popular topic of research in recent times. The present section cannot give a complete overview but focuses on general accounts of frequency changes (2.2.1). The following section (2.2.2) will then focus on the specific question of whether the modals are declining equally in all their functions, whereas the final section deals with the impact of genre on modal use (2.2.3).

2.2.1   *General development and frequency changes*

Krug's (2000) work deals with the starting point of the grammaticalization of the main competitors of the core modals, i.e., the semi-modals (such as *have to, need to*),[2] and provides evidence of the beginning of the decline of the core modals. Based on ARCHER (*A Representative Corpus of Historical English Registers*), he shows that, after grammaticalizing in the Middle English and Early Modern English periods, the semi-modals increase in frequency in the Late Modern English period, with their frequency rise becoming more and more pronounced in the 19th and 20th centuries (Krug 2000: 76–83). Comparing the American and British English data from the 17th to 20th centuries, Krug observes that it might be American English that is in the vanguard of the change (Krug 2000: 78), as corroborated later by Collins's (2009a, b) findings.

Based on the core-BROWN corpus family, i.e., four comparable cross-genre corpora of written standard British and American English from 1961 (LOB; BROWN) and 1991/1992 (FLOB; FROWN), Leech and Smith (2006) observe that in both major national varieties the core modals decrease during this thirty-year time span, whereas the semi-modals (*have to, had better, need to, be supposed to*, etc.) increase. The decrease of some modals is so dramatic that Mair (2006: 100) declares that *must* and *shall* are basically "on their way out". Mair and Leech (2006: 327) see a common denominator determining individual modals' degree of resilience to this trend: those modals which already have low-frequency status in the mid-20th century decline the most sharply, i.e., *shall*, while mid-frequency modals (*may, must*)[3] also undergo a clear, though somewhat less dramatic decline, whereas the high frequency modals (*can, will*) remain stable. Leech's (2009) study, however, shows that this description does not capture the trend completely accurately when

---

2.   To avoid terminological confusion here: The *emergent modals* Krug (2000) discusses, and the terms *semi-modals* and *quasi-modals* can all be found with reference to the same constructions. Collins (2009a: 16–18) distinguishes between *semi-modals* and *quasi-modals* on formal grounds. In the remainder of the present paper, the term *semi-modals* will be used for all grammaticalized periphrastic competitors to the core modals, i.e., *have to, have got to, need to, be able to, be allowed to, be supposed to, had better*, etc. The core modals or simply the modals, by contrast, are the established modal auxiliaries which mostly go back to the earlier preterite-present verb class, i.e., *can, could, may, might, will, would, shall, should, must*.

3.   It seems indeed, as pointed out by an anonymous reviewer, somewhat contradictory that in Mair (2006: 100) *must* is seen as basically on its way out, while in Mair & Leech (2006: 327) it is listed among the mid-frequency modals. However, the corpus data in the present paper shows both statements to be correct – it depends on the temporal perspective. *Must* is mid-frequency in the 19th century, but has been in clear decline since, ending up at the beginning of the 21st century as the second least frequent modal. The only modal whose loss is more advanced is *shall*.

looking at a larger corpus. Studying the development of the modals in COHA, Leech (2009: 553) shows that there are also high frequency modals, namely *could*, that do not merely remain stable, but actually increase slightly between the beginning of the 20th and the beginning of the 21st century, while there are also low frequency modals, such as *might*, that do not undergo a sharp, but only a moderate decline. Daugs (2017) also stresses that grouping the modals into frequent, mid-frequent and infrequent is not as straight-forward as Mair and Leech (2006) presented it to be, when taking a longer time-period into account. Thus, on the basis of the COHA data also used by Daugs (2017), *can* and *may* are almost of the same frequency in the earliest decade in COHA, yet while *can*'s frequency even shows a slight increase over time, *may* decreases sharply. Interestingly, Mair also calls into question the earlier BROWN-corpora-based findings in a later study. Using the B-BROWN corpus, which is parallel in make-up to BROWN and FROWN, but contains data from the 1930s, Mair (2015) shows that the modals in the 1930s were actually less frequent than in the 1960s, and that the drop in frequency visible in the 1990s basically brings them back to the level of the 1930s. However, all in all, the picture remains that the core modals as a class have been significantly declining in the course of the 20th century and continue to do so. Considered individually, however, they decline at very different rates and some do not partake in the general trend at all. Furthermore, individual modals do not decline in the same way in their different functions, nor do they decline uniformly in different text types, as the following two subsections will make evident.

2.2.2 *Frequency changes in the different semantic domains*

Leech (2003) is the first study, to my knowledge, that seeks to answer the question to what extent the modals are declining in their different functions. He carried out an analysis of *may*, *should*, and *must* in British English data, and produces the following insights: concerning *may*, its epistemic uses make up 52% of all occurrences in the written 1960s data (LOB), but 67% in the written 1990s data (FLOB). In spoken data from 1959–1965 (based on the Survey of English usage data), *may* is used epistemically 45% of the time, while in the 1990s (ICE-GB, spoken), this proportion rises noticeably to 82%. Deontic meaning, i.e., permission, is expressed by *may* in only 5% (LOB) and 7% (FLOB) in the written data, thus not showing a great change, but drops from 44% to 8% in the spoken data.

These findings find confirmation in a study of the use of *may* in COHA by Hilpert (2016), using a methodologically very different approach. Hilpert analyzes diachronic changes in collostructional patterns, i.e., changing preferences concerning the lexical verbs *may* tends to combine with. These preferences change over time in such a way that, broadly speaking, the association with concrete activity verbs, such as *see* or *say*, grows weaker, whereas associations with more abstract, stative verbs, such as *depend, exist, indicate* become stronger over time (cf. Hilpert 2016: 81). These changes in co-occurrence patterns allow one to assume that epistemic uses (e.g., *This may indicate...*) are increasing, whereas non-epistemic uses (e.g., *you may see him now*) decrease, since concrete activities under subject control are likely to combine with deontic *may*, while non-control, stative, abstract verbs tend to combine with epistemic *may* (cf. Wärnsby 2009, 2016). In a similar line of argumentation, we may interpret findings by Aarts, Wallis and Bowie (2015) as supporting the stronger decline in the deontic than in the epistemic domain. Presenting findings on frequency changes in spoken British English (1960s vs. 1990s based on London-Lund Corpus and the spoken section of ICE-GB), they focus on frequency developments in different syntactic environments and patterns. Their findings show for instance a stronger decline of the core modals in interrogatives than declaratives (Aarts et al. 2015: 69). As modals are more often deontic or dynamic than epistemic when used in questions (one rather asks *May I come in?* than *May this be true?*), their findings also seem to support the stronger decline of the deontic usage of the core modals. The change observed by Leech in British English with the help of manual semantic classification thus finds corroboration in the purely quantitative/form-oriented approaches by Aarts et al. (2015) (for the same time span and variety) and Hilpert (2016) (for 19th and 20th century American English).

In Leech's (2003) study of *must,* similar tendencies to those of *may* are brought to light in that it shows an increase in epistemic uses (from 25% to 34% in the written data, and from 40% to 49% in the spoken data), and a decrease of the deontic uses (from 69% to 61% in the written, and from 53% to 51% in the spoken data).[4] However, the changes in the distribution are less pronounced. *Should*, by contrast, shows the opposite development, and exhibits a rise in the proportion of its deontic uses and a fall in the proportion of epistemic uses, presumably because in the deontic domain it is replacing *must* in many contexts. Leech's semantic analysis thus shows that the individual modals behave quite differently from one another, a finding that is confirmed by Collins's (2009a) synchronic study.

---

4.   Some further supporting evidence for this development comes from pragmatic studies. Analyzing pragmatic uses of the different modal verbs with a small corpus of spoken interactions among British students, Döhler (1984) states that *must* is hardly ever used in his data in speech acts such as requests, orders, suggestions, where *have to* and *have got to* are vastly preferred, leading him to the tentative conclusion that *must*, just like he supposes for *may*, is specializing to the epistemic domain (Döhler 1984: Section 3.2.4). This conclusion is supported by Kranich, Hampel and Bruns's (2020) findings regarding requests in British, American and Indian English, where *may* and *must* were also rare in all varieties and in all age groups.

Several authors, such as Myhill (1995), Smith (2003) and Mair (2006) have linked such changes in functional distribution to socio-cultural changes and changes in politeness conventions. Modals such as *must* have been argued to have a stronger association with the speaker as deontic source than the semi-modals (cf. Palmer 2001: 10f.; Westney 1995: 54–59).[5] This association may make a modal like *must* less palatable than an expression with e.g., *have to* or *need* in times of democratization, where we increasingly wish to avoid stressing hierarchical power differences and where contexts in which explicitly putting a strong obligation on someone else seems appropriate therefore become fewer and fewer (cf. also Farrelly & Seoane 2012: 393). Mair (2006: 108) also points out that politeness may be the reason why deontic *need to* is on the rise and replacing *must*, as telling someone they 'need to' do something rather stresses the aspect that the action they are obliged to undertake is beneficial for themselves (compare *You must hand in your homework* – implying that this is because I, the speaker, say so – with *You need to hand in your homework* – implying e.g., that this is something you need for reaching your own goals) (cf. Mair 2006: 108).

2.2.3   *Importance of genre*

The crucial importance of genre and of genre-specific stylistic conventions for the development and frequency of the modals has been highlighted by several studies, e.g., Smith (2003), Biber (2004), Collins (2009a), Bowie et al. (2013), Kranich (2016: 153–162), and is also shown very clearly by the dispute between Millar (2009) and Leech (2011) (which is a response to Millar (2009)). Millar (2009) investigated the frequency development of the modals in the TIME corpus (Davies 2007), consisting of articles published in TIME magazine from its first edition from 1923 to 2006. His results show that, while some modals, such as *shall* and *must*, decline, others, like *can* and *may*, are actually on the rise. Millar interprets this partial discrepancy between his findings and previous results based on the BROWN corpora (Leech 2003) as a sign of the greater reliability of the larger data basis he used, stressing that "a diachronic comparison based on two data points [i.e., 1961, LOB, vs. 1991, FLOB, as in Leech (2003), S.K.] may present an inaccurate picture of the overall trend" (Millar 2009: 191). Leech's (2011) long-term perspective based on a broad data basis, i.e., COHA shows, however, that "[t]he modals ARE declining" (as stated in the title of the study) between 1900 and the

---

5.   Note, however, that an association of *must* with subjective deontic modality and of *have to* with objective deontic modality only represents tendencies, not an absolute contrast, as Westney (1995: 55–67) and Collins (2009a: 28–30) have pointed out (cf. also the critical discussion of this view in Depraetere & Verhulst 2008).

beginning of the 21st century. Leech argues that this shows that the TIME Corpus is not the best data source for uncovering general trends in language use, as it may well be influenced by trends in the specific in-house style.

The divergent results of Millar (2009) and Leech (2011) can serve to highlight the great extent to which the use of individual modals is influenced by genre and style. The importance of genre and textual function is furthermore highlighted by studies of modality in ESP (English for specific purposes) research, such as Caliendo's (2004) study on expressions of modality in EU law. In her data basis of EU laws and regulations, *shall* is by no means the most infrequent modal, as in all other studies referred to so far, but is, in fact, the ninth most frequent word in the entire corpus (Caliendo 2004: 244, Table 3) and eleven times more frequent than in the BNC (*British National Corpus*). Furthermore, she shows that the deontic uses of *must*, *shall* and *should* show important differences in her data, with *shall* lending the utterance a performative value that the other modals do not. Her results thus highlight both the importance of considering genre and taking a more fine-grained perspective on textual function, which is what the present study also sets out to do.

3.   Losses in the modal domain in recent English

3.1   Decline and loss in COHA (with a focus on *may* and *must*)

3.1.1   *General background*

The general picture of decline of the modals in American English[6] can be gathered from Figure 1, which presents the frequency development in COHA (cf. also Daugs (2017: Chapter 2), who offers a comparison of COHA and BROWN data).

In order to shed more light on the question in how far the modals are decreasing to different extents in their different functions, a case study of *must* and *may* based on COHA was carried out. *Must* and *may* were chosen because they fulfill the following conditions: they are clearly declining in recent English; however, they have not yet completely fallen out of use, allowing us to witness the steps leading up to loss; and they both have clear-cut deontic and epistemic uses (and more marginal dynamic ones), which makes an investigation into the role of different functions and different modal constructions and their implication in the declining usage fruitful. Furthermore, the changing distribution across functions

---

6.   The core modals are declining in all varieties of English that have been investigated (cf. Collins 2009b), but the decline is most pronounced in American English, hence this variety was chosen for the present investigation.

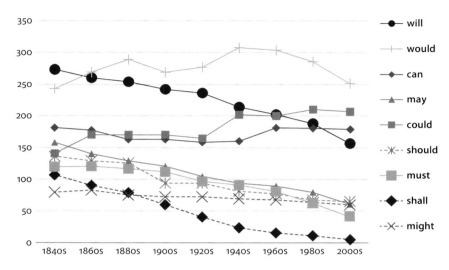

Figure 1. Frequency development of the modals in COHA (normalized per 100,000 words)

in data from the 1960s and the 1990s of *may* and *must* have been investigated by Leech (2003) for British English, who found differences in the extent of the decline in deontic as opposed to epistemic uses, with deontic uses showing a more pronounced decline. This makes it interesting to test to what extent the same trend is also visible, perhaps even more pronounced, in American English. Another study, Hilpert (2016), has also presented interesting insights on diachronic changes in usage of *may*, using COHA, but in contrast to the present approach, Hilpert's analysis is purely quantitative and only presents indirect evidence of the changing distribution of *may*'s function, as it analyzes changes in the preferred lexical verbs combining with the modal verb. Thus, it seems promising to analyze the functions of *may* and *must* in COHA manually, using similar points in time to the ones chosen by Leech (2003) in order to compare the findings (1) to Leech's (2003) findings on British English using a similar approach on both *may* and *must* and (2) to Hilpert's (2016) findings on *may* using a different methodology. Another benefit is that with these modals, the findings gathered present two modals coming from the opposite ends of the permission-obligation / possibility-necessity spectrum.

3.1.2 Data and methods

For this study, the Corpus of Historical American English, COHA, provided the data. It consists of more than 400 million words, covers the time span 1810–2009 and contains fiction (FIC) (short stories, novels, drama) and non-fiction (ACAD: academic and popular scientific texts, MAG: magazine articles, and NEWS: newspaper articles) (cf. Davies 2010). In order to avoid possible pitfalls of just considering two time points, which may distort the overall picture (cf. Mair 2015; Daugs 2017), while at the same time wishing to allow for comparison with seminal studies based on the BROWN-family of corpora, the present paper approaches the decline of modals with varying degrees of diachronic focus: the bigger picture is presented above, while the focus of 3.1.2 is on a comparison of the 1960s with the first decade of the 21st century, allowing for a closer comparison with studies based on the BROWN-family of corpora. For the study of the 'we may say'-construction at the end of Section 3, by contrast, which is unique to the present paper and thus does not allow for a close comparison with previous, BROWN-FROWN-based studies (such as Leech 2003; Mair & Leech 2006; Mair 2006; Leech & Smith 2006), a somewhat larger lens has been used again in order to get an impression of the whole development in 20th and early 21st century American English.

Due to the size of the corpus, a functional analysis is only possible for a sample. For this purpose, random samples of 400 instances of each *may* and *must* were created along the following criteria: 200 instances were collected from the 1960s. Of these 200 instances, 100 were taken from the fiction component (FIC), the other 100 from the non-fiction component (NF). The remaining instances were gathered from the same two *genre groups*[7] from the 2000s. Table 1 below gives an overview of the sample:

Table 1. Overview of the sample analyzed. Data from COHA (Davies 2010), using the random sample function of the interface

Timespan	Must		May		Total
	FIC	NF	FIC	NF	
1960–1969	100	100	100	100	400
2000–2009	100	100	100	100	400
Total	200	200	200	200	800

FIC and NF were selected as the two genre groups in COHA that were most likely to be clearly distinct from one another, as the findings in Kranich and Gast (2015) suggested that the greatest differences exist between the genre group of popular science/science writing (roughly corresponding to NF) and fiction data, whereas news data were rather situated in the middle between these extremes.

---

7. I speak of *genre groups* rather than genres because clearly the categories distinguished in COHA each contain several genres (e.g., FIC consists of novels, short stories, plays, etc.; NF consists of various non-fiction publications, which can be assigned to scientific and popular scientific genres; cf. Davies 2012 for a complete overview).

In the next step, the functions – dynamic, deontic and epistemic – of the modals were analyzed, following the procedure used by Leech (2003) in his analysis of British English data. After the patterns of decline of these three broad functions were established for this data set, the data were scrutinized manually once again in order to see which different modal constructions seemed to be characteristic of the different time frames and which ones might have a particularly important share in the overall decline. On this basis, the 'we may say'-construction was singled out and a further quantitative analysis of its frequency development in the whole course of the 20th and beginning of the 21st century was undertaken.

The coding of functions was carried out using a replacement test. For *must*, the question was: Can the modal be replaced, without significantly changing the original sense, by *have an internal need to* (dynamic), *have to* (deontic), or *very likely (based on existent evidence)* (epistemic, with some evidential connotations[8])? For *may*, the replacement items were *have the ability / the potential to* (dynamic), *be allowed to* (deontic), or *perhaps* (epistemic) (cf. also Collins's (2009a: 34–41, 92–96) discussion of the meaning of *may* and *must*). A three-way distinction epistemic vs. dynamic root vs. deontic root modality (as e.g., in Larreya & Rivière 2014) was deemed more useful than a two-way distinction into root and epistemic (as e.g., in Coates 1983) because of the role democratization has been suggested to play: since the avoidance of overtly hierarchy-emphasizing expressions of deontic modality is one reason proposed for the decline of *must*, it makes sense to try to filter out uses of *must* that would be affected by this tendency, and this concerns only deontic *must*. Thus, a dynamic use of *must* is recognized here, which is, as fits the definition of dynamic modality, concerned with physical possibility as opposed to obligation (deontic) or probability of the truth of the proposition (epistemic). Example (1) shows such an instance of dynamic *must*, which is clearly neither a case of an obligation that is somehow imposed on light, nor is it a question of estimating the probability of the truth (i.e., it cannot be paraphrased as "it is highly probable that the light travels…"). The contrast can be seen clearly in Example (2), which exhibits a deontic use, with *may* expressing permission, and in Example (3), showcasing an example of epistemic *must*, as it expresses the estimation of high probability. Example (4) represents one of the – fortunately – rare ambiguous cases.

---

8.   Evidential connotations of English *must* have been recognized by e.g., Mortelmans (2010) and Kranich (2010), who both show that *must* in what is generally called its epistemic use has evidential undertones, as it implies that the speaker has evidence that allows him to arrive at the logical conclusion that the proposition expressed in the sentence modified by *must* is true. However, this question is not in the focus of the present investigation and will be left aside.

(1)   In order for light to pass from the moon to earth, it *must* now travel a
      somewhat longer distance than would have been necessary if the planets …
                              (ScienceTheNever-Ending, 1960s, NF)

(2)   … I'll be honored to be your host, if I *may*.
                              (A Spaceship named McGuire, 1960s, FIC)

(3)   …Zelack *must* have known that Phil was already dead.
                              (Wishbones, 2000s, FIC)

(4)   With all the books we're taking, we *may* sink the island.
                              (New Song, 1960s, NF)

Example (4) is ambiguous, since here both dynamic and epistemic paraphrases
seem plausible. The speaker either expresses dynamic modality ('[…] we have the
potential to sink the island.') or epistemic modality ('[…] we will perhaps sink the
island.'). In the given context, it is not really important for a hearer to be able to
distinguish between dynamic and epistemic modality, as the whole expression is
hyperbolic and the intended message, from a pragmatic perspective, simply is 'we
are taking too many books'. The use can thus also be classified as *merger* in Coates's
(1983: 15–17) terminology.

3.1.3   *Quantitative findings and their implications*
The present section presents the results on the frequency changes of *may* and *must*
with regard to the distribution of dynamic, deontic and epistemic uses. Figure 2
provides an overview of the general changes in the functional distribution.[9]

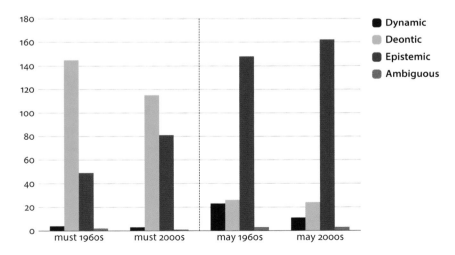

Figure 2. Overview of the general changes in the functional distribution of *may* and *must*

---

9.   The exact numbers can be found in Appendix 1.

Figure 2 shows a general tendency for both *must* and *may* of an increasing proportion of epistemic uses over time. This tendency is highly significant for *must*, but, for *may*, it falls short of statistical significance (see Table 2 at the end of this section). While deontic uses are still predominant in the data for *must*, even in the later time frame, non-epistemic uses of *may* are comparatively infrequent already in the 1960s data.

A closer look at the distribution across the two genre groups adds an interesting perspective (cf. Figures 3 and 4).

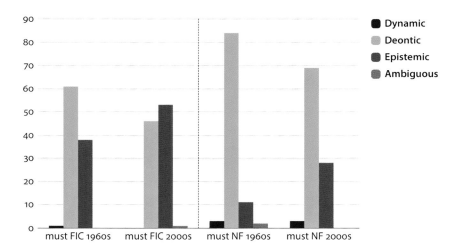

Figure 3. The changes in the functional distribution of *must* according to genre

Figure 3 shows that the changes occurring in the science genre group (NF) are more pronounced than the changes in the fiction genre group (FIC). Considered separately, each is significant at the 0.05 level. The use of *must* with dynamic function is negligible in terms of frequencies in the sample in both genre groups. The function whose proportion declines most sharply is the deontic uses, thus lending some support to the idea of democratization as a driving force of *must*'s demise.

Concerning the impact of genre on the use of *may*, we see much more pronounced differences:

In the FIC genre group, the changes in the proportion of epistemic and non-epistemic *may* actually seem to go in the opposite direction, with *may* becoming less commonly used with epistemic meaning in the 2000s fiction data. The difference in distribution is, however, not statistically significant (p=0.09). In stark contrast to this, there is a clear increase of the proportion of epistemic uses in the NF sample. While the 1960s sample of non-fictional (scientific/popular scientific) data contained 35 non-epistemic uses (including

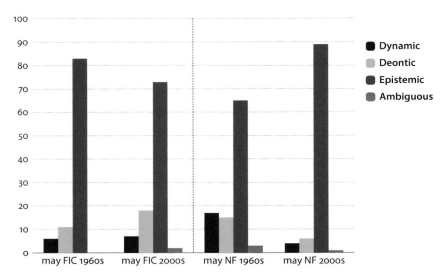

Figure 4. The changes in the functional distribution of *may* according to genre

the ambiguous ones) vs. 65 epistemic uses, the 2000s NF sample has a proportion of 11 non-epistemic to 89 epistemic uses. Both, dynamic and deontic uses of *may*, are responsible for this sharp decrease. This change is highly significant (see Table 2). The development of *may* in the two genres thus seems to be quite different: while it does not present significant changes overall or in fiction, there is a clear, statistically highly significant increase of epistemic uses in the scientific writing genre group. Taking into account effect size, we can see in Table 2 that for both *may* and *must* the effect size concerning the changes between the 1960s and the 2000s is overall relatively small, but it is highest (coming close to medium effect size) in the NF sample for both modals. Genre thus seems to play a decisive role.

Table 2. Statistical significance of the frequency changes between the 1960s and the 2000s sample

		chi-square	significance	Cramer's V
MAY	all	2.810035842	0.093676283	0.083815808
	FIC	2.913752914	0.087827284	0.120701137
	NF	16.26199887	5.51592E-05	0.285149074
MUST	all	11.66951567	0.000635325	0.170803364
	FIC	4.536747656	0.033174566	0.150611216
	NF	9.205287466	0.002413171	0.214537729

3.1.4   *The role of individual modal constructions*

When looking at the data in more detail, it becomes clear that both *must* and *may* are used in many cases in particular modal constructions (in the construction grammar sense, cf. Cappelle & Depraetere (2016) for more details on modal constructions). The benefits of a constructional approach to studying diachronic change have been highlighted e.g., by Hilpert (2013), who explains that "constructional subtypes may differ in their respective values of productivity" (Hilpert 2013: 209). He refers to morphological constructions in this quote, but the same can be assumed to apply to modal constructions. Not only do different modals undergo frequency changes at different rates, as we have seen, but it seems as if some modal constructions resist the decline better than others, while other modal constructions rather seem to be partially responsible for the overall decline and appear to be vanishing from use. This assumption is also in line with findings by Aarts et al. (2015), who have shown that the modals decrease to very different extents in different syntactic environments, and with Johansson's (2013) observations on specific constructions with *must* and *need to*.

The first type of modal construction that, based on the sample analysis, seems to be relatively resistant to decline is the use of the modal *must* with a passive. This pattern has also been identified as typical by Cappelle and Depraetere (2016), and is commonly found in my sample, both in the earlier and the later time frame. An example can be seen in (5):

(5)   Special use permits *must* be obtained through a formal application

(EnvirAffairs, NF, 2000s)

Since it has been argued that deontic *must* is declining because of its association with the speaker as origin of the deontic force, it would make sense that *must* + passive is less affected by the decline. Using *must* with a passive infinitive backgrounds the source of the deontic force, as it rather states an objective rule or regulation that is not associated with a particular person as imposer of the rule. It would thus be conceivable that present-day deontic *must* has found a niche in the combination with passives, as the following passive makes the inference unlikely that it is the speaker imposing the obligation. A search in COHA shows, however, that *must* + passive is not declining less sharply than *must* in general. On the contrary, the decline is even somewhat sharper, as the findings in Table 3 (below) show:

Table 3. Frequency change of *must* + passive vs. *must* overall in COHA (normalized per 100,000 words)

	1960	2000	decline in percent
must + passive	11.2	3.4	−69.6%
must	80.9	40.6	−49.8%

In this case, the prediction based on the sample analysis was thus not borne out by a large-scale quantitative analysis. Quite to the contrary, this modal construction rather turns out to be more vulnerable to loss than *must* overall. A possible explanation might be that even though the speaker is not presented as source of deontic obligation, *must* + passive is still a very authoritative way of phrasing an obligation, one that stresses particularly "social decorum, norms, principles, morals, etc." (Myhill 1995: 173), which is said to be regarded as less and less often appropriate in the wake of Western societies' democratization process (cf. Myhill 1995; Smith 2003; Mair 2006).

The second noteworthy construction in the sample seems to be an instance of a particular vulnerability to loss. As could be gathered from Figure 4, non-epistemic *may* is exhibiting a sharp decline only in the non-fictional data set. Taking a closer look at the data, we can see that non-epistemic *may* is used to a large extent in a very specific construction in these scientific text types. The 'we may say'-construction[10] seems to be relatively popular in the 1960s, with 19 of the 35 non-epistemic instances in NF belonging to this construction type. In the 2000s, by contrast, the construction is only used twice (among the total of eleven non-epistemic uses). The demise of this specific modal construction could thus even be one factor in the overall decline of *may* over time.

In this modal construction, the value of *may* can be said to be mostly deontic, as in Example (6), but is also sometimes rather ambiguous between deontic and dynamic, as in Example (7).

(6)   If we distinguish between sensation, sensory perception, and sensory observation, we *may* regard these as levels of sensory encounter …
(Metaphysics of Natural Complexes, 1960s NF)

(7)   Sounds *may* be divided into musical sounds and noises
(The Science of Language, 1960s NF)

What we see in these examples is definitely a rather untypical use of deontic or dynamic modal *may*. While normally, deontic *may* is used to give permission to

---

10.   A formally similar construction has been discussed by Johansson (2013) and Cappelle and Depraetere (2016), namely the use of *must* with verbs of saying and reasoning. *Must* with verbs of saying and reasoning, however, has a different functional profile than the 'we may say'-construction. It does not occur in classification or labeling contexts as hedge, but generally with the function of expressing concession, and the verbs of saying it combines with typically tend to be speech act verbs that refer to this function, such as *admit*, *confess*, or *warn* (cf. Johansson 2013: 376). It is thus of a different nature in terms of its function. I will not further consider it here, but we discuss it in a paper generally dedicated to *we + MOD + say* (Kranich & Scholz 2020).

someone else, in this construction, authors rather give themselves permission to pursue a certain argumentative step, use a certain label, propose a certain idea, etc. Example (6) could thus be paraphrased as "If we distinguish…, then we are allowed to regard…". For Example (7), one could propose paraphrasing it as "it is generally possible to divide sounds…", i.e., assign a dynamic interpretation to *may*. However, this also does not constitute a very prototypical use of dynamic *may* to describe a neutral ability or possibility since it clearly seems that the overall impact of the utterance is that the author favors this classification rather than stating the mere possibility of its existence. Regardless of whether *may* in isolation would be regarded as deontic or dynamic, the overall function of the construction *we + may + verb of speaking/reasoning* is clear: in all these combinations, the overall contribution to meaning of the combination is to function as hedge, i.e., as a means of softening the force of the assertion (cf. Markkanen & Schröder 1997: 7). The fact that this combination is recurrent and has a function not completely predictable from its components allows us to regard it as a specific modal construction.

Verbs used in this modal construction are rather varied. Besides *say* we find a broad spectrum of verbs in the relatively small sample analyzed, referring to processes of reasoning, arguing, classifying or other discursive moves typical of scientific writing, e.g., *call, conceive, take* (in the meaning 'understand', see Example (8)). Passive forms of the construction also occur, as can be seen in Examples (9) and (10).

(8)　We *may* take these two dresses as representing his official dress for ordinary and special occasions.　　　　　　　　　　　　　(Legal Dress in Europe)

(9)　Another example *may* be given to illustrate D' and P'.
　　　　　　　　　　　　　　　　　　　　　(Principles of the Jewish Faith)

(10)　The basic question *may* be rendered in the form, "Why is all that ever prevails and is alescent what does prevail and is alescent"?
　　　　　　　　　　　　　　　　　　　　　(Metaphysics of Natural Complexes)

The demise of this specific modal construction seemed so extreme (on the basis of this relatively small data set) that it led to the hypothesis that this particular construction is actually not just declining, but is on its way to getting lost. The following section describes the results of the further investigation into the 'we may say'-construction.

3.2　The demise of the 'we may say'-construction

3.2.1　General definition

The construction under investigation has been defined to consist of the first person plural pronoun + *may* + a verb of saying or thinking or arguing, and the construction's function has been determined to be that of a hedge, i.e., a marker that softens the force of the proposition. As a conventionalized form-meaning pair whose meaning is not fully predictable by looking at its individual components, it thus fulfills the criteria for a construction as laid out e.g., by Goldberg (1995, 2006).

3.2.2 *Data and methods*

In order to investigate the long-term trends in the usage of this construction in American English, the 20th and 21st century data in COHA (i.e., 1900–2009) has been taken as basis. Since the idea was to retrieve as many instances of the partially filled construction as possible, the potential fillers for the slot 'verb of saying/reasoning/thinking' had to be determined. This is potentially a very large class of items. In order to come up with a representative and broad set, a large online thesaurus of English (www.thesaurus.com) was consulted for typical words of stating and arguing in academic writing (since this seemed to be the main domain of use of the construction, based on the previous findings presented in Section 3.1). Altogether, 48 verbs were eventually included in the search, a list of which can be gathered from Appendix 2. The search was then conducted for *we may* + any of the 48 verbs (such as e.g., *add, argue, claim, conclude, consider, exclude, explain, note, recognize, wonder*).[11] The occurrences retrieved by this search were then manually checked. The retrieval seems to have worked as intended, as all instances did indeed represent the intended construction. Instances were found with all 48 verbs searched for, in all three semantic categories (saying, reasoning, thinking).

3.2.3 *Quantitative findings and their implications*

The findings confirmed the hypothesis that the use of the construction is going down and the construction is close to becoming obsolescent in present-day English.

The overall results are depicted in Figure 5:

---

11. No intervening words were allowed for, which means uses of the construction with intervening words, e.g., *we may truly consider*, were not retrieved. We considered allowing for intervening words but discarded the idea for two reasons: first, to keep noise in the data low, and second, because with the BYU corpora, it is not possible to use a wildcard that allows for actual optionality. This means that for each verb we would have had to run three individual queries (i.e., *we may say, we may * say, we may * * say*) and then add all values. Surely, it would be possible to do this, but data collection would be cumbersome, and presumably, not a very considerable number of uses of the construction actually occur with intervening words (none were found in the COHA samples of *may* analyzed manually, discussed in 3.1).

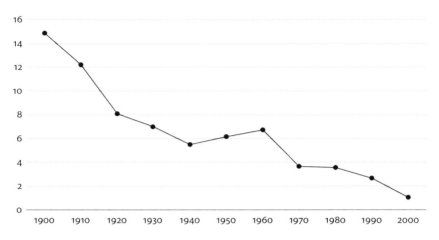

Figure 5. Frequency (pmw) of all verbs investigated based on COHA (1900–2009)

While not extremely frequent to begin with, with 15 occurrences per one million words in 1900,[12] the construction can be seen to decline sharply in frequency, being used fewer than five times per one million words from the 1970s onwards and reaching its all-time low in the first decade of the 21st century. Though by no means representative, it might be interesting to note that native and near-native speakers of English (and scholars of English literature and linguistics) commented on the present findings that the construction has indeed an old-fashioned touch and that they advise students against using it (e.g., Diana Lewis, Irina Dumitrescu, both p.c. 2018).

Furthermore, the findings show that the prototypical verb to be used in the slot of 'say' in the 'we may say'-construction does, indeed, turn out to be *say*, by a

---

12.   The construction gave the impression of being more entrenched in usage, based on the manual analysis of the sample, where it accounted for 19 out of 200 uses of *may*, whereas on the whole, it does not seem very frequent. This difference may, on the one hand, be due to a random accumulation of the not extremely frequent usage pattern in the (relatively small) sample. On the other hand, the sample contained uses of *may* with all types of verbs, while the corpus search for the construction was limited to uses with 48 verbs that were estimated to be typical in the construction, as they represent common verbs of saying and reasoning in the genre, based on the thesaurus list. For future studies, it seems worthwhile to approach the study of the 'we may say'-construction differently, by combining an approach as taken by Hilpert (2016) considering changes in mutual information scores with a fine-grained qualitative analysis of the actual textual functions of different we *may* + verb combinations.

large margin.[13] Figure 6 illustrates this distribution, showing the results for the 13 most common verbs in the construction.

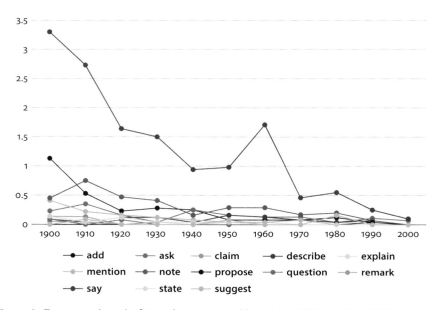

Figure 6. Frequency (pmw) of 13 verbs investigated based on COHA (1900–2009)

Finally, the construction also seems to be or to have been most established with verbs of saying, followed closely by verbs of thinking (cf. Figure 7). By contrast, verbs of reasoning/arguing (though probably also quite frequent in the types of texts in which this particular construction is most established) occur rather infrequently in the 'we may say'-construction.

---

13. Furthermore, *may* is the predominant modal used in the construction, as a corpus-based study that extends the present findings to other modals (charting the development of *we MOD say*) shows (Kranich & Scholz 2020). What we also see in that study is that it cannot be the decline of first person pronoun *we* in professional science writing that is responsible for the decline of the 'we may say'-construction, because other modals in this pattern, e.g., 'we can say' (with the same verbs of saying and reasoning) remain relatively stable. This different development can be linked to the different preferred readings of the modals. Thus, in 'we can say', *can* typically carries its ability meaning and the construction overall does not seem to function as a hedge, but rather emphasizes the authors' achievements (Kranich & Scholz 2020).

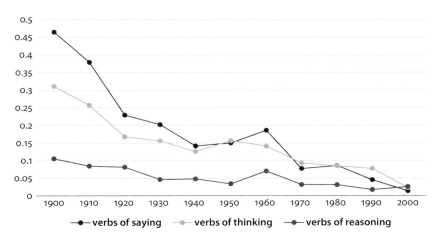

Figure 7. Frequency (pmw) of three groups of verbs investigated based on COHA (1900–2009)

4.   General discussion

The results firstly show that modal verbs decline at different rates in their different basic functions (i.e., dynamic, deontic, epistemic), confirming what Leech's (2003) study has shown for British English to also hold true for American English, a trend already suggested by Hilpert's (2016) collostructional analysis. What is perhaps more interesting and certainly more novel, is the finding that not only individual modals, but even individual modal constructions (such as the 'we may say'-construction) appear to decline at different rates and thus bear impact to different extents on the overall decline. The 'we may say'-construction, as the study presented in Section 3.2 shows, even seems to be on its way to getting completely lost.[14] Furthermore, the findings show that the effect of genre can hardly be overestimated. The findings on *may* and *must* using data from COHA show this, as fiction and non-fiction data behave very differently, especially when it comes to the

---

14.   Certainly, the present findings only show the rapid decline of one specific partially filled construction, which is overall not very frequent in the data, and the findings would have to be extended in order to establish to what extent different constructions at the meso level exhibit more rapid decline or more stability compared to the higher-level construction MOD-V. However, what the present paper clearly shows, is that a fine-grained constructional approach can bring to light interesting, previously undiscovered nuances in the recent history of the modals in English.

use of *may*. The genre sensitivity of the change, the different rates of decline in different functions, the differing rates of decline not only of the large-scale functions, but also of individual modal constructions with very specific discourse functions all allow us to assume that the decline and potential losses in the modal domain in recent English can be linked to the way authors interact with readers. First, the finding that *must* declines most sharply in its deontic function can be related to the suggestion that *must* is associated more with the speaker as the source of the deontic force. Furthermore, the decline of the specific hedging construction 'we may say' in scientific writing can be related to socio-cultural processes, such as democratization, as well. Hedging in academic writing has been explained as being motivated by "deference, humility, and respect for colleagues' views" (Hyland 1998: 351). In the wake of democratization, the need to express or pretend to have such feelings can be assumed to have gone down. The conventions concerning acceptable writer personae for a scientific author in a text may have turned more into a persona characterized by self-confidence, proclaiming one's own argumentative steps without fear, rather than being cautious and employing a lot of hedging, in order to not offend and show humility.[15] This conclusion remains, however, somewhat speculative merely on the basis of this one construction. It would require a more large-scale investigation of hedging strategies in scientific writing in order to be confirmed. It does, however, seem plausible to see the demise of the 'we may say'-construction as connected to changes in conventions concerning author-reader-interaction in these text types and to see its decline and potential loss, just like the other changes in the modal domain discussed in this paper, as related to overall socio-cultural changes.

5.   Concluding remarks and outlook

The changes in the modal domain analyzed, i.e., the changes in functional distribution of *must* and *may* and the decline and near-loss of the 'we may say'-construction, indicate a tendency for modal constructions to be sensitive to changes in sender-receiver interaction, i.e., in the case of scientific writing in the way an author simulates interaction with their audience. Changes in the way authors interact with their audience, in turn, are likely to be caused by more large-scale socio-cultural

---

15.   The fact that more and more scientific writing relies on empirical, verifiable approaches may also play a role, as pointed out by an anonymous reviewer, which could lead to less caution being necessary than in studies containing more speculation. This would have to be verified by a closer, more qualitative approach to modal usage in the corpus data.

changes concerning e.g., social hierarchies. Whereas up to the 1960s, hierarchical relations were more stable and it was acceptable to bring them to the foreground in discourse, hierarchical relations have become flatter or at least, it has become more the norm to gloss over them and act as if we are all on the same level (cf. also Fairclough 1992: 1–29). In general, this can be seen in the decline of deontic *must*. Concerning the 'we may say'-construction, one could assume that authors of scientific prose were more cautious in the 1960s and before to not offend anyone with new insights and new suggestions, as more prominent actors in their scientific field might be among their addressees. In present times, on the other hand, scientists (be they at an earlier or later stage of their career) might feel more encouraged to bring forward their new findings and ideas in a self-confident manner, and a use of previously considered polite hedging patterns, such as the use of the 'we may say'-construction, might be deemed excessively humble.

In order to put these suggestive conclusions on more solid empirical foundation, it seems necessary to go beyond the 'classic' tool kit of investigations into recent change in English, i.e., beyond corpus-based investigations of frequencies. To be able to correlate the declining frequencies of individual modals, individual modal functions and individual modal constructions with more global socio-cultural trends and ensuing changes in politeness conventions and genre norms, it seems necessary to correlate corpus data with e.g., changes in preferred speech act realizations. First steps in this direction have been undertaken by Kranich and Gast (2015), Kranich and Neuhäuser (2017), and Kranich, Hampel and Bruns (2020) as well as Kranich, Bruns and Hampel (2021). Furthermore, apparent time studies of changing attitudes, e.g., towards hierarchies in society, could lead to a substantialization of tentative claims concerning a relation between modal frequencies and socio-cultural changes, such as the notion that a decrease in the use of *must* is influenced by changes in politeness norms. First studies in this direction have brought to light interesting connections, e.g., a trend towards making expert-laymen communication less hierarchical has been uncovered by a combination of corpus-based studies of written discourse and the analysis of the speech act *criticizing* in spoken discourse (Kranich & Neuhäuser 2017).

Connecting the frequency changes in specific genres with changes in the contexts conditioning these genres, especially socio-cultural changes influencing author-reader and speaker-hearer interaction, by using multi-method approaches (combining corpus-based studies, DCTs, questionnaires and spoken discourse analysis) thus seems to be the way forward to fully understand patterns of decline and losses – in the modal domain in recent English, but also in studies into ongoing loss in general.

What we may take away from the present study concerning the more general question of causes and motivations in the loss of linguistic constructions and categories, is the importance that socio-cultural factors can have (as also shown in Kempf, this volume). The way that speakers and hearers interact as well as the way authors simulate interaction (cf. Thompson & Thetela 1995) can be assumed to undergo important changes whenever we witness socio-cultural changes in norms in society concerning politeness, hierarchies, participation and which values are considered important. Paying close attention to genre distribution as well as to contextual analysis, focusing on more fine-grained functions, can be considered key to a better understanding of such processes.

References

Aarts, Bas, Wallis, Sean & Bowie, Jill. 2015. Profiling the English verb phrase over time: Modal patterns. In *Developments in English. Expanding Electronic Evidence*, Irma Taavitsainen, Merja Kytö, Claudia Claridge & Jeremy Smith (eds), 48–76. Cambridge: CUP.

Biber, Douglas. 2004. Modal use across register and time. In *Studies in the History of the English Language II*, Anne Curzan & Kimberly Emmons (eds), 189–216. Berlin: Mouton de Gruyter. https://doi.org/10.1515/9783110897661.189

Bowie, Jill, Wallis, Sean & Aarts, Bas. 2013. Contemporary change in modal usage in spoken British English: Mapping the impact of 'genre'. In *English Modality. Core, Periphery and Evidentiality*, Juana I. Marín-Arrese, Marta Carretero, Jorge Arús Hita & Johan van der Auwera (eds), 57–94. Berlin: Mouton De Gruyter. https://doi.org/10.1515/9783110286328.57

Caliendo, Giuditta. 2004. Modality and communicative interaction in EU law. In *Intercultural Discourse in Domain-specific English*, Christopher Candlin & Maurizio Gotti (eds), 241–259. Frankfurt: Peter Lang.

Cappelle, Bert & Depraetere, Ilse. 2016. Short-circuited interpretations of modal verb constructions: Some evidence from The Simpsons. In *Modal Meaning in Construction Grammar*, Bert Cappelle & Ilse Depraetere (eds). *Special issue of Constructions and Frames* 8 (1): 7–39. https://doi.org/10.1075/cf.8.1.02cap

Coates, Jennifer. 1983. *The Semantics of the Modal Auxiliaries*. London: Croom Helm.

Collins, Peter. 2009a. *Modals and Quasi-modals in English*. Amsterdam: Rodopi. https://doi.org/10.1163/9789042029095

Collins, Peter. 2009b. Modals and quasi-modals in world Englishes. *World Englishes* 28 (3): 281–292. https://doi.org/10.1111/j.1467-971X.2009.01593.x

Daugs, Robert. 2017. On the development of modals and semi-modals in American English in the 19th and 20th centuries. In *Big and Rich Data in English Corpus Linguistics. Methods and Explorations* [Studies in Variation, Contacts and Change in English 19], Turo Hiltunen, Joe McVeigh & Tanja Säily (eds). Helsinki: VARIENG. <http://www.helsinki.fi/varieng/series/volumes/19/daugs/> (19 February 2020).

Davies, Mark. 2007. TIME Magazine Corpus (100 million words, 1920s-2000s). <http://corpus.byu.edu/time> (10 November 2015).

Davies, Mark. 2010. The Corpus of Historical American English (400 million words,1810–2009). <http://corpus.byu.edu/coha/> (10 November 2019).

Davies, Mark. 2012. Expanding horizons in historical linguistics with the 400-million word Corpus of Historical American English. *Corpora* 7 (2): 121–157. https://doi.org/10.3366/cor.2012.0024

Declerck, Renaat. 2009. 'Not-yet-factual at time t': A neglected modal concept. *In Modality in English. Theory and Description*, Raphael Salkie, Pierre Busuttil & Johan van der Auwera (eds), 31–54. Berlin: Mouton de Gruyter. https://doi.org/10.1515/9783110213331.31

Depraetere, Ilse & Verhulst, An. 2008. Source of modality: A reassessment. *English Language and Linguistics* 12 (1): 1–25. https://doi.org/10.1017/S1360674307002481

Döhler, Per N. 1984. Semantik und Pragmatik der Modalität im Englischen. MA thesis, <http://www.triacom.com/archive/semprag.de.html> (10 November 2019).

Fairclough, Norman. 1992. Introduction. In *Critical Language Awareness*, Norman Fairclough (ed.), 1–29. Abingdon: Taylor & Francis.

Farrelly, Michael & Seoane, Elena. 2012. Democratization. In *The Oxford Handbook of the History of English*, Terttu Nevalainen & Elizabeth Closs Traugott (eds), 392–401. Oxford: OUP.

Goldberg, Adele E. 1995. *Constructions. A Construction Grammar Approach to Argument Structure*. Chicago IL: The University of Chicago Press.

Goldberg, Adele E. 2006. *Constructions at Work. The Nature of Generalization in Language*. Oxford: OUP.

Hilpert, Martin. 2013. *Constructional Change in English. Developments in Allomorphy, Word Formation, and Syntax*. Cambridge: CUP. https://doi.org/10.1017/CBO9781139004206

Hilpert, Martin. 2016. Change in modal meanings: Another look at the shifting collocates of may. In *Modal Meaning in Construction Grammar*, Bert Cappelle & Ilse Depraetere (eds), *Special issue of Constructions and Frames* 8 (1): 66–85. https://doi.org/10.1075/cf.8.1.05hil

Hyland, Ken. 1998. Boosting, hedging, and the negotiation of academic knowledge. *Text* 18 (3): 349–382. https://doi.org/10.1515/text.1.1998.18.3.349

Johansson, Stig. 2013. Modals and semi-modals of obligation in American English: Some aspects of developments from 1990 until the present day. In *The Verb Phrase in English. Investigating Recent Language Change with Recent Corpora*, Bas Aarts, Joanna Close, Geoffrey Leech & Sean Wallis (eds), 372–380. Cambridge: CUP.
https://doi.org/10.1017/CBO9781139060998.016

Kranich, Svenja. 2010. Evidentielle Ausdrücke als Übersetzungen epistemischer Ausdrücke: Eine Korpusanalyse populärwissenschaftlicher Übersetzungen aus dem Englischen. *Talk presented at the workshop Modalität und Evidentialität*, University of Hannover, Germany, 31 May-2 June.

Kranich, Svenja. 2016. *Contrastive Pragmatics and Translation. Evaluation, Epistemic Modality and Communicative Styles in English and German* [Pragmatics & Beyond New Series 261]. Amsterdam: John Benjamins. https://doi.org/10.1075/pbns.261

Kranich, Svenja & Gast, Volker. 2015. Explicitness of epistemic modal marking: Recent changes in British and American English. In *Thinking Modally. English and Contrastive Studies on Modality*, Juan Rafael Zamorano-Mansilla, Carmen Maíz, Elena Domínguez & M. Victoria Martín de la Rosa (eds), 3–22. Newcastle upon Tyne: Cambridge Scholars.

Kranich, Svenja & Neuhäuser, Wera. 2017. Some effects of democraticization on the performance of face-threatening acts in expert-layman communication. *Talk presented at the 15th International Pragmatics Conference (IPrA)*, Ulster University, Belfast, Northern Ireland, 16–21 July. <https://www.lets.uni-bonn.de/uploads/research/presentations/kranich-neuhaeuser -2017> (19 February 2020).

Kranich, Svenja & Scholz, Anna-Katharina. 2020. 'What we may conclude without fear of contradiction' - The demise of a hedging construction in 20th century English. Unpublished working paper, LETS, University of Bonn.

Kranich, Svenja, Bruns, Hanna & Hampel, Elisabeth. 2021. Requests across varieties and cultures: Norms are changing (but not everywhere in the same way). *Anglistik* 32 (1)

Special Issue Focus on English Linguistics: Varieties Meet Histories (Daniela Kolbe-Hannah & Ilse Wischer, eds): 91–114.

Kranich, Svenja, Hampel, Elisabeth & Bruns, Hanna. 2020. Changes in the modal domain in different varieties of English as potential effects of democratization. *Language Sciences* 79: 1–15. https://doi.org/10.1016/j.langsci.2020.101271

Krug, Manfred G. 2000. *Emerging Modals. A Corpus-based Study of Grammaticalization*. Berlin: Mouton De Gruyter. https://doi.org/10.1515/9783110820980

Larreya, Paul & Rivière, Claude. 2014. *Grammaire Expliciative de l'Anglais*, 4th edn. London: Pearson.

Leech, Geoffrey. 2003. Modality on the move: The English modal auxiliaries 1961–1992. In *Modality in Contemporary English*, Roberta Facchinetti, Manfred Krug & Frank Palmer (eds), 223–240. Berlin: Mouton de Gruyter. https://doi.org/10.1515/9783110895339.223

Leech, Geoffrey. 2011. The modals ARE declining: Reply to Neil Millar's "Modal verbs in TIME: Frequency changes 1923–2006". *International Journal of Corpus Linguistics* 14:2 (2009), 191–220. *International Journal of Corpus Linguistics* 16 (4): 547–564.

Leech, Geoffrey. 2013. Where have all the modals gone? An essay on the declining frequency of core modal auxiliaries in recent standard English. In *English Modality. Core, Periphery and Evidentiality*, Juana I. Marín-Arrese, Marta Carretero, Jorge Arús Hita & Johan van der Auwera (eds), 95–115. Berlin: Mouton De Gruyter. https://doi.org/10.1515/9783110286328.95

Leech, Geoffrey & Smith, Nicholas. 2006. Recent grammatical change in written English 1961–1992: Some preliminary findings of a comparison of American with British English. In *The Changing Face of Corpus Linguistics*, Antoinette Renouf & Andrew Kehoe (eds), 186–204. Amsterdam: Rodopi.

Leech, Geoffrey, Hundt, Marianne, Mair, Christian & Smith, Nicholas. 2009. *Change in Contemporary English. A Grammatical Study*. Cambridge: CUP. https://doi.org/10.1017/CBO9780511642210

Mair, Christian. 2006. *Twentieth Century English. History, Variation and Standardization*. Cambridge: CUP. https://doi.org/10.1017/CBO9780511486951

Mair, Christian. 2015. Cross-variety diachronic drifts and ephemeral regional contrasts: An analysis of modality in the extended Brown family of corpora and what it can tell us about the New Englishes. In *Grammatical Change in English World-Wide* [Studies in Corpus Linguistics 67], Peter Collins (ed.), 119–146. Amsterdam: John Benjamins.

Mair, Christian & Leech, Geoffrey. 2006. Current change in English syntax. In *The Handbook of English Linguistics*, Bas Aarts & April McMahon (eds), 318–342. Oxford: Blackwell. https://doi.org/10.1002/9780470753002.ch14

Markkanen, Raija & Schröder, Hartmut. 1997. Hedging: A challenge for pragmatics and discourse analysis. In *Hedging and Discourse. Approaches to the Analysis of a Pragmatic Phenomenon in Academic Texts*, Raija Markkanen & Hartmut Schröder (eds), 3–18. Berlin: Walter de Gruyter. https://doi.org/10.1515/9783110807332.3

Martin, James R. 1997. Analysing genre: Functional parameters. In *Genre and Institutions. Social Processes in the Workplace and School*, Frances Christie & James R. Martin (eds), 3–39. London: Continuum.

Millar, Neil. 2009. Modal verbs in TIME: Frequency changes 1923–2006. *International Journal of Corpus Linguistics* 14 (2): 191–220. https://doi.org/10.1075/ijcl.14.2.03mil

Mortelmans, Tanja. 2010. Falsche Freunde: Warum sich die Modalverben must, müssen und moeten nicht entsprechen. In *Modalität / Temporalität in kontrastiver und typologischer Sicht*, Andrzej Kątny & Anna Socka (eds), 133–148. Frankfurt: Peter Lang.

Myhill, John. 1995. Change and continuity in the functions of the American English modals. *Linguistics* 33 (2): 157–211. https://doi.org/10.1515/ling.1995.33.2.157

Nuyts, Jan. 2005. The modal confusion: On terminology and the concepts behind it. In *Modality. Studies in Form and Function*, Alex Klinger & Henrik Høeg Müller (eds), 5–38. London: Equinox.

Palmer, Frank R. 2001. *Mood and Modality*, 2nd edn. Cambridge: CUP. https://doi.org/10.1017/CBO9781139167178

Smith, Nicholas. 2003. Changes in the modals and semi-modals of strong obligation and epistemic necessity in recent British English. In *Modality in Contemporary English,* Roberta Facchinetti, Manfred Krug & Frank Palmer (eds), 241–266. Berlin: Mouton de Gruyter. https://doi.org/10.1515/9783110895339.241

Thompson, Geoff & Thetela, Puleng. 1995. The sound of one hand clapping: The management of interaction in written discourse. *Text* 15: 103–127. https://doi.org/10.1515/text.1.1995.15.1.103

Trousdale, Graeme. 2008. Constructions in grammaticalization and lexicalization: Evidence from the history of a composite predicate construction in English. In *Constructional Approaches to English Grammar*, Graeme Trousdale & Nikolas Gisborne (eds), 33–67. Berlin: Mouton de Gruyter.

van der Auwera, Johan, Schalley, Ewa & Nuyts, Jan. 2005. Epistemic possibility in a Slavonic parallel corpus: A pilot study. *In Modality in Slavonic Languages. New perspectives*, Petr Karlík & Björn Hansen (eds), 201–217. München: Sagner.

Wärnsby, Anna. 2009. On controllability as a contextual variable. In *Studies on English Modality. In Honour of Frank Palmer*, Anastasios Tsangalidis & Roberta Facchinetti (eds), 69–97. Berlin: Peter Lang.

Wärnsby, Anna. 2016. On the adequacy of constructionist approach to modality. In *Modal Meaning in Construction Grammar*, Bert Cappelle & Ilse Depraetere (eds), *Special issue of Constructions and Frames* 8 (1): 40–53. https://doi.org/10.1075/cf.8.1.03war

Westney, Paul. 1995. *Modals and Periphrastics in English*. Tübingen: Niemeyer. https://doi.org/10.1515/9783110958904

Appendix 1

Modal		Function	1960s	2000s
must	FIC	Dynamic	1	0
		Deontic	61	46
		Epistemic	38	53
		Ambiguous	0	1
	NF	Dynamic	3	3
		Deontic	84	69
		Epistemic	11	28
		Ambiguous	2	0
may	FIC	Dynamic	6	7
		Deontic	11	18
		Epistemic	83	73
		Ambiguous	0	2
	NF	Dynamic	17	4
		Deontic	15	6
		Epistemic	65	89
		Ambiguous	3	1

Appendix 2

Verbs of saying	Verbs of thinking	Verbs of reasoning
add	accept	agree
ask	acknowledge	argue
claim	assume	conclude
describe	classify	consider
explain	compare	debate
mention	correct	deny
note	define	disagree
propose	estimate	discuss
question	exclude	postulate
remark	expect	refute
say	find	return
state	identify	
suggest	include	

Appendix 2 (*Continued*)

Verbs of saying	Verbs of thinking	Verbs of reasoning
	infer	
	interpret	
	perceive	
	recall	
	recognize	
	regard	
	suppose	
	think	
	understand	
	view	
	wonder	

CHAPTER 10

German *so*-relatives

Lost in grammatical, typological, and sociolinguistic change

Luise Kempf
Universität Bern

The paper presents a corpus-based analysis of the loss of the relativizer *so* in New High German. The corpus data show that the frequencies dropped in the 18th century, with significant differences among regions and genres. The distributions underpin a relation to chancery language (as assumed in the literature), but the particle was also used in all other domains when sophisticated style was aimed at. Since the demise of chancery language does not fully account for the disappearance of *so* relatives, a broader socio-historical background and general language change of the time needs to be taken into account. Large-scale developments, such as increasing literacy and the Enlightenment, are shown to have induced fundamental language changes. Overall, written German underwent a typological drift to overt, morphosyntax-based complexity. This is evidenced by a number of general grammatical developments. Specifically, the increase of nominal concord conflicted with *so* relativizers, as they were uninflected. Overall, aggregative and indistinct structures were given up in favor of more integrative and precise constructions. The study reveals the fundamental importance of considering the entire language system and general socio-cultural and socio-linguistic changes in the study of grammatical obsolescence.

Keywords: German, grammatical obsolescence, corpus study, relativizer, genre, socio-cultural factors

1. Introduction

The present study investigates a case of grammatical obsolescence: the loss of the German relative particle *so*. The particle was very frequent in Early New High German but started falling out of use in the subsequent period. Eventually, the

https://doi.org/10.1075/slcs.218.10kem
© 2021 John Benjamins Publishing Company

decline resulted in a complete loss of the construction, so that present-day speakers of German do not even have any passive knowledge of it, e.g., as an archaic phrasing. This rapid and complete decline of a once seemingly omnipresent construction renders *so*-relative clauses an interesting case example for the study of obsolescence. The examples below give a first impression, and they also illustrate the two usages of *so*, i.e., in a subject (cf. (1)) or a direct object position (cf. (2)) of the relative clause (i.e., in the two leftmost and most accessible positions of Keenan and Comrie's 1977: 66 accessibility hierarchy).

(1)   Ein Papagoy, <u>so</u> dieses alles gesehen hatte, fieng darauf an: ...
      a parrot *so* this all seen had started thereupon: ...
      'a parrot <u>who</u> had seen all this started thereupon: ...'
      (1744, Fabeln, GerManC: Narrative prose, West Upper German)

(2)   die Gelder/ <u>so</u> ihr fordert/ [...] sollen euch [...] geliefert werden
      the funds <u>so</u> you$_{pl}$ demand [...] shall to.you [...] delivered be
      'the funds <u>that</u> you demand shall be delivered to you'
      (1659, Herkules, GerManC: Narrative prose, North German)

Originating in a comparative conjunction, *so* begins to be used as a relativizer in the Middle High German period – its first attestations date back to the 12th century (Reichmann & Wegera 1993: 447; Ágel 2010: 202). In the 14th and 15th centuries, *so*-relativizers are used predominantly in official language/administrative texts before spreading to other genres such as sermons, letters, and narrative prose in the 16th century and onwards (Reichmann & Wegera 1993: 447). Their heyday is assumed to have been in the 15th to 17th centuries (Ágel 2010: 202), while the 18th century witnessed their demise (Semenjuk 1972: 139, 145; Lefèvre 1996: 71; Brooks 2006: 132–135).

The case of *so*-relatives can be classified with respect to types of obsolescence as follows: In the introduction to their workshop on obsolescence, Kranich and Breban (2018) propose to "distinguish losses with regard to their scope". The loss of *so*-relatives constitutes the loss of an individual construction as opposed to the loss of a "distinction within a category" or of a whole category (see also Kranich & Breban, this volume, p. 3, Table 1). Furthermore, the present case can be classified as grammatical obsolescence (as opposed to lexical losses). For grammatical obsolescence, Rudnicka (2019: 4) specifies that "[t]he function of the obsolescent construction may discontinue or continue to be (fully or partially) expressed by alternative means." In the present case, the function – i.e., introducing relative clauses – survives unharmed, thus it can be viewed as an obsolescence of form. It needs to be added, though, that the form itself persists, just not as a relativizer. The effects of the multifunctionality of *so* on its loss will be discussed in more detail in Section 6.1.

Previous accounts of the *so*-relativizer have suggested various factors for its loss, including both sociolinguistic and grammatical factors, or combinations of both. Many of the considerations are plausible, most are based on some empirical data (e.g., from individual authors or regions, see below); but no broad diachronic survey encompassing all regions and multiple genres has been conducted yet. The present study seeks to fill this gap by analyzing the German Manchester Corpus (henceforth: GerManC; Durrell et al. 2007), a balanced corpus of the relevant period (1650–1800). Based on the results of the corpus analysis, the scenario of obsolescence will be refined.

The paper is structured as follows: Section 2 gives an overview on the state of research, Section 3 describes the corpus, data, and methods. Section 4 presents the corpus results pertaining to regions, genres, and styles. As these results point to the importance of the historical context, Section 5 provides the relevant information on socio-historical, cultural, and associated cognitive changes. Section 6 provides grammatical, systemic, and typological analyses building on the broader changes described in Section 5. Section 7 sums up the findings and evaluates them with respect to recent work on obsolescence.

2. State of research

This section will summarize the state of research, focusing on those studies that deal with *so*-relative clauses as (one of) their main subject(s). Semenjuk (1972) traces the development of grammatical norms in periodicals in East Central German in the first half of the 18th century. As for the *so*-relativizer, she suggests that some of its grammatical features – e.g., being restricted to a subject or direct object position, or having been highly polysemous – may have contributed to the loss (1972: 130). While Semenjuk (1972) does not elaborate in detail on why polysemy may have been a critical property, Sections 5 and 6.1 will argue that polysemy was less of an actual problem in concrete contexts, but rather became problematic in connection with new language ideals that favored the clearest possible expression.

Schieb (1978), by contrast, puts forth stylistic arguments. In her survey of attributive relative clauses of 16th-century agitation texts, she comes to the conclusion that *so*-relativizers were avoided because they were stylistically marked as *Kanzleisprache* ('chancery language', the officialese of the governing authorities at the time) (1978: 508). This is a plausible argument considering that chancery language, formerly the prestige variety of German, lost its model character after its heyday and was subsequently even actively avoided (see Sections 4 and 5 for more detail).

Baldauf (1982) observes high frequencies of *so*-relatives in Martin Luther's (mainly private) letters and accordingly argues that *so*-relative clauses were by no means confined to official, bookish language. In a similar vein, Lefèvre (1996: 71) observes remarkably high rates of *so*-relative clauses in Princess Elisabeth

Charlotte's private letters around 1700 and suggests a connection between the spoken-like character of the letters and the uninflected particle *so*. Jakob (1999), who analyzes linguistic amendments in East Central German lexicon series in the 18th century, notes frequent replacing of *so* by its rival relativizers *d-* and *welch-*. He ascribes these changes to the period grammarian J. C. Gottsched, who recommended avoiding the relative particle *so*.

Morisawa (2004) investigates relativizers in private writings (letters and diaries) of young patrician women and men of 16th-century Nuremberg. Male writers, on average, use *so* even more frequently than administrative writings do (which may have been due to hypercorrection, 2004: 191), while female writers only start using it in the second half of the 16th century, when their education had improved in the wake of the Reformation. Brooks (2006) examines East Upper German prints from various genres from the 16th to 18th centuries. The distribution of *so* across genres brings him to the conclusion that *so* was indeed stylistically marked as chancery language. Accordingly, he assumes that when chancery language lost its prestige, the particle was discarded along with it (2006: 232–234). Additionally, he deems the impact of leading grammarians such as suggested by Jakob (1999) to be plausible (2006: 134).

Hennig (2007) analyzes *so* (with all its numerous functions) in a corpus covering the period 1650–2000. For each half-century, the corpus contains one text that represents *language of immediacy* and one representing *language of distance*. These terms can be described in a nutshell as follows: language of immediacy is also termed *conceptually spoken language*; regardless of whether it is (medially) spoken or written, it is characterized by features that typically occur when the interlocutors are in the same time and place – such as spontaneity and cooperation. Language of distance, also termed *conceptually written*, is characterized, e.g., by monologic structures and an elaborate progression of topics (for more detail see also, e.g., Raible 1994; Ágel & Hennig 2006, 2007, Oesterreicher & Koch 2016). As for relative *so*, Hennig (2007) finds that it is used until 1700 in language of immediacy and up until 1800 in language of distance.

Ágel (2010) compares the fate of relative *so* with that of the surviving relative particle *wo* (literally 'where'). He suggests that a number of factors, including both systemic and socio-historical factors, account for the loss of *so*. Essentially, he argues that while both relative particles share(d) their *aggregative* nature, this feature was problematic only with *so*, as it belonged to the language of distance, while the feature was unproblematic with (more or less) dialectal *wo*. The term *aggregative* contrasts with *integrative*:[1] While integrative techniques interweave

---

1. Ágel (2010) adopts the terms *aggregative/integrative* from Köller (1993), but see also Raible (1992). Opposing aggregation and integration can already be found in Schlözer (1772: 18–19) in an (abstractly) related sense.

("integrate") their propositions into strongly cohesive texts (i.e., they formally indicate the relations among the propositions), *aggregative* structures present the facts in a more loose and associative rather than formally elaborate manner. This can be illustrated with the simple examples in (3) and (4), taken from Raible (1992: 14–16; for more detail on this dichotomy see, e.g., Ágel 2007 and Czicza & Hennig 2013).

(3) aggregative: *Peter geht nicht zur Schule. Er ist krank.*
    'Peter is not going to school. He is ill.'

(4) integrative: *Peter geht nicht zur Schule, weil er krank ist.*
    'Peter is not going to school because he is ill.'

To the modern reader, whose mind is influenced by integrative structures, aggregative phrasings may appear to be redundant, illogical (as in double negation, cf. the related phenomenon in (5)), or ambiguous, or seem to violate grammatical concord or cohesion (e.g., *apo koinu* constructions or the example in (6)).

(5) *darinnen fande ich / [...] / mehr Thorheiten / als mir bißhero noch nie vor Augen kommen*
    'in there I found more follies than I had ever (lit.: never) seen before'
    (17th century, cited in Ágel 2007: 41)[2]

(6) *meine Mutter mit ihren Kindern stehen an der Hausthüre*
    'my mother with her children are standing by the door'
    (19th century, cited in Ágel 2015: 132)[3]

At a closer (and more neutral) look, however, aggregative structures can be understood as semantically or pragmatically conditioned (cf. the plural form *are standing* in (6)), whereas integrative structures are form-governed (see Ágel 2015: 132 et passim). For the history of *so*-relativizers, both ambiguity (apparent or actual) and lack of formal concord are relevant aggregative features, see discussion in Section 6.

Pickl (2019)[4] investigates the relativizers *so*, *d-* and *welch-* as a case example of selection in a standardization process. A data analysis using the DTA corpus

---

2. This example illustrates aggregative structures more intricately than (3) does. The phrasing 'I had never seen before' bears witness of both propositions being viewed separately: 'In there, I found many follies' and 'I had never seen so many follies before'.

3. In present-day German, verbal concord is strongly formally conditioned so that a plural verb form would not be grammatical in this structure, at least not in writing.

4. I thank Simon Pickl for sharing a pre-print version of his paper. The study has been conducted incidentally at the same time as the present one. The corpus studies are nicely complementary (Pickl investigates the large, but unbalanced DTA corpus with a search query, while the present study examines the small but perfectly balanced GerManC using in-depth semi-manual searches).

shows that the decline of *so* occurred by and large in the 18th century. As for factors accounting for the loss of *so*, Pickl considers Ágel's (2010) line of reasoning and also highlights the role the decline of chancery language must have played (as put forth by Schieb 1978 and Brooks 2006), reflected in "a prescriptivist negative attitude towards *so*" (Pickl 2019: chapter 2.4).

As this outline of the state of research shows, many factors for the loss of relative *so* have been suggested, based partly on empirical studies, partly on general considerations. They can be summarized and evaluated as follows: Certain grammatical and semantic features of (relative) *so* – prominently its restriction to subject or direct object positions and its ambiguity – have been deemed relevant for the loss, but this connection has not been spelled out in detail yet. It looks very promising, however, to follow Ágel's (2010) idea to view the grammatical behavior of the relativizer as aggregative and evaluate this with respect to a general drift of German towards integrative structures (this general drift is argued for by Czicza & Hennig 2013). Ágel's (2010) account presupposes that *so*-relativizers belonged to the language of distance, since the similar relativizer *wo* survived in dialects, i.e., (by and large) language of immediacy. Classifying *so*-relatives as belonging to language of distance seems controversial: While Baldauf's (1982), Lefèvre's (1996), and Morisawa's (2004) data show high rates of *so*-relatives in private writings, the distributions among subcorpora in Brooks's (2006), Hennig's (2007), and Pickl's (2019) studies suggest that they belong to the language of distance. This can likely be reconciled by considering that all relevant authors of private letters were highly educated and may have been hypercorrecting. If a connection between *so*-relativizers and the language of distance is corroborated, Schieb's (1978) argument of the relativizer having declined along with chancery language gains in plausibility and deserves closer inspection. Another open question pertains to the role of period grammarians such as Gottsched, especially in connection with the decreasing prestige of chancery language.

In the present study, a fine-grained analysis of a balanced corpus is carried out to deliver more precise empirical information about regions, genres, and styles (specifically about the pace of decline in either of these varieties) and about semantic and (other) grammatical properties of concrete usages. This kind of information can help assess the arguments put forth by previous studies. Specifically, this study aims at connecting the distributional and grammatical properties of *so*-relativizers with general language change and socio-historical developments at the time.

3. Corpus, data, and method

The GerManC spans the period between 1650–1800, which is structured into three sections of fifty years each. The corpus covers the entire German-speaking area, structured into five major regions (Northern German, East and West Central German, East Upper German including Austria, and West Upper German including Switzerland). As a third dimension, the corpus is structured into eight different genres (drama, humanities, legal texts, letters, narrative prose, newspapers, scientific texts, and sermons). Each slot defined by these three dimensions is represented by three texts of a little over 2,000 words each, resulting in a corpus size of nearly 800,000 words in total. The corpus offers part-of-speech tags, lemma tags, and morphological annotation (for more detail see the GerManC documentation as well as Durrell et al. 2007).

For the present study, the corpus was analyzed in its entirety, with the exception of the subcorpus 'letters'.[5] The goal was to determine the number of *so*-relative clauses for each text as well as the number of all relative clauses introduced by the competing relativizers *d-* and *welch-* for comparison. For the latter, the POS-tagging ("PRELS" = relative pronoun) was of sufficient accuracy. As for *so*, the tagging ("PTKREL" = relative particle) was too inaccurate – which bears witness to the polyfunctional nature of the word that rendered it a difficult candidate for automatic parsing. Therefore, all occurrences of *so* were surveyed manually, except for those followed by a finite verb (*so*-relative clauses in written German of that period are either verb-final or drop the finite verb altogether).[6] In addition to the verb position, the following criteria were applied to determine *so*-relative clauses: The clause needs to refer to a head in the matrix clause. Typically, this head is a noun phrase,[7] and in the majority of cases, the *so*-clause follows immediately after this head. As shown in (1) and (2), *so* occurs either in the subject or direct object position of the relative clause (with a few exceptions, see Section 6.1).

Taking both syntactic and semantic context into consideration, almost all occurrences could clearly be identified as relative clauses vs. other usages, with virtually no cases remaining ambiguous. This annotation experience is noteworthy

---

5. The subcorpus 'letters' is not available in the download version; it is also incomplete in that a few slots are not represented by three individual texts. Moreover, it lacks part-of-speech tags as well as morphological annotation. This would have made it difficult to identify all instances of *so* relatives.

6. Verb-second order is attested for older stages of German, but not with relative clauses introduced by relative particles (Axel-Tober 2012: 235).

7. It can also, quite rarely, be a state of affairs, e.g., *Einige glauben daß er sich selbst getödtet habe / so aber ungewiß ist.* (1701, hanau1, News, West Central German) 'Some believe he may have killed himself, which is, however, uncertain.'; see (12) for another example. There was one instance of a formally headless *so*-relative clause in the corpus: *Aldieweil aber [...] die Krancken und so bey ihnen im Hause wohnen / verschlossen sind [...]* (1680, ConsiliumMedicum, Science, North German) 'While the sick and [those] who live with them in their houses are locked away...'. As can be seen from the translation, this relative clause logically refers to a (non-overt) element in the matrix clause.

with respect to the role of polysemy in the loss of *so* as a relativizer (see discussion below). The ratios of both types of relative clauses will be presented with respect to periods, regions, genres, and individual texts. In addition to the quantitative investigation, selected qualitative analyses were carried out, e.g., stylistic analyses of narrative prose texts or syntactic analyses of a number of sample cases. The results of the qualitative analyses will be presented in Sections 4.3 and 6.1–6.3.

4. First results: Regions, genres, and styles

Before delving into the specifics of the subcorpora, I will briefly discuss the overall picture arising from the collective data. In order to determine the pace of the decline, I grouped the data into smaller periods (thirty-year periods instead of the original fifty-year periods).[8] Figure 1 shows that in the collective data, *so*-relative clauses start out at about 16% of the relative clauses, increase to about 20% at first, but subsequently drop continuously throughout the 18th century, holding merely 2% in the end.

Figure 1. Share of *so*-relativizers (vs. relative pronouns) in the GerManC (1650–1800), N=7,136 relative clauses[9]

---

8.   To gain a realistic picture, it is reasonable to compare various temporal groupings, as will be done in the text below; for reasons of space, only the thirty-year-periods will be shown. Using twenty-year periods instead yields the same basic results (for the collective data as well as for the subcorpora), but the graphs are jagged due to the smaller amount of data underlying each point. Note that re-arranging the periods messes with the balanced design of the corpus (the smaller the periods, the bigger the impact, obviously).

9.   The absolute numbers underlying this chart as well as all the following charts are given in Table 1 in the Appendix.

The overall shape of the curve conforms to both Brooks's (2006: 135) and Pickl's (2019) surveys of different corpora.[10] Both studies set in earlier, and their results suggest, overall, that there were only minor fluctuations in the frequency of relative *so* between 1600 and 1650. As for the bump around 1700, both studies show it as well, even though it is quite minor in Pickl's study. In the GerManC data, the bump appears in all seven genres and in four of the five regions when the data are grouped in twenty-year periods (thus, it is not a specific of Upper German, as Brooks 2006: 134 assumes). These findings suggest that there was indeed an ephemeral upward trend before the decline set in.[11] As is known, the loss should remain permanent in the centuries to come. The changes in the 18th century fully conform to Rudnicka's (2019: 6, 24, 60) core necessary condition of obsolescence (which captures what one would expect intuitively): a "visible negative correlation between the time and the frequency of use." (cf. also Rudnicka, this volume).

The knowledge of the precise curve of decline enables us to evaluate Jakob's (1999: 36) assessment that the contemporary grammarian J. C. Gottsched had a major influence on the abandonment of *so*-relativizers: As Gottsched's relevant grammars were published in 1748 and 1762, they cannot have been the or a cause of the demise. Rather, his criticism may be viewed as an epiphenomenon of the language development and linguistic attitude at the time (see below).

4.1 Regions

Figure 2 shows the frequency developments for the five regions.[12] The differences among the regions are highly significant.[13] From early on and almost until the end, East Upper German is leading in the use of *so*-relative clauses. West Central German follows closely, while West Upper German and East Central German make less use of *so*-relatives throughout the period under investigation. Northern German shows the lowest rates on average, with the exception of the period

---

10. The overall percentage is somewhat lower than in Brooks's (2006: 135) or Pickl's (2019) data. This is most likely due to the facts that a) Brooks's (2006) corpus focuses on East Upper German, which uses *so* relative clauses more frequently than average (see below) and b) Pickl's (2019) corpus contains a larger share of scientific and functional texts, while the present corpus contains a higher share of dramas and sermons (which use *so* relative clauses less frequently than average).

11. While it is difficult to determine the factors accounting for this ephemeral trend, the fact itself seems worth mentioning, especially for purposes of comparison with other phenomena of obsolescence.

12. Again, calculated for thirty-year periods. For each region, all genres are merged into one curve. Separating both regions and genres would leave too small an amount of data for each period.

13. A chi-square test conducted for the five regions yields a p-value < 0.00001.

1680–1709, where it skyrockets to 24%, leaving all other regions behind. This turns out to be a short-lived trend, though, as the region displays the steepest decline just afterwards. Note that the trend does not appear to be an artifact of the composition of periods. Each period is represented by about 11–14 individual texts, and no clustering of genres that might have skewed the curve could be found.

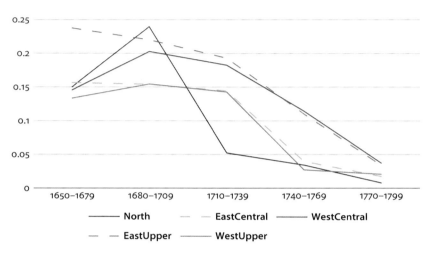

Figure 2. Share of *so*-relativizers (vs. relative pronouns) per region (GerManC, 1650–1800), N=7,136 relative clauses

These findings pertaining to the regions can be taken to hint at the importance of style, prestige, and the evolution of a written standard: The language of Central and Upper German chanceries used to be the prestige variety in the 16th and 17th centuries (e.g., Brooks 2001: 292; Schwitalla 2002: 387). It was a symbol of power and sophisticated style (Schwitalla 2002: 379, 387) and had a vast influence beyond official language. It spread to various genres, becoming the supra-regional linguistic ideal. In the 18th century, chancery language lost its prestige due to various socio-historical and sociolinguistic developments (see, e.g., Brooks 2001; Schwitalla 2002: 387; Schuster &Wille 2015 as well as Section 5 below). East Upper German was the region to adhere the longest to the old linguistic ideal (see Reiffenstein 1992: 486–488; Wiesinger 1995: 329; Schwitalla 2002: 393). Thus, the region's high rate of *so*-relatives and its reluctance to give them up are in concord with the view of *so*-relatives being strongly connected with chancery language.

In the Northern German territories, the Low German written variety had been given up in connection with the decline of the Hanse and was replaced by the emerging High German written standard. Even though High German remained the language of writing, the linguistic dominance of the Southern chancery language became fragile when the South lost its political, economic, and cultural predominance (Brooks 2001: 295). Schildt (1984: 158–159) points out how losing the Seven-Year War (1756–1763) had weakened the political power and cultural influence of Austria and Saxony and strengthened that of (the Northern regions) Prussia and Brandenburg. Another, more linguistic factor came into play as well: As the evolution of a standard had taken place in writing, there was still a wide variety of regional ways of pronunciation in the 18th century. The search for the "best" pronunciation strengthened the linguistic status of the North: Since North-erners had to acquire the (High German) written standard almost like a foreign language, their pronunciation was closest to the written norm. Supported by influential advocates of the maxim "speak as you write" (such as Johann Leonhard Frisch or Barthold Heinrich Brockes), Northern German gained prestige in the early 18th century (cf. Schildt 1984: 174). In connection with these socio-historical developments, the rapid drop of *so*-relatives in the Northern German subcorpus can be read as an epiphenomenon of the North shaking off the political, cultural and linguistic dominance of the Southern chancery language.

4.2   Genres

Figure 3 shows the data grouped according to genre.[14] The caption lists the genres in descending order by their average percentage of so-relativizers. The differences among the genres are dramatic:[15] Legal texts are clearly in the lead, only matched by newspapers until about 1700. Both genres peak at about 31%, but newspapers quit using *so*-relativizers quite rapidly after 1709, while legal texts do so more reluctantly. Scientific texts fall in the midrange, with an average usage of 12%. Humanities, narrative prose and dramas follow in this order, and they display remarkably similar developments from 1710 onwards. Sermons, finally, rank last, never reaching a ratio higher than ca. 6%.

Some of the results about genres are also corroborated by Pickl's (2019) study. The genres of the DTA corpus, however, are broader and less balanced. Legal texts are not represented as a category, but as for newspapers and academic writing, Pickl observes high percentages of *so* – which is in accordance with the findings of the present study. Furthermore, he notes that fiction shows the lowest rate of *so*. Fiction in the DTA by and large corresponds with 'narrative prose' in the present corpus, but additionally includes some dramas. Thus, the findings from both corpora are quite in line with one another (sermons do not form a category of the DTA).

---

14.   For this chart, the regions are merged. Each point has 5–14, on average 9 individual texts from various regions underlying it. No suspicious clustering of regions could be found. However, with this small amount of individual texts, idiosyncratic characteristics of a single text (see below) may have visible influences on the curve.

15.   A chi-square test conducted for the seven genres yields a p-value < 0.00001.

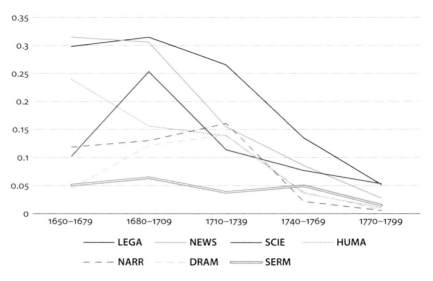

Figure 3. Share of *so*-relativizers (vs. relative pronouns) per genre (GerManC, 1650–1800), N=7,136 relative clauses

As a first and most striking conclusion, we can take the data presented in Figure 3 to lend further evidence to the link between chancery language (represented here by legal texts) and *so*-relativizers. In Brooks's (2006: 132–133) corpus of East Upper German prints, similar tendencies emerge: Legal texts show a preference for *so*, while historical and medical treatises do not seem to display any clear tendencies, and religious texts tend to avoid this relativizer. Brooks (2006: 133) ascribes this avoidance to *so* being 'stylistically marked' as chancery language. The data of the present study add to this picture: just like sermons, dramas are written for oral delivery; yet, they attain a much higher mean rate of *so* than sermons do. Thus, the problem does not seem to lie in the oral medium but indeed in the 'stylistic' quality of the construction, or, to be more precise, in its affiliation to a communicative domain very different from the ecclesiastical sphere. Further evidence of the link between chancery language and the use of *so* can be derived from the initially high rate of *so* in newspapers; it is a well-known fact that early newspapers imitated chancery style (Korhonen 1988: 242; Polenz 22013: 398–401; Schuster & Wille 2015).

   It should be emphasized, though, that *so*-relativizers were not exclusive to chancery language. This can be seen in the fact that all seven genres surveyed here do make use of the construction. Additionally, there is evidence from investigations of private letters that needs to be considered in this context. Baldauf (1982: 185), Lefèvre (1996: 71), and Morisawa (2004) determine very high rates of *so*-relative clauses in the private letters of Luther, Princess Elisabeth Charlotte, and 16th-century Nuremberg patricians, respectively. Both Baldauf and Lefèvre draw the remarkable conclusion that *so*-relative clauses were closely connected to spoken language. In Morisawa's (2004) study, however, it becomes clear that the abundance of *so* is closely connected to higher education and may even be a sign of hypercorrection. This connection to educated style is corroborated by the following qualitative analyses of individual texts in the corpus.

4.3   Styles

The genres vary strongly not only in their average rate of *so*, but also in how continuously or discontinuously the demise of *so* takes place, in other words: how homogeneous or heterogeneous they are. The two highest ranking genres, legal texts and newspapers, display more even developments than the other genres. Specifically, in narrative prose, drama, and sermons, the rates of *so* among individual texts are quite diverse and not necessarily in line with the general trend of the time. These differences are exemplified by Figure 4 and Figure 5, contrasting the genres 'legal texts' and 'narrative prose'.

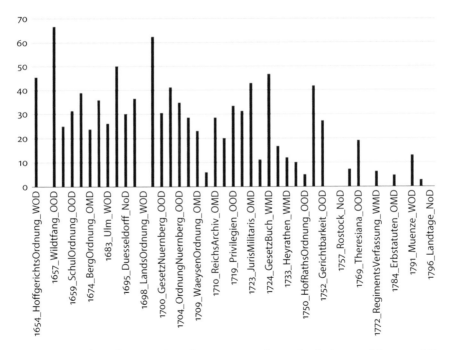

Figure 4.   Share of *so*-relativizers (vs. relative pronouns) in individual texts of the genre LEGAL TEXTS (GerManC, 1650–1800), N=866 relative clauses[16]

---

16.   Note that the x-axis is not an exact linear time scale, but simply shows the texts in chronological order. For reasons of space, not all individual texts are labeled. The titles of each text

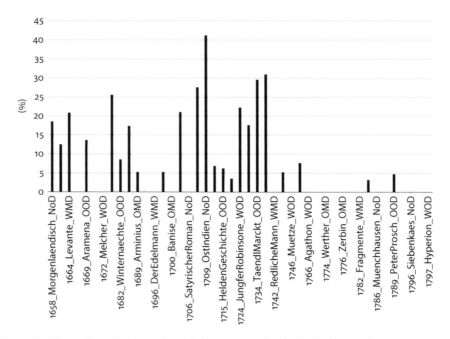

Figure 5.   Share of *so*-relativizers (vs. relative pronouns) in individual texts of the genre NARRATIVE PROSE (GerManC, 1650–1800), N=1,141 relative clauses

While in the legal texts the decline proceeds more or less continuously, there are more outliers among the narrative prose texts: Quite a number of text exemplars do not use any *so* relatives even in the 17th century. On the other hand, some texts from the 18th century show frequencies far above the average of their time. These outliers cannot be explained by regional characteristics, as the texts originate in various regions and do, for the most part, not reflect their regions' tendencies. Instead, a closer analysis of the texts in terms of their style and *conception* (i.e., language of distance vs. language of immediacy) proves quite fruitful. The stylistic analysis shows clearly that *so*-relatives are frequent in texts that instantiate educated style and language of distance; conversely, *so* is rare in those texts or text passages that aim at a spoken-like style and language of immediacy. This connection will be exemplified on the basis of two texts that deviate from the average of their time. Example (7) shows a passage from 'Schelmuffsky' – a text that uses *so*

---

are not essential in the current context. If need be, they could be identified with the help of Table 1 in the appendix or the GerManC documentation.

in only about 5% of the relative clauses, even though it has been written in the 17th century.[17]

(7)   [during a carriage ride…] *so schmiß der Postilion/ ehe wir es uns versahen/ den Post-Wagen um/ daß er wohl den einen Berg hinunter über 1000. mahl sich mit uns überkepelte und nahm der Tebel hohl mer keiner nicht den geringsten Schaden. Ausgenommen zwey Räder/ die gingen an der Post-Calesse vor die Hunde.*

'thus the stage-coachman / before we realized it / over-turned the stage coach / that it flipped over with us inside surely over a thousand times all the way down the hill, and – may the devil come and get me! – nobody didn't suffer the slightest damage. Except for two wheels / they broke off the carriage and went to the dogs.'
(1696, Schelmuffsky, GerManC: Narrative Prose, West Central German)

This text displays numerous features that are typical of language of immediacy: The use of first person pronouns and exclamations (*der Tebel hohl mer* 'the devil come and get me') signal involved style and render the narrative lively – as does the colloquial lexis (e.g., *schmiß* 'knocked over'); significant grammatical features are, for example, double negation (*keiner nicht* 'nobody didn't') and aggregative conjunctions (*daß* 'that' instead of the more specific final conjunction *so daß* 'so that'). The example in (8) – a passage from 'Tändl=Marckt' – could not be any more different. This text was published 35 years later than the previous one, yet it applies *so* in almost a third of its relative clauses.[18]

(8)   *erstbenannte Bibliotheck bestehet in viel tausend Büchern, sonderbahr aber in denen urältisten Manuscriptis, <u>so</u> in allerhand Sprachen zu finden, höchstgedachte Römisch. Kayserl. Mayestät haben solche zu allgemeinen Nutzen der Studirenten wie auch andere Gelehrten an und auf geführet …*

'The first-named library consists of many thousand books, specifically however of the most ancient manuscripts <u>that</u> can be found in all languages; the most highly esteemed [or: afore-mentioned] Roman imperial Majesty have collected and displayed these for the general benefit of the students as well as of other scholars.'
(1734, Tändl=Marckt, GerManC: Narrative Prose, East Upper German)

---

17.   The translation tries to convey the stylistic flavor of the original text as far as possible. Please note that there is no *so*-relative clause in the example. It merely serves to illustrate the stylistic qualities of the text.

18.   Again, the translation tries to come as close to the original as possible, at the expense of overstretching the grammar of contemporary English in some places.

The text is characterized as sophisticated style not only by its respectful conduct, but also by its precise conjunctions and conjunctional adverbs (*sonderbahr aber* 'specifically however', *wie auch* 'as well as'), by its textual deixis (*erstbenannte* 'first-named', *höchstgedachte* 'most highly esteemed aforementioned'), and by its use of coordination ellipsis (*an geführet und aufgeführet* 'collected and displayed').

The analyses so far have shown that *so*-relatives were, in terms of communicative domains, closely linked to chancery language, but not exclusive to it. Instead, they were used in all genres investigated here as well as in previous studies. Regardless of what genre they were used in, they are used in an attempt to achieve sophisticated style.

5.   Socio-historical, cultural, and cognitive context

From what we have seen so far, it is clear that the loss of *so*-relatives is closely linked to the demise of chancery language as a linguistic ideal. However, assuming the relativizer simply fell out of fashion along with chancery language does not capture all the relevant connections. Schieb (1978: 508), who is a proponent of this argument, considers an attempt to get rid of stilted bookish German to be a decisive factor. While such an attempt was definitely a trend of the 18th century, this account leaves some explanatory gaps: it does not explain why some constructions of chancery language survived and became part of the written standard while others were deselected. In specific: Why did this tendency affect the relativizer *so*, even though it was not stilted at all in its grammatical properties? In fact, relative particles are typically a feature of dialects and spoken varieties (Fleischer 2004; 2005, Nübling & Kempf 2020, § 4.3), while inflected relative pronouns are a quirk of written European standard languages (Comrie 1998; Haspelmath 2001: 1494–1495). The situation becomes even more puzzling considering that some of the surviving chancery constructions display fairly complex, written-like grammatical properties. These constructions include, e.g., the (famous German) bracketing constructions (Admoni 1990: 178; Betten 2000: 1657),[19] the related phenomenon of preposed complex attributes with centripetal structure (consider for illustration: *die in Frankreich gefertigten Kleidungsstücke* lit. "the in France

---

19.   For example: *Anna hat das Klavier von einem freundlichen alten Mann gekauft.* lit.: "Anna has the piano from a friendly old man bought." The two components of the periphrastic verb form, *has* and *bought*, form the sentence bracket.

produced garments"; Lötscher 1990), or the order infinite–finite verb in the right-hand bracket of dependent clauses (Ebert 1981; Brooks 2001: 299).[20]

Given the nature of these examples, it seems plausible to assume that abstract syntactic constructions stood a better chance of surviving, while concrete lexical constructions were more saliently marked as chancery style – and therefore avoided, for instance: bookish loan words in *-ieren* (e.g., *debarquieren* 'to debark') or honorific superlatives such as *allergnädigst-* 'most merciful' and honorific textual deixis like *höchstgedacht-* 'most highly esteemed aforementioned' (Schuster 2017: 39; Kempf 2020). As for the relative particle *so*, one can certainly assume that it was marked as sophisticated; however, due to its brevity and simplicity, it was most likely not perceived as stilted and cumbersome as much as the examples above.

To gain a more profound understanding of the obsolescence of *so*-relatives, it is necessary to consider the socio-historical context that surrounded the fading of chancery language and brought about new language ideals. Obviously, even a condensed account of the political and cultural situation in the German-speaking territories of the time would go beyond the scope of this paper. Instead, some developments pivotal for the topic will be highlighted.

The socio-historical situation in the 18th century is shaped by the Enlightenment and its increasing conflict with the old absolutist system. In this system, progress was impeded and poverty was high, especially after the Thirty Years' War (1618–1648). The absolutist monarchs of the numerous territories made their subjects obedient not only by institutional and military power, but also by means of socially repressive systems of privileges and protection for those serving the court (parts of aristocracy and civic society, who served, e.g., as clerics, artists, secretaries, diplomats; Polenz 2013: 4). Considering this political situation, the use of deferential linguistic means as sketched above (e.g., (8)) can be understood not only as a matter of attitude, but as vital for maintaining one's societal and economic status. Similarly, the widespread imitation of chancery language can be seen as an attempt to boost one's status and power (cf. Schwitalla 2002: 379). Also, the linguistic properties of chancery language become understandable in this context: (overly) deferential forms are used to please the sovereign on whose goodwill the writers were existentially dependent; complicated and unnatural means of expression may have been chosen to boost the value of texts and to exclude lower classes from knowledge and power (see, e.g., Lötscher 1990: 22–23; Eichinger 1995: 315–317; Schwitalla 2002: 394; Schuster & Wille 2015: 10; Lötscher 2016: 369).

---

20. For example: *dass Anna das Klavier von einem Freund gekauft hat.* lit.: "that Anna the piano from a friend bought has."

However, with the advance of the Enlightenment in the early 18th century, it became difficult for the old elites to maintain their traditional systems of power. To prevent revolutions, they induced reforms 'from above' and transformed their reign into 'enlightened absolutism' (Polenz 2013: 13–14). Societal structures had become more permeable, and the middle-classes had gained more power. It is understandable that in this altered societal situation, language users (to be more precise: those who participated in writing) felt less need to use the old, stilted, and unnatural practices of chancery language. The new linguistic ideals – advocated by writers and grammarians – were naturalness, frankness, brevity, intelligibility, and clarity (Blackall 1966: 121–124; Reichmann 1995; Linke 2006: 53–54; Betten 2012: 20; Schuster & Wille 2015: 12–16).

A related and equally important factor is the advance of written language use in growing parts of society. This factor reciprocally relates to the Enlightenment, for instance: increased reception of written information – prominently of newspapers (since around 1600) and periodicals (since around 1700) – paved the way for democratization, as it gave people more knowledge and power (Polenz 2013: 21, 34–35); agents of the Enlightenment, in turn, encouraged the improvement of education. Compulsory schooling was introduced in the 17th and 18th centuries (depending on the state), resulting in literacy rates of over 60% in some regions (Polenz 2013: 27; Szczepaniak 2015: 107).

Beyond such historical and culture-specific implications, the use of written language generally has a deep influence on cognition, culture, and linguistic structures.[21] As communication is increasingly practiced via writing and across temporal and spatial distances, it creates a disconnect between immediate situational experience and utterance (Ágel 1999: 199; Polenz 2000: 115). In writing, utterances are no longer fleeting and dynamic; instead, they have become static and material – a symbolic duplication of reality ("symbolische Verdopplung der Realität", Maas 1985: 59), a conservation of thoughts for the future reader. These circumstances make it necessary to anticipate the reception (Raible 1992: 194; Ágel 1999: 213–214), i.e., to mentally shift to the perspective of the readers and to design the text according to their needs. This process raises the awareness of communicative roles as well as metalinguistic thought in general.

The linguistic ideals of the Enlightenment need to be understood in the context of the social, medial and cognitive changes of the time. The principles of naturalness, brevity, and intelligibility can be viewed as a renunciation of the exclusive and cumbersome style of chancery language. The principles of intelligibility and clarity are specifically interesting in the interactional view of written

---

21.   For a comprehensive elaboration on this idea see Ágel (1999, 2015 and references therein).

communication. Writing lacks the rich para- and extra-linguistic context of spoken communication, in specific: intonation, facial expressions, gesture, situational embedding (Raible 1992: 194; Koch & Oesterreicher 2012). To compensate for this lack, writing needs to be clearer and more distinct than speech. With growing proportions of society participating in written discourse, writing is increasingly shaped by this necessity (as can also be seen from the fact that the graphemic system became more reader-friendly in the 16th–18th centuries, see Ruge 2004: 234). This adaptation to readers' needs likely occurred in part as an invisible hand phenomenon (boosted by economic competition – reader-friendly texts sell better); but also, contemporary grammarians and language critics strongly advocated unambiguousness in the *rationalist* line of metalinguistic reflection (see Reichmann 1995). The rationalist ideal was an entirely logical and precise grammar with clear relations between form and meaning. Since the process of standardization was not fully completed yet, these ideals still had a great impact on the development of the standard language.

The new developments – growing literacy and meta-linguistic reflection – led to an increased use of integrative structures (e.g., precise and unequivocal conjunctions) and an avoidance of aggregative structures (such as double negation), which fell out of use in the written standard and were continued only in dialects and language of immediacy (Ágel 2010: 208, 2015: 129). In that sense, the principle of naturalness was overridden by the principle of clarity. The view of enlightened, natural language use as overcoming 'stilted bookish German' thus sees only half the picture. Chancery language is often viewed as written language par excellence, due to its complex syntax. But in many respects, it was not (see, e.g., Polenz 2013: 301 for examples of conjunctions that seemed specific, but were in fact rather vague). Sentences were long and hypotactic, but they were often not integrative or cohesive, but instead aggregative and merely concatenative – sometimes even failing to close a bracket opened up many lines ago; they would also concatenate long strings of subordinate clauses without ever offering a matrix clause to embed them in (see also Admoni 1985: 1539–1540; Eichinger 1995). Taking this into account helps reassess why some of the chancery language constructions made it into the New High German standard, while others did not. Bracketing constructions (when correctly designed) as well as some of the conjunctions (e.g., *obwohl* 'although') were integrative and were retained. Others, such as *apo koinu* constructions or vague conjunctions, were given up eventually.

These aspects are important for the fate of the relativizer *so*: due to its grammatical properties (uninflectedness, see below), it was less distinct than its competitors, the inflecting relative pronouns *d-* and *welch-*. Brooks's (2006: 135) and Pickl's (2019) data show how both competitors increased in frequency in the 18th century, as *so*-relativizers declined. The difference in explicitness among the three relativizers, arguably, would not have been a problem in and of itself: The relativizer *so* had worked for centuries, reached all genres, and attained similar frequencies as the other two forms. It is only in connection with the 18th-century attempts at unambiguousness and the rise of integrative structures in advancing literacy, that the grammatical properties of *so* became problematic. These connections will be corroborated by the grammatical analyses of corpus data in Section 6.

The role of the Enlightenment in the loss of *so*-relatives is reflected in the genre-specific corpus results pertaining to fiction and humanities. In Semenjuk's (1972: 131–133) study of periodicals, it is the group of literature journals that shows the fastest decline of *so*-relative clauses (as opposed to newspapers, historical-political, and scientific journals); similarly, in Pickl's (2019) study, fictional texts reduce the use of *so*-relatives faster than 'functional texts', 'academic writing', and newspapers. In the data of the present study, narrative prose (which also contains a few non-fictional texts) shows average values until the period 1710–1739; but in the subsequent two periods, the values for narrative prose drop dramatically, and in a strikingly similar way as those of 'humanities' and 'drama' (see Figure 3 above). From 1740 until the end of the 18th century, the three genres show the lowest rate of *so*-relatives – ranking even lower than sermons.

6.   Grammatical, systemic, and typological analysis

This section will explore the grammatical properties of the relativizer *so*. The main focus will be on the implications of its indistinct, aggregative nature. The indistinct nature was brought about by both its inability to inflect and its strong polysemy. It will be argued that while the vagueness of *so* did sometimes lead to indistinct phrasings, the structural ambiguities can usually be dissolved by pragmatic inference. It is only in the historical context of German becoming a written standard language that the vagueness became a problem. Related grammatical developments (e.g., the increases of morphological concord and of bracketing constructions) are in line with this general development of German – and they can be shown to have conflicted with *so*. Together, these changes bear witness to German having undergone a drift towards *morphosyntax-based maturity* or an *overt complexity* language (see Bisang 2015 for this concept, which he contrasts with economy-oriented and pragmatics-based *hidden complexity*).

6.1   Indistinctness of *so*

It was mentioned above that the relativizer *so* was less distinct than its competitors, the inflecting relative pronouns *d-* and *welch-*. As is typical of relative pronouns, they express three functions simultaneously (Lehmann 1984: 246–252; Pittner 2009: 747; Zifonun 2011: 80). In addition to marking subordination, they also express the syntactic function within the relative clause via case marking (e.g., accusative −> direct object as in (9)) and the referential identity with the head through gender and number agreement (e.g., masculine singular as in (9)).

(9) *der*   *Mann,*   *den*   *ich sah*
     DEF:MASC.SG.NOM man(MASC.SG) REL.MASC.SG.ACC I   saw
     'the man whom I saw'

As *so* relatives do not inflect, they cannot express the latter two functions explicitly. Since the referential identity with the head is not marked morphologically, *so*-relative clauses are usually positioned immediately after the head.[22] In those cases where they are not, the referential identity has to be inferred pragmatically; for instance in Example (10), only semantic-pragmatic inference can help resolve that it was the 'crabs' that 'crawled around on the graves'.

(10) *Er hat am Charfreytag bey der Nacht etliche Krebs auff den Kirchhoff bringen lassen/ denselben brennende Wachskertzlein zwischen die Scheren gegeben/ so auff den Gråbern damit herumb gekrochen/ und dieweiln es bey der Nacht schrecklich anzusehen gewesen/ …*

'He had a number of crabs be brought to the churchyard on Good Friday at nightfall and put burning candles between their claws, which crawled around on the graves with them; and as this was a horrible sight in the dark…'

(1654, Rosetum, GerManC: Humanities, East Central German)

As was mentioned in the introduction, *so*-relatives were restricted to the first two positions of Keenan and Comrie's (1977: 66) Accessibility Hierarchy, i.e., to the subject or the direct object of the relative clause. This can be seen as a consequence of being uninflected; the competing relative pronouns use their inflection to realize the position of indirect object (e.g., *dem, welchem* 'whom, to which') and, in the case of *d-*, also the position of genitives (e.g., *dessen* 'whose'). Additionally, they can occur in oblique positions by combining with prepositions, e.g., *das Haus, in dem/welchem* sie wohnte 'the house, in which she lived'. Unfortunately for *so*, it did not combine with prepositions (Lefèvre 1996: 71, 2013: 351).[23] Interestingly, the corpus data feature sporadic (functional) transgressions of these limitations.

---

22. In Schieb's (1978: 507) 16th-century data, all 111 instances are positioned after the head; in Baldauf's (1982: 183) corpus of Luther's writings, 94% of the *so*-relatives occur in contact position, while for all relative clauses in total, the proportion is only 68%.

23. Note that the dialectal relative particle *wo* does combine with prepositions and pronominal adverbs, see Fleischer (2004: 227).

(11)   *Dise Action ist in Festo S. Ladislai [...] vnd am Tag/ <u>so</u> Jhro Kayserl. Majest.*
       die Vngarische Cron empfangen/ vorbey gangen.

       'This event took place during the festivity of St. Ladislaus and during the
       day <u>on which</u> Her Imperial Majesty received the Hungarian crown'
                            (1684, Muenchmerc, GerManC: News, East Upper German)

(12)   *Unterdessen hatte Bŏckgen [...] einen Schlŭssel zum Pferde-Stall von der*
       Schrauben genommen, und das Schloß erŏffnet, <u>so</u> niemand gewahr worden,
       weiln inwendig noch zwey Riegel an der Thŭren

       'Meanwhile, Boeckgen had taken a key to the horse stable off the hook and
       opened the lock, <u>which</u> no one became aware <u>of</u>, as there were still two
       locking bolts on the inside'
       (1724, JungferRobinsone, GerManC: Narrative prose, West Upper German)

In (11), the *so*-relativizer stands in the position of an adverbial (that would otherwise be realized with a preposition), and in Example (12), it corresponds to a
genitive.[24] Since it can neither express the genitive nor combine with a preposition, these syntactic relations have to be inferred pragmatically. As the examples
show, the inferences work without any problems. Thus, usages like these are not
dysfunctional – they only violate formal grammatical regularities. This is precisely
what is unproblematic in oral, aggregative language but becomes problematic in
the context of a literate culture, especially in connection with rationalistic metalinguistic reflection. Thus, the limitations of *so* in terms of syntactic functions were
tightened as the language became more strictly form-oriented.[25]

     Another kind of indistinctness came about due to the strong polysemy of the
word *so*. Both Semenjuk (1972: 130–131) and Ágel (2010: 214) consider that its
polysemy may have been a contributing factor in the loss of relative *so*. Hennig
(2007: 260–261) detects nine different functions of *so* in language of immediacy
and seven different functions in language of distance for the period 1650–1800.
Interestingly, the number of functions is reduced to four in both subcorpora by
the end of the 20th century. This at least points to the form *so* having become more
univocal from a lexicographer's perspective, i.e., semasiologically. It should be

---

24.   As an anonymous reviewer correctly points out, the construction *gewahr werden* 'become
aware' could still occur with an accusative complement in the 18th century.

25.   Note, however, that subject and direct object are by far the most frequent positions rela-
tivized into; thus, this limitation is not as fatal as it may seem, but rather a cog in the wheel
of the overall process. As Lefèvre (1996: 71, 2013: 351) points out, *so*-relatives suffered no
restriction with respect to the semantic class (person, object, abstract concept) of their head
noun; also, Baldauf's (1982) study as well as the present corpus data show that they had no
restriction with respect to number or gender.

considered, however, that in actual language use, the reader does not usually take a lexicographer's perspective, but is rather concerned with decoding the meaning of the present utterance. Therefore, the polysemy of a given sign is not problematic as long as the context disambiguates it. Why, then, should the polysemy of *so* have been a problematic feature? Ágel (1999: 207) gives a very conclusive account of the problem:

> 'Polysemy' constitutes a typical but nonetheless inappropriate projection of a "literal" term [i.e., a term conditioned by a literate culture] on 'oral semantics'. Linguistic signs only appear polysemous to hypostatizing literalized agents. To an oral speaker [i.e., member of an oral culture], any particular connector is only of value in its particular actional context. And in this actional context, it is entirely 'monosemous'.   [translation LK][26]

These theoretical considerations are fully corroborated by the corpus data: As described in Section 3, virtually no occurrence of so in its actual context remained ambiguous as to whether or not it was a relativizer. The status could always be determined using the syntactic and semantic context – primarily the position of the finite verb and the semantic reference to the head. These findings underpin the idea that it is mainly the attitude of "literalized agents" – or a (conscious or unconscious) metalinguistic concern – that conflicts with polysemous forms. A bit further on in the text, Ágel (1999: 215) points out how especially in the Age of Enlightenment, both polysemies and synonymies were perceived as impediments to clear expression and consequently depreciated.

6.2   *so*-relatives and the changing role of concord

As noted above, 18th-century grammarian J.C. Gottsched advised against the use of *so*-relativizers. And in fact, the reason he gives is the strong polysemy of *so* (1748: 238–239, 366). Interestingly, he points out that the particle may be used in cases where the gender of the head is unclear or where the head consists of several coordinated nouns differing in gender. Indeed, many examples of this kind can be found in the corpus data. Especially as the construction is dying out, it appears that usages of this kind constitute one of the last niches of survival. In particular, *so* is used to conceal agreement conflicts that would have become overt if inflecting relativizers had been applied. Agreement conflicts may arise, for instance, from

---

26.   "'Polysemie' stellt eine typische, aber unangemessene Projektion eines literalen Begriffs auf die 'orale Semantik' dar. Polysem erscheinen die Sprachzeichen nur dem hypostasierenden Literalisierten. Für den orale[n] Sprecher hat der jeweilige Satzkonnektor nur in dem jeweiligen konkreten Handlungszusammenhang einen Wert. Und in diesem Handlungszusammenhang ist er eben vollkommen 'monosem.'"

coordinated nouns with differing numbers and genders as in (13), from hybrid nouns (such as *Volck* 'people' in (14)), from the first person pronoun as in (15) (given that none of the relativizers could inflect for first person), or from a head noun occurring in a quantifier construction as in (16).

(13)   *fùr die Ehre/ respective guten Willen/ Trewe/ Gehorsam vnd Dienste/ so sie an jhm […] in wàrender Præsidentschafft geleistet/*

'for the honor$_{\text{FEM.SG}}$, the good will$_{\text{MASC.SG}}$, respectively, the fidelity$_{\text{FEM.SG}}$, the allegiance$_{\text{MASC.SG}}$, and services$_{\text{MASC.PL}}$ that they had bestowed upon him during his regency'

(1658, Morgenlaendisch, Narrative prose, North German)

(14)   *Der Zulauff des Volcks war unbeschreiblich / so in allen Gassen von der Arbeit geloffen / und zusammen geeilet;*

'The flow of the people$_{\text{SING}}$ was incredible, who had run from work and flocked together in all the streets'

(1712, Wien, News, East Upper German)

(15)   *…und mir, so weder solches empfunden noch vermercket, …*

'and to me, who [had] neither perceived nor realized such things, …'

(1750, Teutsche, Narrative prose, West Central German)

(16)   *auch sahe man aus der Menge lockern Sandes, so gemeiniglich um die westliche und nordwestliche Gegend dieser weichen Bànke lag, daß…*

'also, one could see from the amount$_{\text{FEM.SG}}$ of lose sand$_{\text{MASC.SG}}$, which would usually be found around the Western and North-Western areas of these soft banks, that…'

(1778, MineralogischeGeographie, Science, East Central German)

It is interesting to observe that concealing agreement conflicts seems to have been relevant only for a limited time span. Before the 18th century, lack of formal agreement does not seem to have been a problem. One of several phenomena that bear witness to this is the coordination ellipsis of articles in mixed number and gender coordinations (i.e., where the articles would have had different forms). An instance of this can be seen in Example (13) above (*fùr die Ehre/ respective den guten Willen*, etc.); while Early New High German texts provide plenty of instances, it is increasingly harder to find any in texts after ca. 1800 (see also Jakob 1999: 31, who lists passages where these ellipsis have been amended in lexicon series of the 18th century; in a very recent study, Dammel 2020 shows that coordination ellipses with diverging feature combinations drop dramatically in the second half of the 18th century, based on data from the GerManC).

As for concealing agreement conflicts: In post-18th-century (written) German, agreement conflicts by and large cannot be concealed, but must be dissolved explicitly or be avoided altogether; for example with a quantifier construction as in

(16), one would have to explicitly resume either of the two nouns (with semantic nuances). For *so*-relativizers, this means that their being inflectionally unmarked opened up a specific niche only for a limited period but eventually turned into a disadvantage: As inflectional concord became more mandatory in the grammar of German (see also Polenz 2013: 263), the relative particle was no longer in line with the grammatical system.

6.3   *so*-relatives and the reduction of multiple embedding

There is also a syntactic factor to be considered for the loss of relative *so*. As described above, the older, chancery-inspired tradition of writing displayed a highly complex syntax. Sentences were long and hypotactic, often with multiple levels of embedding – especially in the 17th century (Admoni 1985: 1540–1544). Another syntactic phenomenon of the time – the dropping of auxiliary verbs in subordinate clauses – is assumed to have been used to flag the embedded structure. Furthermore, it is assumed that the phenomenon declined as syntactic structures became clearer and shorter in the 18th century and thus this aid for understanding (multiple) embedding was not needed as much anymore (Admoni 1985: 1540–1544). This is interesting with respect to *so*-relatives: In the corpus data, there are plenty of instances in which *so*-relatives occur in the vicinity of auxiliary drop and/or other relativizers. Thus, it can be assumed that variation in the choice of relativizers was another strategy to make multiple embedding easier to parse or at least look less monstrous (see also an according advice pro variation in Adelung 1801: 117).

A mild example of 17th-century syntax is given in (17). The passage contains two *so*-relative clauses, one of them containing another relative clause. This inner relative clause is introduced by a different relativizer (*worinnen* 'in.which') and applies auxiliary drop ("Ø" indicates the missing perfect auxiliary *haben* 'have'). Also, the writer uses numeration (placing one thread of numeration within another), which suggests they tried hard to clarify the relations among the individual propositions.

(17)   (*2.*) *sind die Personen von welchen geredet worden / die / <u>so</u> 1. von denen inficirten Orten her Brieffe anzunehmen pflegen 2. in den Gasthöfen die Mågde / <u>so</u> die Betten / worinnen Passagiers gelegen Ø / gemacht haben.*

‘Secondly are the persons mentioned above those <u>that</u> (1) are wont to receive letters from the infected places and (2) in the guesthouses the maids <u>that</u> have made the beds which travellers have slept in.’[27]

(1680, ConsiliumMedicum, Science, North German)

---

27.   The translation aims for a compromise between intelligible English and maintaining the original structure.

Within the time span covered by the corpus (1650–1800), syntactic complexity reduces notably. A connection with *so*-relative clauses is likely: While three major relativizers could thrive without a problem in the age of excessive embedding – in fact they were needed for variation–, there was less need to have them all in the subsequent period when multiple embedding had reduced in connection with *brevity* and *naturalness*. Also, it should be noted that the variation of relativizers did not effectively clarify the heavily interlaced structures but only made them look less recursive: the relativizers do not appear to have been used for functional oppositions, e.g., for marking 'inner layers' or restrictive relative clauses (Baldauf 1982: 183 observes that *so* tended towards restrictive relative clauses in Luther's writings; the present corpus, however, offers plenty of nonrestrictive uses). Thus, the variation strategy does not agree with the rationalistic ideal of *clarity* conceived of as a one-to-one correspondence between form and meaning.

6.4   Typological drift towards overt complexity

Both the semantic indistinctness of *so* and its inflectional imprecision (and to some degree also the unspecific concatenation of clauses) point to properties of older stages of German: They point to stages when pragmatic inferences played a more important role and formal explicitness and congruence was less mandatory. The subsequent developments – including, inter alia, the obligatorification of inflectional concord, the consolidation of bracketing structures, the specification of subordinators (see Polenz 2013: 263, 299–300), and increasingly formal restrictions on the ellipsis of parts of words (e.g., *Ein- und Ausgang* 'entrance and exit', see Kempf 2010) – can be seen as a path to *morphosyntax-based maturity*, or *overt complexity*. Building on Dahl (2004: 103–115), Bisang (2015: 183–184) describes this path as involving chain reactions in an evolutionary process:

> Seen from the perspective of constant competition between economy and explicitness at any position in an utterance [...], the obligatorification of a category in a given morphosyntactic position may enhance additional overt complexity elsewhere at a next stage if that category is exploited for additional functions (e.g., noun class markers as markers of agreement within the noun phrase) or if its presence necessitates additional rules (e.g., word order, simultaneous presence of another category).

The changes in the history of (Early) New High German can be viewed as interrelated in this way. For instance, the rise of nominal brackets builds on gender agreement between the article (left-hand bracket) and the noun (right-hand bracket);[28]

---

28.   Consider, e.g., *die in Frankreich komponierte Musik* lit. "the$_{\text{FEM.SG}}$ in France composed music$_{\text{FEM.SG}}$."

thus, gender agreement became more important with time; the rising importance of gender agreement did not correspond well with non-inflecting relativizers. Thus, the demise of *so*-relatives needs to be understood in connection with these general systemic developments. When speaking about the *system* of German, though, it is important to bear in mind that a) it is the written standard that conditions the idea of a "system" in the first place (Ágel 1999) and b) the grammatical properties described refer to this written standard. The aggregative, pragmatically conditioned and non-agreeing phrasings found in pre-18th-century writings still persist to some degree in the language of immediacy (even though these registers are also influenced by the developments of the written standard, see Szczepaniak 2015; Czicza & Hennig 2013: 28). The relativizer *so*, however, could not "persist" in the language of immediacy, as it was never part of it.

7.   Summary and outcome for the study of obsolescence

The present study detailed the factors relevant for the loss of *so*-relativizers in three basic steps: The first part of the corpus analysis showed that *so*-relatives decreased in the 18th century and were indeed close to chancery language; but they were also used in all other domains, specifically when a high, sophisticated register was aimed at. The next steps of analysis had to resolve the puzzle of why *so*-relatives went down along with chancery language, while other constructions were maintained. Thus, the second step surveyed the socio-historical context and general tendencies in language change at the time. German in the 18th century underwent fundamental changes. The Age of Enlightenment, first signs of democratization, and the rise of public participation in writing resulted in clearer and more natural expression. Specifically, the increased use of written language shaped cognition and grammar, resulting in a rise of integrative constructions that rely on grammatical precision rather than on pragmatic inference. In a third step, it was shown in which grammatical and semantic respects *so*-relativizers were indeed imprecise. It was also argued that the imprecision was not a problem in and of itself but got into conflict with other developments (rise of agreement, precision of conjunctions) and a general typological drift towards overt, morpho-syntax-based complexity.

   As a first outcome for the study of obsolescence, it can be deduced from this case study that it might be essential to consider a comprehensive picture – including the semantic and grammatical properties of the construction (and of its competitors), the distributions across genres, styles, and regions, the nature and diachronic tendencies of the hosting system, as well as the socio-historical context conditioning it. Beyond this general statement, the case at hand will now be evaluated with respect to a number of specific questions raised in the literature on obsolescence or language change.

With respect to the type of obsolescence, we are dealing with a case of grammatical obsolescence where an individual construction is lost (cf. Section 1). More precisely, it is the specific form–function pairing that is lost, while the function continues to be realized by other forms, and the form *so* continues to be used in other functions. The presence of other functions may in fact have had a negative impact on *so* as a relativizer, specifically in the context of the (rationalist) pursuit of unambiguousness. It is well possible that in other cases, the coexistence of other functions carried out by the same forms helps the construction survive by way of boosting the token frequency of the form and thus its entrenchment (cf. Divjak & Caldwell-Harris 2015 and also Rehn, this volume).

A second strand of questions could be headed 'suspicious epiphenomena'. Obviously, the construction experienced a drop in frequency. It might be noteworthy, though, that prior to its final demise, there is a short-term upward trend, shared by almost all genres and regions. When obsolescent constructions are losing frequency, they tend to retreat to certain (temporary) niches of survival. This *distributional fragmentation*, as Rudnicka (2019: 219) terms it, can be observed for *so*-relativizers: One of the niches – apart from their natural habitat, official language – is sophisticated style in various genres. Two other niches are grammatical (blurring agreement conflicts, providing variation in multiple embedding). Another typical epiphenomenon is competition. While Aronoff and Lindsay (2015: 3) ascribe to it an important role "in the organization of linguistic systems", competition does not need to be a sign of incipient obsolescence (as they show with their case study as well), nor does obsolescence require competition (consider, especially, cases involving functional obsolescence). In the present case, competition did play a certain role, but was not the trigger of the loss. The three major options of the time, *d-*, *welch-*, and *so*, had coexisted peacefully for at least a whole century (see Brooks 2006: 135; Pickl 2019). It was only in the general language changes of the 18th century that the inflectionally richer forms gained 'evolutionary advantages' over *so*.

The aspect of competition additionally falls within the scope of a final set of questions to be addressed: What can be hypothesized to be a recurring tendency in obsolescence? Specifically, what recurring factors can be discerned as candidates for typical or even universal causes of obsolescence? Competition was just mentioned as a typical but not mandatory concomitant phenomenon; in connection with competition, the principle *survival of the frequent* (see Haspelmath 2004: 18 for references) may be considered. The present case can be taken to conform to this principle: In Brooks's (2006: 135) and Pickl's (2019) mixed-genre data, *so* appears just a little less frequently than its competitors, but distributional factors reinforce this ranking. The results of the present study show that *so* attained substantial shares only in newspapers and legal texts; also, *so* was grammatically most restricted (see Section 6). Thus, it can be stated that among the major 17th-century relativizers, the least frequent one lost the competition. Another potential tendency pertains to the types of obsolescence: Referring to the syntactic constructions she examined, Rudnicka (2019: 224) summarizes that "[t]hey all represent what we could call 'obsolescence of form' and not function, as their function is still part of the language". This is true for the present case as well. However, it is hard to tell whether functions are indeed more stable diachronically than forms. This impression might be just an artifact of formal phenomena attracting linguists' attention more than functions do (since forms are easier to grasp). Kuo's study on the loss of the adverse avertive schema in Mandarin (this volume) shows that cases of complete loss of a function do occur.

When it comes to factors accounting for the loss of a construction, it feels safe to hypothesize that obsolescence is rarely ever caused by a single factor and much more likely to be caused by an interaction of several factors. Rudnicka (2019: 223) brings up "the cliché 'to be in the wrong place at the wrong time'", which is very fitting for *so*-relatives as well. Neither their stylistic affiliations nor their grammatical features were fatal by themselves; instead, the combination of these properties got into conflict with general grammatical, conceptual, and typological changes of the time. These changes, in turn, were conditioned to a high degree by socio-cultural and socio-linguistic developments, such as democratization, the Enlightenment, and literalization. Thus, there is not only a multitude of factors but, crucially, a hierarchy of influential factors: The major societal and linguistic changes appear to be fundamental, while more local factors, such as competition and grammatical features, function as contributing factors. This constellation strikingly parallels the scenario Rudnicka (2019: 188) develops for the loss of purpose subordinators in Late Modern English, even though the culture and language-specific developments, of course, differ.[29] From this scenario, Rudnicka (2019: 219) concludes that "only constructions which [...] turn out to be 'against' higher-order processes that are at work at a certain point in time do become obsolescent and obsolete." If a

---

29. Interestingly, mass readership plays a fundamental role in both cases, notwithstanding that it had different effects in English – likely due to different temporal, diatopic, and societal circumstances. In English, mass readership seems to have brought about colloquialization phenomena. In German, mass readership in the 18th century was connected with the (comparatively late) development of a standard language. The development of a standard language and its accompanying linguistic ideals led to an avoidance of dialectal or even colloquial constructions in written German (Polenz [2]2013: 144–145) and to the preference of precise and distinct constructions (as described above, Sections 5 and 6).

fundamental role of higher-order processes indeed proves to be universal to obsolescence, we can acknowledge, as Rudnicka (2019: 221) puts it, that "the constructional level is never separable from the higher-order processes" and that "what we observe on the constructional level is a symptom of higher levels undergoing a change, be it an internally or externally-motivated change". This is precisely what makes scenarios of loss so conclusive for historical linguistics: They can function as a mirror of fundamental language change.

Acknowledgements

I would like to express my thanks to the audiences in Mainz, Salzburg, and Stuttgart for their helpful comments on earlier presentations of this work; to Judith Winterberg and Lena Späth for organizing the literature; to Antje Dammel and Simon Pickl for sharing pre-print versions of their papers; to Mehmet Aydın for proofreading and language-editing this paper; to two anonymous reviewers as well as to the editors for providing constructive feedback. All remaining errors are, of course, mine.

Corpora

DTA = Deutsches Textarchiv. <http://www.deutschestextarchiv.de/
GerManC = German Manchester Corpus. <http://www.ota.ox.ac.uk/desc/2544>

References

Adelung, Johann Christoph. 1801. *Grammatisch-kritisches Wörterbuch der Hochdeutschen Mundart, mit beständiger Vergleichung der übrigen Mundarten, besonders aber der Oberdeutschen* 4. Leipzig: Breitkopf.
Admoni, Wladimir. 1985. Syntax des Neuhochdeutschen seit dem 17. Jahrhundert. In *Sprachgeschichte: Ein Handbuch zur Geschichte der deutschen Sprache und ihrer Erforschung* [Handbücher zur Sprach- und Kommunikationswissenschaft 2], Werner Besch, Oskar Reichmann, and Stefan Sonderegger (eds), 1538–56. Berlin: De Gruyter.
Admoni, Wladimir. 1990. *Historische Syntax des Deutschen*. Tübingen: Niemeyer.
Ágel, Vilmos. 1999. Grammatik und Kulturgeschichte: Die raison graphique am Beispiel der Epistemik. In *Sprachgeschichte als Kulturgeschichte* [Studia Linguistica (SLG) 54], Andreas Gardt, Ulrike Haß-Zumkehr & Thorsten Roelcke (eds), 171–224. Berlin: De Gruyter. https://doi.org/10.1515/9783110807806.171
Ágel, Vilmos. 2010. +/−Wandel: Am Beispiel der Relativpartikeln so und wo. In *Kodierungstechniken im Wandel: Das Zusammenspiel von Analytik und Synthese im Gegenwartsdeutschen* [Linguistik - Impulse & Tendenzen 34], Dagmar Bittner & Livio Gaeta (eds), 199–222. Berlin: De Gruyter. https://doi.org/10.1515/9783110228458.199

Ágel, Vilmos. 2015. Die Umparametrisierung der Grammatik durch Literalisierung: Online- und Offlinesyntax in Gegenwart und Geschichte. In *Sprachwissenschaft im Fokus: Positions- bestimmungen und Perspektiven*, Ludwig M. Eichinger (ed.), 121–55. Berlin: De Gruyter.

Ágel, Vilmos & Hennig, Mathilde (eds). 2006. *Grammatik aus Nähe und Distanz: Theorie und Praxis am Beispiel von Nähetexten 1650–2000*. Tübingen: Niemeyer. https://doi.org/10.1515/9783110944709

Ágel, Vilmos & Hennig, Mathilde. 2007. Überlegungen zur Theorie und Praxis des Nähe- und Distanzsprechens. In *Zugänge zur Grammatik der gesprochenen Sprache* [Reihe germanist- ische Linguistik 269], Vilmos Ágel & Mathilde Hennig (eds), 179–214. Tübingen: Niemeyer.

Aronoff, Mark & Lindsay, Mark. 2015. Partial organization in languages: La langue est un sys- tème où la plupart se tient. In *Proceedings of the 8th Décembrettes, 8th International Confer- ence on Morphology, 6–7 December 2012* [Carnets de Grammaire] 1–14. Toulouse: CNRS & University of Toulouse Jean Jaurès.

Axel-Tober, Katrin. 2012. *(Nicht-)kanonische Nebensätze im Deutschen. Synchrone und dia- chrone Aspekte* [Linguistische Arbeiten 542]. Berlin: De Gruyter. https://doi.org/10.1515/9783110276671

Baldauf, Kunibert. 1982. Die Relativsatzeinleitung in der Luthersprache. *Sprachwissenschaft* 7: 448–80.

Betten, Anne. 2000. Zum Verhältnis von geschriebener und gesprochener Sprache im Früh- neuhochdeutschen. In *Sprachgeschichte: Ein Handbuch zur Geschichte der deutschen Sprache und ihrer Erforschung, 2nd rev. edn*, Werner Besch, Anne Betten, Oskar Reichmann & Stefan Sonderegger (eds), 1646–1664. Berlin: De Gruyter.

Betten, Anne. 2012. Direkte Rede und episches Erzählen im Vergleich: Eine syntaktische Reise durch fünf Jahrhunderte (1500–2000). In *Im Bergwerk der Sprache: Eine Geschichte des Deutschen in Episoden*, Gabriele Leupold & Eveline Passet (eds), 13–34. Göttingen: Wallstein.

Bisang, Walter. 2015. Hidden complexity - The neglected side of complexity and its implications. *Linguistics Vanguard* 1: 177–187.

Blackall, Eric A. 1966. *Die Entwicklung des Deutschen zur Literatursprache 1700–1775: Mit einem Bericht über neue Forschungsergebnisse 1955–1964 von Dieter Kimpel*. Stuttgart: Metzler. https://doi.org/10.1007/978-3-476-99901-6

Brooks, Thomas. 2001. Vom Vorreiter zum Nachzügler: Überlegungen zum Prestigeverlust der Kanzleisprache am Übergang vom 17. zum 18. Jahrhundert. In *Textallianzen: Am Schnitt- punkt der germanistischen Disziplinen*, Alexander Schwarz & Laure Ablanalp Luscher (eds), 291–302. Bern: Peter Lang.

Brooks, Thomas. 2006. *Untersuchungen zur Syntax in oberdeutschen Drucken des 16.-18. Jahr- hunderts* [Schriften zur deutschen Sprache in Österreich 36]. Frankfurt: Peter Lang.

Comrie, Bernard. 1998. Rethinking the typology of relative clauses. *Language Design* 1: 59–86.

Czicza, Daniel & Hennig, Mathilde. 2013. Aggregation, Integration und Sprachwandel. In *Sprachwandel im Neuhochdeutschen* (Language change in New High German), Petra Maria Vogel (ed.), 1–34. Berlin: De Gruyter.

Dahl, Östen. 2004. *The Growth and Maintenance of Linguistic Complexity* [Studies in Language Companion Series 71]. Amsterdam: John Benjamins.

Dammel, Antje. 2020. Absence as evidence - Determination and coordination ellipsis in con- joined noun phrases in (early) New High German. In *Walking on the Grammaticaliza- tion Path of the Definite Article in German: Functional Main and Side Roads* [Studies in

Language Variation 23], Johanna Flick & Renata Szczepaniak (eds), 162–195. Amsterdam: John Benjamins. https://doi.org/10.1075/silv.23.06dam

Divjak, Dagmar & Caldwell-Harris, Catherine L. 2015. Frequency and entrenchment. In *Handbook of Cognitive Linguistics*, Ewa Dąbrowska & Dagmar Divjak (eds), 53–75. Berlin: De Gruyter.

Durell, Martin, Ensslin, Astrid & Bennett, Paul. 2007. GerManC: A historical corpus of German 1650–1800. *Sprache und Datenverarbeitung: International Journal for Language Data Processing (SDv)* 31 (1): 71–80.

Ebert, Robert Peter. 1981. Social and stylistic variation in the order of auxiliary and nonfinite verb in dependent clauses in early New High German. *Beiträge zur Geschichte der deutschen Sprache und Literatur (PBB)* 103: 204–37.

Eichinger, Ludwig M. 1995. Syntaktischer Wandel und Verständlichkeit: Zur Serialisierung von Sätzen und Nominalgruppen im frühen Neuhochdeutschen. In *Linguistik der Wissenschaftssprache*, Harald Weinrich & Heinz L. Kretzenbacher (eds), 301–24. Berlin: De Gruyter.

Fleischer, Jürg. 2004. A typology of relative clauses in German dialects. In *Dialectology meets Typology: Dialect Grammar from a Cross-Linguistic Perspective* [Trends in Linguistics and Monographs 153], Bernd Kortmann (ed.), 211–243. Berlin: Mouton de Gruyter.

Fleischer, Jürg. 2005. Relativsätze in den Dialekten des Deutschen: Vergleich und Typologie. *Linguistik Online* 24 (3): 171–186.

Gottsched, Johann Christoph. 1748. *Grundlegung einer Deutschen Sprachkunst: Nach den Mustern der besten Schriftsteller des vorigen und jetzigen Jahrhunderts*, 2nd rev. edn. Leipzig: Bernhard Christoph Breitkopf.

Gottsched, Johann Christoph. 1762. *Vollständigere und Neuerläuterte Deutsche Sprachkunst*, 5th edn [Ausgewählte Werke VIII]. Leipzig: Bernhard Christoph Breitkopf.

Haspelmath, Martin. 2001. The European linguistic area: Standard Average European. In *Language Typology and Language Universals: An International Handbook* [Handbücher zur Sprach- und Kommunikationswissenschaft 20/1], Martin Haspelmath (ed.), 1492–1510. Berlin: De Gruyter. https://doi.org/10.1515/9783110171549.2.14.1492

Haspelmath, Martin. 2004. On directionality in language change with particular references to grammaticalization. In *Up and Down the Cline: The Nature of Grammaticalization* [Typological Studies in Language 59], Olga Fischer, Muriel Norde & Harry Perridon (eds), 17–44. Amsterdam: John Benjamins. https://doi.org/10.1075/tsl.59.03has

Hennig, Mathilde. 2007. Da klingelt der cantzler mit der glocke so kam der Man hinnein. *Sprachwissenschaft* 32 (3): 249–278.

Jakob, Karlheinz. 1999. Die Sprachnormierungen Johann Christoph Gottscheds und ihre Durchsetzung in der zweiten Hälfte des 18. Jahrhunderts. *Sprachwissenschaft* 24: 1–46.

Keenan, Edward L. & Comrie, Bernard. 1977. Noun phrase accessibility and Universal Grammar. *Linguistic Inquiry* 8 (1): 63–99.

Kempf, Luise. 2010. In erober: vnd plünderung der Statt: Wie die Ellipse von Wortteilen entstand. *Beiträge zur Geschichte der deutschen Sprache und Literatur (PBB)* 132 (3): 343–365. https://doi.org/10.1515/bgsl.2010.052

Kempf, Luise. 2020. Verloren im Wandel der Textgestaltung: Funktionen, Grammatikalisierung und Schwund der -selb-Anadeiktika. In *Textkohärenz und Gesamtsatzstrukturen in der Geschichte der deutschen und französischen Sprache vom 8. bis zum 18. Jahrhundert. Akten zum Internationalen Kongress an der Universität Paris-Sorbonne vom 15. bis 17. November 2018* [Berliner Sprachwissenschaftliche Studien 35], Delphine Pasques & Claudia Wich-Reif (eds.), 417–444. Berlin: Weidler.

Koch, Peter & Oesterreicher, Wulf. 2012. Language of immediacy - Language of distance: Orality and literacy from the perspective of language theory and linguistic history. In *Communicative Spaces. Variation, Contact, and Change: Papers in Honour of Ursula Schaefer*, Claudia Lange, Beatrix Weber & Göran Wolf (eds), 441–73. Frankfurt: Peter Lang.

Köller, Wilhelm. 1993. Perspektivität in Bildern und Sprachsystemen. In *Deutsch im Gespräch*, Peter Eisenberg & Peter Klotz (eds), 15–34. Stuttgart: Klett.

Korhonen, Jarmo. 1988. Zur Textkonstitution und Syntax in der 'Relation' des Jahres 1609. In *Studien zum Frühneuhochdeutschen* [Göppinger Arbeiten zur Germanistik (GAG) 476], Peter Wiesinger (ed.), 227–245. Göppingen: Kümmerle.

Kranich, Svenja & Breban, Tine. 2018. Lost in change: Causes and processes in the loss of constructions and categories. Presentation held at 40. DGfS-Jahrestagung. AG Lost in change: Causes and processes in the loss of grammatical constructions and categories, 7 March.

Lefèvre, Michel. 1996. Die adverbialen Proformen 'so', 'da', 'wo' im späten Frühneuhochdeutschen. In *Pro-Formen des Deutschen* [Eurogermanistik 10], Marie-Hélène Pérennec (ed.), 63–74. Tübingen: Stauffenburg.

Lefèvre, Michel. 2013. *Textgestaltung, Äußerungsstruktur und Syntax in deutschen Zeitungen des 17. Jahrhunderts: Zwischen barocker Polyphonie und solistischem Journalismus* [Berliner sprachwissenschaftliche Studien 29]. Berlin: Weidler.

Lehmann, Christian. 1984. *Der Relativsatz. Typologie seiner Strukturen; Theorie seiner Funktionen; Kompendium seiner Grammatik* [Language Universals Series 3]. Tübingen: Narr.

Linke, Angelika. 2006. "Ich": Zur kommunikativen Konstruktion von Individualität. Auch ein Beitrag zur kulturellen Selbsterfindung des 'neuen' Bürgertums im 18. Jahrhundert. In *Bürgerlichkeit im 18. Jahrhundert*, Hans-Edwin Friedrich, Fotis Jannidis & Marianne Willems (eds), 45–67. Tübingen: Niemeyer. https://doi.org/10.1515/9783110922370.45

Lötscher, Andreas. 1990. Variation und Grammatisierung in der Geschichte des erweiterten Adjektiv- und Partizipialattributs des Deutschen. In *Neuere Forschungen zur historischen Syntax des Deutschen: Referate der internationalen Fachkonferenz Eichstätt 1989* [Reihe Germanistische Linguistik (RGL) 103], Anne Betten & Claudia M. Riehl (eds), 14–28. Tübingen: Niemeyer. https://doi.org/10.1515/9783111708751.14

Lötscher, Andreas. 2016. Komplexe Attribuierung als Element von Textstilen im diachronen Vergleich. In *Komplexe Attribution: Ein Nominalstilphänomen aus sprachhistorischer, grammatischer, typologischer und funktionalstilistischer Perspektive* [Linguistik - Impulse & Tendenzen 63], Mathilde Hennig (ed.), 353–390. Berlin: De Gruyter. https://doi.org/10.1515/9783110421170-010

Maas, Utz. 1985. Lesen - Schreiben - Schrift: Die Demotisierung eines professionellen Arkanums im Spätmittelalter und in der frühen Neuzeit. *LiLi. Zeitschrift für Literaturwissenschaft und Linguistik* 59: 55–81.

Morisawa, Mariko. 2004. Syntaktische Erscheinungen als Spiegel der Gesellschaft im 16. Jahrhundert: Historisch-soziolinguistische Analyse von Relativsatzeinleitungen in der Nürnberger Stadtsprache. *Neue Beiträge zur Germanistik* 3 (1): 183–95.

Nübling, Damaris & Kempf, Luise. 2020. Grammaticalization in the Germanic Languages. In *Grammaticalization Scenarios. Areal Patterns and Cross-Linguistic Variation. A Comparative Handbook*, Walter Bisang & Andrej Malchukov (eds). Berlin: De Gruyter.

Oesterreicher, Wulf & Koch, Peter. 2016. 30 Jahre 'Sprache der Nähe - Sprache der Distanz': Zu Anfängen und Entwicklung von Konzepten im Feld von Mündlichkeit und Schriftlichkeit. In *Zur Karriere von "Nähe und Distanz": Rezeption und Diskussion des Koch-Oesterreicher-Modells*, Helmuth Feilke & Mathilde Hennig, 11–72. Berlin: De Gruyter Mouton. https://doi.org/10.1515/9783110464061-003

Pickl, Simon. 2019. Factors of selection, standard univerals, and the standardisation of German relativisers. *Language Policy* 19: 235–258. <https://doi.org/10.1007/s10993-019-09530-3>

Pittner, Karin. 2009. Relativum. In *Handbuch der deutschen Wortarten*, Ludger Hoffmann (ed.), 727–757. Berlin: De Gruyter.

von Polenz, Peter. 2000. *Deutsche Sprachgeschichte vom Spätmittelalter bis zur Gegenwart*, Band 1: *Einführung, Grundbegriffe, 14. bis 16. Jahrhundert*, 2nd rev. and enlarged edn. Berlin: De Gruyter. https://doi.org/10.1515/9783110824889

von Polenz, Peter. 2013. *Deutsche Sprachgeschichte vom Spätmittelalter bis zur Gegenwart*, Band II: *17. und 18. Jahrhundert*, 3 Vols, 2nd edn. Berlin: De Gruyter.

Raible, Wolfgang. 1992. Junktion: Eine Dimension der Sprache und ihre Realisierungsformen zwischen Aggregation und Integration. *Sitzungsberichte der Heidelberger Akademie der Wissenschaften*. Heidelberg: Winter. Vorgetragen am 4. Juli 1987.

Raible, Wolfgang. 1994. Orality and literacy (Mündlichkeit und Schriftlichkeit). In *Schrift und Schriftlichkeit: Ein interdisziplinäres Handbuch internationaler Forschung - Writing and Its Use* [Handbücher zur Sprach- und Kommunikationswissenschaft 10], Hartmut Günther & Otto Ludwig (eds), 1–17. Berlin: De Gruyter.

Reichmann, Oskar. 1995. Die Konzepte von 'Deutlichkeit' und 'Eindeutigkeit' in der rationalistischen Sprachtheorie des 18. Jahrhunderts. In *Sprachgeschichte des Neuhochdeutschen: Gegenstände, Methoden, Theorien* [Reihe germanistische Linguistik 156], Andreas Gardt, Klaus J. Mattheier & Oskar Reichmann (eds), 169–97. Tübingen: Niemeyer. https://doi.org/10.1515/9783110918762.169

Reichmann, Oskar & Wegera, Klaus-Peter. 1993. *Frühneuhochdeutsche Grammatik* [Sammlung kurzer Grammatiken germanischer Dialekte 12]. Tübingen: Niemeyer.

Reiffenstein, Ingo. 1992. Oberdeutsch und Hochdeutsch in Gelehrtenbriefen des 18. Jahrhunderts. In *Verborum Amor: Studien zur Geschichte und Kunst der deutschen Sprache*, Harald Burger, Alois M. Haas & Peter von Matt (eds), 481–501. Berlin: De Gruyter. https://doi.org/10.1515/9783110858068-027

Rudnicka, Karolina. 2019. *The Statistics of Obsolescence: Purpose Subordinators in Late Modern English* [NIHIN Studies]. Freiburg: Rombach.

Ruge, Nikolaus. 2004. *Aufkommen und Durchsetzung morphembezogener Schreibungen im Deutschen 1500–1770* [Grammatische Bibliothek 19]. Heidelberg: Winter.

Schieb, Gabriele. 1978. Relative Attributsätze. In *Zur Literatursprache im Zeitalter der frühbürgerlichen Revolution: Untersuchungen zu ihrer Verwendung in der Agitationsliteratur* [Bausteine zur Sprachgeschichte des Neuhochdeutschen 58], Gerhard Kettmann, Joachim Schildt & Wolfgang Pfeifer (eds), 445–498. Berlin: Akademie Verlag.

Schildt, Joachim. 1984. *Abriß der Geschichte der deutschen Sprache: zum Verhältnis von Gesellschafts- und Sprachgeschichte*, 3rd revised edition [Sammlung Akademie-Verlag 20]. Berlin: Akademie Verlag.

von Schlözer, August Ludwig. 1772. August Ludwig Schlözers [...] Vorstellung seiner UniversalTheorie, Vol. 1, 2 Vols. Göttingen: Dieterich.

Schuster, Britt Marie. 2017. Elemente einer Theorie des Textsortenwandels: Eine Bestandsaufnahme und ein Vorschlag. In *Textsortenwandel vom 9. bis zum 19. Jahrhundert: Akten zur internationalen Fachtagung an der Universität Paderborn vom 9–13 Juni 2015* [Berliner sprachwissenschaftliche Studien 32], Britt M. Schuster & Susan Holftreter (eds), 25–43. Berlin: Weidler Buchverlag.

Schuster, Britt Marie & Wille, Manuel. 2015. Von der Kanzlei- zur Bürgersprache? Textsortengeschichtliche Betrachtungen zur >Staats- und Gelehrten Zeitung des Hamburgischen unpartheyischen Correspondenten< im 18. Jahrhundert. *Jahrbuch für Kommunikationsgeschichte* 17: 7–29.

Schwitalla, Johannes. 2002. Komplexe Kanzleisyntax als sozialer Stil: Aufstieg und Fall eines sprachlichen Imponierhabitus. In *Soziale Welten und kommunikative Stile: Festschrift für Werner Kallmeyer zum 60. Geburtstag* [Studien zur deutschen Sprache 2], Inken Keim & Wilfried Schütte (eds), 379–398. Tübingen: Gunter Narr.

Semenjuk, Natalia N. 1972. Zustand und Evolution der grammatischen Normen des Deutschen in der 1. Hälfte des 18. Jahrhunderts. In *Studien zur Geschichte der deutschen Sprache* [Bausteine zur Geschichte des Neuhochdeutschen 49], Günter Feudel (ed),, 79–166. Berlin: Akademie Verlag.

Szczepaniak, Renata. 2015. Syntaktische Einheitsbildung - typologisch und diachron betrachtet. In *Handbuch Satz, Äußerung, Schema* [Handbücher Sprachwissen 4], Christa Dürscheid & Jan G. Schneider (eds), 104–124. Berlin: De Gruyter. https://doi.org/10.1515/9783110296037-006

Wiesinger, Peter. 1995. Die sprachlichen Verhältnisse und der Weg zur allgemeinen deutschen Schriftsprache in Österreich im 18. und frühen 19. Jahrhundert. In *Sprachgeschichte des Neuhochdeutschen: Gegenstände, Methoden, Theorien* [Reihe germanistische Linguistik 156], Andreas Gardt, Klaus J. Mattheier & Oskar Reichmann (eds), 319–367. Tübingen: Niemeyer. https://doi.org/10.1515/9783110918762.319

Zifonun, Gisela. 2011. Sprachtypologische Fragestellung in der gegenwartsbezogenen und der historischen Grammatik des Deutschen, am Beispiel des Relativsatzes. In *Neue historische Grammatiken: Zum Stand der Grammatikschreibung historischer Sprachstufen des Deutschen und anderer Sprachen* [Reihe germanistische Linguistik 243], Anja Lobenstein-Reichmann & Oskar Reichmann (eds), 59–86. Berlin: De Gruyter.

Appendix Absolute numbers of relative clauses in total (introduced by relative pronouns or relative particles) and *so*-relatives for all texts of the GerManC (except for subcorpus 'letters')[30]

Subcorpus, year, and text title	Rel. sum	Rel. *so*	Subcorpus, year, and text title	Rel. sum	Rel. *so*
DRAM NoD:			1764_Maegera	8	
1673_Leonilda	10		1782_Serail	11	1
1699_Euridice	20	1	1798_Donauweibchen	9	
1700_Freyheit	15	2	DRAM WMD:		
1707_SchaeferSpiel	36	1	1662_Tomyris	5	
1711_Croesus	12		1668_ChristRuehmendes	13	1
1749_AlteJungfer	16		1670_Comoedianten	20	
1764_Salomo	19	1	1742_Bookesbeutel	12	3
1767_Minna	4		1743_DieGeistlichen	19	
1776_Zwillinge	22		1745_Zuegellose	11	
DRAM OMD:			1773_Goetz	12	
1657_Cardenio	21	1	1780_Hausvater	12	
1661_Cleopatra	12		1787_Verbrechen	4	
1683_Masaniello	12		DRAM WOD:		
1732_Cato	10	3	1663_Carle	13	
1736_Fischbein	7		1687_Joseph	7	1
1747_Schwestern	20		1699_LiebesStreit	14	8
1774_Hofmeister	21		1702_Helvetia	7	
1775_LeidendeWeib	8		1737_Verehrung	5	
1788_Egmont	13		1748_Hoelle	13	1
DRAM OOD:			1762_Evander	16	1
1675_Pirrus	17	3	1781_Raeuber	10	
1682_Abraham	29	4	1783_Elfride	26	
1725_Venceslao	7		HUMA NoD:		
1733_Ciro	16	5	1663_HaubtSprache	22	4
1749_Schaeferinsel	17				

30. The abbreviations spell out as follows: DRAM = drama, HUMA = humanities, LEGA = legal texts, NARR = narrative prose, NEWS = newspapers, SCIE = scientific texts, SERM = sermons; NoD = Northern German, OMD = East Central German, OOD = East Upper German, WMD = West Central German, WOD = West Upper German; Rel. sum = relative clauses total (PRELS + PTKREL), Rel. *so* = *so* relative clauses.

Appendix (*Continued*)

Subcorpus, year, and text title	Rel. sum	Rel. *so*	Subcorpus, year, and text title	Rel. sum	Rel. *so*
1667_Ratseburg	19	10	1737_Curiositaeten	31	6
1674_NaturalienKammer	14		1739_Stollberg	34	7
1720_Remarques	22	3	1748_Samuel	31	3
1737_Koenigstein	2	2	1772_Baukunst	32	
1739_MusicalischInterval	21		1777_Homburg	26	1
1762_Kreuzzuege	35		1789_Italien	25	
1772_Ursprung	24		HUMA WOD:		
1788_Menschen	45	2	1662_Musurgia	21	6
HUMA OMD:			1686_Betrachtung	19	3
1654_Rosetum	20	9	1698_Mythoscopia	26	6
1680_Bericht	22		1740_Poesie	27	1
1685_ChristenStat	21	2	1741_Antiquitaeten	53	
1717_DienstMaegde	22	3	1744_Pfaltz	19	2
1725_Hass	28		1768_Roemer	26	1
1729_Biedermann	28	6	1784_Weibs	15	
1774_Roman	37		1795_Dichtung	23	
1777_Dichtkunst	17		LEGA NoD:		
1798_Sondershausen	48		1657_Luebeck	28	
HUMA OOD:			1673_BergOrdnung	18	7
1680_MercksWienn	30	6	1695_Duesseldorff	10	3
1689_Crain	26	9	1700_Braunschweig	8	5
1690_Proteus	21	3	1707_Reglement	14	4
1704_WasserKunst	39	8	1724_StadtRecht	27	3
1707_HundertNarren	13	1	1751_FeuerOrdnung	12	5
1731_Antiquitaeten Schatz	21	2	1757_Rostock	19	
1774_Emil	36		1796_Landtage	19	
1778_Pons	32		LEGA OMD:		
1792_Alterthuemer	21	1	1659_Hexen	12	3
HUMA WMD:			1674_BergOrdnung	21	5
1674_BilderSchatz	29	1	1680_Dreszden	14	5
1692_Christus	18	1	1709_WaeysenOrdnung	13	3
1699_KetzerHistorie	34	3	1710_ReichsArchiv	7	2
			1723_JurisMilitaris	14	6

(*Continued*)

Appendix (*Continued*)

Subcorpus, year, and text title	Rel. sum	Rel. *so*	Subcorpus, year, and text title	Rel. sum	Rel. *so*
1767_ProcessOrdnung	14	1	1787_Cameralrecht	32	
1777_MuehlenOrdnung	15		1791_Muenze	54	7
1784_Erbstatuten	21	1	NARR NoD:		
LEGA OOD:			1658_Morgenlaendisch	27	5
1657_Wildtfang	18	12	1659_Herkules	16	2
1659_SchulOrdnung	16	5	1682_Mandorell	43	11
1700_GesetzNuernberg	23	7	1706_SatyrischerRoman	18	
1704_OrdnungNuernberg	26	9	1709_OstIndien	17	7
1709_Promptuarii	17	1	1715_Africa	29	2
1719_Privilegien	36	12	1786_Muenchhausen	22	
1750_HofRathsOrdnung	20	1	1790_AntonReiser	28	
1752_Gerichtbarkeit	22	6	1796_Siebenkaes	25	
1769_Theresiana	21	4	NARR OMD:		
LEGA WMD:			1671_Ruebezahl	16	
1694_RathsSatzung	16	8	1689_Arminius	19	1
1698_BergkRecht	22	8	1700_Banise	23	
1700_LandRecht	34	14	1708_Affecten	29	8
1720_VatterMord	16	5	1731_Seefahrer	17	3
1724_GesetzBuch	30	14	1738_Lebens Beschreibung	29	9
1733_Heyrathen	25	3	1774_Werther	29	
1756_StaatsArchiv	11		1776_Zerbin	18	
1772_Regiments Verfassung	16	1	1782_Volksmaerchen	23	
1792_Reichshofrath	35	1	NARR OOD:		
LEGA WOD:			1667_Simplicissimus	24	
1654_Hoffgerichts Ordnung	11	5	1669_Aramena	22	3
1683_Ulm	23	6	1682_Winternaechte	35	3
1698_LandsOrdnung	12		1703_Narrennest	19	4
1711_HalsGericht	15	3	1715_HeldenGeschichte	32	2
1729_WechselRecht	12	2	1734_TaendlMarckt	27	8
1738_Constantz	10	1	1787_Aglais	35	
1769_ZunftOrdnungen	7		1789_PeterProsch	21	1
			1796_Quintus	33	

Appendix (*Continued*)

Subcorpus, year, and text title	Rel. sum	Rel. *so*	Subcorpus, year, and text title	Rel. sum	Rel. *so*
NARR WMD:			1798_danzig	25	
1664_Levante	48	10	NEWS OMD:		
1696_DerEdelmann	22		1666_leipzig1	15	3
1696_Schelmuffsky	19	1	1666_leipzig2	9	2
1716_Fleurie	28	1	1683_breslau	11	
1742_RedlicheMann	20		1684_breslau	20	3
1750_Teutsche	26	2	1687_leipzig	27	8
1775_Bacchidon	5		1722_leipzig1	19	2
1782_Fragmente	32		1722_leipzig2	1	
1783_Moralische Erzaehlungen	31	1	1724_halle	16	3
NARR WOD:			1744_erfurt1	10	
1672_Melcher	16		1744_erfurt2	9	
1682_Feuermaeuer	23	4	1769_erfurt	17	
1689_Miranten	33		1784_gotha	22	
1724_JungferRobinsone	18	4	1789_gotha	19	1
1744_Fabeln	19	1	1790_gotha	11	
1746_Muetze	26		NEWS OOD:		
1766_Agathon	47		1659_muenchen1	4	2
1771_Usong	40		1659_muenchen2	6	4
1797_Hyperion	12		1659_muenchmerc	5	1
NEWS NoD:			1679_nuernberg1	14	5
1666_berlin1	12	4	1679_nuernberg2	13	6
1666_berlin2	14	3	1684_muenchmerc	14	10
1673_hamburg	13		1702_muenchen1	16	7
1698_altona	22	7	1702_muenchen2	9	5
1702_hamburg	27	11	1712_wien	13	3
1735_berlin	10	1	1713_wien	6	1
1740_berlin1	29		1744_graz	19	5
1740_berlin2	3		1780_wien	19	4
1786_wolfenbuettel1	8		1790_erlangen	20	1
1786_wolfenbuettel2	8	1	1791_bayreuth	29	1
1796_stettin	18		NEWS WMD:		
			1662_koeln	9	4

(*Continued*)

Appendix (*Continued*)

Subcorpus, year, and text title	Rel. sum	Rel. *so*	Subcorpus, year, and text title	Rel. sum	Rel. *so*
1663_koeln	11	6	1744_Cometen	25	
1671_frankfurt1	22	7	1761_Menschlich	15	1
1671_frankfurt2	6	1	1775_Chemie	25	
1699_koeln	20	6	1799_Gasarten	40	
1701_frankfurt	14	4	SCIE OMD:		
1701_hanau1	15	7	1664_StraussStern	16	2
1701_hanau2	8	2	1672_Handwercke	20	2
1750_frankfurt	26	7	1700_BergBau	31	9
1784_mannheim	17		1717_Materialist	39	
1793_mainz	31		1731_HarnRuhr	22	1
1797_hanau	31	1	1737_Medica	31	12
NEWS WOD:			1778_Mineralogische		
1662_strassburg1	18	5	Geographie	34	4
1662_strassburg2	10	4	1781_Akademie	26	
1681_zuerich	21	2	1781_Chymie	12	1
1685_lindau	16	4	SCIE OOD:		
1689_lindau	18	3	1665_Feldmessen	16	1
1722_zuerich	21	1	1681_CometenGespoetts	25	5
1723_augsburg1	16	3	1689_PferdKunst	34	5
1723_augsburg2	14	4	1705_WerckSchul	8	1
1749_loerrach1	23		1722_NordScheines	23	2
1749_loerrach2	4		1745_Mathematicus	25	
1781_heilbronn	17		1780_Zeichen		
1784_freiburg1	7		Instruments	42	
1784_freiburg2	12		1786_Polizey	31	4
1798_tuebingen	30		1788_Chimie	23	1
SCIE NoD:			SCIE WMD:		
1672_Prognosticis	9	1	1676_ArtzneyBuch	14	4
1680_Consilium			1680_Epidemica	26	3
Medicum	32	17	1687_ArtzneyKunst	22	2
1684_Durchfall	15	3	1702_Armuth	33	13
1734_Barometer	20		1714_Kleinod	37	5
1736_Anweisung	18		1744_SelbstArtzt	36	5

Appendix (*Continued*)

Subcorpus, year, and text title	Rel. sum	Rel. *so*	Subcorpus, year, and text title	Rel. sum	Rel. *so*
1753_ProbierSteins	29	5	1790_Unruhen	25	
1777_Logik	38		SERM OOD:		
1781_Forstwissenschaft	22	8	1660_EinweihungsPredigt	24	1
SCIE WOD:			1663_Amaradvlcis	23	5
1663_KunstSpiegel	16	1	1686_Klagseufftzendes Ach	20	3
1665_Cometen	36	2			
1693_Kranckheit	19	6	1700_FeyerTag	7	2
1708_WunderbarenWelt	31	6	1709_Orgel	16	1
1720_FangSchlaeussen	21	4	1728_Verstellte	21	4
1741_Erden	52	3	1751_Elisabetha	22	1
1774_Hygrometrie	41		1782_Erloeser	25	
1780_Instrument	18	1	1792_Sonntagen	25	
1787_Botanik	23	1	SERM WMD:		
SERM NoD:			1662_Funeralia	19	
1666_Erbteil	20		1674_Trost	37	
1677_LeichSermon	24	1	1699_Solms	35	1
1690_WilleGottes	23		1702_Leben	22	
1715_Klugheit	22	1	1721_HeilBronnen	29	1
1715_Seeligkeit	25		1743_TrostPredigt	23	3
1730_JubelFeste	21		1774_Gewohnheit	43	
1765_Trauerrede	27		1780_Feuersbrunst	33	
1770_Gottesdienst	40		1780_LottoSucht	35	5
1798_LetztePredigt	32		SERM WOD:		
SERM OMD:			1654_Eytelkeit	29	2
1672_Advent	23	2	1660_LeichPredigt	17	
1680_Balcken	23		1683_TrostPredigt	18	
1680_SursumDeosum	18	1	1708_Zotten	30	
1706_GedaechtnisPredigt	22	7	1730_SeelenLiecht	18	
1715_Beerdigung	39		1739_Kranckentrost	11	1
1734_Evangelisch	24	1	1751_DreiKoenig	34	
1756_Trost	34	1	1790_Strassburg	37	
1760_Folgen	21	3	1792_Hegel	37	

CHAPTER 11

Loss of object indexation in verbal paradigms of Koĩc (Tibeto-Burman, Nepal)

Dörte Borchers

Karl-Franzens Universität, Graz

Koĩc ([kɔĩts]; English: Sunwar) is a Kiranti language spoken in eastern Nepal. In the past, Koĩc had a biactantial indexing system with transitive verbs indexing subjects and objects, a typical feature of Kiranti languages.[1] In modern Koĩc, transitive verbs are not indexed for object. A comparison shows connections in form and function between old and new argument indexes. Now Koĩc has a system of different conjugations, and for the majority of verbs membership in a conjugation is lexically fixed.

Most speakers of Koĩc are bilingual with Nepali (Indo-Iranian), and the longstanding Nepali influence will be discussed as one possible cause of language change.

Keywords: Kiranti language, transitivity, finiteness, person indexation, participle

1. Introduction[2]

1.1 Overview

This paper investigates the case of loss of object indexation in the modern Koĩc language, a Tibeto-Burman language spoken traditionally in eastern Nepal. Koĩc is one of the Kiranti languages, which typically have complex transitive verbal paradigms with biactantial indexes and a differentiation between inclusive and exclusive dual and plural indexes. Modern Koĩc, as documented in texts recorded since the 1990s (Rapacha 2005; Borchers 2008a), has no biactantial indexation but

---

1. Arguments of verbs are labelled here subject and object. This terminology refers to syntactic relations and makes no statement about the roles of the arguments.

2. I thank two anonymous reviewers for their critical comments on an earlier version of this paper.

https://doi.org/10.1075/slcs.218.11bor

© 2021 John Benjamins Publishing Company

subject indexes, which are not the same for all verbs. Verbs belong to different con-jugations, which are distinguished on the basis of their singular indexes. Modern Koïc has three transitive, one intransitive and one reflexive conjugation. For most verbs, membership in one of the conjugations is fixed, and transitive verbs can be transformed into reflexives.

I will demonstrate how complex subject and object indexes are connected with the subject indexes occurring in the different conjugation patterns of modern Koïc.

After introducing the language and its sociolinguistic context (Section 1), I will present the data that led to the investigation of the loss of biactantial indexes in Koïc. These data include the verbal paradigm with subject and object indexes, a verbal paradigm with only subject indexes collected by Carol Genetti (1988), and finite verbs with subject indexes, (which differ slightly from the paradigm in Genetti (1988)), presented in Borchers (2008a). A comparison of the biactantial and the subject indexing paradigms draws attention to morphological and seman-tic connections between the two systems (Section 2). Further literature with data about argument indexing in Koïc is introduced in the next section (Section 3) in order to clarify the process of language change that resulted in the loss of biac-tantial indexes, and to determine the sociolinguistic factors of geographic and temporal distribution. With the additional data the picture becomes rather more complex. Interestingly, however, one source (Bieri & Schulze 1973) features biac-tantial indexes occurring side by side with subject indexes.

There is a discussion of the possible reasons for the language change in Koïc in Section 4. Autonomous development will be considered as well as contact induced language change. The literature about contact induced language change suggests that structural change occurs predominantly in environments with intensive bilin-gualism (van Coetsem 2000; Heine & Kuteva 2005; Matras 2009; Thomason & Kaufman 1988). The frameworks of Kusters (2003) and Silva-Corvalán (1994) will be introduced because both these sources present detailed studies of structural language change in communities similar to that of the Koïc speakers. Kusters's model is based on the hypothesis that community structure and language com-plexity correlate. His comparison of four varieties of each of the languages in ques-tion allows him to closely track the factors that are decisive in language change.

Silva-Corvalán (1994) shows how the sociolinguistic situation of Spanish in Los Angeles resulted in the loss of gender distinguishing morphology. The case of Spanish in Los Angeles shows some overlap with the sociolinguistic situation of Koïc in Nepal, but there are also differences between the two. Koïc is, for example, not an official language anywhere and there is no large-scale production of Koïc movies or books.[3]

---

3.   Connections between language contact situations and different forms of language change have been described already by Thomason and Kaufman (1988). The works by Kusters

A summary (Section 5) concludes by pointing out promising directions for further research.

1.2   Koĩc, a Kiranti language

The language Koĩc belongs to the Kiranti group of Tibeto-Burman languages that are spoken predominantly in eastern Nepal. The speakers of Koĩc and their children refer to themselves as *Koĩc* or *Koĩcmur* 'Koĩc' or 'Koĩc people'.

In the English literature, the Koĩc language and its speakers are also referred to with the term 'Sunwar' or 'Sunuwar', based on their name in Nepali, सुनुवार *sunuvār*. This name was derived from the name of the river Sun Koshi, which runs south of the Koĩc speaking area. Koĩc has about 37,000 speakers (Central Bureau of Statistics 2012: 37), most of whom live in villages along the river *Likhu Khola*, about a hundred kilometres east of Nepal's capital Kathmandu (cf. Map 1, 2).

Languages belonging to the Kiranti branch of the Tibeto-Burman language family typically have biactantial indexing systems, indexing not only the subject but also the object on transitive verbs. This contrasts with other languages in the Tibeto-Burman language family, like Chinese, Tibetan or Burmese, which do not have any verbal morphology referring to arguments of the verb (Michailovsky 2017: 13).[4]

Kiranti languages employ case marking morphemes and follow the ergative pattern of marking subjects and objects (Michailovsky 2017: 2). Case markers are not syntactically obligatory and are not employed when they are not necessary pragmatically.

In Koĩc, case marking generally follows the ergative pattern but there are examples of the ergative marker and the object marker occurring in the same phrase. Nouns or pronouns referring to subjects of transitive verbs may remain without overt case marking or may be marked by the suffix *-mi* 'SBJ', objects of transitive verbs may remain unmarked or may be marked by the suffix *-kali* 'OBJ' (cf. Example 1). Subjects of intransitive phrases are unmarked for case. The presence or absence of Koĩc case markers for subjects and objects does not result in an obvious change in meaning to the phrase in question. This tendency towards

---

and Silva-Corvalán corroborate Thomason and Kaufman's results and fine-tune them with detailed case studies.

4.   The larger language family of which Kiranti languages are a subgroup is labelled here Tibeto-Burman in accordance with the linguistic literature, which treats Sinitic as a branch of Tibeto-Burman on the basis of historical linguistic developments (cf. DeLancey 2014: 41, footnote 2). In the linguistic literature, the traditional label Sino-Tibetan is also used to refer to the same larger language family (Michailovsky 2017: 2–3).

differential case marking has also been observed in other Tibeto-Burman languages in Nepal and Northeast India (DeLancey 2011: 14–15).

(1)   ge-mī   miʃal-kali sari ma-phe-di
       you-SBJ   girl-OBJ   Sari NEG-put.on-PRT.2SG
       'You didn't dress the girl in a Sari.'   (Borchers 2008a: 137)

Koïc speakers don't index the object on verbs anymore.[5] Subject and object indexing morphology was recorded in the 1980s, and a few phrases containing subject and object indexes were documented in the 1970s. There is no recent evidence of the subject and object indexing system, and in elicitations, speakers of the language were not able to precisely identify the meaning of verb forms with complex morphology (Borchers 2008a: 158). In modern Koïc, only the subject is indexed on the verb. In modern Koïc, the dual and plural subject indexes are the same for all transitive and intransitive verbs but the singular subject indexes show conjugation specific variation. Singular subject indexes indicate whether a verb is intransitive or transitive. In addition, singular subject indexes show to which of three transitive conjugations a verb belongs. Conjugation membership is lexically fixed for most verbs.

1.3   The sociolinguistic situation

In Nepal, Koïc is spoken in villages in eastern Nepal and in Kathmandu. Outside of Nepal, there has been a Koïc community in Sikkim (India) since the beginning of the 18th century (Shneiderman & Turin 2006: 54). In Sikkim, the language has a semi-official status.[6] In addition, there is a Koïc diaspora in Hong Kong and in Great Britain and there are Koïc people living temporarily or permanently in Malta, Portugal and other countries, where they went for work or education.

In a few villages in Nepal, Koïc is the dominant language spoken by the majority of people, for example in Bhuji (Ramechap) and in Khiji (Okhaldhunga). In other villages, which are rather removed from the river Likhu, Koïc is one of several languages spoken, for example in villages on the banks of the river Khimti (Ramechap district) on the northern fringe of traditional Koïc settlements, or in Katunje (Okhaldhunga district).

---

5.   There are no recent records of object indexing morphology in Koïc but it should be kept in mind that recordings were not made with speakers from every village.

6.   Koïc, which is called Mukhia in Sikkim, is there one of ten "Additional Official Languages" (Commissioner for Linguistic Minorities 2011: 84). The official language of Sikkim is English.

In most Nepali villages several languages are spoken. Among the other languages spoken in predominantly Koïc villages are the Tibeto-Burman languages Newar, Sherpa, Tamang and Thangmi.

Like the majority of the inhabitants of Nepal that speak languages other than Nepali (Indo-Iranian) with their families, most speakers of Koïc are bilingual with Nepal's national language and *lingua franca* Nepali. Nepali is the dominant language of instruction in schools, with English language education catching up very fast. There are radio programmes in several of the bigger minority languages of Nepal, but most programmes on the radio and TV are in Nepali. The longstanding contact between Nepali and the other languages spoken in Nepal has resulted in language change on both sides.

In Koïc families in the countryside, members of all generations speak Koïc at home and with Koïc neighbours. The same is true of families that move from their village to Kathmandu, with children who are at that time already old enough to speak Koïc. Most children born in the city will at best acquire a passive knowledge of their parents' mother tongue but grow up with Nepali as their first language. Most parents find it natural that children born in the city don't learn the language of the village. In the city, only a few parents make the effort to consciously support their children in to acquiring their own mother tongue.

In villages without a Koïc majority, Nepali is used in daily interactions with most neighbours and at the weekly market. Kubukastali (Ramechap), for example, is a village with a linguistically mixed population. In this village Nepali is dominant. It was observed there during a visit in winter 1997/98 that members of the local teacher's family, which was Koïc speaking, would not always use dual verb forms to refer to dual actants. When talking about these forms, however, the same speakers would produce the dual forms actively.

In villages with a Koïc majority, Koïc is used in more domains and there is less often cause to switch between languages. One such village is Bhuji (Ramechap district), which is dominantly Koïc speaking, and where Koïc is also the language of the village's weekly market. In a sociolinguistic survey of Koïc Lal Rapacha (1996) included a small-scale quantitative study on loan words in the language of Bhuji and in the language of a village with a Koïc minority, namely Katunje (Okhaldhunga district). The result of this study was that the dataset from Katunje included more Nepali loan words than that from Bhuji.

In Nepal's villages with a single major linguistic and cultural group, members of other groups may feel some societal pressure to adapt. Atit Mukhiya[7] reported that during his video documentation of the annual Candi festival in different villages,

---

7. Atit Mukhiya is a laywer and Koïc poet, who is originally from Ragani (Okhaldhunga).

he encountered Brahmins who had acquired a basic competence in Koĩc, and he observed Brahmins participating in minor functions in the religious ceremonies.[8]

Koĩc speakers in villages as well as in the city do not see Nepali as a threat to their mother tongue but as useful and just another one of their languages. One result of the sociolinguistic survey conducted by Lal Rapacha (1996) in villages in eastern Nepal shows that, at least at the time of the survey, Koĩc speakers of various ages had a very positive attitude towards their mother tongue (Rapacha 1996: 64, 68, 70). The people interviewed were all bilingual with Nepali and also wanted their children to learn both these languages (Rapacha 1996: 70). At the same time of Rapacha's survey in the 1990s, Koĩc speakers in Kathmandu tried to hide the fact that they came from the countryside and were speaking an indigenous language. They would use their clan name as family name, instead of the last name Sunuwar and would avoid letting their colleagues know they were Koĩc and that they could speak the Koĩc language. This attitude changed in the city during and after the civil war, in the mid-2000s, when it became prestigious to be indigenous.

Koĩc speakers easily switch between their mother tongue and Nepali, depending on the audience and the topic. In Kathmandu, code switching is common even in groups of competent Koĩc speakers. Traditional ceremonies will be talked about in Koĩc but Nepali politics are discussed in Nepali.

Since the early 1990s, Koĩc has been a written language in Nepal and Sikkim, making use of two writing systems, namely Devanagari (in Nepal) and Jĕticha (Sikkim, India) (see Rapacha (2020) for an overview of texts in and about Koĩc). In Nepal, publications in Koĩc include poetry, newspaper articles and works about language and culture. In Sikkim, the Koĩc community produces a newspaper and schoolbooks for mother tongue education in public schools.

Koĩc has no clearly defined standard variety but speakers tend to identify the area of Bhuji and Khiji on the river Likhu, which is dominantly Koĩc speaking, as the centre of their language and culture. The Koĩc language shows some regional variation, and community members are able to identify the place of origin of other speakers based on their pronunciation and to a lesser extent on differences in the lexicon. The word for chicken, for example is *ba* in Okhaldhunga, and *bwa* or *ba* in Ramechap. The differences between the varieties of the language don't hinder communication (Rapacha 2009: 120).

Speakers of different varieties of Koĩc meet in marriage. In Koĩc culture, spouses have to belong to different clans, and in each village one clan is dominant. After marriage, the women live in the household of their parents-in-law, which

---

8.   Candi is the major goddess of the Kiranti people and her annual festival is celebrated in larger Koĩc villages for one week in spring (Egli 1999: 251–252).

is often located in another village and thus might be located in another dialectal area. Speakers of different varieties also meet during major festivals which are celebrated exclusively in larger villages and attract visitors from smaller places. Nowadays Koïc speakers from different villages also meet in Kathmandu.

Intermarriage with members of other linguistic groups occurs in the villages and is common among young people in the city. In the case of intermarriage, Nepali is more likely to become the family language than any of the parents' other languages.

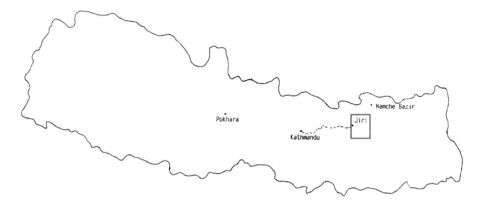

Map 1. Nepal with the square indicating the area traditionally inhabited by Koïc speakers.

1.4   Literature about Koïc person and number indexes

The publications about Koïc argument indexes as well as publications with Koïc texts are few. The data analysed in Section 2 were collected at four different points of time and at five different places. First, in the data and analysis of Stan Konow in the Linguistic Survey of Nepal, there are no biactantial indexes on the verbs. Konow's data was collected in the 19th century in Sikkim (India). The Koïc language of the Linguistic Survey of India differs from any Koïc data collected later.

In the 1970s, Dora Bieri and Marlene Schulze (1973) published a collection of Koïc texts from the village of Sabra (Ramechap district) and organised the translation of the Bible into Koïc. The text collection contains three sentences with biactantial agreement indexes, and in the Bible translation three examples were detected. The data allow a glimpse of the syntactical structure of phrases with biactantial indexes.

In the 1980s, Carol Genetti (1988) collected more than 50 paradigms of verbs with biactantial indexes with the help of a young man from Khiji (Okhaldhunga district). About 15 years after the publication of Genetti's analysis, Lal Rapacha

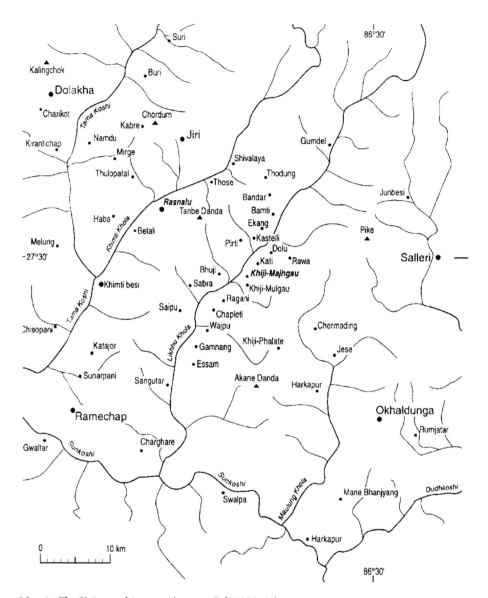

Map 2. The Koĭc speaking area (source: Egli 1999: 40)

(2005) published a grammar of Koĭc. Rapacha's grammar contains paradigms of verbs with subject indexes and texts collected with speakers from the villages of Khiji and Ragani (both Okhaldhunga district) and with a speaker in Sikkim (India), which contain no biactantial indexes.

I collected Koïc language data in the villages of Kubukastali and Bhuji (Ramechap district) and in Kathmandu with people from Saipu (Ramechap) and Khiji (Okhaldhunga) (Borchers 2008a), and those data contain no verbs with complex verbal inflection, i.e., no verbs indexing an object. Instead, the subject indexes show similarities to the complex paradigms in Genetti's data. The subject indexes of transitive verbs in the preterite tense are not the same for all verbs but follow one of three patterns, depending on the verb they are affixed to.

The data do not present a coherent picture of the regional distribution of complex forms (though of course the data set is rather small). The only full paradigm with complex verb indexes comes from Khiji (Okhaldhunga), which is also the source of a text without any biactantial form. In the material from Sabra (Ramechap), there are a few examples of biactantial indexes in texts, but not in other data from the same district. In addition, the biactantial forms are rather rare, even in the texts where they occur, compared to the number of other finite verb forms.

2.   Person and number indexes in Koïc

2.1   Biactantial indexing

Example (2) shows a biactantial form from Genetti (1988), indexing a second person dual subject and a first person singular object.

(2)   *gēē-tisi*
       give-PRT.2DU > 1SG'
       'You two gave me (something)'   (Genetti 1988: 71, Example 12)

In Surel, a language closely related to Koïc, biactantial indexing occurs though only rarely. Surel is spoken by descendants of Koïc who left one of the central Koïc villages around the end of the 19th century to migrate about 30 kilometres northwest, to a village in the Dolakha district.

In Surel, as in Koïc, verbs are as a rule only indexed for subjects, but the data from freely spoken texts collected between 2007 and 2013 contain one example of a verb with object as well as subject indexes (cf. Example 3).

(3)   *bak   pha   al-pishi   ge-da-ŋ-mi*
       chicken wing   child-PL   give-PRT-1SG(SBJ)>3PL(OBJ)
       'I gave some of the chicken, the wings [chicken curry] to the children.'
                                   (Topindrakumari Surel 2008: Chicken Curry)

The example above shows a finite transitive verb indexed for first person subject and third person plural object with suffixes that are the same in form and meaning as the equivalent Koĩc markers collected in the 1980s by Genetti (1988). In the example above, the subject is not mentioned explicitly. The object – *al-pishi* (child-PL) 'children' – is not marked by the object marker – *kali* 'OBJ', which may be suffixed to nouns, especially when the object is animate and not known from the context. Case marking in Example (3) does not differ from case marking in phrases with subject indexing only.

2.2   Subject and object indexes (Genetti 1988)

Carol Genetti (1988) published the first analysed data about Koĩc verb forms, collected about a hundred years after the data in the Linguistic Survey of Nepal. Genetti collected the data with the help of a linguistically interested and talented young speaker of Koĩc in Kathmandu, who had grown up in Khiji village in the district of Okhaldhunga in eastern Nepal. Genetti's informant wrote down 52 verbal paradigms with affirmative preterite forms showing subject and object indexing (cf. Table 1) as well as paradigms showing subject indexing only (Genetti 1988: 62; cf. Table 2).

In Table 1, each field is filled with two short suffix strings, one above the other. The upper suffix string represents Genetti's Conjugation 1, the lower suffix string represents Genetti's Conjugation 2. The two conjugations identified by Genetti differ with regard to the preterite tense marker that is the first suffix in each suffix string in Table 1. Verbs of Genetti's Conjugation 1, have a preterite tense marker that always has the same form -*tā*, and that is used in affirmative as well as in negative preterite tense forms. Verbs of Genetti's Conjugation 2 have a preterite tense marker with initial /t/ followed by a vowel, /a, i, e, u/, and have no preterite tense marker in negated preterite tense forms.

The tense marker is followed by one or two morphemes, which are the person and number indexes of the verb's subject and object.

A comparison of the transitive paradigm in Table 1 with the subject only indexing paradigm in Table 2 shows that the subject only indexing paradigm is included in the complex paradigm, namely in the row with third person singular object indexes.

The subject only indexing forms that were labelled by Genetti as structurally intransitive forms are also employed in transitive constructions. According to Genetti's informant, the subject and object indexing forms (cf. Table 1) might have been preferred when the object was to be emphasised, and the subject indexes (cf. Tables 2, 3) when the subject was to be emphasised (Genetti 1988: 81–82).

In the paradigm with only subject indexes, the indexes for a first person singular stand out because there is no form indexing a first person singular subject only, without also indexing the object. The first person singular subject and third

Table 1. Preterite tense, person and number indexes on stems of transitive verbs (Genetti 1988: 74). Parentheses mark items occurring occasionally and rather in slowly spoken language.

	O=1s	1d	1p	2s	2d	2p	3s	3d	3p
S=1s	Sunwari Transitive Past			tā-n	tā-n-si	tā-n-ni	tā-ŋ	tā-ŋ-si	tā-ŋ-mi
	Verb Forms (Affirmative)			ta-n	ta-n-si	ta-n-ni	tā-(ŋ)	tā-(ŋ)-si	tā-(ŋ)-mi
1d	Conjugation 1			tā-sku					
	Conjugation 2			ta-sku					
1p				tā-k(a)					
				ta-k(a)					
2s	tā-yi	tā-(yi)-ski	tā-(yi)-				tā-yi	tā-m-si	tā-mi
	ti-yi	ti-(yi)-ski	ki				ti-yi	ti-m-si	ti-mi
			ti-(yi)-						
			ki						
2d	tā-yi-si	tā-si					tā-si		
	ti-yi-si	ti-si					ti-si		
2p	tā-yi-si	tā-ni					tā-ni		
	ti-yi-si	ti-ni					ti-ni		
3s	tā-yi	tā-ski	tā-ki	tā-ye	tā-(ye)-si	tā-(ye)-	tā-u	tā-m-si	tā-mi
	ti	ti-ski	ti-ki	te	te-si/ti-si	ni	tu	ti-m-si	ti-mi
						te-ni/			
						ti-ni			
3d	tā-(yi)-si	tā-s(e)		tā-ye-si	tā-s(e)				
	ti-si	te-s		te-si	te-s				
3p	tā-(yi)-mi	tā-m(e)		tā-ye-mi	tā-m(e)				
	ti-mi	te-m		te-mi	te-m				

person singular object (1SG>3SG) index is only used, when the object is indeed a third person singular. For indexing a first person singular subject, the appropriate index from the complex paradigm has to be chosen. With, for example, a first person singular subject and a second person plural object (1SG>2PL), the index on the verb can only be the appropriate form from the complex paradigm, namely -tānni (Genetti's Conjugation 1) or -tanni (Genetti's Conjugation 2).

The table with the complex paradigm (Table 1) shows that there is not a specific, unambiguous index for every possible subject and object combination. This means that also by employing forms from the complex paradigm, the object might not be indexed at all, or the person and number of the object might not be indexed unambiguously.

With a first or a third person singular subject, there is a distinct form to index the person and number of each possible object. This is different for indexes for first person dual and first person plural subjects, which each have one single form. For first person dual and first person plural subjects, there is no object indexing on the verb.

For a second person dual subject, the complex paradigm (Table 1) contains two indexes. One indexes a second person dual subject and a first person singular object (2DU>1SG). The other one indexes a second person dual subject and any object that is not a first person singular (2DU>non1SG).

Genetti's paradigm contains optional morphemes and optional word final vowels in parentheses. The presence of the optional morphemes disambiguates subject and object indexes, which without the optional vowels would have the same form. For example, a second person singular subject and a first person plural object (2SG>1PL) are indexed by -tā-(yi)-ki (Conjugation 1) or -ti-(yi)-ki (Conjugation 2). Without the optional morpheme, the index has the form -tā-ki (Conjugation 1) or -ti-ki (Conjugation 2), which also indexes a third person singular subject and a first person plural object (3SG>1PL). According to Genetti, the optional morphemes may be omitted in quick speech and in that case the form of the verb would not indicate whether the subject acting upon a first person object is a second or a third person singular.

Table 2. Subject only indexing suffixes – structurally intransitive morphemes that are used with transitive verbs (Genetti 1988: 82)

1SG	[complex forms from Table 1]
2SG	-yi
3SG	-u
1DU	-sku
2DU	-si
3DU	-s(e)
1PL	-k(a)
2PL	-ni
3PL	-m(e)

The Koĭc paradigm in Table 1 is not unique among Kiranti languages in not having a specific form for every possible subject and object combination.

A look at Khaling (Jacques et al. 2012: 1102), Hayu (Michailovsky 1988: 82; Michailovsky 2003: 521) and Bahing (cf. Table 7, Table 8; van Driem 1991 with data from Hodgson 1858 and Michailovsky 1975) shows that these languages also have the most unambiguous subject and object indexing forms for singular subjects.

For Bahing, a comparison of the paradigm with data from Hodgson (1858) with data collected by Michailovsky (1975; both as cited in van Driem 1991: 339–340) shows a decline in the variety of forms between the older and the newer paradigm. In the paradigm based on Michailovsky's data (1975), there is only one index for a first person plural exclusive and a second person object (1PL>2) of any number. In the paradigm based on Hodgson's data, the indexes for the same relationships still distinguish the number of the object (cf. Table 7, Table 8).

A similar development, namely the syncretism of indexes resulting in a smaller number of forms that are more ambiguous, might have also happened in Koïc before the language was documented.

2.3 Subject indexing in modern Koïc (Borchers 2008a)

Finite verbs in modern Koïc have tense markers followed by subject indexes that contain information about the subject's person and number. Objects are not indexed.

Table 3. Person and number indexes for subjects in modern Koïc in the affirmative preterite tense. Suffixes for the singular, indicated here by [variety] are presented in Table 5. The left column shows Genetti's subject indexing suffixes for comparison.

	(Genetti 1988)	(Borchers 2008a)
1SG	[see first person singular subject and object indexing forms in Table 3]	[variety; see Table 5]
2SG	-yi	[variety; see Table 5]
3SG	-u	[variety; see Table 5]
1DU	-sku	-sku
2DU	-si	-si
3DU	-s(e)	-s(e)
1PL	-k(a)	-k(a)
2PL	-ni	-ni
3PL	-m(e)	-m(e)

The major differences between Genetti's data and the more recent data from villages in the Ramechap district concern the singular person indexes. In Genetti's data, the first person singular is the only person that is always indexed by combined subject and object markers.

In modern Koïc, each verb belongs to one of five conjugations. There are three transitive (Conjugation 1–3), one intransitive (Conjugation 4) and one reflexive (Conjugation 5) conjugation, which differ with regard to the singular person indexes in the preterite tense forms.

Most intransitive and transitive verbs conjugate according to one of the intransitive or transitive conjugation patterns only. There are a few verbs that conjugate according to the reflexive conjugation pattern only. With a reflexive suffix, transitive verbs can be transformed into reflexive verbs.

Interestingly, a few verbs conjugate according to transitive Conjugation 1 or intransitive Conjugation 4, depending on the presence or absence of an object in the same phrase, for example the verb *kīcā* 'to stretch'. Verbs that can take Conjugation 1 as well as Conjugation 4 indexes can also be transformed into reflexive verbs and conjugate according to reflexive Conjugation 5. In that case, the verb indicates an increased effort in performing the activity referred to (Borchers 2008a: 120–122). Most verbs belonging to one of the transitive conjugations have transitive indexes, independent of the presence or absence of an explicit reference to an object in the same phrase (Borchers 2008a: 120–122).[9]

Most transitive verbs belong to Conjugation 1. The verbs of Conjugation 3 (Genetti's Conjugation 1) occasionally occur with the tense, person, and number markers of Conjugation 1, which might be an indication of another ongoing language change.

The verbs of Conjugation 3 feature an unvarying preterite tense marker /-tā/ (cf. Example 7), which differs from the tense marker /-tV/ for Conjugations 1 and 2 (cf. Example 8 for Conjugation 2). In addition, Conjugation 3 is the only conjugation that has a tense marker for negated preterite tense forms. Conjugations 1 and 2, intransitive Conjugation 4 and reflexive Conjugation 5 do not have a tense marker for negated preterite tense forms. The small group of Conjugation 2 verbs have singular person indexes that are almost the same as those of Conjugation 1 in the affirmative preterite tense forms. The negative preterite forms indexing first or third person singular are different. In addition, Conjugation 2 verbs have stems that show regular stem variations, unlike the verbs of other conjugations.[10]

Table 3 illustrates the person and number suffixes for preterite tense forms in modern Koīc. The dual and plural forms are the same for the transitive and

---

9.   Like other Tibeto-Burman languages, Koīc has transitive and intransitive verb pairs, which share the same form except for the initial. Transitive verbs in these pairs have an unvoiced initial plosive, and intransitive verbs have a voiced initial plosive of the same place of articulation (Borchers 2008a: 122). These verbs behave like other transitive or intransitive verbs that have no transitive or intransitive counterpart.

10.   An example of stem variation of Conjugation 2 is the verb *pa-cā* (do-INF) 'to do', that has a stem *pam-* (do-) in *pam-te-me* (do-PRT-3PL) 'they did' with the 3rd person plural affirmative preterite tense form.

intransitive conjugations. The conjugations differ with regard to singular person and number indexes (cf. Table 4; cf. Examples 4, 5, 6). The negative preterite tense person indexes are included in Table 5 to illustrate the difference in person indexing between Conjugations 1 and 2, which is not present for the affirmative preterite person indexes. Please note that the differences between the forms of the argument indexes of the different conjugations are small, but occur regularly in freely spoken texts as well as in elicited paradigms.

Table 4. Koĩc singular person indexes in the preterite tense (Borchers 2008a: 118).

	affirmative					negative				
	C1tr	C2tr	C3tr	C4itr	C5rf	C1tr	C2tr	C3tr	C4itr	C5rf
1SG	ta	ta	ŋ	tī	ŋ(a)	u	ŋ	tu	ŋa	ŋ(a)
2SG	tī	tī(wi)	ī	te	e	ī	ī(wi)	tī	e	se
3SG	tu	tu	u	t(a)	u	a	u	ta	—	se

(4) ca   sat   kḷas   pare-tā-ŋā
     six seven class learn-PRT-1SG
     '… and I went to school up to about class seven.'   (Borchers 2008a: 250)

(5) saṃsa go   ka   me   pā-tā
     world 1.SG/DU/PL one what do-PRT.1SG
     'what could I do alone…'   (Dalkumari Sunuwar, Rec 2008)

(6) min nole didi   yo   kathmandu pi-ta
     and later older.sister also Kathmandu come-PRT.3SG
     'and then sister also went to Kathmandu.'   (Borchers 2008a: 250)

2.4   The former and the current system of indexing arguments

There is a regular relation between the forms and functions of subject and object indexes and subject indexes (cf. Table 5, 6). Forms that index singular subjects and a third person singular object (1/2/3SG>3SG) in the complex paradigm are transitive subject indexes in the paradigm with only subject indexes (cf. vertically outlined forms in Table 5 below and columns for C1, 2, 3 in Table 6). Biactantial indexes for a third person singular subject and singular object indexes (3SG>1/2/3SG) are the current intransitive singular subject indexes (cf. Example 14, and the horizontally outlined forms in Table 5, and the column for C4 in Table 5). For example, a first person singular subject index for a transitive verb of C1 or C2 has in the affirmative preterite the form -ta(ŋ), which indexes in the complex paradigm a first person singular subject and a third person singular object (1SG>3SG).

Table 5. Person and number indexes of subjects and objects on stems of transitive verbs (based on Genetti 1988: 74)

	P=1s	1d	1p	2s	2d	2p	3s	3d	3p
A=1s	Sunwari Transitive Past			-n	-n-si	-n-ni	-ŋ	-ŋ-si	-ŋ-mi
	Verb Forms (Affirmative)			-n	-n-si	-n-ni	-(ŋ)	-(ŋ)-si	-(ŋ)-mi
1d	Conjugation 1						-sku		
	Conjugation 2						-sku		
1p							-k(a)		
							-k(a)		
2s	-yi	-(yi)-ski	-(yi)-ki				-yi	-m-si	-mi
	-yi	-(yi)-ski	-(yi)-ki				-yi	-m-si	-mi
2d	-yi-si	-si						-si	
	-yi-si	-si						-si	
2p	-yi-si	-ni						-ni	
	-yi-si	-ni						-ni	
3s	-yi	-ski	-ki	-ye	-(ye)-si	-(ye)-ni	-u	-m-si	-mi
	-ti	-ski	-ki	te	-si/ti-si	-ni/ti-ni	tu	-m-si	-mi
3d	-(yi)-si	-s(e)		-ye-si			-s(e)		
	-si	-s		-si			-s		
3p	-(yi)-mi	-m(e)		-ye-mi			-m(e)		
	-mi	-m		-mi			-m		

Table 6. Person and number indexes of subjects in modern Koĭc in the affirmative preterite tense. The vertical column on the left side indicates the person indexed by the markers in the modern subject indexing paradigm. The columns filled by numbers and arrows indicate the same form's function in the former biactantial argument indexing paradigm, e.g., first person subject and third person object (1 > 3).

	C1, C2 (transitive)		C3 (transitive)		C4 (intransitive)		C5 (reflexive)	
1SG	ta(ŋ)	1 > 3	ŋ	1 > 3	tī	3 > 1	ŋ(a)	1 > 3
2SG	tī	2 > 1/3	ī	2 > 1/3	te	3 > 2	e	3 > 2
3SG	tu	3 > 3	u	3 > 3	ta	[zero]	u	3s

Historical evidence from Bahing (cf. Section 2.4 and Appendix) shows that a reduction of forms and unambiguous distinctions is not a process observable uniquely in Koĭc.

The simplification of complex verbal paradigms seems to also happen in other Kiranti languages even though it is not clear whether this is part of a process resulting in the loss of morphology or just a switching between more and less finite forms. Michailovsky (2017: 16–17) mentions that it was observed for several Kiranti languages that some speakers had difficulty producing specific biactantial forms. They would instead use simpler indexes, in which the number of the subject or object might not be distinguished, or they would even use non-finite forms.

While the morphological and semantic relationship between the biactantial indexes and the subject indexes of Koĭc is undeniable, the process that resulted in the loss of object indexing cannot be reconstructed on the basis of data from

Genetti (1988) and Borchers (2008a). There are a few more sources about Koĭc collected at different times and at different places, which might help to understand the historical development resulting in the loss of object indexation. These are introduced in section 3.

3. Person and number indexes - Additional data

3.1 Konow (1909), Bieri & Schulze (1973) and Rapacha (2005)

In the previous section, the Koĭc argument indexing system was introduced by summarising the data from Genetti (1988) and Borchers (2008a). The result of the change in Koĭc (namely the loss of object indexation), was demonstrated, but not the process that led to this result. In order to shed light on this process, I will now discuss further sources with Koĭc data, collected at different times and in different places.

3.2 Linguistic Survey of India (Konow 1909)

In an early description of Himalayan languages in the Linguistic Survey of India (Konow 1909), Himalayan languages are divided into two categories, pronomi-nalised languages and non-pronominalised languages. Pronominalised languages have a complex argument indexing system with subjects as well as objects being indexed on transitive verbs. Koĭc (called Sunwār or Sunuwār in the survey) was classified as a non-pronominalised language, together with the Tibeto-Burman languages Newar, Magar, Lepcha and others (Konow 1909).

In the subchapter on Koĭc, Konow provides a short description of grammatical features of the language and a glossed Bible text translated from English. The text was collected in Kathmandu (Nepal) and forms the basis of Konow's description of the language, along with a vocabulary list compiled in Darjeeling (India).

Konow (1909: 201) states that Koĭc verbs in the sample text do not have subject indexes. The text, however, does contain verbs with subject indexes that are the same as those employed in the modern Koĭc language in Nepal (cf. Example 7). The finite verb in Example (7) could occur in the same form with the same meaning in a modern Koĭc text. The text collected by Konow contains other person and number suffixes, which index the subject but which differ from modern indexes. An example is the verb form *gep-to* (give-PRT2/3SG) 'she or he gave', 'you gave'. The morpheme *<-to>* indexes a second as well as a third person singular subject (cf. Example 8a, b). In modern Koĭc there are two different suffixes for indexing a second person singular and a third person singular subject respectively illustrated with the same verb, *gep-ti* (give-PRT.2SG) and *gep-tu* (give-PRT.3SG). The verbal morphology in the text collected and analysed by Konow does not cover all forms necessary to fill a paradigm of subject indexes. What becomes clear, however, is that the language in the text, does contain subject indexes.

(7)   *tup-ni-mi*
      beat-NPRT-3PL
      'they beat'   (Konow 1909: 202)

(8)   a.   *meko wāilī   jawab   gep-to*   ...
           that   servant answer give-PRT.2/3SG ...
           'That servant answered ...'   (Konow 1909: 205)

      b.   *aur ga   genāi gep-to*   ...
           and you ever   give-PRT.2/3SG ...
           'And you gave ...'   (Konow 1909: 205)

Konow points out that the translation of the English Bible text into Koïc reproduces English word order and might not represent the language well (1909: 181).

Konow (1909: 181) remarks in the Linguistic Survey of India that Brian Houghton Hodgson had classified Koïc as a pronominalised language and suggests that it may still be pronominalised even though his data seem to contradict this possibility. Konow claims that the apparent loss of subject and object indexes on finite verbs is a result of language change triggered by contact with Tibetan languages.

The Koïc data in the Linguistic Survey of India were collected before 1909 in Kathmandu (Nepal) and in Darjeeling (India), outside of traditionally Koïc speaking villages. These data are not accompanied by any metadata about the linguistic and social background of those who provided the language data. It was not recorded whether Koïc was spoken regularly in the family and in the neighbourhood of the informants and which other language(s) might have had an influence on the informants' variety of Koïc – be it at work or in community affairs.

At the time the data for the Linguistic Survey of India were collected, the Koïc language in villages in Nepal was undocumented. The differences between the Koïc language data in the Linguistic Survey of India and more recent data cannot be explained by language change over time alone. The word order with the object more often following than preceding the verb as well as the absence of object indexes and similar linguistic peculiarities might very well be due to the fact that the translator tried to produce a Koïc text structurally close to the English original, as suggested by Konow (1909: 181).

The argument indexing system documented in this early source on Koïc differs from the systems documented later. Even though the section about Koïc in the Linguistic Survey of India provides no evidence for a complex paradigm with subject and object indexes for the language, the biactantial indexing system must have been in use in other places, as the later documentation of such a system shows.

3.3   Subject and object indexes (Bieri & Schulze 1973)

In 1973, Dora Bieri and Marlene Schulze from the Summer Institute of Linguistics published a collection of 11 glossed and translated texts, which they collected with the help of Koĩc speakers from the village of Sabra in Ramechap district. They also coordinated the translation of the Bible into Koĩc, which is the largest written Koĩc text (Without Author 2011).[11]

Bieri and Schulze's text collection contains three finite verbs that are glossed as being indexed for two actants, and in the translation of the Bible four verbal forms were detected, which match forms of the complex paradigm published by Genetti (1988). Of the four complex forms in the Bible, three are identical, *śētānnī* 'I taught you' (plural; 1SG>2PL) and occur in two sentences (Example 9, Example 10) following each other in the same paragraph.[12]

Bieri and Schulze did not publish paradigms of the verb forms they encountered in Sabra, and the complex forms in their texts and in the Bible cover only a small part of a possibly larger complex paradigm.

Case marking in this rather small collection of six sentences with complex verbs shows no significant difference to case marking in phrases with only subject indexes. Actants known from the context are not mentioned explicitly (Examples 9, 10, 11, 12, 13, 14), and there is a case marker suffixed to the only mentioned actant. Only in Example (9) are there pronominal forms referring to subject and object of the biactantial verb, and the one referring to the object is marked as such.

Bieri and Schulze's forms of the complex verbal morphology differ slightly from Genetti's complex forms with regard to a final glottal stop in the tense marker where Genetti's equivalent morpheme shows a nasal, which is optional in one of the two conjugations. This difference might be due to dialectal variation.

(9)   ...*meko as-kali rim-sho pa*
      ...these two-benefactor well-adverbializer do

---

11.   Translated texts are not an ideal basis for the linguistic analysis of a language. A few of the problems with the language of translations are mentioned in Section 2.2 with regard to the Linguistic Survey of India. As the translation of the New Testament is the longest written text in Koĩc, the few complex verbal forms detected in this publication are still presented here.

12.   The digital version of the Bible translation was searched for forms that in Genetti's complex paradigm (1988) and in Bieri and Schulze's texts (1973) index subject and object unambiguously. The Bible translation might contain further subject and object indexing verbs with indexes that differ in shape from those searched for.

woyk-taak-si[13]
put-1SG-3DU,undergoer,past
'… I let the two girls settle in.' (Bieri & Schulze 1973: 436; Text 1, Sentence 9)

(10)   *Minu aphis kaam pa nga min,*
and office work do and then

marlen didi nu dori didi -m
Marlene big.sister and dori big.sister agent

tsutti ge-ti-si
leiasure time give 1SG undergoer -3DU.agent.past

'After I had done the office work Marlene and Dori let me go.'
(Bieri & Schulze 1973: 441; Text 2, sentence 5)

(11)   *Minu meko -puki -m laak -tsa*
And these -plural -agent go -infinitive

ma-ge-yi-mi
negative-give-1SG,undergoer -3PL,agent

'They did not allow me to pass.'
(Bieri & Schulze 1973: 441; Text 2, sentence 7)

(12)   बाक्नीनी। मनु परमप्रभु यावे, आं परमप्रभुमी आं कली अरेशो खोदेंशो पा,
गो इन कली आ फुल्लुम मुशा ब्रेक्शो लोव् नु आ निसाफ पतीक लोव् शेंतान्नी।[14]
bāk-nī-nī. minu paramprabhu yāve, ā paramprabhu-mī ā kali
see-NPRT-IMP.POLITE and Lord Yave, my Lord-SBJ me OBJ

are-śo khodēśo pā,
order-PTCP such do

go in kalī ā phullu-m mu-śā brek-śo lov' nu
I you OBJ his stone-LOC engrave-PF write-PTCP word and

nisāph pa-tīk lov' śē-tā-nnī.
justice do-NZN word teach-PRT-1SG>2PL

'Please see! As Yave, my Lord ordered me to do, I taught you his written
word, engraved in stone, about his commands and his word about justice.'
(Without Author 2011: page 291; 5. Moses 4, Section 5)

(13)   मारदे शेंतान्नी देंशा हना, गेजाक्शा इन के सेल्चा चक्शिो रागीमी मेको
नेल्ल पचा, दे शेंतान्नी।

mārde śē-tā-nnī dē-śā hanā, ge jāk-śā in ke sel-cā
why teach-PRT-1SG>2PL say-PF if, you go-PF you GEN build-INF

---

13.   Bieri and Schulze use the sign 'k' to represent in writing a syllable final glottal stop in
spoken language. The glosses of the examples (9, 10, 11) are Bieri and Schulze's.

14.   I thank Lal Rapacha for his assistance with glossing the sentences from the Koïc Bible.

cikā-śo rāgī-mī meko nell pa-cā, de śē-tā-nnī
dare-PTCP kingdom-LOC that all do-INF say teach-PRT-1SG>2PL

'I taught you so that you, after going to the kingdom, which you are going to build, do all this.'   (Without Author 2011: page 291; 5. Moses 4, Section 5)

(14)   मनु गे लने। भेडा पाठा आन कली फर आन दातेमी सोइश्शो खोदेंशो पा सोइक्तानूनी।

minu ge la-ne bheḍā pāṭhā ān kalī
and you go-IMP sheep lamb them OBJ

phar ān dāte-mī soiś-śo khodēśo pā soik-tā-nnī.
jackal them middle-LOC send-PTCP such do send-PRT-1SG>2PL

'And go! I sent you like lambs having been sent among jackals.'
(Without Author 2011: page 1564 Lukas 10:3)

3.4   Subject indexing in modern Koĭc (Rapacha 2005)

In two sections (2005: 200, 204) of his grammar of the Koĭc language, Lal Rapacha (2005) presents affirmative preterite tense paradigms of two transitive verbs, which have, with small phonological differences,[15] the same indexes as those presented in Table 3 in the first column. In Rapacha's transitive paradigm, the first person singular subject index is *-ŋ*, which indexes a first person singular subject and a third person singular object (1SG>3SG) in the complex paradigm. Rapacha (2005: 183–184) distinguishes a transitive and an intransitive verb class based on their first person subject indexes but he doesn't provide a paradigm of the intransitive paradigm. The first person subject index for transitive verbs is *-ta-ŋ* and for intransitive verbs *-ti*.

Rapacha does not discuss biactantial indexes of Koĭc. The grammar contains three Koĭc texts (Rapacha 2005: 363–391) that were collected with two speakers from the villages of Khiji and Ragani in Okhaldhunga and one text collected with a speaker from Bhusuk (Sikkim, India). These texts do not contain a single example of a verb that would feature an unambiguous complex subject and object index.

3.5   More data – Better explanations?

The additional data provide additional information but instead of clarifying the process that resulted in loss of object indexing, they rather reveal complexity.

Konow's (1909) language sample, which does not contain any biactantial indexes, might not be representative of the language use at his time, as he himself points out, and therefore might be disregarded here.

---

15.   One of the small differences is, for example, the index for a third person plural subject, which is *-t?*(*m*) in Rapacha 2005: 200, 204), and *-te*(*m*) in Genetti (1988) and Borchers (2008a).

Bieri and Schulze (1973) and Rapacha (2005) present data collected in the 1970s and 1990s in different places in eastern Nepal and Sikim.

Rapacha (2005) mentions different sets of transitive and intransitive subject person and number indexes for Koïc, similar to Borchers (2008a). He (2005: 183–184) points out that Koïc has a transitive and an intransitive verb class, which are distinguished by the first person subject indexes -ta-ŋ and -ti respectively, but he doesn't provide more information about the intransitive conjugation pattern. Borchers (2008a: 144–151, 158–159) provides paradigms for the three transitive, the intransitive, and the reflexive conjugations, collected with Koïc speakers from Saipu, Bhuji (both Ramechap) and Khiji (Okhaldhunga).

In the text collection of Bieri and Schulze (1973), verbs occur with transitive and intransitive subject indexes, for example la-ti (go-PRT1SG) 'I went (away)' (1973: 433; text 1, 5). The same texts also contain verbs indexed for both, subject and object (cf. Section 23.3). This shows that both, the complex paradigm and different subject conjugation patterns, were part of the repertoire of Koïc speakers in Saipu in the 1970s. When and how the different conjugation patterns emerged is unknown. They are not mentioned in Genetti's (1988) study, which mentions only one subject indexing conjugation pattern that is used with all verbs.

The additional data do not answer the question as to how object indexing in Koïc was lost. They do not provide insights into the geographical or temporal diffusion of the loss. With the additional data the picture becomes even less clear. And even with the additional data, it has become clear that the data are too limited to answer the questions about the process behind the loss of morphology.

4.   Loss of morphology – Language change

The loss of object marking in Koïc deserves an explanation because such a loss of verbal morphology has not been reported to have happened in other Kiranti languages, which are spoken in similar sociolinguistic settings to Koïc. Autonomous language change and change triggered by language contact will be considered as possible causes as well as the possibility of the change being limited to one regional variety or to a specific generation.

The loss of morphology may happen with or without language contact. The employment of plural indexes instead of appropriate dual indexes in the village of Kubukasthali (Ramechap) (see 1.3) could be the beginning of a language change caused by contact with Nepali, which has no dual category. There is more contact with Nepali in Kubukasthali than in villages with a Koïc majority. Examples from other languages, such as modern Arabic varieties, show, however, that the loss of the category dual is not always the result of language contact but may be an autonomous development (Kusters 2003: 157, 365).

In the case of Koĩc, the systematic connection between the complex and the subject indexing paradigm is considered to be the result of a historical development. The morphology in both paradigms shows systematic connections in form and function. A loss of morphological diversity also took place in Bahing (Section 2.4; Appendix). Tendencies to morphological loss and simplification have also been reported for other Kiranti languages (Michailovsky 2017: 17; Section 3). Even though the changes in the verbal inflection systems of other Kiranti language are less extensive than in Koĩc, the direction of the changes towards fewer formal distinctions is the same.

Language contact is a likely reason for the observed changes in Koĩc. According to the literature about language change, grammatical change occurs in the context of widespread and long-standing bilingualism (Heine & Kuteva 2005; Kusters 2003; Matras 2009; Thomason & Kaufman 1988; van Coetsem 2000). Heine and Kuteva (2005: 13) state that grammatical structures may be copied in both directions, from the bilinguals' dominant language into their other language, or in the opposite direction. Other linguists note that the likely direction is a copying from the bilinguals' dominant language into their other language, which is likely to be a socially or politically dominant language (Matras 2009; Thomason & Kaufman 1988; van Coetsem 2000). In the case of Koĩc, most speakers are bilingual with Nepali and this has been the case for a long time. However, Koĩc does not have a large group of people learning the language as a second language. Theoretically, there could be a group of bilinguals with Koĩc and Nepali whose dominant language is Nepali, who transfer language structures from Nepali to Koĩc. These new structures could then be copied by other Koĩc speakers. There is, however, no evidence for the existence of such a group. At the moment, the loss of object indexing seems to be a language change initiated by people for whom Koĩc is the dominant language.

The parallel use of the biactantial and the subject indexing forms with the former being much rarer than the latter has been documented by Bieri and Schulze (1973). Such a co-occurrence of older and newer grammatical structures with similar and overlapping functions is what Heine and Kuteva (2005: 44–54) label major and minor usage patterns, with the older pattern being used less and less and the newer one occurring more and more often and also occurring in contexts, in which once the older forms were formerly more appropriate (46, 50).

The evidence from Koĩc can be – to some extent – accommodated by the framework of Wouter Kusters (2003) and shows parallels to Spanish in Los Angeles, as presented by Carmen Silva-Corvalán (1994), with regard to both, the sociolinguistic situation and the loss of grammatical categories.

Kusters (2003) analysed the role that the structure of a society plays in the complexity or the simplicity of verbal inflection on the basis of several varieties of four languages, which include Scandinavian as a group of closely related languages.[16] According to his study, small, close-knit societies have rather complex verbal inflection systems, whereas languages with many first and second language speakers distributed over a large geographic area tend to have simpler inflection systems (Kusters 2003: 365). A factor causing the simpler structure of a geographically widespread language would be the adaptation of native speakers to the simpler version of their language spoken by non-native speakers, in order to be better understood by the latter. This simpler variety might be learned by the community's children (Kusters 2003: 110).[17] Kusters shows how object indexing was lost in such scenarios in Ecuadorian Quechua and in Katanga Swahili, which lost object indexing for one of several noun classes (Kusters 2003: 74).

The loss of object indexing in Koĩc can be compared to the examples discussed by Kusters as simplification, but the sociolinguistic situation of Koĩc is different. Koĩc is neither spoken by a close-knit society nor in a rather loosely connected society, which would include second language speakers. Koĩc speakers who live in the villages are not all in close contact with each other but there is communication and there are visits between the villagers. Certainly, the loss of object indexing in Koĩc cannot be explained by any scenario, in which second language learners' mistakes or simplifications influence the language use of competent mother tongue speakers of the language. The number of people who spoke or are speaking Koĩc as a second language is unknown, but certainly the number is low. On the other hand, the Surel, whose forefathers and -mothers left one of the larger Koĩc villages around the beginning of the 20th century, use biactantial indexes.[18] The centre of Surel social life is the village of Suri-Mulgaon. The speakers of Surc, as they call their language, are related to each other, are neighbours and meet about daily (Borchers 2008b). Therefore, the two closely related languages, Koĩc and Surc,

---

16.   Matras (2005) also focusses on sociolinguistic factors influencing language change in contact situations. For Matras the place of language change is more limited than for Kusters, namely the communicative event, in which people adapt their linguistic behaviour to a specific situation and to a specific communication partner.

17.   This connection between community size and language retention is not dissimilar from Thomason and Kaufman's claim that speakers of a dominant contact language are likely to integrate the mistakes made by large numbers of second language learners into their language, which thereby undergoes change (1988: 50).

18.   Members of the Surel and the Koĩc community confirm independently of each other that their community split at the beginning of the 20th century.

confirm the conclusion of Kusters's study that small communities tend to have more complex verbal inflection patterns. Kusters's framework is likely be useful for further research into the change of verbal inflection in varieties of Koĭc, as already the small comparison with Surc shows.

Silva-Corvalán's (1994) sociolinguistic study of Spanish in Los Angeles addresses language change in a very diverse community. The members of the Spanish speaking community live in an environment that is to some extent comparable to that of a Koĭc village in Nepal. The loss of morphology observed in Koĭc may be caused by similar factors to those responsible for changes in Spanish in Los Angeles. The Spanish speakers in Los Angeles are confronted with English as the dominant language of administration, education and in the media, which has been spoken as a second mother tongue by many community members for generations. There are young community members who are incomplete learners of Spanish, and new community members might be Spanish monolinguals.

Silva-Corvalán (1994: 4–5, 133) observed that two groups of Spanish speakers in Los Angeles spoke a non-standard variety of the language, namely the young incomplete leaners as well as the competent bilinguals. The incomplete learners in Silva-Corvalán's study didn't acquire, for example the category of nominal gender. The competent bilinguals tended to diverge from the standard language by transferring features from one language to the other.[19] In addition, the bilinguals used Spanish in fewer and fewer domains of life.

The linguistic situation in a Koĭc village is comparable with that of Spanish in Los Angeles, in that there is a long-standing bilingualism with the politically dominant language Nepali and bilinguals switch between both languages regularly. Especially young people in Nepal use Nepali in more and more domains. Unlike earlier generations, they have access to education, radio, maybe even TV, which is all available in Nepali, and they travel more than their parents' generation.

The loss of object indexing in Koĭc seems not to have influenced the syntactic structure of the language but rather triggered the emergence of new verbal inflection patterns. What remains unclear is when and where the process of the loss of object indexes began and how it proceeded. In this paper, it was argued that the structural loss was initiated by the linguistic behaviour of Koĭc-Nepali bilinguals, who transferred structures from the dominant administrative language to their mother tongue.

---

19. Thomason and Kaufman (1988: 47–48) already pointed out that competent bilinguals tend to transfer structural features from the socially or politically dominant language to their first language, and might thereby cause their first language to change substantially.

5. Summary

The loss of object indexing in Koĩc is the result of a grammatical change that can only be observed in other Kiranti languages to a much lesser extent. Due to the heterogeneity and scarcity of Koĩc data, the process that resulted in the change of the language is not reconstructable. The speakers of Koĩc are bilingual with Nepali, and it was argued here that the loss of object indexation happened under the influence of Nepali, which does not feature biactantial indexes.

Hypotheses about the process of language change, which can be tested only with additional data, are that the initiators of change were bilinguals with Nepali as their dominant language or that they were competent speakers, who adapted their language to that of less competent speakers.

Abbreviations

1, 2, 3 = 1st, 2nd, 3rd person, 1SG>2SG = first person singular subject and second person singular object, DU = Dual, IMP = imperative, IMP.POLITE = polite imperative, INF = infinitive, INS = Instrumental, NEG = negative, NPRT = non preterite tense, NZN = nominalisation, LOC = locative, OBJ = object, PF = perfect gerund, PL = plural, PRT = preterite tense, PTCP = preterite tense participle, SBJ = subject, SG = singular, / = or

References

Bieri, Dora, Schulze, Marlene & Hale, Austin. 1973. An approach to Sunwar discourse. In *Clause, Sentence, and Discourse Patterns in Selected Languages of Nepal*, Austin Hale (ed.), 433–462. Norman OK: Summer Institute of the University of Oklahoma.

Borchers, Dörte. 2008a. *A Grammar of Sunwar. Descriptive Grammar, Paradigms, Texts and Glossary* [Languages of the greater Himalayan region 5.7]. Leiden: Brill.

Borchers, Dörte. 2008b. Surelgãũko surelbhãṣā (The Surel language in the village of Suri). *Sirmī* 7 (6): 63.

Central Bureau of Statistics. 2012. *National Population and Housing Census 2011*. Kathmandu: Government of Nepal.

Commissioner for Linguistic Minorities. 2011. *48th Report of the Commissioner for Linguistic Minorities in India (July 2010 to June 2011)*. Allahabad: Ministry of Minority Affairs, Government of India. <http://nclm.nic.in/shared/linkimages/nclm48threport.pdf> (14 April 2017).

DeLancey, Scott. 2011. "Optional" "ergativity" in Tibeto-Burman languages. *Linguistics of the Tibeto-Burman Area* 34 (2): 9–20.

DeLancey, Scott. 2014. Creolization in the divergence of the Tibeto-Burman languages. In *Trans-Himalayan Linguistics. Historical and Descriptive Linguistics of the Himalayan Area* [Trends in Linguistics. Studies and Monographs [TiLSM] 266], Thomas Owen-Smith & Nathan Hill (eds), 41–68. Berlin: De Gruyter Mouton.

van Driem, George. 1991. Bahing and the Proto-Kiranti verb. *Bulletin of the School of Oriental and African Studies LIV*(2): 336–356. https://doi.org/10.1017/S0041977X00014828

Egli, Werner M. 1999. *Bier für die Ahnen. Erbrecht, Tausch und Ritual bei den Sunuwar Ostnepals.* Frankfurt: Verlag für Interkulturelle Kommunikation (IKO).

Genetti, Carol. 1988. Notes on the structure of the Sunwari transitive verb. *Linguistics in the Tibeto-Burman Area* 11 (2): 62–92.

Hodgson, Brian Houghton. 1858. Comparative vocabulary of the languages of the broken Tribes of Nepál. *Journal of the Asiatic Society of Bengal XXVII*: 393–456.

Jacques, Guillaume, Lahaussois, Aimée, Michailovsky, Boyd & Bahadur Rai, Dhan. 2012. An overview of Khaling verbal morphology. *Language and Linguistics* 13(6): 1095–1170. <http://crlao.ehess.fr/docannexe/file/1739/khaling_verb.pdf> (3 October 2019).

Heine, Bernd & Kuteva, Tania. 2005. *Language Contact and Grammatical Change* [Cambridge Approaches to Language Contact]. Cambridge: CUP. https://doi.org/10.1017/CBO9780511614132

Konow, Stan. 1909. Sunwār or Sunuwār. In *Linguistic Survey of India, Vol. III: Tibeto-Burman Family, Part I: General Introduction, Specimens of the Tibetan Dialects, the Himalayan Dialects, and the North Assam Group*, George Abraham Grierson (ed.), 198–205. Calcutta (Kolkata): Superintendent of Government Printing, India. <http://dsal.uchicago.edu/books/lsi/lsi.php?volume=3-1&pages=670#page/29/mode/1up> (18 March 2019).

Kusters, Wouter. 2003. *Linguistic Complexity. The Influence of Social Change on Verbal Inflection.* Utrecht: LOT. <https://www.lotpublications.nl/documents/77_fulltext.pdf> (12 October 2019).

Matras, Yaron. 2009. *Language Contact* [Cambridge Textbooks in Linguistics]. Cambridge: CUP.

Michailovsky, Boyd. 1975. Notes on the Kiranti verb (East Nepal). *Linguistics of the Tibeto-Burman Area II* (2): 183–218.

Michailovsky, Boyd. 1988. *La Langue Hayu.* Paris: Editions du Centre National de la Recherche Scientifique.

Michailovsky, Boyd. 2003. Hayu. In *The Sino-Tibetan Languages* [Routledge Language Family Series], Graham Thurgood & Randy J. LaPolla (eds), 518–532. London: Routledge.

Michailovsky, Boyd. 2017. Kiranti Languages. In *The Sino-Tibetan Languages*, 2 edn. [Routledge Language Family Series], Randy LaPolla & Graham Thurgood (eds.), 646–679. Oxford & New York: Routledge. halshs-01705023. <https://halshs.archives-ouvertes.fr/halshs-01705023/document> (19 August 2019).

Rapacha, Lal. 1996. Sunwar Language. A Sociolinguistic Profile. MA thesis, Central Department of English, Kirtipur.

Rapacha, Lal. 2005. A Descriptive Grammar of Kirānti-Kõits. PhD dissertation. Jawaharlal Nehru University.

Rapacha, Lal. 2009. *Vanishing Ethnicity, Cultures and Languages of Nepal.* Kathmandu: Institute of Kirantology.

Rapacha, Lal. 2020. *Kirā̃nti-Kõits (Sunuwār/Mukhiyā) Pahicān tathā bhāṣā-sāhityako aitihāsik sarbhekṣaṇ* (A Historical Survey of Kiranti-Koits (Sunwar/Mukhiya) Identity and Language-Literature). Kathmandu: Kirānti vijñān adhyayan sāsthān.

Shneiderman, Sara & Turin, Mark. 2006. Seeking the tribe. Ethno-politics in Darjeeling and Sikkim. *Himal Southasian*, March-April 2006: 54–58. https://hcommons.org/deposits/download/hc:31462/CONTENT/2006seeking-the-tribe_-ethno-politics-in-darjeeling-and-sikkim.pdf/ (19 August 2019).

Silva-Corvalán, Carmen. 1994. *Language Contact and Change. Spanish in Los Angeles* [Oxford Studies in Language Contact]. Oxford: Clarendon Press.

Thomason, Sara G. & Kaufman, Terrence. 1988. *Language Contact, Creolization, and Genetic Linguistics.* Berkeley CA: University of California Press.

van Coetsem, Frans. 2000. *A General and Unified Theory of the Language Transmission Process in Language Contact* [Monographien zur Sprachwissenschaft 19]. Heidelberg: Winter.

Without Author. 2011. *The Word of God. The Holy Bible Sunuwar.* Kathmandu: Wycliffe Inc. & Ekta Books Distributors. <https://scriptureearth.org/data/suz/pdf/wholebible.pdf> (29 September 2019).

Appendix: Bahing paradigms

Table 7. Bahing transitive paradigm with data from Hodgson (1858: 408–409) as cited in van Driem (1991: 339).

	PATIENT 1 s.	1 d.i.	1 d.e.	1 pl.i.	1 pl.e.	**PATIENT** 2 s.	2 d.	2 pl.	**PATIENT** 3 s.	3 d.	3 pl.
1 s.						Σ-ná Σ-[n]tana	Σ-nási Σ-[n]tanasi	Σ-náni Σ-[n]tanani	Σ-gna/Σ-ǎ Σ-toŋ	Σ-gnasi/Σ-usi Σ-tóŋsi	Σ-gnami/Σ-ǔmi Σ-tòŋmi
A 1 d.i.									Σ-sa Σ-tǎsǎ	Σ-sasi Σ-tǎsǎsi	Σ-sami Σ-tǎsǎmi
1 d.e.						Σ-esi Σ-tesi	Σ-sisi Σ-tasisi	Σ-nisi Σ-tanisi	Σ-suku Σ-tǎsúku	Σ-sukusi Σ-tǎsikisi	Σ-sukumi Σ-tǎsikimi
G 1 pl.i.									Σ-ya Σ-[n]tǎyo	Σ-yasi Σ-[n]tǎyosi	Σ-yami Σ-[n]tǎyómi
1 pl.e.						Σ-emi Σ-temi	Σ-simi Σ-tasimi	Σ-nimi Σ-tanimi	Σ-ka Σ-[k]tǎko	Σ-kasi Σ-[k]tǎkosi	Σ-kami Σ-[k]tǎkómi
E 2 s.	Σ-i Σ-ti		Σ-siki Σ-taniki		Σ-ki Σ-[k]taki				Σ-i Σ-[p]teu	Σ-ist Σ-[p]teusi	Σ-imi Σ-[p]teumi
2 d.	Σ-isi Σ-tisi		Σ-sikisi Σ-tasikisi		Σ-kisi Σ-[k]takisi				Σ-si Σ-tasi	Σ-sisi Σ-tasisi	Σ-simi Σ-tasimi
N 2 pl.	Σ-ini Σ-tini		Σ-sikini Σ-tasikini		Σ-kini Σ-[k]takini				Σ-ni Σ-[n]tani	Σ-nisi Σ-[n]tanist	Σ-nimi Σ-[n]tanimi
3 s.	Σ-i Σ-ti	Σ-so Σ-taso	Σ-siki Σ-tasiki	Σ-so Σ-taso	Σ-ki Σ-[k]taki	Σ-e Σ-te	Σ-si Σ-tasi	Σ-ni Σ-[n]tani	Σ-a Σ-[p]ta	Σ-asi Σ-[p]tasi	Σ-ami Σ-[p]tami
T 3 d.	Σ-isi Σ-tisi	Σ-sasi Σ-tasosi	Σ-sikisi Σ-tasikisi	Σ-sasi Σ-tasosi	Σ-kisi Σ-[k]takisi	Σ-esi Σ-tesi	Σ-sisi Σ-tasisi	Σ-nisi Σ-[n]tanisi	Σ-se Σ-tase	Σ-sesi Σ-tasesi	Σ-semi Σ-tasemi
3 pl.	Σ-imi Σ-timi	Σ-somi Σ-tasami	Σ-sikimi Σ-tasikimi	Σ-somi Σ-tasomi	Σ-kimi Σ-[k]takimi	Σ-emi Σ-temi	Σ-simi Σ-tasimi	Σ-nimi Σ-[n]tanimi	Σ-me Σ-[m]tame	Σ-emesi Σ-[m]tamesi	Σ-memi Σ-[m]tamemu

Table 8. Bahing transitive paradigm with data from Michailovsky (1975), as cited in van Driem (1991: 340).

	PATIENT 1 s.	1 d.i.	1 d.e.	1 pl.i.	1 pl.e.	**PATIENT** 2 s.	2 d.	2 pl.	**PATIENT** 3 s.	3 d.	3 pl.
1 s.						Σ-na Σ-[n]tana	Σ-nasi Σ-[n]tanasi	Σ-nani Σ-[n]tanasi	Σ-ŋa/Σ-u Σ-iɔŋ	Σ-ŋasi/Σ-usi Σ-tɔŋsi	Σ-ŋami/Σ-umi Σ-tɔŋmi
A 1 d.i.									Σ-sa Σ-tasɵ	Σ-sasi Σ-taso	Σ-sami Σ-tasɵ
1 d.e.						?Σ-si Σ-tasu			Σ-su Σ-tasu	Σ-susi Σ-tasu	Σ-sumi Σ-tasu
G 1 pl.i.									Σ-ja Σ-[N]taja	Σ-jasi Σ-[N]taja	Σ-ja(mi) Σ-[N]taja
1 pl.e.						Σ-ka Σ-[k]takɵ			Σ-ka Σ-[k]takɵ	Σ-kasi Σ-[k]takɵ	Σ-ka(mi) Σ-[k]takɵ
E 2 s.	Σ-i Σ-ii		Σ-si		Σ-ki Σ-[k]taki				Σ-i Σ-[p]ii	Σ-isi Σ-[p]iisi	Σ-imi Σ-[p]iimi
2 d.	Σ-isi Σ-iisi		Σ-tasi		Σ-ki Σ-[k]taki				Σ-si Σ-tasi	Σ-si(si) Σ-tasi	Σ-simi Σ-tasimi
N 2 p.	Σ-ini Σ-iini		Σ-sikini Σ-tasi(kini)		Σ-ki Σ-[k]takini				Σ-ni Σ-[n]tani	Σ-ni(si) Σ-[n]tani	Σ-ni(mi) Σ-[n]tani
3 s.	Σ-i Σ-ii					Σ-e Σ-te	Σ-si	Σ-ni Σ-[n]tani	Σ-a Σ-[p]ta	Σ-asi Σ-[p]tasi	Σ-ami Σ-[p]tami
T 3 d.	Σ-isi Σ-iisi	Σ-so Σ-taso	Σ-si Σ-tasi	Σ-so Σ-taso	Σ-ki Σ-[k]taki	Σ-esi Σ-test	Σ-tasi	Σ-nisi Σ-[n]tani(si)	Σ-se Σ-tase		
3 pl.	Σ-imi Σ-iimi					Σ-emi Σ-temi	Σ-si(mi) Σ-tasi	Σ-ni(mi) Σ-[n]tani(mi)	Σ-me Σ-[m]tame		

Index